# PACIFIC NORTH COAST

---

### HOW TO USE THIS GUIDE

The first section consists of useful general information—Facts at Your Fingertips—designed to help you plan your trip, as well as local facts, business hours, time zones, and customs that will be of use while you are traveling.

Next are essays to help you with the background of the area that this Guide covers—the cultural scene, some historical insights, regional food and drink, and so on.

Following these essays comes the detailed breakdown of the area, geographically. Each chapter begins with a description of the place or region, broadly describing its attraction for the visitor; this is followed by Practical Information to help you explore the area—detailed descriptions, addresses, directions, phone numbers, and so forth for hotels, restaurants, tours, museums, historical sites, and more.

Two vital ways into this book are the Table of Contents at the beginning and the Index at the end.

## FODOR'S TRAVEL GUIDES

are compiled, researched, and edited by an international team of travel writers, field correspondents, and editors. The series, which now almost covers the globe, was founded by Eugene Fodor in 1936.

## OFFICES
New York & London

**Fodor's Pacific North Coast:**

Area Editors: RALPH FRIEDMAN, LINDA LAMPMAN, ARCHIE SATTERFIELD, NORMA SPRING, JULIE STERLING, DAVID WISHART
Editorial Contributors: BARRY ANDERSON, HILDA ANDERSON, YVONNE ROTHERT
Editor: DEBRA BERNARDI
Editorial Associate: STEPHEN BREWER
Illustrations: BRIAN DEINES, MICHAEL KAPLAN, SANDRA LANG
Maps and Plans: DYNO LOWENSTEIN, BURMAR

# FODOR'S

# PACIFIC NORTH COAST

**FODOR'S TRAVEL GUIDES**
New York

All the following Guides are current (most of them also in
the Hodder and Stoughton British edition.)

CURRENT FODOR'S COUNTRY AND AREA TITLES:

| | |
|---|---|
| AUSTRALIA, NEW ZEALAND AND SOUTH PACIFIC | ISRAEL |
| AUSTRIA | ITALY |
| BELGIUM AND LUXEMBOURG | JAPAN |
| BERMUDA | JORDAN AND HOLY LAND |
| BRAZIL | KOREA |
| CANADA | MEXICO |
| CARIBBEAN AND BAHAMAS | NORTH AFRICA |
| CENTRAL AMERICA | PEOPLE'S REPUBLIC OF CHINA |
| EASTERN EUROPE | PORTUGAL |
| EGYPT | SCANDINAVIA |
| EUROPE | SCOTLAND |
| FRANCE | SOUTH AMERICA |
| GERMANY | SOUTHEAST ASIA |
| GREAT BRITAIN | SOVIET UNION |
| GREECE | SPAIN |
| HOLLAND | SWITZERLAND |
| INDIA | TURKEY |
| IRELAND | YUGOSLAVIA |

CITY GUIDES:

| | |
|---|---|
| BEIJING, GUANGZHOU, SHANGHAI | PARIS |
| CHICAGO | ROME |
| DALLAS AND FORT WORTH | SAN DIEGO |
| HOUSTON | SAN FRANCISCO |
| LONDON | STOCKHOLM, COPENHAGEN, OSLO, HELSINKI, AND REYKJAVIK |
| LOS ANGELES | |
| MADRID | TOKYO |
| MEXICO CITY AND ACAPULCO | WASHINGTON, D.C. |
| NEW ORLEANS | |
| NEW YORK CITY | |

FODOR'S BUDGET SERIES:

| | |
|---|---|
| BUDGET BRITAIN | BUDGET ITALY |
| BUDGET CANADA | BUDGET JAPAN |
| BUDGET CARIBBEAN | BUDGET MEXICO |
| BUDGET EUROPE | BUDGET SCANDINAVIA |
| BUDGET FRANCE | BUDGET SPAIN |
| BUDGET GERMANY | BUDGET TRAVEL IN AMERICA |
| BUDGET HAWAII | |

USA GUIDES:

| | |
|---|---|
| ALASKA | HAWAII |
| CALIFORNIA | NEW ENGLAND |
| CAPE COD | PENNSYLVANIA |
| COLORADO | SOUTH |
| FAR WEST | TEXAS |
| FLORIDA | USA (in one volume) |

# CONTENTS

# FOREWORD

Magnificent wilderness, luxury resorts, and sophisticated cities can all be part of a visit to the Pacific North Coast. This book covers the coastal areas of Oregon, Washington, British Columbia, and southeast Alaska; the cities of Portland, Seattle, and Vancouver, B.C.; and the most important inland recreation areas. Your trip to the Pacific Northwest might consist of soaking up the sun on Oregon's beautiful beaches, skiing high on the slopes of Mt. Hood, or camping in Washington's rugged Olympic National Park. It could mean stopping for a drink atop Seattle's Space Needle as you watch the sun sink into Puget Sound, browsing in Vancouver's cosmopolitan shops, or cruising up Alaska's Inside Passage. And everywhere you go there seems to be a backdrop of mountains to take your breath away.

*Fodor's Pacific North Coast* is designed to help you to plan your own trip to the Northwest, based on your time, your budget, your energy, your interests—your idea of what this trip should be. Perhaps having read this guide you'll have some new ideas. We have, therefore, tried to offer you the widest possible *range* of activities and within that range *selections* that will be safe, worthwhile, and of good value to you. The descriptions we provide are designed to help you make your own intelligent choices from among our selections.

All selections and comments in *Fodor's Alaska* are based on personal experiences. We feel that our first responsibility is to inform and protect you, the reader. Errors are bound to creep into any travel guide, however. Much change can and will occur even while we are on press, and also during the succeeding twelve months or so that this edition is on sale. We sincerely welcome letters from our readers on these changes, or from those whose opinions differ from ours, and we are ready to revise our entries for next year's edition when the facts warrant it.

Send your letters to the editors at **Fodor's Travel Guides, 2 Park Avenue, New York, N.Y. 10016.** Continental or British Commonwealth readers may prefer to write to Fodor's Travel Guides, 9-10 Market Place, London W1N 7AG, England.

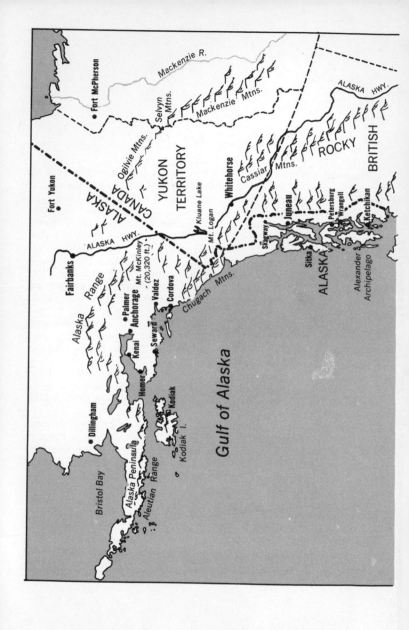

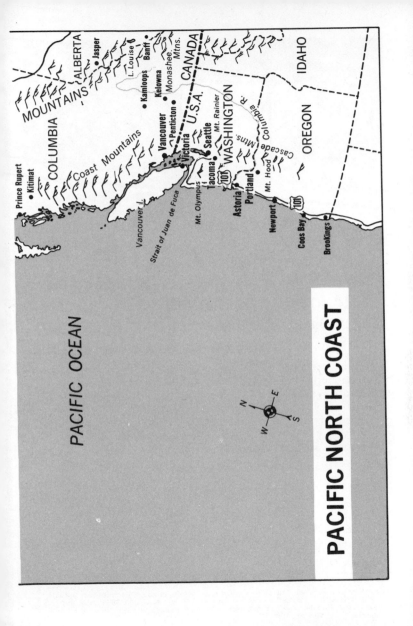

**PACIFIC NORTH COAST**

# FACTS AT YOUR FINGERTIPS

 **DEFINING THE AREA.** This book covers the northwest coastal area of the United States and Canada: the states of Oregon and Washington; the most westerly Canadian province, British Columbia; and the southeast region of the state of Alaska. We focus on the "coast"—taken to include the mainland, attached peninsulas, and a myriad of offshore islands to the west—and also cover impressive mountain areas that attract skiers, climbers, and hikers. From south to north the Cascades connect with Canadian mountains that merge with Alaskan ranges. These follow closely along the Gulf of Alaska to provide a scenic backdrop for Alaska's southeastern communities.

But mountains and sea are not all the Pacific North Coast offers. If you choose to fly to this area, you'll probably come into one of the area's major cities: Portland, Oregon, on the banks of the Columbia River; Seattle, Washington, on Puget Sound; Vancouver, B.C., on the Straits of Georgia. The cities here manage to combine cosmopolitan environments with natural settings that are nothing less than breathtaking.

 **TIPS FOR BRITISH VISITORS. Passports.** You will need a valid passport (cost £15) and a U.S. Visa (which can be put only in a passport of the 10-year kind). The visa will be good for multiple entries for the life of the passport. You can obtain the visa either through your travel agent or directly from the *United States Embassy*, Visa and Immigration Department, 24 Grosvenor Sq., London W1; 01–499 3443.

No vaccinations are required for entry into the U.S.

**Customs.** If you are 21 or over, you can take into the U.S.: 200 cigarettes, 50 cigars, or 3 pounds of tobacco; 1 U.S. liter of alcohol; duty-free gifts to a value of $100. Be careful not to try to take in meat or meat products, seeds, plants, fruits, etc. And avoid narcotics like the plague.

**Insurance.** We heartily recommend that you insure yourself to cover health and motoring mishaps, with *Europ Assistance*, 252 High St., Croydon CR0 1NF; 01–680 1234. Their excellent service is all the more valuable when you consider the possible costs of health care in the United States.

**Tour Operators.** The price battle that has raged over transatlantic fares has meant that most tour operators now offer excellent budget packages to the United States. Among those you might consider as you plan your trip are—

*American Express*, 6 Haymarket, London SW1.

*Thomas Cook Ltd.*, Thorpe Wood, Peterborough, PE3 65B.

*Cosmos*, Cosmos House, 1 Bromley Common, Bromley, Kent BR2 9LX.

*Cunard*, 8 Berkeley St., London W1.

*Jetsave*. Sussex House, London Rd., East Grinstead RH19 1LD.

*Page and Moy*, 2 Hatfields, London SE1.

*Speedbird,* Alta House, 152 King St., London W6.

**Air Fares.** We suggest that you explore the current scene for budget flight possibilities. Unfortunately, there is no longer standby service on any of the major airlines; but do check their APEX and other fares at a considerable saving over the full price. Quite frankly, only business travelers who don't have to watch the price of their tickets fly full-price these days—and find themselves sitting right beside APEX passengers!

**Hotels.** You may have need of a fast booking service to find a hotel room. One of the very best ways to do this is to contact HBI-HOTAC, Kingsgate House, Kingsgate Pl., London NW6. They book rooms for most of the large chains (Holiday Inns, Hilton, Ramada, etc.), so you can have a multiple choice with only one contact. HBI-HOTAC specializes in booking for business firms, but also deals with the general public.

 **WHEN TO GO.** Generally, the best seasons are late spring, summer, and early fall, though ski resorts and excellent snow lure a growing number of winter visitors.

There are fringe benefits to going in the fringe seasons, late and early, and avoiding the busy summer. These "thrift seasons" offer lower prices for accommodations, transportation, and tours. There is more likely to be space available in campgrounds, hotels, and motels. Aesthetically, the bonus may be in the form of beauty, as found in autumn color, bluer skies, and fresh dustings of snow on the glaciers and mountains, making them even more beautiful.

A drawing card for Alaska in summer is daylight, long hours of it, the farther north the lighter. However, Alaskans claim that they have more time to play *after* the long, light summer when they are preparing for winter and are busy with the tourist season. This may be true of the other coastal regions as well.

Actually, the entire year is considered delightful by the residents because of the mildness of the climate. Check on what is happening in the way of sports, cultural events, and celebrations (see *Practical Information* sections). You're likely to find something to catch your eye among *Seasonal Events;* residents don't miss many chances to celebrate, including such times as Alaska Day in Sitka, Seafair in Seattle, and Rose Festival in Portland, to name but a few possibilities.

 **CLIMATE.** Tempered by the warm Japan Current and protected by mountains, the coastal climate is quite uniformly mild. It rarely drops below freezing nor climbs much above the mid-seventies. On the few occasions when it snows (usually December–January), everyone is thrown into a tizzy. Adults don't know what to do with it, but the kids, reprieved from school, are delighted.

Residents admit that record rainfalls may dampen human spirits at times, but they rally quickly in defense of precipitation. In Ketchikan, Alaska, they are prone to boast about having had as much as 164 inches. Elsewhere they point out that rain, mist, and fog keep everything so fresh looking, green, and blooming. Residents' advice to visitors is to come prepared with your favorite raingear for use if needed. Then, do as the "natives" do: dress for it—and enjoy!

 **MONEY.** The Canadian dollar, like the U.S. dollar, is divided into 100 cents, and coins and bills exist in the same denominations as in the U.S.—i.e., 1¢, 5¢, 10¢, etc.; $1, $2, $5, $10, etc.

Actual exchange rates fluctuate from day to day but the Canadian dollar is usually worth about $1.20 U.S. In order to get the most for your money, convert it before you leave home. Though U.S. money is accepted in Canadian stores, waiting until you get to Canada can create problems. The banks, which are generally open only from 10 A.M. to 3 P.M. Monday through Friday, are sometimes not prepared to exchange foreign currency, and, even if you find one that will, it is not always convenient to go to a bank. Furthermore, hotels, stores, and restaurants may offer something less than the best rate. The best exchange rate is usually paid at B.C. government-owned liquor stores. Another good policy is to find the nearest Deak-Perera foreign exchange office. There is a Deak bureau in Vancouver (555 Howe St.).

There are no restrictions on the amount of money you may bring into or take out of Canada. Both Canadians and foreign visitors may convert money from Canadian tender to another currency or from a foreign currency to Canadian dollars as often as they want, in amounts as great as they want, either inside or outside Canada.

Neither Canadian coins nor paper money are accepted by American businesses at this writing. They must be exchanged at a bank or other valid office.

 **CROSSING BORDERS.** Customs regulations between the United States and Canada are among the most liberal in the world. Passing from one country to the other is usually a simple matter of presenting some valid and acceptable form of identification and answering a few simple questions about where you were born, where you live, why you are visiting Canada, and how long you will stay.

The identification need not be a passport, although this is certainly acceptable. You can also use a driver's license, birth certificate, draft card, Social Security card, certificate of naturalization, or resident alien ("green") card. Entry procedure for citizens of Great Britain, Australia, and New Zealand is similarly simple.

Canada allows British and American guests to bring their cars (for less than six months), boats or canoes, rifles and shotguns (but not handguns or automatic weapons) and 200 rounds of ammunition, cameras, radios, sports equipment, and typewriters into the country without paying any duty. Sometimes they will require a deposit for trailers and household equipment, but this is refundable when you cross back over the border. (This is to guarantee that you do not sell these items in Canada for a profit.) Needless to say, you may bring clothing, personal items, and any professional tools or equipment you need (if you work in Canada) without charge or restriction. It is also a good idea to carry your medical insurance and insurance for boats, vehicles, and personal luggage.

Some items are restricted, however. You need the contract for a rented car. And, if you are going to return home and leave behind a car you rented in the States, you have to fill out an E29B customs form. Tobacco is limited. Dogs, for hunting or pets, are duty-free, but you must bring a certificate from a veterinary inspector to prove that the dog has no communicable diseases. (Cats may enter without restriction.) All plants must be examined at the customs station to preclude the entry of destructive insects. Most important, Canadian officials are diligent in pursuing smugglers of narcotics and other illegal items.

It is up to Americans to be able to assure U.S. immigration of their right to reenter the United States. They are allowed to bring back personal or household merchandise for their own use up to a value of $25 without duty if they have stayed up to 48 hours. People staying longer than 48 hours are entitled to an exemption up to $300. Families traveling together can pool their exemptions, i.e., a family of four could have a total exemption of $1,200. Keep receipts handy.

For more information on U.S. customs, contact your nearest U.S. customs office or write to *U.S. Customs Service,* Washington, DC 20229.

For Canada, contact *Revenue Canada Customs & Excise,* Public Relations Branch, Ottawa, Ont., Canada K1A 0L5; (613) 593–6220. Or, Revenue Canada Customs & Excise, 1001 West Pender St., Vancouver, B.C. Canada V6E 2M8; (604) 666–1456.

When leaving Canada, be sure to give yourself extra time at the airport to deal with customs before your flight.

**HOTELS AND MOTELS.** The possibilities range from wilderness lodges and cabins to high-rise suites. There are small hideaway resorts and posh ones, and a growing number of hostel and bed-and-breakfast accommodations. It's always wise to reserve rooms in advance.

Hotels and motels in this guidebook are divided into standard categories based on their prices—*deluxe, expensive, moderate, inexpensive,* and, in some chapters, *basic budget.*

Although the names of the various hotel and motel categories are standard, the prices listed under each category may vary from area to area. This variance is meant to reflect local price standards, and take into account that what might be considered a *moderate* price in a large urban area might be quite *expensive* in a rural region. In every case, however, the dollar ranges for each category are clearly stated before each listing of establishments.

Some of the establishments listed under "Hotels and Motels" in the *Practical Information* sections are actually *wilderness lodges* that provide facilities for fishing, boating, and other outdoor activities. (Note however that these are listed separately in the Alaska chapter.)

*Bed-and-breakfast* establishments, mainstays of European travel, are fast becoming a popular alternative for U.S. travelers. Most are private homes and apartments or small guest houses that have one or more rooms available, usually with shared bath, on a nightly basis. Breakfast, as might be expected, is included in the charge. The quality of accommodations and the range of prices vary widely, but at least one national and many regional organizations exist to help tourists sort out the type of lodging they want.

*Bed & Breakfast Registry,* P.O. Box 80174, St. Paul, MN 55108; (612) 646–4238. This is a reservation service covering North America. Prices range from $12-$90 per night, with the Registry requiring a $10 per room/night deposit. The deposit is refundable if the traveler is not satisfied with the accommodations after inspection. Also worth contacting is the *American B & B Association,* P.O. Box 23486, Washington, DC 20024; (703) 379–4242. Unlike the Registry, the B & B Association offers no guarantee, but its $3 listing of bed-and-breakfasts throughout the U.S. is a good companion for the free-wheeling traveler. People with rooms to let might consider joining *InnTer Lodging Co-op,* P.O. Box 7044, Tacoma, WA 94807; (206) 756–0343. InnTer Lodging is a network of bed-and-breakfasts (alas, often without the breakfasts). You pay $35 to be listed in a directory, agree to accept guests for three months out of the year, and you are entitled to guest privileges for $4-$5 per night in the homes of other registrants. The network covers most of the U.S. and Canada. *Sweet Dreams & Toast, Inc.,* P.O. Box 4835-0035, Washington, DC 20008; (202) 483–9191. This service provides current listings of local B & B networks by state.

In larger towns and cities a good bet for clean, plain, reliable lodging is a *YMCA* or *YWCA.* These buildings are usually centrally located, and their rates tend to run to less than half of those of hotels. Nonmembers are welcome, but may pay slightly more than members. A few very large Ys may have accommodations for couples but usually sexes are segregated. Decor is spartan and the cafeteria fare plain and wholesome, but a definite advantage is the use of the building's pool, gym, reading room, information services, and other facilities. For a directory, write to *National Council of the YMCA,* 291 Broadway, New York, NY 10007; and the *National Board of the YWCA,* 600 Lexington Ave., New York, NY 10022.

*Youth hostels* also offer inexpensive lodging alternatives. A guide and handbook comes with hostel memberships. Write to *American Youth Hostels, Inc.,* 1332 I St., N.W., Suite 800, Washington DC 20005; and the *Canadian Hostelling Assn.,* 3425 W. Broadway, Vancouver, B.C., Canada V6R 2B4; (604) 736–2674.

**DINING OUT.** Food and dining along the coast is much the same as elsewhere, with fast-food and restaurant chains, and simple to elegant meals in hotels and resorts that feature international cuisines. Like lodging, eating out, except in the fanciest places, tends to be quite informal in dress and in service.

Restaurants are divided into price categories as follows: *deluxe, expensive, moderate,* and *inexpensive.* As a general rule, expect restaurants in metropolitan areas to be higher in price, but many restaurants that feature foreign cuisine are surprisingly inexpensive. We should also point out that limitations of space make it impossible to include every establishment. We have, therefore, listed those which we recommend as the best within each price range.

Although the names of the various restaurant categories are standard, the prices listed under each category may vary from area to area. This variation is meant to reflect local price standards and take into account that what might be considered a *moderate* price in a large urban area might be quite *expensive* in a rural region. In every case, however, the dollar ranges for each category are clearly stated before each listing of establishments.

**SENIOR CITIZEN AND STUDENT DISCOUNTS.** Many attractions—and many hotels, motels, and restaurants—offer discounts to senior citizens and students. In most cases, showing a driver's license, passport, or some other proof of age will suffice—"senior" generally being defined as 65 or over. Museums, movie theaters, and even some stores will often post special senior-citizen rates. Airlines normally give seniors a 10 percent discount on air travel. Those places offering student discounts are generally more stringent in their proof requirements—a high school or college ID, international student travel card, or evidence of age may be requested. Persons under 22 get a discount of up to 25 percent on air travel on a standby basis. The Days Inn chain offers various discounts to anyone 55 or older. Holiday Inns give a discount to members of the NRTA (write to *National Retired Teachers Association,* Membership Division, 406 Grand Ave., Ojai, CA 93023) and the AARP (write to *American Association of Retired Persons,* Membership Division, 215 Long Beach Blvd., Long Beach, CA 90801). Members of the AARP, the NRTA, The Catholic Golden Age of United Societies of U.S.A., the Old Age Security Pensioners of Canada, and similar organizations benefit increasingly from a number of discounts, but the amounts, sources, and availability of these change, so it is best to check with either your organization or the hotel, motel, or restaurant chain you plan to use. The *National Council of Senior Citizens,* 925 15th St., N.W., Washington, DC 20005, works especially to develop low-cost travel possibilities for its members.

**DRINKING LAWS.** Rules and regulations governing what kinds of alcoholic beverages may be sold, at what hours, and to whom, vary in the coastal regions:
Nearly all bars in **Oregon** serve until the legal closing time of 2:30 A.M. The minimum age for consumption of alcohol is 21. ID cards are for sale for a $2 fee at state liquor stores.

The legal drinking age in **Washington** is also 21. Bars, all of which are connected with restaurants, can stay open until 2 A.M. Taverns sell beer and wine; grocery stores sell them by the bottle. Hard liquor, heavily taxed, is sold at state stores.

The drinking age in **British Columbia** is 19. Liquor, beer, and wine can be served in "licensed premises," dining rooms, and pubs, or bars. Some may still have separate ladies' entrances. Taverns are open until 1 A.M.; bars and cabarets until 2 A.M.

Consumption rules, especially serving hours, are quite broad in **Alaska**. The only time bars are required to be closed is for the three hours between 5 A.M. and 8 A.M. The legal drinking age is is 19, but children may enter bars with a parent or guardian. Beware of local drinking laws; you may have to bring your own or go thirsty if you are in a village that voted to be "dry" in its last election.

 **BUSINESS HOURS AND LOCAL TIME. Washington, Oregon,** and **British Columbia** (except for a small chunk of its northeast border) are on *Pacific Standard Time.* Southeast **Alaska** observes *Yukon Time,* one hour earlier that P.S.T. There is one hold-out, however: the Indian residents of Metlakatla, on Annette Island 15 miles from Ketchikan, have declared that they are staying on Pacific Standard Time for community reasons.

All communities, though, including Metlakatla, switch to Daylight Saving Time in summer.

 **ROUGHING IT.** There are many ways to rough it pleasurably while exploring the coastal areas. Camping by tent, trailer, or recreational vehicle is an inexpensive way to go. More and improved camping facilities keep springing up. Some may be simple roadside turnoffs, but they often have sweeping views. If all you need in a pinch is a patch of ground to pitch a tent you can set up camp just off the road on Canada's Crown lands. Likewise in Alaska's public lands, but be sure to restore the spot to mint condition.

The best choice is among camping areas in national parks, national forests, state parks, provincial parks, and in private camping areas and trailer parks offering hookups, showers, laundromats, recreational facilities, and stores.

 **HINTS TO HANDICAPPED TRAVELERS.** There are millions of handicapped people who are physically able to travel and who do so enthusiastically when they know they will be able to move about with safety and comfort. A growing number of travel agents specialize in this market. Generally, their tours parallel those of the non-handicapped traveler but at a more leisurely pace, with everything checked out in advance to eliminate inconvenience. It is essential that handicapped people who need special help inform cruise companies and tour operators when they start to plan their trip. Some companies require a medical certification for their protection. Important sources of information in this field are: *The Travel Information Center,* Moss Rehabilitation Hospital, 12th St. and Tabor Rd., Philadelphia, PA 19141; *Easter Seal Society,* Director of Education and Information Service, 2023 Ogden Ave., Chicago, IL 60612; and *ASSIST,* 67 Yonge St., Toronto, Ont.

Important sources of information in this field are the books: *Travel-Ability,* by Lois Reamy, published by Macmillan; and *Access to the World: A Travel Guide for the Handicapped,* by Louise Weiss, available from Facts On File, 460 Park Ave. South, New York, NY 10016, $14.95 including postage. A publication that gives valuable information about motels, hotels, and restaurants (rating them, telling about steps, table heights, door widths, etc.) is *The Wheelchair Traveler,* by Douglass R. Annand, Ball Hill Road, Milford, NH 03055. Many of the nation's national parks have special facilities for the handicapped. These are described in *National Park Guide for the Handicapped,* available from the U.S. Government Printing Office, Washington, DC 20402. TWA publishes a free 12-page pamphlet entitled *Consumer Information about Air Travel for the Handicapped* to explain available special arrangements and how to get them. Transport Canada publishes *A Guide for the Disadvantaged.*

**MAIL.** There is no separate air mail rate for letters or postcards posted in Canada for delivery within the country or to the United States, nor for those posted in the U.S. delivery within the United States or posted to Canada. Mail for distant points is automatically airlifted. Canadian postage is $.30 for the first ounce; U.S. postage is $.20.

**TELEPHONES. Alaska:** The area code throughout the state is 907. Pay phones cost $.10.

**British Columbia:** The area code for the province is 604. (The Rocky Mountain area around Banff discussed in the British Columbia chaper is in Alberta; the area code is 403.) Phones in British Columbia cost $.25 (Canadian).

**Oregon:** The area code for Oregon is 503; local pay phones cost $.25.

**Washington:** The area code for most of the western part of the state is 206 (elsewhere it's 509). Pay phones cost $.25 for local calls.

# NOURISHED BY WATER

*An Introduction to the Pacific North Coast*

by
**NORMA SPRING**

*Norma Spring is a Seattle-based freelance writer, whose books include*
Alaska, Pioneer State *and* Alaska, the Complete Travel Book. *She is
also the author of numerous newspaper and magazine articles on Alaska,
as well as round-the-world travel, including a book on travel in the
U.S.S.R.—*Roaming Russia, Siberia, and Middle Asia—*illustrated with
photographs by husband Bob.*

Chinese philosopher Lao-Tze, reflecting on nature some 2,500 years
ago, wrote that "water is good; it benefits all things and does not
compete with them." Residents living in the Pacific northwest coastal

9

regions of Oregon, Washington, British Columbia, and southeast Alaska seem to concur.

In fact, they agree that the abundance of water, both fresh and salt, adds up to a major boon—whether precipitating, flowing in numerous streams and rivers, held captive in plentiful lakes, or caressing (sometimes pounding) their varied coastlines. Of all the elements, including gold, that played a part in the settlement, then the development of industries, recreation, and a distinctive lifestyle, West Coast dwellers credit water as the most influential.

## The Columbia

As early as the 1500s exploring ships from Spain were sizing up the west coast of the continent, naming passageways and islands to the north. They were followed by the British, who established trading companies to lay claim to western Canada, and the Russians, who, seeking furs, discovered and claimed Alaska. The United States, fresh from the Revolutionary War, was a latecomer.

In the early 1800s, President Jefferson dispatched a pair of captains and their "corps of discovery" to blaze and map a feasible overland and river route from the Missouri to the Pacific Ocean. The plan was to make contact with a rumored mighty river that emptied into the ocean. The final leg would be accomplished in dugout canoes, to be portaged around such hazards as falls and rapids.

It took two years, round trip, including wintering near the mouth of that rumored river, the Columbia, but as a result of the reports of Lewis and Clark, the United States put in its claim for what was to become the Oregon Territory.

Today, the Columbia River forms most of the boundary between the states of Oregon and Washington. Highways and railroads follow it inland on both banks. Its rapids and falls have been tamed by a series of dams. The reservoirs behind them provide areas for recreation and water to irrigate productive farmlands reclaimed from desert land. Assorted river traffic—pleasure boats, freight-carrying tugs, and barges —plies the river today.

The river also has a Canadian connection. It rises in British Columbia's Kootenay (Indian for water people) region, and makes a big bend to the north before heading south for the United States. Fed by many tributaries, the Columbia drains much of the area covered in this book.

As a watery common denominator, the river continues on through Washington state, dammed at the Grand Coulee, then proceeds to carve a magnificent gorge through the Cascade Mountains, flowing west to its rendezvous with the Pacific Ocean.

## More Water

The activity surrounding the Columbia is heavy, and British Columbia's Fraser River is also tamed for commerce and has a rich delta. But the winner has to be Puget Sound and northward along the thousand-mile-long Inside Passage, the marine highway well used for centuries by all manner of craft.

Before white men came, the Indians plied the passage in canoes, hand-hewn from the large and abundant cedar tree trunks, trading with, and often warring with, other tribes. Next came the explorers, in sailing ships, and word spread of undetermined wealth in the form of furs. Trading ships from many countries followed. Competitive trading posts were established. They developed into settlements that were the basis for territorial claims, to be settled later by treaties, cash, and arbitration.

The discovery of gold in various areas accessible via the Inside Passage prompted sporadic "rushes." The wildest one occurred at the turn of this century, when the rich strike in Canada's Klondike made the news. Then the avid argonauts crowded on almost anything that would float to the passage's dead end at gold-rush–founded Skagway. From there, the gold seekers risked the grueling trek over the mountains and rafted down streams and rivers to reach the "city of gold" at Dawson, gateway to the goldfields.

Today the Inside Passage continues its popular and busy role as water-bearer of an amazing assortment of marine transportation, including ferries that carry both vehicles and passengers. The Washington State Ferries criss-cross Puget Sound and make regular calls at ports in the San Juan Islands. They are a necessity for commuters who opt for island living and a pleasure for vacationers who want to island-hop and spend time exploring in favorite places.

British Columbia Ferries are the vital link for the Canadian islands and mainland ports as far as Prince Rupert, British Columbia. From there, Alaska State Ferries carry on to the end of the passage. Though not connecting with the southeastern system, another branch of Alaska ferries connects communities of the Gulf of Alaska, some of which have highway access to the largest city, Anchorage.

Periodically for decades there have been rumors of schemes for digging a canal that would connect Puget Sound (and the Inside Passage) with the Columbia River and Oregon . . . and the rumors continue.

In summer, well known world-class cruise ships join the traffic. They promise their several hundred passengers the utmost in comfort and luxury while viewing wildlife and wilderness, and they call at the larger southeast Alaska ports. The smaller *Explorer Class* ships offer the same amenities, plus they take their fewer-than-a-hundred passengers where the bigger ships cannot go. Some advantages are venturing up glacial fjords that extend far into the coast, easing in close to seal and bird rookeries, and adding a variety of small, friendly communities (along with the bigger ports) to their flexible itineraries.

Adding to the interest of a cruise along the Inside Passage are sightings of assorted-size craft, bent on doing their own thing, but ready with a friendly toot of greeting. The "work horses" are the sturdy tugboats of practical, no-nonsense design, towing rafts of logs, and barges with loads of sawdust or huge containers full of whatever goods and supplies are in demand. Some are headed for far-north Prudhoe Bay, Alaska, accessible by sea only in summer when Arctic waters thaw.

Fishing boats give a clue to their mission by the equipment they carry: nets and floats, stacks of crab pots, and other essential gear. Pleasure craft run the gamut: rubber rafts, canoes, foldboats, outboards, inboards, cabin cruisers, yachts, and sailing ships of all sizes. They display their flags and indicate their ports of origin with pride. Each appears to be trying to outdo the other in coming up with a clever name for the bow: "Pic-Sea"; "Skookumchuck" (Indian for strong, swift water); "Rock Bottom"; "Fish Killer"; "Our Li'l Stinker."

## The Beach Scene

Considering the amount of shoreline that borders the ocean, sound, lakes, rivers, and that surrounds uncounted islands, the possibilities for pursuing beach-related activities appear inexhaustible. They vary from well used beaches near the bigger population centers to vast uncrowded stretches, some barely visited as yet.

Some of the most accessible and photogenic ocean beaches lie along the winding Oregon Coast. With great foresight, and the desire that this resource be enjoyed to the maximum, the state set aside most of the shoreline as public property. There are liberally spaced forest camps, waysides, state parks, and rest areas, plus towns and resort communities with the finest facilities.

Driving the highway that parallels the coast is a soul-renewing experience. Photographers are drawn to the graceful curves of coves with breaking surf and to vistas that include picturesque lighthouses, rolling sand dunes, rocky points and headlands, high-splashing waves, fleets of fishing boats headquartered in protected bays. The action is brisk in prime season, with deep-sea charters bringing in record catches, both in size and in quantity.

Fishing is a major attraction in all the coastal areas, and fishermen and women don't have to go out to sea to fish. Freshwater lakes and streams are handy, and from the very edge of the salt water, large nets can be cast out to scoop up smelt or a line thrown to hook surf fish.

Capturing crabs requires some wading and a crabnet. With a clam gun (shovel) as a weapon, digging the tasty mollusks, including giant sized, fast-digging geoducks (pronounced goo-ee), is also great sport. The reward for dropping a well baited line from rocks and jetties may be a salmon, often sizable.

The Northwest Coast Indians lived easily and well off the sea and forests. It left them time to develop their distinctive art, including woodcarving and other crafts. Early settlers also appreciated the bountiful and readily available seafood, claiming, "When the tide is out the table is set." The variety appreciated by anglers continues to exist in "hot spots" all the way from the Oregon shores through those of southeast Alaska. But along with fishing, there's a wide choice of other water-oriented activities as well.

Vacationers can beachcomb for provocatively shaped driftwood, gather shells, and sometimes find a well traveled glass float that escaped from a Japanese fishing net—considered a real treasure. Rockhounds find beauties, well polished by the sea. People interested in marine life find fascinating specimens temporarily trapped in tide pools.

There are places to camp and hike, swim, boat, and surf. Resorts offer such activities as exploring by dune buggy, scuba diving and snorkeling, and golf.

A shoreline pride of British Columbia is the Pacific Rim National Park, on the west coast of Vancouver Island, largest of the offshore group. Vancouver Island was named for the intrepid explorer-captain who sailed around it while mapping and marveling that " . . . nothing can be more striking than the beauty of these waters. . . . "

Vancouver Island's Long Beach, 12 miles of it, lures visitors with the promise of bountiful driftwood cast up by winter storms and Pacific rollers to challenge surfers. Added attractions nearby are trails leading into rain forests and even to an old gold mine. The islands scattered over the mouth of Barkley Sound are rich in sea life. They support thousands of birds and sea lions, and gray whales migrate there annually.

The "Lifesaving Trail," built as an access route along the stormiest forty-five miles of Vancouver Island's west coast, intrigues hikers. At one time there was even a telegraph connection with the two lighthouses. The keepers reported the frequent shipwrecks to Victoria, the provincial capital at the southern tip of the island. Survivors, if any, who made it to shore could find this trail and make their way to emergency cabins, supplies, and phones. It's a fortitude-testing trail, and though it's no longer needed for lifesaving, hardy hikers take to it. They should be prepared to judge time and tide where necessary, to battle through dense forest growth, and on occasion to wade a chilly stream. There are also fantastic beach hiking opportunities elsewhere in British Columbia, as well as along the shorelines of Oregon and Washington.

But there are less rugged ways to enjoy the beaches. There are lakes within city boundaries or within reach for a day's recreation. All it takes is free time and the promise of sun to coax town and city dwellers out for a picnic by water that warms up enough in summer, even in Alaska, for swimming and water skiing.

Speaking of warmer water, the area abounds in hot springs. Indians enjoyed the therapeutic pleasures of a hot soak whenever and wherever they encountered the steaming springs. Today, some of these thermal pools are the "mainsprings" of year-round resorts. In summer, they are relaxing relief after more strenuous activities in surrounding wilderness. In winter, what could be better as a warm-up after a day on the ski slopes?

Coastal dwellers share another hot feature, and no one is sure yet of its potential: volcano power. Scientists monitor rumblings and belchings of certain peaks, which are pinpointed as part of the Pacific "rim of fire." Mostly sleeping, but restless, they may be candidates for eruption.

Washington and Oregon had a sample of volcano power in 1980, when Mount St. Helens blew its top, devastating considerable terrain and taking human life. The blast ruined a favorite subject for photographers: the symmetrical, snow-covered cone, mirrored in a picture-perfect mountain lake. Though St. Helens appears to be settling down now to rebuild its dome and become a tourist attraction, there are signs that other volcanic peaks might put on a show sooner or later.

Some lava cones and mountain peaks in Alaska's Aleutian Island chain, which divides the Pacific Ocean from the Bering Sea, are still smoking. Mt. Baker at the border of British Columbia and Washington, enjoyed as a popular hiking, skiing, and recreational area, occasionally lets off steam. Climbers on Oregon's Mt. Hood detect sulphurous fumes at certain elevations. Even hoary Mt. Rainier, standing alone and rising to heights that make it a dominant feature of Puget Sound scenery, may be vulnerable. Climbers, stranded overnight on top, have been grateful for the warmth of steaming caves at the summit.

## The Mountains

Mountains are on a grander scale here than anywhere else on the North American continent. In Oregon and Washington, sea level delights are not far from the Cascade Mountain heights that are the backbone of the two states. Though snow rarely falls on the milder, moister west side of the Cascades, outdoor enthusiasts can easily find the white stuff nearby. There is superb winter skiing in mountain resort areas, with plenty of tows, as well as trails for cross-country treks.

In summer, hikers take to wilderness trails in national parks and forests and accept the challenge of climbing major and minor peaks. Others choose family camping expeditions in view of the high-rising, snow-clad volcanic crests.

The defining mountain ranges continue northward to serve as the border between Canada's most westerly province and southeast Alaska, which is dubbed the "Panhandle." These Alaskan mountains are beautiful and rugged with limited roads designed so as to pass through the most scenically spectacular areas. They lead to popular interior resorts and attractions in river valleys with flourishing farms and orchards. However, they have competition—offshore, and paralleling the mainland, are the unusual mountains of the Alexander Archipelago. Actually, they are mountain remnants from about 25 million years ago. Just the tops of this long-submerged mountain mass are visible. Transformed by time and nature, they are a sheltered island paradise, treasured by the boating set and by all who seek the pleasures of sun and sea. There are myriad bays and waterways to explore, excellent fishing, camping, hiking, and opportunities for intriguing port calls, from millionaires' mansions and gardens to totem-pole-studded Indian villages.

This string of islands of the Alexander Archipelago and the strip of coastline between mountains and sea make up the Alaskan Panhandle. It has more in common with its southern coastal neighbors than with the rest of Alaska—contained in a huge, pan-shaped peninsula jutting northwest, its shores washed by the Pacific Ocean, the Arctic Ocean, and the Bering Sea. These are only a few of the attractions—and the islands and Canada's "Sunshine Coast" have exceptionally good weather.

The International Boundary zigzags between these pleasure islands from the 49th Parallel, then heads westward down the middle of the Strait of Juan de Fuca, between Vancouver Island and the Olympic Peninsula. This land division settled a long-standing stalemate over title to the San Juan Islands, occupied and claimed by both the United States and Britain.

What was known as the "Pig War" was triggered in 1859 by a British pig plundering an American potato patch. Only one shot was fired, and only the porker was killed, but the Englishman demanded British trial for the American defendant, who asked for U.S. government jurisdiction and protection. Subsequent events included warships positioned in the harbor of San Juan Island and garrisons and troops stationed at opposite ends of the island. Over the years, relations remained friendly —even convivial—between camps. Finally, in 1872, arbitration by Kaiser Wilhelm I of Germany gave the San Juan Islands to the United States, leaving the Gulf Islands to Canada.

## Color It Green

It's not presumptuous that Washington claims the title "Evergreen State" and that "Emerald City" is the nickname chosen for Seattle. Green is the predominant color in Puget Sound country, as it is in Oregon, British Columbia, and Southeast Alaska. Restful green, all shades of it, is a trademark in towns and cities, farmlands, and forest lands.

Trees grow big—and fast—on densely-forested islands and steep mainland slopes. They provide a renewable resource that supplies the timber industries, so important to the economy of all four regions.

Logging operations, especially at high elevations, are fascinating and carried out with ingenuity that involves helicopters and giant balloons. Marine traffic may pause to watch awhile. Up inlets and bordering bays, there'll be busy mills, surrounded by small logging settlements. Where there have been timber harvests, bright green regrowth is quick to start up. But for the most part, this green wilderness remains as pristine as when the first mariners admired it, marked only occasionally by small pockets of civilization.

Logging skills are honed through practice, and communities from Alaska to Oregon hold festivals for show off. There are prizes for such contests as bucking (sawing), tree-topping, tree-felling, log-rolling, and axe-throwing. Celebrations usually start with a bang-up parade. Visitors who happen to be in the vicinity for forest or other local celebrations are always welcome to join in.

Trees, unharvested, are a major benefit to recreation in national, state, and provincial parks. Rain forests are favorite walking grounds; some prize ones are in Glacier Bay National Park, Alaska, and the Olympic National Park, Washington.

The rain forest surrounding the lodge at Glacier Bay, Alaska, is an easy walk, well explained by a park ranger. It's a most unusual experience to go from there, traveling up-bay by boat, for a "return to the Ice Age." Again, with the help of a naturalist aboard, visitors learn about the wildlife and the vegetation. It becomes increasingly sparse as you approach the high sheer face of a tidewater glacier, until there is no vegetation, or just the start of primary plants, the lichens. Amazing, when you consider that where a lodge and rainforest stand now, the land was being released from its icy wraps only a hundred years ago!

Washington's Olympic Peninsula rain forest flanks a unique mountain mass at the center of the peninsula. Unlike Washington's volcanic mountains, this range of sandstone and slate rock composition has an icy core, topped by Mt. Olympus. Though king of these mountain peaks, it doesn't stand out like other snowy peaks that rise alone from lower horizons. It blends in with a chain of snowy crests that are almost as high. Here, in the glaciers that continue to flow from the summit of Olympus on all sides, the "Ice Age" is perpetuated.

Though a few roads touch on the rain forest, it's best explored by trails. The forest's most famous residents, Olympic elk, browse the bushes there in winter, helping to keep it open for sunlight to filter through and reflect in soft green tones from the feathery hanging mosses.

Unlike Glacier Bay, this "Ice Age" requires considerable up-and-down hiking to reach. Through the ages, streams and glaciers have cut through the rock, separating the terrain into high ridges and valleys. It takes stamina for the deep descents, steep climbs, and long stretches along high, scenic ridges to get to the top.

The Olympic Mountains affect the climate, causing Pacific winds to drop some 140 inches of rain a year, thus nurturing the windward, west-side rain forests. In snow, that means the mountains might take on as much as 200 inches. But there are places on the east side of the mountains that are protected by the mountain barrier. For example, along the Strait of Juan de Fuca, bordering the north side of the peninsula, there is no snow and rarely more than seventeen inches of rain a year.

## Cities and People

A common denominator of the cities throughout the four coastal regions is their age—generally young, as cities are judged. Most of them are barely starting their second hundred years. There's a feeling of the frontier and a vibrancy that is a clue to the social and cultural climate.

Populations are cosmopolitan, made up of descendants of the earliest people—Indian tribes—and perhaps of explorers, and the descendants of pioneering settlers, plus native-borns and transplants from everywhere. All display their vigor as they work and play.

Though people appear to lean toward participation sports and outdoor recreation, they are also responsive to the arts. They seem especially attuned to music of all kinds. Vancouver, British Columbia, and the neighboring college town Bellingham, across the border in Washington, are considered to be *avant garde* musically and artistically. But most all communities, besides supporting local endeavors, give a warm and lively welcome to top entertainers, from pop musicians to symphony orchestras, who periodically tour the coastal areas.

Appreciative of the natural beauty of the settings of their cities, citizens complement it by maintaining public and private parks, gardens, and home yards. They create showpieces, aided by the favorable climate and "green thumbs" that, from the results, must extend up to the elbow.

A common trait shows in the high number of fine museums, treasured by even the smallest towns: these people are savers, and they extend their efforts to preserving whole, historically significant sections of cities. At the same time, businesses are encouraged to locate in the refurbished buildings.

Residents as well as visitors are pleased with the distinctive restaurants that serve international food specialties, and original shops that feature locally created products, as well as imported goods from all over the world.

Some treasures from the past are left to be admired at the site. Petroglyphs, rock carvings from what were probably early fishermen, are found at many favorite Indian fishing grounds, such as along the Columbia River, on Vancouver Island, and in Alaska.

English is the common language, give or take some local idioms here and there. However, you can count on it, anyone who says "bean," "oot," "agayn," and "aboot," for "been," "out," "again," and "about," is bound to be a Canadian.

## Summing Up

"It's the water," brags a company famous for its brew. They concoct it near the Washington state capital, Olympia, at the end of an inlet just off Puget Sound. The company is speaking about the readily available pure artesian water, used in making their Olympia Beer by falls at Tumwater, the oldest settlement in Puget Sound country. The Hudson Bay Company considered these falls for a possible sawmill site. Mid–nineteenth-century American settlers saw other possibilities and called the town "New Market." But the name that won out came from the Chinook Indians in the area. The rhythm of the falls reminded them of a throbbing heart—thum-thum-thum—thus, in their jargon, "thum-water."

There's a message in that slick slogan that goes beyond tiny Tumwater. Throughout these coastal regions, it *is* the water, in all its forms and many uses, that paces the heartbeat of both land and people.

# OUTDOOR RECREATION ON
# THE NORTH COAST

by
**BARRY and HILDA ANDERSON**

*Barry and Hilda Anderson are freelance writers living outside Seattle. They write a weekly column for the* Seattle Post-Intelligencer *and contribute to numerous other publications.*

Recently, a southern telephone operator, on learning she was talking to a party in Seattle, exclaimed, "Oh, how lucky you are to live up there. I've always wanted to come to the Northwest and homestead."

Pacific Northwesterners are often amused by the perception of many from other parts of the country that the whole region is one vast, howling wilderness, punctuated by a few primitive communities. In actuality, thousands of travelers visit Portland, Seattle, Vancouver, and Anchorage and only glimpse the wilderness from an airplane window at 30,000 feet.

The perception, however, is not totally inaccurate. Nowhere else in the country is so much of the great outdoors so untrammeled and so close to many urban centers. Vast conifer forests grow right to water's edge all along this coast. The woodlands begin just beyond the suburbs and rise through the foothills to crest in the snow-capped Cascade and Coast Ranges. Saltwater arms of the Pacific punctuate the land mass in hundreds of places, creating thousands of miles of saltwater beaches, forested islands, coves, and inlets.

Whether the many migrants who have come here since World War II were outdoor enthusiasts already or whether the availability of all those wild lands and waters made believers of them is a moot point. But you'll be hard pressed to find a resident that doesn't sail, or ski, or hike, or fish.

During the winter months city streets are dotted with cars bearing ski racks and skis. Business people want to get away quickly after work for an evening on the slopes. On summer evenings and weekends, lakes and bays are white with the sails of amateur yachtsmen out for a few hours of cruising. And on weekends, trailheads in the mountains, where hikers have left their cars before strapping on backpacks and heading into the woods, look like supermarket parking lots.

Participating in all this outdoor activity is no trick at all for the visitor. The largest outdoor equipment and clothing manufacturers are located here and many stores will rent you anything from a pair of snowshoes to a backpack and mountain tent. Dozens of small companies offer guided bird watching, hiking, cruising, horse packing, cross-country skiing, river rafting, and other outdoor trips. Though most are not big enough to advertise nationally, you can contact them through state and provincial tourist offices.

### Getting Out on the Briny

Salmon, the premier saltwater sportfish, triggers a regional mania when the season opens in late spring. As the homeward-bound Chinooks and Cohos gather off the river mouths to begin their upstream spawning runs, squadrons of charter boats put out from every small harbor and marina along the coast. Dozens of salmon derbies attract cash-hungry weekend fishermen, and one Washington auto supply chain even releases a tagged salmon into Puget Sound that, if caught, is worth $1 million.

Hydroelectric dams, pollution, overfishing and, in recent years, the warm ocean current known as *El Niño,* have put a serious crimp in the runs in Oregon and Washington waters, but your chances of bringing home a couple of hefty specimens are still pretty good if you go during the peak of the season in July and August. You'll find the best selection of charters around the mouth of the Columbia River (Warrenton and Astoria, Oregon; Ilwaco, Washington) and at Westport, Neah Bay, and Sekiu, Washington. Seattle and Portland radio stations broadcast regular reports on where the fish are biting.

The action gets better as you move north. Charters depart from Port Alberni, Campbell River, and several other small ports on both Vancouver Island and the British Columbia mainland to fish the rich waters of the Strait of Georgia and the long, fjordlike inlets that penetrate the coastal mountains.

Serious anglers head for Alaskan waters where 50-pound Chinooks, 20-pound Cohos, and 225-pound halibut are not uncommon. All of the Panhandle ports from Ketchikan to Juneau, as well as the ports on Cook Inlet and Prince William Sound, have extensive charter fleets.

Spring's low tides bring hordes of visitors to coastal beaches in search of succulent razor and butter clams. The accepted procedure is to rent or buy a long, narrow clam shovel or a hollow metal tube called a clam gun, don your oldest clothes and wet weather gear, and head for the beach. You stomp along just at water's edge until you spot the telltale squirt of a clam burrowing. Then it's down on your knees, digging furiously to unearth the elusive bivalve before he jets away. It's cold, messy work, but the rewards of sitting around a beach fire consuming a bucket of steamed clams is worth the effort. (Note: a virus decimated the Washington clam population during the winter of 1983/84, requiring beaches to be closed for the 1984 season, but the clams are expected to return in subsequent years.)

Oregon's Tillamook Bay and the shallow harbors of Washington, British Columbia, and Alaska are prime destinations for crabbers, who fish for the native Dungeness crab with crab traps from small boats. Many marinas in the area rent the necessary gear. Oyster fanciers head for the rocky beaches of Washington's San Juan Islands and the Canadian islands just to the north.

What do you do for fun where it rains all winter? Residents in the Pacific Northwest have developed the fine art of storm watching. For sheer power and drama, few other acts of nature can match the great winter storms that lash this coast from November through March. Even as Coast Guard stations hoist the twin red gale-warning pennants, dedicated storm watchers are headed for the coast.

The key element is comfort. Find a cozy hotel and snuggle down to sounds of wind howling around the eaves and rain lashing against the windows. Add the crackle of a driftwood fire, the mournful call of a foghorn, and the wink of a lighthouse in the gloom and you have a front-row seat for nature's production.

The best winter storm-watching takes place along the central Oregon coast, where dramatic headlands jut from the sea and there is a wide variety of accommodations with a view of the action.

During the periodic lulls typical of these storms, it's time to go beachcombing. High surf and tide cast all manner of flotsam and jetsam onto the beaches—broken packing crates with Oriental markings, cork floats, colored glass bottles, shells, contorted driftwood, gem-quality agate, jasper, and garnet, and the highly prized Japanese glass fishing floats.

With the depressed fishing industry and a need to find other sources of income, charter skippers along the Oregon coast and around Westport, Washington, have organized whale-watching expeditions to view the massive California gray whales as they migrate northward in the spring. Excursion boats get within touching distance of the leviathans who, out of curiosity, may come up and nuzzle the vessel and eyeball the passengers.

Dotted with hundreds of islands, the protected reaches of Puget Sound in Washington and the Strait of Georgia in British Columbia form miles and miles of tranquil waterways ideal for cruising. Schooners, sloops and ketches, outboards, and cabin cruisers ply these waters from the first of the good sailing weather in April through the end of October. You can anchor in a secluded cove in the San Juans or Gulf Islands, explore the quiet reaches of Canadian inlets, or pit your skills against the winds and tidal rips of the Strait of Juan de Fuca.

Many of the islands are uninhabited; boat-only public parks are available on others. In the more remote waters of British Columbia, you may cruise alongside a pod of playful killer whales or confront deer, bear, and other wildlife close at hand on wilderness shorelines. Well-equipped marinas throughout the region offer rentals, marine charters, and equipment, and sometimes first-class lodging and dining.

For the truly stout-of-heart there's scuba diving and ocean kayaking. Though the waters are chilly and require a wet suit, experienced divers say the underwater fishing and exploring are outstanding. (The world's largest octopus, a monster with a tentacle spread of 25 feet 7 inches, was wrestled to the surface in Washington's Hood Canal in 1973.) Ocean kayakers lead expeditions in these Eskimo craft through the Straits and on the seaward side of Vancouver Island during the summer months.

## Into the Hills

It's no coincidence that the nation's leading outdoor clothing and equipment dealers are located in the Pacific Northwest. Everything from freeze-dried food to snowshoes is developed and field-tested in the forests and mountains of the region.

Whether or not you intend to buy, a visit to one of the big outlets in Seattle or Portland (such as REI or Eddie Bauer) is an eye-opener. Mountains of backpacks, pitons, nylon rope, maps, guidebooks, cooking gear, portable stoves, thermal underwear, parkas, boots, and other outdoor paraphernalia are crammed into every available foot of space. Shoppers range from coeds to senior citizens. You'll overhear such esoteric discussions as the merits of Gore-tex versus rip-stop nylon or down insulation versus fiberfill.

In Washington and Oregon, late April usually marks the beginning of the hiking season. As the snowline retreats to higher elevations more and more mountain trails open up, until all of the high country is snow free by about the Fourth of July.

The western slopes of the Cascade Range are densely forested with Douglas fir, cedar, and hemlock, while the eastern slopes are more sparsely forested, chiefly with Ponderosa pine.

Virtually all of the prime hiking and backpacking country in the Cascades is administered by the U.S. Forest Service and open to the public. The forest service maintains trailhead parking areas (many of them just a few hundred yards off main highways), keeps the trails cleared and signed, and even provides portable toilets in remote areas.

You have a wide choice of easy day hikes of six or seven miles roundtrip or longer expeditions overnight or for several days. Typically, these trails follow mountain valleys or climb ridges to pristine Alpine lakes and stunning mountaintop viewpoints.

The Cascade Crest Trail, which begins at the Mexican border and ends in Canada, is the primary north-south access route. In both states the trail crosses each of the trans-mountain highways, so you can hike segments of it by having someone drop you off on one highway and pick you up at the next.

Mt. Rainier National Park is a hiker's paradise, with dozens of trails that cross Alpine meadows resplendent in wildflowers in mid-summer and bring you face-to-face with the mountain's glaciers. The ninety-mile-long Wonderland Trail encircles the base of the mountain with very little elevation gain.

North Cascades National Park is virtually roadless, but laced with hiking trails. One favorite route takes you aboard the sightseeing boat, *Lady of the Lake,* fifty-five miles to the upper end of Lake Chelan, then up the Stehekin River Valley, over 5,392-foot Cascade Pass, and down to the Skagit River.

These states offer some fine coastal hiking as well. Though some segments are still unfinished, the Oregon Coast Trail stretches from the Columbia River to the California border. Because coastal towns are numerous, you can choose from a number of short hikes between towns. Climbing over massive headlands and descending to follow the beach, this trail offers some magnificent views of the coast as well as rare opportunities to see sea lion colonies and other marine mammals close offshore.

Olympic National Park encompasses a roadless stretch of wilderness coast punctuated with picturesque offshore sea stacks. Because access is difficult, most hikers schedule at least three days for this trip, camping along the beach. Inclement weather and the rugged nature of the terrain can make this hike difficult. It's not recommended for beginners.

The main body of the park includes the Olympic Mountains and several river valleys that are lush with rain forests. Good trails penetrate the area and bring you close to resident elk and mountain goat herds, but the weather is usually wet and good rain gear is recommended. Many of Olympic's trails also have enclosed trail shelters for overnight hikers.

On Vancouver Island, Pacific Rim National Park has turned an old coastal lifesaving trail into a fine hiking route. The West Coast Trail runs forty-five miles from Port Renfrew to Bamfield, where you board the thrice-weekly freight boat to return to road's end at Port Alberni. The scenery along the trail is wild and incredibly beautiful, but the hike is recommended only for experienced backpackers.

In southwestern British Columbia, Whistler Resort makes a good base for hiking into adjacent Garibaldi Provincial Park. Manning and Cathedral Provincial Parks, along the Washington border, are also good destinations.

Because so much of Alaska is true wilderness, recreational hiking opportunities are somewhat limited and hikers are cautioned against hiking without a guide. One favorite trip of several days duration takes you from Dyea, near Skagway, over the Chilkoot Pass Trail, famous as the route of the Klondike Gold Rush in 1898.

The Mountaineers (719 Pike St., Seattle, WA 98101) publishes an excellent series of guides to hiking trails in the Northwest. This club also offers guided trips in a whole range of outdoor activities.

If hiking is not your strong suit, you may want to try horse packing. Experienced outfitters lead trips into the Cascades, Olympics, and the mountains of British Columbia every summer. You need not have ridden before. Horses are gentle and the guide does all the work—

saddling up, loading the pack animals, making camp, and cooking on the trail. You need only supply a sleeping bag and an appetite.

Jim Whittaker, a Washingtonian, was the first American to reach the summit of Mt. Everest, on May 1, 1963. He and his fellow mountain climbers trained on Mt. Rainier, as do virtually all American mountaineering expeditions today. Jim's brother, Lou, operates the Rainier Guide Service that conducts guided climbs to the 14,410-foot summit three times a week during the summer months. You need not have mountain climbing experience to join one of these two-day trips, but you must be in good shape for some strenuous hiking. The service requires a one-day course in the basic skills of climbing on ice, relaying, rappelling, crevasse rescue techniques, and use of the ice axe before you go.

In Portland and Seattle, the Sierra Club, Mountaineers, Mazamas, other outdoor clubs, and some city and county parks departments conduct mountaineering classes and lead regular climbs to mountains all over the Northwest and Alaska.

## Camping

With hundreds of state, provincial, and national parks, as well as those administered by lumber companies and local governments, the region offers a myriad of camping opportunities. Early in this century a forward-looking Oregon governor, Oswald West, managed to secure the state's 400 miles of coastline in public ownership. As a result, Oregon has the best and most numerous coastal parks in the West. There are more than fifty of them along U.S. 101, seventeen of which have full camping facilities that often include hot showers and coin-operated laundries. Numerous county parks and private recreation vehicle parks round out the camping picture.

Though summer months bring crowds to the coast, the best months for camping are often September and October, when the weather is likely to be calm and sunny.

Inland, the Rogue River Valley and the foothills of the Cascades have fine state park camping along rushing streams while the jewellike lakes along the Cascade crest are dotted with the more primitive forest service campgrounds.

The Washington, British Columbia, and Alaska coasts are much less developed for camping. Washington state parks on Puget Sound and some British Columbia provincial parks on Vancouver Island and north of Vancouver provide campsites on salt water.

You'll find some of the best camping in units administered by the National Park Service—Oregon Dunes, Crater Lake, Mt. Rainier, Olympic, North Cascades. In addition to fine facilities, these campgrounds often have guided nature hikes and campfire programs that are conducted by naturalists. (Most state, provincial, and national parks charge a modest fee for camping; most national forest sites do not.)

## Hunting

Both the coastal mountains and the Cascades have deer hunting; the season is usually in October. Many of the lakes and coastal estuaries support large waterfowl populations hunted during the fall months.

For big game you must journey to Canada and Alaska. Bear, elk, deer, and mountain goats are available in the Canadian mountains. Sitka, Valdez, Wrangell, and many other coastal communities, as well as Anchorage, have hunting guides who will fly you in, outfit you, and guide you in hunting moose, goat, and bear. There are moose on the Kenai Peninsula and the fearsome Kodiak bear, world's largest carnivorous animal, on Kodiak Island.

## Freshwater Recreation

All of the North Coast is washed by copious amounts of precipitation, which feed hundreds of westward flowing creeks and rivers, during the winter and spring months. These rivers, short and swift for the most part, plunge from the slopes in cataracts of white water ideal for river rafting.

Several companies offer guided trips during the spring on the rivers of Washington and Oregon. On some trips you help paddle; on others you relax while someone else does the work. Most are single-day trips, but there are a few that run two and three days. You need no prior experience or equipment, except a wet suit (which you can rent) to protect you from the chilly waters.

Southern Oregon's Rogue River and Washington's Skagit River pass through bald eagle sanctuaries and raft trips here specialize in eagle watching. Boatmen on Oregon's McKenzie River have developed a double-ended, high-prowed dory that turns on a dime and is ideal for the white-water trips they conduct. The eastward flowing Wenatchee River is a favorite late-spring trip in Washington. Several raft companies operate the large Grand Canyon–style pontoon rafts on British Columbia's wild Fraser River from Lytton and Boston Bar. Some cruise ships plying the Inside Passage also offer river runs as optional shore excursions on Alaska's short coastal rivers.

Veteran anglers rate the freshwater streams and lakes of the North Pacific Coast as "good" to "outstanding." Trout is the primary gamefish, while northern pike and Arctic grayling dominate the colder waters of British Columbia and Alaska.

Most Oregon and Washington streams and lowland lakes open in late April. In Oregon the Rogue, Umpqua, and McKenzie rivers are popular, as are the Lewis, Skykomish, Stillaguamish, and Skagit in Washington. Some of the finest trout fishing in these two states is found in the Alpine lakes above 3,000 feet. You must hike in to the best spots and trails are often not snow-free until late June.

Hardiest (some say foolhardy) of northwest fishermen are the steelheaders, who brave frigid waters, snow, wind, and rain for the chance to catch this elusive fish. The steelhead is a sea-run trout that grows to twenty pounds or more and returns to fresh water during the winter months. Those who have caught them affirm the quarry is well worth the hardship it takes to catch them.

The most prodigious fishing tales come from the north country, where anglers tell of lakes teeming with trout eager to be caught. Fly-in fishing is the way to do it in both British Columbia and Alaska. Typically, you arrange with a bush pilot to fly you into a wilderness lake and return to pick you up at a pre-set time. Some of these remote lakes have comfortable lodges and you can arrange a package that includes transportation, lodging, meals, and gear.

## Winter Sports

It's a rare child who grows up in the Pacific Northwest without learning how to ski. From the time the first snow flies in the mountains in late October or early November through late April, the slopes are busy with skiers on weekends and weekday evenings. Dozens of ski areas, ranging from single rope-tow operations to full-scale resorts, lie scattered along the mountain spines from Mt. Ashland on the California-Oregon border to Mt. Aleyska outside of Anchorage. Most are adjacent to cross-mountain highways.

Despite advertising claims to the contrary, the snow that falls on the mountains of the North Pacific Coast is not powder. Laden with moisture from Pacific storms, it's rather wet and heavy. Northwesterners who seek the ideal condition of deep powder head for the resorts in the Rockies (like everyone else in the country).

What the Northwestern ski areas do have is accessibility. In Portland, Seattle, Vancouver, and Anchorage, the slopes are less than an hour's drive from downtown. Many visitors to these cities wedge a day or two of skiing into their sightseeing itineraries. Business travelers often opt for night skiing at the end of the business day. With half a dozen exceptions, all of the ski areas in Oregon, Washington, British Columbia, and Alaska are day- and evening-use areas with no overnight accommodations.

Oregon's major resort is Mt. Bachelor, near Bend on the eastern slope of the Cascades. Mt. Bachelor, with ten chair lifts and miles of downhill slopes and cross-country trails, is about three hours from Portland.

Granddaddy of them all is Timberline, high on the southern slopes of Mt. Hood about fifty miles east of Portland. Whether or not you ski, the lodge itself is worth the visit. A project of the Depression-era W.P.A. using local materials and craftsmen, Timberline Lodge is an architectural masterpiece of stone, timber, and ironwork. Skiing often continues on the upper slopes of Mt. Hood well into July. Snowcats take you over the glaciers.

Most of the action in Washington is focused on White Pass, Crystal Mountain (near Mt. Rainier), four small operations clustered around Snoqualmie Pass, just east of Seattle, and Stevens Pass. Olympic National Park has a small ski area at Hurricane Ridge near Port Angeles. At Mt. Baker, on the Canadian border, skiing lasts into summer, with the Slush Cup (skiing across a slush-filled lake) held on the Fourth of July.

Skiers on Grouse Mountain are within sight of downtown Vancouver. Many non-skiers ride the gondola to the restaurant at the top for dinner and watch the sun go down and see the lights come on in the city below.

The most complete ski resort in the region is Whistler, located in the coastal mountains seventy miles north of Vancouver. Designed in the European tradition, a village of condominiums, hotels, restaurants, and other visitor facilities is strung along the base of two mountains, Whistler and Blackcomb. A number of interconnected lifts permits you to ski the entire length of the valley, ascending one mountain and descending to the base of the next.

Alaska's Mt. Alyeska is located about 40 miles southeast of Anchorage.

Though they're outside the coastal region, Sun Valley in Idaho and Banff–Lake Louise in Alberta are the closest major ski resorts. Both offer superb skiing, a long season, plenty of powder snow, and some of the finest resort facilities in North America. Sun Valley, one of America's oldest ski resorts and popular as the subject of several motion pictures, has two sizable mountains on which to ski. If you choose not to drive, you can reach this area by air, with connections from the east through Salt Lake City and from the west through Boise.

Noted for their elegant hotels—Banff Springs and Chateau Lake Louise—Banff and Lake Louise in Alberta offer three areas for downhill skiing. Access by air is through Calgary, but many visitors prefer to take the incredibly scenic train ride through the Canadian Rockies on VIA Rail Canada's *Canadian*. Both of these resort complexes offer a whole range of winter activities including ice skating, skiing behind horses, sleigh rides, snowmobiling, cross-country skiing, and winter wildlife viewing.

Skiers who've tried everything else come from all over the world to ski by helicopter in British Columbia's Bugaboo Mountains. The typical helicopter skiing package (for experts only) airlifts you into remote but well-appointed mountain lodges. Each day a helicopter takes you to a different mountaintop for miles of downhill runs through unbroken snow. It's the ultimate in wilderness skiing.

Snow-covered logging roads and forest trails in all of the northwest mountains provide plenty of cross-country skiing as well. Local forest ranger districts provide maps and, in some cases, sign the trails. You'll find some of the best cross-country skiing, as well as snowshoeing, in Mt. Rainier National Park.

# FOODS OF THE PACIFIC NORTHWEST

### by
### YVONNE ROTHERT

*Yvonne Rothert has been food editor for* The Oregonian *and is currently an editor at* Northwest Magazine. *She contributed the Portland chapter to the book* Where to Eat in America.

Fresh is the word for the foods of the Pacific Northwest, as fresh as the rain-cleaned atmosphere and the political ideology of this last frontier of continental North America. The same rain that keeps the country on the coastal side of the mountains green year-round also waters an abundance of food crops that must have seemed heaven-sent to nineteenth-century pioneers. They reached the end of the arduous Oregon Trail to find fertile land, fish-filled streams, and, finally, the Pacific Ocean with its bounty of seafood.

To understand the foods of the Pacific Northwest, it is necessary to be at least a little familiar with the area's geography. Oregon, Washington, and British Columbia are divided roughly north to south by mountain ranges. West of the mountains are the rolling, fertile lands filled with orchards, vineyards, and vegetable field crops. East of the mountains are range lands for beef cattle and lamb, vast wheat fields, and thousands of acres planted in potatoes—many of the potatoes served elsewhere as "Idaho" potatoes actually come from eastern Washington and Oregon. The annual crop of "Walla Walla Sweet" onions is eagerly awaited.

Another look at the map shows the hundreds of miles of coastline in this country, making it readily apparent why fine fish and seafood restaurants abound in all the major cities of the Northwest, and why many of these restaurants offer on their menus special "catch of the day" listings that enable diners to order the best of the freshest.

## Salmon and Sturgeon

Mention the Columbia River, Puget Sound, and more northern waters, and salmon immediately comes to the mind of the knowledgeable diner. Ever since those first travelers west found the native American Indians landing the fish from river banks or in coastal waters from Oregon to Alaska, salmon has been *the* fish of the Northwest. Baked or barbecued whole, filleted or cut into steaks, it offers an unmatched culinary experience. Lucky is the traveler who is privileged to attend a traditional Indian salmon "bake," where fillets of the fish are woven on slender branches stuck into the ground and cooked around fires of the seasoned wood of the native northwest alder.

Less known to the world, but almost equally fine, is sturgeon, a white-fleshed fish that grows to enormous proportions. During its limited season, when this scarce fish appears on menus and in fish markets, it is a delicacy diners may find a treat surpassing even salmon for delicate flavor.

Both salmon and sturgeon are available smoked, too, and some specialty shops, particularly along the coast, will pack and ship smoked fish to the folks back home.

In recent years, a new food industry has developed around the processing of sturgeon roe for caviar, and the coral-colored salmon roe, often used as bait by northwest sport fishermen, is also processed and shipped to the Orient, particularly to Japan, where it is considered a great delicacy.

Salmon catches have been dwindling in recent years, and commercial fishermen have turned to other species, especially the bottom fish of coastal waters: sole, some flounder, black cod, hake (marketed euphemistically as Pacific whiting), and several varieties of rockfish. Pacific red snapper, one of the rockfish and a different breed entirely from Atlantic red snapper, makes good eating in its own right and is often less expensive than other varieties of fish.

### Shellfish

Shellfish lovers offered Dungeness crab and Olympia or Yaquina Bay oysters might be hard-put to make a choice. Every lover of fine food, however, should have the experience at least once of dining on sweet, succulent Dungeness crab meat, whether it's served in a predinner crab cocktail, presented whole—"cracked"—for the diner to pick out the meat himself, or used as a stuffing for native rainbow trout. For its finest—and probably most costly—presentation, try Dungeness crab legs sauteed in butter and laced with cognac or dry sherry.

From more northern coastal waters come the much larger and more plentiful King crab and snow crab, commonly shipped to other parts of the United States and Canada. Given a choice, however, most Northwesterners opt for Dungeness.

Pacific Northwest oysters are smaller than many varieties found in other waters, but what they lack in size they make up for in distinctive flavor. Found growing naturally, of course, they are also produced in oyster "farms" in shallow, protected coastal waters.

Shrimp are abundant, too—the tiny ones often marketed as "salad" shrimp—as are clams, from small "butter" clams for steaming to the much-larger razor clams usually served fried, and the really large geoducks (pronounced "gooey-ducks").

For years one of the greatest unused resources of these waters has been the millions of mussels attached to the underwater rocks and harvested at low tide only by natives in the know. In recent years they have been made available commercially by fish marketers in the know. If smoked mussels appear on a menu, be sure to give them a try.

### About the Meats

Red meats have their place in the Northwest, of course, and steak houses still are among the most popular restaurants. Many of the beef cattle raised on Pacific Northwest ranches get to the table here only after they have made a trip to Midwestern feed lots for their final fattening-up. Northwest veal is not as pale and tender as the Wisconsin variety; many restaurants serve the shipped-in Wisconsin product.

Fresh lamb is available year-round from northwest ranches, but it has never reached the height of popularity among natives that it enjoys in some other areas.

## Home-Grown

Apples, peaches, apricots, pears, and cherries fill Northwest orchards, and the quality of strawberries, raspberries, and blueberries grown in the Northwest is unmatched. Most restaurants feature them seasonally fresh. Motorists should watch for fresh fruits in the roadside stands that dot the highways in growing areas.

Hazelnuts—more often called filberts by Northwesterners—are an important crop in Oregon. Often appearing as a recipe ingredient, they can be found tinned in specialty shops—roasted, toasted, flavored, sugared, or plain.

## Fine Dining

In spite of the abundance of native foods, fine dining has really come into its own only during recent decades. Formerly even the most loyal Northwesterners felt they had to travel—to San Francisco, say—for their experiences in fine dining. For the present generation, however, the story has changed considerably, and myriad restaurants worthy of the area's fine foods are well-established throughout the Northwest, particularly in the major cities. Off the beaten track, too, the traveler can find eating places that far exceed the banality of the clichéd "roadside diner." Restaurants specialize in an assortment of ethnic cuisines, and excellent apprenticeship programs and culinary schools in community colleges are turning out home-trained chefs who are beginning to vie with their European-trained colleagues. Northwest varietal wines have also been competing with their European counterparts in recent years. Produced by wineries considered small in comparison to those of Europe and California, they nonetheless are of a quality that is making itself felt in international wine competitions. Pinot noirs, chardonnays, white rieslings, and merlots, among others, are being noted by visiting wine connoisseurs and are also being marketed in major East Coast cities. Most upper-echelon northwest restaurants have special listings of the northwest wines on their wine lists. (For a complete list of vineyards and visiting hours, write Oregon Winegrowers Association, Box 2134, Salem, OR 97310.)

# OREGON

*Fine City, Awesome Scenery*

**by**
**RALPH FRIEDMAN, LINDA LAMPMAN, and JULIE STERLING**

*Ralph Friedman has spent much of his life writing about Oregon. A Portland resident, he is the author of* Oregon for the Curious, Tales Out of Oregon, Northwest Passages, *and* A Touch of Oregon, *among other titles.*

*Linda Lampman and Julie Sterling, who covered Portland for this book, met when they were reporters for* The Oregonian. *Together they have written* The Portland Guidebook *and* Oregon for All Seasons.

34

French Canadian voyageurs seeking better prices for beaver pelts, the British who built the trading posts to receive the furs, southern families fleeing the certain Civil War, mountain men with a yearning for a new land, New England sea captains searching for a safer harbor, and suffragettes with a vision a hundred years before ERA are all part of Oregon's historical tapestry. And the diversity that helped build a territory into a state remains abundantly evident today—physically and philosophically.

In one day a visitor can dig razor clams at the beach during an early morning low tide and carry them, still salty and cold, to bubble up for chowder after a sunset ski run in the Cascade Range. Or he or she can join an evening audience of hundreds sitting under the stars in an exact replica of the Globe Theater in Ashland to watch one of the nation's best ̀Shakesperian companies, and by dawn, with just half-an-hour drive, stand in isolated timber casting a fly out to tempt a giant trout in the rapids of the Rogue River. Portland itself—a growing city with fine restaurants, intriguing galleries, and what some have termed "new-wave" architecture—is but a short drive from the 400-plus–mile coastline guaranteed by statute to be open to everyone who yearns for sand between the toes.

The spread of political opinions seems to keep the state's Congressional leaders half hawks and half doves. National pollsters keep a careful eye on Oregon's election returns, which consistently reflect national trends toward either party.

Preserving the state's natural beauty, however, does seem an issue on which all can agree. A clean air act, adopted by the state in 1983, prohibits smoking in public places and sets up designated smoking areas in restaurants, shopping centers, and public buildings. The first bottle bill, placing a deposit on soda and beer cans and bottles in order to keep them off the street and have them recycled, was passed in Oregon a decade ago. The Department of Environmental Quality monitors both air and water quality daily and has the power to enforce clean emissions whether they be from factories or residential chimneys.

Visitors will find Oregonians friendly and helpful—but if you don't want to be immediately classified as an outsider, be advised that the state name is pronounced "ORY-gun," the Willamette Valley is "Will-AM-utt," and the beautiful Deschutes River in Southern Oregon is always referred to as the "Da-Shoots." Even if you get your pronunciations right, there's little chance that any Oregonian will consider you a native; publically they accept only residents of 25 years or more as "semi-native" and actually seem to subscribe to the idea that no one is a native who did not travel by hardship to Oregon before its statehood in 1852. But if you're happy being a tourist, then Oregon is a wonderful place in which to be one.

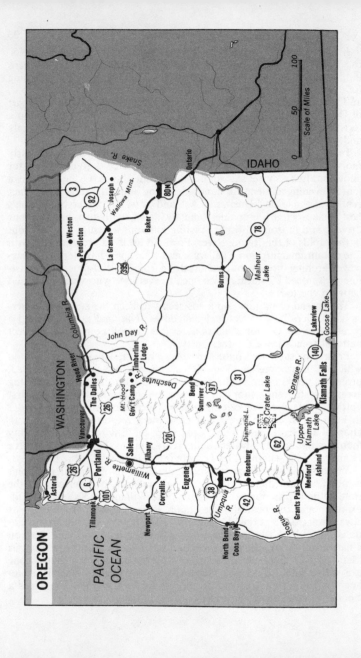

# EXPLORING PORTLAND

Not so many years ago the pedestrian on Portland's downtown streets could know this city easily by checking his bearings by siting Mt. Hood, rising over the east side, and knowing that the Willamette River rested below, dividing the city's east side residential from west side urban areas.

Today the clatter of jackhammers and the bright arcs of welding torches span newly rising buildings as the port city soars toward a totally new cosmopolitan community; now to really get to know Portland it is necessary to put on some comfortable shoes and walk. It's still a small town at heart and an easy gait will carry the curious through all the main urban streets in one day with plenty of time for lunch, coffee or tea breaks, shopping stops, and photo opportunities.

## At the Center of Downtown

Pioneer Courthouse Square, filling a city block from Sixth Avenue to Broadway between Morrison and Yamhill, remains the center of the downtown area. It also tells the story of Portland's present growth. Originally the site of the grand old Portland Hotel, where old-timers say President Taft was wedged in his bathtub for an uncomfortable period of time, the site brought tears to the eyes of Portland when the gracious grey-stone Queen Anne–style hotel was razed in 1950 to make way for an asphalt parking lot. Several decades later, newer city fathers decided to turn the block back into a gathering spot, this time creating an open space bedecked with bronze pillars, a glass conservatory, and benches in the sun—all laid out on bricks individually inscribed with the names of the citizens who paid for them.

West, across the square, is Nordstrom, the city's largest fashion outlet for men, women, and children, in front of which coffee and fresh pastries are sold on the sidewalk, rain or shine. Heading south on Broadway, look for the old Jackson Tower, a reminder of the old Broadway style of building with its clock tower topped by flagpoles and its rim of lights that twinkle every night. The building formerly housed the *Oregon Journal,* for years Portland's afternoon newspaper. Farther south on Broadway, between Taylor and Salmon, rises the great, grey monolith that is the Hilton Hotel. Portland was both enthralled and appalled when the hotel first rose in its midst, but just a couple of decades of Oregon weather has subdued its tones and caused greenery

# Points of Interest

1) Art Museum
2) Benson Hotel
3) City Hall
4) Civic Auditorium
5) Civic Theater
6) County Justice Center
7) Hilton Hotel
8) Ira's Foundation
9) Japanese Garden
10) Lownsdale/Chapman Squares
11) Marriott Hotel
12) Memorial Coliseum
13) Multnomah Civic Stadium
14) Multnomah County Courthouse
15) Nordstrom
16) O'Bryant Square
17) Oregon Historical Society
18) Oregon Museum of Science & Industry
19) Performing Arts Center
20) Pioneer Courthouse/Square
21) Portland Building
22) Portland Motor Hotel
23) Portland Police Museum
24) Portland State University & Architectural Preservation Gallery
25) Post Office; Meier & Frank
26) Trailways Bus Depot
27) Tri-Met Customer Service
28) Union Station
29) Waterfront Park
30) Willamette Center (Visitors Info)
31) Yamhill Market
32) Zoo

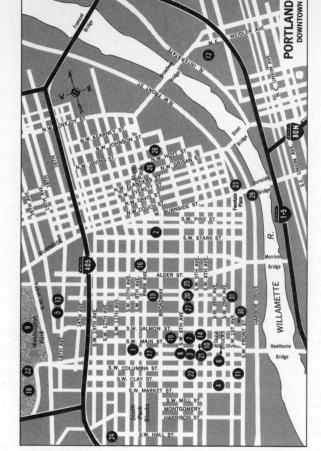

to cover its sides, giving this member of the international chain a very Northwest appearance. Across the street is Metro Broadway, a clutch of counter-service eateries, and next door to Metro is the Portland outlet for the Lawrence Gallery, one of the finest outlets for Northwest artists.

## The Park Blocks

Farther south up the rise beginning at Taylor is the site of the new Performing Arts Center, a three-building complex already under construction. Take a right, to the west, at S.W. Jefferson. On the corner is Abernethy's, an excellent spot for lunch or supper, and across Broadway is The Oregonian Building, a show-stopper in tinted green glass when it was constructed in the 1950s. It houses the offices of the local paper of the same name. Just west of Broadway is Park, the only north-south street bearing a name instead of a number in downtown Portland (it takes the place of Ninth Avenue). Park, or the Park Blocks, was set aside by early settlers in the 1850s as a public roadway through the city. At the corner of Jefferson and Park are the Oregon Historical Society on the east side and the Portland Art Museum on the west. The Historical Society includes three floors of Oregon history open free of charge to the public every day but Sunday. The main floor is devoted to rotating shows of Northwest historic importance; the second floor includes a wonderful series of dioramas of Northwest Indian life, complete with artifacts; and the third floor holds the reference library, also open to the public.

The Portland Art Museum, just across the street, was designed by Pietro Belluschi in 1930 and gave the architect an international reputation. His skill is ably demonstrated by the fact that he returned to design the museum's Hoffman Wing 40 years later, giving the brick and marble building its present façade with no clues to the addition. The museum, open Tuesday through Saturday, includes an excellent display of Northwest Indian art as well as permanent collections of Renaissance, African, Asian, and Pre-Columbian art, and traveling shows of importance.

A short walk north (that's downhill) through the Park Blocks will give you an appreciation for settlers who set the property aside from commercial construction. Bronze statues centered in each block, as well as ancient elms sheltering seasonal flowers, provide a pleasant walk or stop for the visitor, as well as for the Portland State University students who attend classes at the south end. The tree-lined stroll ends abruptly with the brick face of the Arlington Club, Portland's last all-male bastion. To the north is O'Bryant Square, an urban plaza popular for outdoor lunches and concerts.

## Downtown Mall

Turn right toward the river on Salmon Street and walk past the side of the Hilton Hotel until you reach the brick-lined mall of S.W. Sixth Avenue. Cross the street on Sixth and walk south (right) past the Orbanco Building, the city's first reflecting building, which reflects black images of the new and the old upon its sleek facade. Photographers will enjoy the imaginative results of images caught in its glassy sides. A terra cotta gazebo on the west side of the building is all that is left of the block's former resident, the old Congress Hotel. Step through its gates and descend to Harrington's Bar and Grill below, a lively stop for lunch, dinner, cocktails, or dancing.

Turning toward the river again on Main Street, pass the Standard Plaza, one of the first Portland buildings thoughtful enough to withdraw itself from the sidewalks to open up wider spaces for pedestrians. This is a more common occurrence today; builders often win a construction bid in the city by providing improved conditions for pedestrians, allowing for more flowers, trees, and art. Rian's Breadbasket, on the Standard Plaza main level, is a good stop for coffee and fresh blueberry muffins.

## Architecture: Past and Present

Just east of the Standard Plaza, between Fourth and Fifth and stretching from Main south to Columbia, are two buildings that could be seen to symbolize Portland's movement from the past to the future. Between Madison and Jefferson is the historic city hall, designed by William Whidden and built in 1895. Whidden came to the city to work on the Portland Hotel and stayed to leave his imprint on many of the municipal buildings. The old building, with its Italian *palazzo* air, is almost overwhelmed by Michael Graves's new Portland Building to the north, the new center for city services that drew international attention with its completion in 1983. The building is nothing less than outrageous: the blue-tiled lower regions give way to imaginative orange garlands along the upper stories and the entire structure is blessed by the marble carving "Portlandia," who kneels above the main floor, arms extended. Everyone has an opinion about the Graves building, which has already starred in a Japanese commercial. If you stand south of the Whidden version of city hall, looking north toward Graves's version, you will find some form and color repetitions which may or may not be coincidental.

Before heading north, take a short sprint south on Third to Clay through the rosy brick Fountain Plaza project to Portland's Civic

Auditorium. The auditorium is faced by another ingenious work of art, loved by the entire city and nicknamed "The People's Fountain." Officially dedicated "Ira's Fountain" for the late Ira Keller, the block-square sculpture in cement is covered with rushing waterfalls and rimmed by many freshly filled ponds. As part of the total artistic concept, people are encouraged to step behind the waterfalls and into the ponds. The watery art is so popular that lifeguards are employed in the summer months.

Returning Oregon's rivers to its people has been a main concern of city and state leaders for the past decade. In 1984 the original Columbia River Highway was named a historic landmark, ensuring that its twisting curves touching the Columbia Gorge and providing breathtaking views would remain intact. If you continue east on S.W. Clay, past the Marriott Hotel, you will come to another venture toward personalizing the Willamette River. In the building is a giant esplanade, capable of holding the Oregon Symphony for summer concerts at the river's edge. Abutting the public gathering place will be a series of condominiums and retail spaces all opening on the river's front. In addition, a greenway law allows public access to all river edges, whether the land above is private or not.

Heading back north again, take Third Avenue and you will come to the new Multnomah County Justice Center, between Main and Madison. By state law, one percent of all revenues must go toward art in public places and this new center, opened in the winter of 1983, is abundantly ornamented by local artists—from the columns at the doorway on S.W. Third to the bronze exterior lights, glass ceiling ornaments, and sculpture in the main lobby. The building also houses the Multnomah County Jail in a new concept of open living now under national study.

The two parks facing the Justice Center, Lownsdale and Chapman Squares, as well as the Portland Building, were dedicated in 1852 and have always provided a spot for public debate. Originally designated by block as "Men's" and "Women's," the two parks are now totally integrated, but local debate on every other issue continues at noontime rallies. The statue of the elk that lifts its antlers mid-street between the two blocks marks a long-ago grazing ground for a bull elk who lived in the nearby hills. A popular photographic study, the statue was given to the city in 1900 and neither time nor traffic, which must maneuver beneath the hoofs, has changed its position.

Heading north toward Yamhill Street, be sure to look east at the corner of Salmon Street where the glass Portland General Electric complex gives everyone a lift on an antique merry-go-round spinning on the street level at First Avenue. If you do continue down Yamhill, you'll find visitors information available near the waterfront at the southwest corner of Front and Salmon.

The Yamhill Market, a designated stop for the city's new light rail system, is open seven days a week on Yamhill at Second. Four stories are well designed in what appears to be an old two-story building. The third floor is devoted to superior fast-food outlets, including a mix of cuisines from France, Italy, South America, south Chicago, and the Far East. On the main floor the air is filled with the aroma of fresh-baked cookies, hand-dipped chocolates, and fresh seafood still damp from the Pacific Ocean.

The Yamhill Market is on the border of Portland's Old Town, which stretches north along Second through N.W. Everett Street. The iron-front buildings, many carefully restored, house specialty shops, excellent restaurants, and boutiques. Saturday or Sunday, when area artists gather under the Burnside Bridge, is an excellent time to explore Old Town.

### Old Town

To visit Portland's Old Town, continue north on Second Avenue toward Ankeny. (Don't complain about the eight-block distance; the city's hardy founding fathers walked daily to their businesses here from their homes on S.W. King Street, a block of Historic Landmark houses just off Salmon at S.W. 21st.) At the corner of Second and Stark is Victoria's Nephew, a good stop for light lunch or high tea in an atmosphere of Winston Churchill's finest hour. A block to the west on S.W. Third and Oak is the Portland Outdoor Store, a one-of-a-kind enterprise for western and eastern riding gear. Texans fill their shopping bags here at every visit. As you continue north to Second you will pass the Hazeltine Building on the west side between Pine and Ash. The old stone façade still bears the high-water mark from Portland's great flood of the 1800s. The main floor is the home of Crêpe Faire, an excellent spot for breakfast, lunch, dinner, or a late night snack.

You will be approaching Ankeny now, the first in a long list of alphabetized streets and the last of the narrow old Portland cobblestone streets. Just west off Second on Ankeny is Dan and Louis Oyster Bar, a Portland landmark in itself and the spot to stop for fresh Yaquina oysters on the half shell or in steamy stew. The building once housed Portland's city government, and the preservation-minded Wachsmiths, who own the restaurant, have left the upper story intact, including dias, meeting hall, and Victorian city offices. Toward the river on the right is the New Market Street Theater, where the traveling guests played to early Portland and even President Grant joined in the applause. Recently renovated, the elegant brick and cast-iron building is a cluster of small shops and eateries. Captain Ankeny's Well on the second level honors the seagoing captain who made Portland his final stop. The Well serves beer, wine—and ginger ale at the behest of the teetotaling owner. The new glass addition to the Market Street Theater provides a glittering frame for Skidmore Fountain, a gift to Portland by Stephen Skidmore in 1888. The fountain is dedicated to the thirst of men, horses, and dogs, and true to its period, the women were left to do the work, as evidenced by the three lovely bronze ladies who hold the fountain bowl.

Just beyond the fountain's splash, across Front Street, Waterfront Park begins with the contemporary aluminum sculpture by Bruce West, a backdrop for lively music most warm Saturdays and Sundays in the city when Saturday Market surrounds the public with art, food and spontaneous entertainment under the Burnside Bridge. Just below the seawall here is a floating dock for fishing and river watching.

Walking under the Burnside Bridge is the best way to cross the busy throughway of Burnside. You'll pop up to a safe sidewalk and pass several fine restaurants, including the tropical Key Largo, with its nighttime live music, and the elegant Norton House, which offers continental cuisine and live opera.

Just beyond Couch Street is Import Plaza, the largest of the direct shipment stores in the city. But before you encumber yourself with baskets, piñatas, and other bulky imports fresh off the ship, turn left on Couch to visit three museums on one of the newest of the Old Town restorations—Capt. John H. Couch Square, at the southeast corner of Second and Couch. The Oregon Preservation Resource Center, The Advertising Museum, and the Portland Police Museum are all here.

Couch and Davis are lined with many fine small shops selling everything from food to clothing to Indian artifacts. On a warm day stop by Jazz De Opus at Second and Couch for a sidewalk luncheon or climb the stairs to La Patisserie for espresso, desserts, or late-night snacks and a neighborhood window view of old Portland.

Old Town returns with a shiny nudge to the twentieth century, whether walkers turn west toward the rosy new tower of U.S. Bancorp at S.W. Sixth and Pine or to One Pacific Square, the cool glass-and-aluminum environment for Northwest Natural Gas Company on N.W. First and Flanders.

## Pioneer Courthouse

Return to city center via Morrison Street, at the north end of Yamhill Market, and you can stop for your post card stamps at the city's most historic business site, the Pioneer Courthouse, on S.W. Fifth between Morrison and Yamhill. Built in 1869, during the Andrew

Johnson administration, the building is topped by a cupola that remains open to the public at times; here visiting dignitaries were taken for a bird's-eye view of a young Portland. The first federal office building in the Pacific Northwest, the courthouse is the oldest public building in the region. Completely renovated and true to the nineteenth-century design, all offices, including the elegant Victorian courtroom home of the Ninth U.S. Circuit Court of Appeals, are in operation and may be viewed by the public. The U.S. Post Office occupies the main floor. Just across the street on Morrison is Meier & Frank Co., the city's largest department store, with ten floors of general merchandise, several spots for eating, and an Oregon gift shop, which is located on the main floor.

## PRACTICAL INFORMATION FOR PORTLAND

**HOW TO GET THERE. By Air.** Major airlines that fly into Portland International Airport are *Air California (AirCal); Alaska; American; Continental; Delta; Eastern; Frontier; Northwest Orient; Pacific Southwest (PSA); Republic; TWA; United; Western;* and *Wien Air Alaska.*

Two commuter airlines, also flying into Portland International, serve points in Oregon, Washington, Idaho, and elsewhere in the Pacific Northwest. They are *Cascade,* (800) 541–5552,with service from spots in Oregon, Washington, Idaho, Montana, Utah, and Canada; and *Horizon Air,* (800) 547–9308, serving Oregon, Washington and Idaho, including seasonal service to Sun Valley.

For information on getting into town from the airport, see *How to Get Around,* below.

**By train.** Considering the cutbacks AMTRAK has suffered in recent years, Portland is favored with relatively good service to points north, south, and east, including Seattle, San Francisco, Los Angeles, Salt Lake City, and Chicago via Pasco and Spokane, Washington, or via Denver. The toll-free number for AMTRAK Intercity Rail Passenger Service Information and Reservations is (800) 872–7245.

**By bus.** Two transcontinental lines, *Greyhound* and *Trailways,* serve Portland.

**By car.** Travelers to Portland by automobile will follow the approximate route of the Oregon pioneers if they take route I-84, which enters the state from Idaho at Ontario, Oregon. From California, motorists can take efficient I-5, which crosses the state line just south of Ashland, or scenic U.S. 101, which travels along the coast, with offshoots east to Portland.

**HOTELS AND MOTELS.** Hotel and motel accommodations in Portland are developing as fast as new foundations can be poured. As this edition goes to press, a new deluxe hotel will open its doors directly adjacent to the also-new Performing Arts Center on S.W. Broadway at Salmon. Beyond the planning board stage as well as two more deluxe hotels, one in the Fountain Plaza complex across from Civic Auditorium and another in the four-block Morrison Street project between Morrison and Yamhill streets. Throughout the city other facilities for visitors continually undergo complete renovations, which sometimes include changes in name or ownership.

Most deluxe rates will be found in the city center. A price listed as "expensive" in an outlying area may offer all the luxuries to be found in the more central location. Unless otherwise noted, these hotels can be expected to have air conditioning and TVs and to accept most major credit cards. All rates given are based on double occupancy and and are categorized as follows: *Deluxe,* $70 and up; *Expensive,* $50 to $70; *Moderate,* $30 to $50; *Inexpensive,* $20 to $30; *Basic Budget,* under $20. Hostels and bed-and-breakfasts follow the regular listings; these are all in the *Basic Budget* category.

## AIRPORT AREA

### Deluxe

**Sheraton-Portland Airport.** 8235 N.E. Airport Way; (503) 281–2500. 215 rooms. Located right at the edge of Portland's International Airport, this inn is so well soundproofed that guests will forget the proximity until it is time for free airport delivery. Luxurious accommodations include king-size and double beds, an indoor swimming pool with Jacuzzi and fitness center, restaurant, two lounges—one with live entertainment. Free parking.

### Expensive

**Chumaree Comfortel,** N.E. 82nd and Sandy Blvd.; (503) 256–4111. 119 rooms. The owners will drive visitors to the airport and store their cars free of charge for four weeks. Complimentary drinks at sunset and complimentary breakfast. Restaurant and lounge with live entertainment, suites with fireplaces, outdoor pool, sauna, Jacuzzis in some rooms, TV with movie channel.

**Cosmopolitan Airtel.** 6221 N.E. 82nd; (503) 255–6511. 96 rooms. Travelers with extra energy will especially appreciate this hotel, with its outdoor swimming pool, mineral bath, saunas, outdoor tennis courts, putting green, and horseshoe courts. Airport transportation, restaurant and lounge. Free parking.

**Holiday Inn at the Airport.** 8439 N.E. Columbia Blvd.; (503) 256–5000. 286 rooms. Amenities include indoor pool, Jacuzzi, and game room. Restaurant and lounge with disc jockey. Free airport transportation and free parking.

### Moderate

**Flamingo Best Western Motel.** 9727 N.E. 82nd; (503) 255–1400. 173 rooms. Extras include heated pool, therapy pool, and four Jacuzzi suites. Free parking, restaurant and lounge with live entertainment, long-boy beds.

**Fortniter Best Western Motel.** 4911 N.E. 82nd; (503) 255–9771. 52 rooms. Guests presenting key from this motel may use all the facilities of the Oregon Athletic Club, one mile away. Free parking, airport transportation, TV including movies and sports channels, complimentary coffee. Restaurant nearby.

**Nendels Motor Inn-Airport.** 7101 N.E. 82nd; (503) 255–6722. 136 rooms. Newly renovated French colonial–style inn includes restaurant and lounge, outdoor pool, whirlpool bath, two suites with sitting rooms. Free parking for one week, 24-hour on-call airport service, TV with in-room movies.

*Inexpensive*

**Best Western Capri Motel.** 1530 N.E. 82nd; (503) 253–1151. 42 rooms. Outdoor pool, free parking, complimentary coffee, restaurant and lounge adjacent, air conditioning in some rooms only.

**Cabana Motel.** 1707 N.E. 82nd; (503) 252–0224. 42 rooms. Offers a sleep/park/fly package, which includes a night's lodging for two, free parking while away for four weeks, and free transportation to and from airport. Restaurant and lounge nearby, free coffee.

**Cameo Motel.** 4111 N.E. 82nd; (503) 288–5981. 41 rooms. Coffee shop and steak house nearby. TV with movie channel.

**Chumaree Motor Inn/Holgate.** 4511 S.E. 82nd; (503) 774–8876. 40 rooms. Four units totally designed for handicapped. Free parking and airport transportation. Restaurant nearby.

# DOWNTOWN

As you may expect, downtown is the most convenient area to stay; but you'll probably have to pay for parking.

*Deluxe*

**Hilton Hotel.** 921 S.W. 6th; (503) 226–1611. 475 rooms. Ideally and centrally located, with the Performing Arts Center to the south, city shopping east and north, Oregon Historical Society and Portland Art Museum to the west, this urban inn especially caters to foreign travelers, with room service menus printed in Spanish, Japanese, German, and English, and a currency exchange at the registration desk. Facilities include outdoor pool, sauna, locker room. Hotel will gladly provide joggers with map of best city routes. Three restaurants, including the private *International Club,* which also accepts guests of the hotel, and the *Panorama,* which offers one of the best views of the city from the hotel's 23rd floor. Three lounges. Valet parking with daily charge, bus service to airport, TV with movie channel.

**Marriott Hotel.** 1401 S.W. Front; (503) 226–7600. 506 rooms. Balcony views of the Willamette River and Portland's esplanade are offered by this newer facility seemingly designed for the active set. Facilities include health club, indoor pool, sauna, Universal gym, whirlpool bath, and video parlor. The hotel is across the street from Civic Auditorium. Valet parking, bus airport service, two restaurants and two lounges, TV with in-house movies.

**Westin Benson.** S.W. Broadway at Oak; (503) 228–9611. 330 rooms. Built by Portland lumberman Simon Benson in 1913, this historic hotel has added a new wing but retains the lavish splendor of the early era, as well as the same tradition of personal service. The lobby lounge, set among potted palms, paneled in Russian Circassian walnut and lit by sparkling chandeliers, is a great place to watch for visiting celebrities. Hotel restaurants include *Trader Vic's* and the award-winning *London Grill.* Valet parking, bus airport service.

### Expensive

**Red Lion Motor Inn-Portland Center.** 310 S.W. Lincoln; (503) 221–9450. 238 rooms. Luxurious, sprawling, motel-style development within short, downhill walk to city center. Courtesy limo to airport. Restaurant and lounge with live entertainment. Free parking, pool.

**Imperial Hotel.** 400 S.W. Broadway; (503) 228–7221. 145 rooms. Spacious, comfortable city-center hotel often frequented by cattle ranchers who appreciate the room to spread out. Children stay free on rollaways. Free parking, bus transportation to airport. Restaurant and lounge.Free local calls.

**Mallory Motor Hotel.** 729 S.W. 15th; (503) 223–6311. 160 rooms. Comfortable older hotel, across from Portland Civic Theatre. Home away from home for Portland's James Beard. Dining room, lounge, free phones.

**Portland Motor Hotel.** 1414 S.W. 6th; (503) 221–1611. 178 rooms. Businessmen visiting the city often opt for this convenient motor hotel located across from The Oregonian building. Personal shuttle picks up guests from airport bus at downtown stop. Free parking, restaurant, lounge, TV with in-room movies, outdoor heated pool, non-smoking sections.

**Riverside West Motor Hotel.** 50 S.W. Morrison; (503) 221–0711. 138 rooms. At Front Avenue, with some rooms overlooking Willamette River. Shuttle for airport bus passengers. Free parking, unusually fine restaurant: *The Park Place.* Lounge, big-screen Monday night football.

### Inexpensive

**Caravan Motor Hotel.** 2401 S.W. 4th; (503) 226–1121. 40 rooms. Caters to businesspeople; executive suites and family units. Free parking, restaurant and lounge, free coffee, video player for movies in room on request. Across street from 12-acre park and jogging track.

**Corsun Arms Motor Hotel.** 809 S.W. King; (503) 226–6288. 82 rooms. Older hotel/motel in Portland's West Hills neighborhood. Clean and comfortable. Some suites with kitchens. Indoor and outdoor pools, TV with movie channel.

## EAST SIDE

The Lloyd Center mall and the Memorial Coliseum have spawned a number of east side inns and convention centers.

### Expensive

**Red Lion/Lloyd Center.** 1000 N.E. Multnomah; (503) 281–6111. 520 rooms. Newest and largest facility in Oregon for this northwest chain that stresses luxurious comfort. This Lloyd Center shopping-area inn has a pool, exercise room, suites, including lanai suites that open directly to the pool, and vast public areas—three restaurants and three lounges, one with live entertainment. Limosine service to airport. A popular convention center.

**Cosmopolitan Hotel.** 1030 N.E. Union; (503) 235–8433. 176 rooms. Adjacent to Memorial Coliseum and near Lloyd Center shopping area, this establishment draws many regular customers. Free parking, two restaurants (one with rooftop view of the city), two lounges, swimming pool.

**Holiday Inn at the Coliseum.** 10 N.E. Weidler; (503) 239–9900. 179 rooms. Completely renovated inn with indoor pool, Jacuzzi, and workout area. Free airport transportation, restaurant and lounge, TV with in-room movies.

*Moderate*

**Best Western King's Way Inn.** 420 N.E. Holladay; (503) 233–6331. 96 rooms. Across the street from the Holiday Inn, this comfortable, older establishment offers bus airport transportation, free parking, restaurant, TV with in-room movies, whirlpool baths, Jacuzzi, and sauna.

**Best Western Sunnyside Inn.** Intersection of I-205 and S.E. Sunnyside Rd., Milwaukie; (503) 652–1500. 137 rooms. Next to Kaiser Permanente Hospital and a mile from Clackamas Town Center Shopping Center, this is a country inn with city connections just outside of Portland. Free parking, free airport transportation, restaurant and lounge, Jacuzzi and hot tub, outdoor pool, and some Jacuzzi suites.

**Hyatt Lodge.** 431 N.E. Multnomah; (503) 233–5121. 80 rooms. Located three blocks from Lloyd Center shopping area, this family-operated lodge serves free coffee, hot chocolate, doughnuts and danish from 6–11 A.M. and free cocktails from 7–9 P.M. Free parking, restaurants adjacent, TV with movie channel.

**Imperial 400 Motel.** 518 N.E. Holladay; (503) 234–4391. 35 rooms. Family rates are featured at this east-side motel. Free parking, restaurant, lounge, and airport transportation all available directly across the street. Outdoor pool.

**International Dunes Motel.** 1980 Clackamette Dr., Oregon City; (503) 655–7141. 120 rooms. This motel is on the banks of the Willamette River and directly adjacent to Clackamette Park, where children can feed the ducks or run in the open spaces. Free parking, restaurant and lounge. About 10 miles outside of Portland.

**Jade Tree Motel.** 3939 N.E. Hancock; (503) 288–6891. 48 rooms. Family-run and very clean, this motel allows small pets as well as children. Airport transportation is provided by the owner. Restaurant across the parking lot provides room service if meals are charged on credit card accepted by motel (AE, CB, DC, MC, VISA). TV with in-room movies.

**Nendels Motor Inn-Troutdale.** I-84 Troutdale Interchange; (503) 667–6212. 78 rooms. Adjacent to Burns Brothers Truck Stop, this is a good stop for travelers continuing to eastern Oregon via Mt. Hood. Free parking, free airport transportation on call, restaurant and lounge adjacent, swimming pool. About 20 minutes from downtown Portland.

**Portland TraveLodge.** 949 E. Burnside; (503) 234–8411. 78 rooms. Refurbished totally in 1983, this all-new facility offers complimentary tea and coffee in the lobby, 24-hour airport transportation, TV with movies, and outdoor swimming pool. Adjacent to the Lloyd Center shopping area and five minutes from city center.

**Shilo Inn.** 1506 N.E. 2nd; (503) 231–7665. 44 rooms. Near Lloyd Center shopping area, with free parking, free airport transportation, restaurant and lounge nearby, free continental breakfast. A favorite with businessmen, this motel also provides free popcorn for in-room movie viewing.

**Thunderbird Motel Inn-Coliseum.** 1225 N. Thunderbird Way; (503) 235–8311. 214 rooms. Directly across from Portland's Memorial Coliseum, many rooms look directly onto the Willamette River, as does the elegant dining room. Coffee shop and lounge also on premises, free parking, swimming pool.

*Inexpensive*

**Coliseum Motel.** 305 N.E. Broadway; (503) 284–5181. 20 rooms. Convenient east-side motel with airport transportation, restaurant and lounge in neighborhood, TV with movies.

**Friendship City Center Motel.** 3800 N.E. Sandy Blvd.; (503) 287–1107. 60 rooms. On a direct route to Portland airport, this motel offers free parking, restaurants adjacent to building, TV with movie and sports channel, some king water beds.

*Basic Budget*

**Motel 6.** 3104 S.E. Powell Blvd.; (503) 233–8811. 70 rooms. Centrally controlled air conditioning, pay TV in black and white, no phones, pool. No credit cards.

 **HOSTELS AND BED-AND-BREAKFASTS.** Bed-and-breakfast and hostel facilities are beginning to make an impact on the Portland area. *Betty Gallucci* operates a bed-and-breakfast at 1328 S.E. Division, (503) 231–0602, which also has a cellar dormitory for students. Rooms upstairs, furnished with antiques (which are for sale), with shared baths are modestly priced at under $20 for a double. Students may rent a cot for $5 per night in the cellar, but should be warned that the outside door will be locked at 8 P.M., and they must be out by 8 A.M. the next morning. Mrs. Gallucci enforces a lights-out at 11 P.M. rule for students but provides plenty of soap and towels for showers. Call her at *Lake Grove Realty,* (503) 636–6933, for other accommodations of this type in the Portland area.

 **CAMPING.** There are no camping facilities in the immediate vicinity of Portland other than some RV parks. The state parks with camping facilities closest to Portland are *Ainsworth,* on the Columbia River Scenic Route, 37 miles east of Portland; *Champoeg,* off U.S. 99W, about 28 miles south of Portland; and *McIver,* off Oregon 211, about 25 miles southeast of the city. An *Oregon Parks* map and directory is published by the state and is available at most travel information centers. For additional information about camping call the state *Travel InformaCenter,* (503) 285–1631, which operates from May through October.

 **HOW TO GET AROUND. From the airport:** You can reach downtown Portland from the airport via *DART (Downtown Airport Rapid Transportation) bus,* not the cheapest but probably the most efficient way; *Tri-Met bus* (metropolitan mass transportation), definitely the cheapest; and *cab,* the most expensive. DART, 231–7606, leaves the airport every 20 minutes on weekdays and every 30 minutes on weekends and holidays between 6 A.M. and midnight. (Service from downtown to the airport is between 5:30 A.M. and 12:30 A.M.) Fare is $3.50 for adults and $1.25 for children ages 6–12. Children under 6 ride free. The DART buses deliver and pick up at the Benson, Hilton, and Marriott hotels. To travel Tri-Met, catch a #72 (82nd Ave.) bus at the airport's bus zone and transfer at 82nd and Sandy to a #14S (Sandy) to the Portland Mall, which is a stone's throw from the Hilton Hotel. At $.75 (at press time) the price is right. Cabs can be found easily at the airport and charge around $14 for a trip between the airport and downtown.

*Avis* (800) 331–1212; *Budget* (800) 527–0700; *Dollar* (800) 421–6868; *Hertz* (800) 654–3131; *National* (800) 328–4567; and *Thrifty* (800) 367–2277 *rental cars* have counters at the Portland International Airport. In addition, some of the smaller rental agencies provide shuttle service between their offices and the airport. Two of these are *Nickel Rent-a-Car,* 8500 N.E. Columbia Blvd. (225–0393) and *Rent-A-Dent,* 7510 N.E. Killingsworth (257–9831).

**By bus:** Tri-Met, the Portland area's public transportation system, will transport you free in the downtown area. Its Fareless Square service covers hundreds of downtown blocks on the west side of the river. Best place to catch a bus downtown is generally on the Portland Mall (5th and 6th avenues) for north-south travel or on Washington and Salmon streets for east-west travel. You'll find that Tri-Met drivers are helpful about directing you to the right bus. If you're traveling by bus outside the downtown area, the fare at press time for riding in one or two zones (much of the City of Portland) is $.75 (youth, $.50, all zones). Rides beyond the first two zones cost $1. Exact change is required. For additional information about Tri-Met, visit the Customer Assistance Office in the heart of downtown at Pioneer Courthouse Square, on 6th between Morrison and Yamhill; it is open weekdays from 8 A.M. to 6 P.M.: 233–3511. Self-service help with Tri-Met routes is provided at eight trip-planning kiosks on the Mall. Each is equipped with a map and a computer that will display routes and schedules.

**By car:** Portland is a divided city, its east and west portions separated by the Willamette River. Downtown Portland is neatly contained, like the eye of a hurricane, within a freeway system delineated on the west by I-405 and on the east by I-5. The interstate freeway river crossings of the Willamette River are the Fremont Bridge on the north and the Marquam Bridge on the south. Between these two bridges are five others that stitch Portland's east and west sides together. North of Portland is the great Columbia River, which divides

Oregon and Washington. Travelers to Seattle and other points in Washington may cross the Columbia via the Interstate Bridge on I-5 or the Glenn Jackson Bridge on I-205, east of the Portland International Airport.

Before attempting to get around Portland, stop at the *Greater Portland Convention and Visitors' Association Information Center* at the southwest corner of S.W. Front and Salmon (222–2223), in downtown Portland near the river. Short-term parking for visitors is available across Front. Maps and printed brochures are dispensed by a friendly, knowledgeable staff. Hours are Monday–Friday, 8:30 A.M.–5 P.M.

If your gateway to Portland is the Interstate Bridge (I-5), you can stop at a *Travel Information Center* on the Portland side at 12345 N. Union, Jantzen Beach; 285–1631. It is operated by the state from May–November 1.

For names and phone numbers of the major car rental companies, see *From the airport,* above.

**By cab:** In Portland you don't hail a cab. You phone for one or try to find one at any downtown hotel or major department store. Cab companies charge $1 for a pickup plus $1.20 per mile. Oldest and largest cab company is *Broadway,* 227-1234. Others include *New Rose City,* 282–7707, and *Radio,* 227–1212. Special phones are provided in many busy locations for ordering cabs.

 **TOURIST INFORMATION.** The *Greater Portland Convention and Visitors' Association* is in downtown Portland at the southwest corner of S.W. Front and Salmon. Maps and brochures are available here; questions are answered by a friendly staff. Open Monday–Friday, 8:30 A.M.–5 P.M.; 222–2223.

 **SEASONAL EVENTS.** Portland has long had a reputation as a city in which people gather in the streets to celebrate the moderate climate and lush gardens. Foremost on the annual events list is the *Portland Rose Festival,* a week of activities held the second week in **June.** Most of these events, scheduled to honor the city's first flower, are free. The week begins with the selection of a queen. One of Portland's fairest high school seniors is selected to reign over the festivities. The arrival of the U.S. and Canadian navies raises most of the city bridges during the early part of the week as the huge vessels line the city harbor. Tours of the ships are open to the public and free. A parade for children, complete with younger bands, household pets, and a junior court, winds its way through the N.E. Hollywood district of the city early in the week. The International Rose Show draws blossoms from all over the world for the annual competition at the Lloyd Center, and for less-sedate folks a carnival atmosphere is maintained at Waterfront Park during the week. The climax of the festival is the Grand Floral Parade, held the last Saturday of the week, when flower-laden floats and national bands march through the Memorial Coliseum and trail through the city's downtown streets, providing plenty of free curbside viewing.

Runners will enjoy the 15-kilometer *Cascade Run-Off* in late June. It starts and ends in downtown Portland. (See "Participant Sports," below in this section.)

*Jazz* is offered annually during the summer months. From **July** through **August,** pack a picnic lunch and visit Washington Park Zoo for a weekly jazz night just next to the elephant pavilion. Admission is by ticket to the zoo. (See "Zoos," later in this section.) Two days of international jazz greats performances are held in August at Mt. Hood Community College in Gresham. (See "Music" in this *Practical Information* section. Tickets may be by reservation or general admission. (On a very warm day, general admission tickets may be the best buy, since they are the only seats in the shade of the outdoor field area.)

Everyone gathers at Waterfront Park during the month of **July** for a weekend festival called *Neighborfair.* This folk festival celebration stresses the city's neighborhoods, ethnic and social service groups, and includes two days of music (that last into the night), a variety of ethnic foods, and a city-carnival atmosphere.

The Oregon Historical Society sponsors a *Wintering-In* in the truest pioneer tradition at the Bybee Howell House on Sauvie Island (just north of Portland off U.S. 30) the last Saturday of each **September.** Special games for children, music for adults, and a glimpse of the pre–Civil War farm home are included in the end-of-summer party, open to the public and free of charge.

The Portland Marathon, normally run in late **September** or **October,** sends runners across the Willamette River twice on a 26.2 mile course that snakes through downtown, the northwest industrial area, and the cozy neighborhoods of north Portland.

A *Christmas Cheer and Author's Party,* the first Sunday in **December,** at the Oregon Historical Society (1230 S.W. Park; 222–1741), draws more than 100 Oregon authors and their books to the society's main floor exhibition area. Admission is free and hot cider punch is served.

 **TOURS.** *Gray Line* offers city tours as well as trips to Mt. Hood, the Columbia River Gorge, the Oregon Coast, and Mount St. Helens—the Northwest's active volcano. Summer and winter schedules differ so phone (503) 226–6755 for up-to-date information as well as reservations. All tours originate at the Imperial Hotel, 400 S.W. Broadway, where Gray Line has its office. Pickups are made at downtown hotels and in the Coliseum and Jantzen Beach areas.

 **ARCHITECTURAL WALKING TOURS.** *Portland Walking Tours* will guide any number from one to a busload, on foot or by bus, through four segments of Portland. Founder and leader Persis Schmeer, who has done her homework on architects and architecture, offers visitors a particularly well-informed and Oregon-opinionated discussion of the city, both old and new.

All tours are two hours in length. Walkers will see more of one individual area; bus riders will receive a thorough overview of the entire city in one ride.

Tours include "Old Portland," beginning at the urban plaza block of O'Bryant Square, continuing through the old U.S. National Bank building, past the Lee Kelly fountain to see the new U.S. Bank building with its rosy tinted windows, on to the contemporary naked lady sculpture, the Dekum Building, Bishop's House, and through the beautifully restored New Market Theater to Waterfront Park, the Skidmore Fountain, and the Architectural Preservation Gallery, with a finish at the old Merchants Hotel.

The "City Walk" includes tours of the new Justice Center, the controversial Portland Building, Willamette Center, the Federal Building, Yamhill Market, Pioneer Courthouse, and concludes at the Portland Art Museum. "City Walk South" includes urban renewal areas, the Halprin fountains, parks, gardens, and Portland State University. "Northwest Portland" shows that neighborhood's renovation of Victorian homes, as well as several churches of particular interest, including Trinity Episcopal.

To schedule a tour, or for more information, contact Portland Walking Tours, P.O. Box 4322, Portland, OR 97208; (503) 233-1017. Tours are available year-round with a $3 per-person charge and a $30 minimum per group tour.

**PARKS.** Tall Douglas firs, so characteristic of Oregon, hover protectively over many of Portland's spectacular parks and add to their splendor. *Washington Park,* at the end of Park Place near Vista Avenue in the city's southwest area, is indeed a splendid place. Within its 145 hilly acres are, in addition to the tall, green sentinels, the International Rose Test Garden, the Japanese Garden, a garden theater, and romantic statuary, including a depiction of Sacajawea, the Indian guide who helped explorers Lewis and Clark find the transcontinental route to Oregon. The statue is not far from the park's main entrance at Park Place, where a Lewis-and-Clark column rises above a formal garden. Also in the southwest area of the city is *Council Crest Park,* at 1,073 feet the highest viewpoint within the city, with some of Portland's most elegant homes at its feet and views of Mt. Hood and Mt. St. Helens off in the distance. To the north, still on the west side of the river, huge *Forest Park,* with its 30 miles of hiking trails, sprawls from N.W. 29th and Upshur to N.W. Skyline and St. Helens Road.

Downtown parks and fountain plazas are alive with music and brown-baggers on summer days. Among the most inviting are *O'Bryant Square,* between S.W. 9th and Park, Washington and Stark, which features a large, contemporary fountain, and the old-fashioned *South Park Blocks,* which form a corridor east of S.W. 10th from Salmon south to and through the campus of Portland State University.

In Portland Center, an urban renewal complex built on the site of one of Portland's old neighborhoods, the best stops are at *Ira's Fountain,* a park of waterfalls, facing the Civic Auditorium at the north end of Portland Center between Market and Clay; *Pettygrove Park,* an artificially contoured hideaway within the Center (south of Ira's Fountain), presided over by a 7,000-pound bronze sculpture, "The Dreamer," by Manuel Izquierdo; and *Lovejoy Fountain,* a serene arrangement of watery stairsteps.

In the Old Town area, hugging the Willamette River seawall at the foot of Ankeny Street, is the floating dock of *Waterfront Park,* a staging area for many civic functions and festivals. To the west is historic *Skidmore Fountain plaza;* the plaza is of rounded cobblestones said to have come to the city as ballast on ships.

Across the river, *Mt. Tabor Park,* east of S.E. 60th between Yamhill and Division, contains an extinct volcano that graciously provides an outdoor amphitheater for summer concerts. *Westmoreland Park,* S.E. 22nd and Bybee, is an aesthetic array of ponds, duck-filled canals, a fly-casting pool, and large playing fields, while *Laurelhurst Park* to the north, at S.E. 39th and Oak, offers a generous lake for the city's duck population. In the extreme northern section of the city is one of its most unusual parks, *Cathedral,* a riverside park under the gothic arches of the St. Johns Bridge, Portland's only suspension bridge. A boat ramp provides access to the river for boating and fishing.

Most city parks close from midnight to 5 A.M.; call 796–5193 for city park information.

Near Lake Oswego, south of Portland, is *Tryon Creek State Park,* a 600-acre wilderness area for hikers, cyclists, and horseback riders (bring your own horse). A nature center keeps a full schedule. Call 636–4550 for information.

 **ZOOS.** Animals at the *Washington Park Zoo* thrive in the simulated natural habitats provided for them in a hillside setting three miles from downtown Portland (just off U.S. 26 [westbound], at the Zoo–OMSI–Forestry Center exit). Nationally known for its elephant herd, the zoo is the lifetime home of Pachy, whose birth there was reported around the world in 1962. Pachy has sired several of the present herd and is famous as the first second-generation captive bull elephant to become a successful father. Among many other impressive exhibits are the Cascade Stream and Pond habitat, a simulated environment for river otters, beavers, waterfowl, and fish, and Night Country, where nocturnal felines cavort in an atmosphere of reversed light cycles. There is a gift shop and food service. Admission is charged except after 3 P.M. on Tuesday. Members are admitted free. The zoo is open every day, including Christmas. Open 9:30 A.M.–7 P.M. in summer; 9:30 A.M.–4 P.M. in winter; 9:30 A.M.–5:30 P.M. in spring and fall; 226–1561. Free parking is plentiful. Zoo bus service (Tri-Met) is available downtown on #63 (look for the roaring tiger painted on the back), which stops on Washington at the 5th Avenue Mall.

When visiting the zoo, save time for a visit to the *Oregon Museum of Science and Industry,* the *Western Forestry Center,* and *TERA One,* a demonstration solar home, which are all within walking distance.

**GARDENS.** Because Portland is known as the Rose City, a visit to the *International Rose Test Gardens* in Washington Park in summer or early fall is mandatory. The 400 varieties of roses planted there are conveniently charted at a kiosk near the entrance. Call 796–5193 for information. West of the Rose Garden is the serene *Japanese Garden,* featuring the five traditional garden forms. Admission is charged. Call 223–1321 or 223–4070 for hours, which change with the seasons. The garden is closed Thanksgiving, Christmas, and New Year's days.

Visitors can take a self-guided tour of the *Hoyt Arboretum,* which lies between Washington Park and the Washington Park Zoo at 4000 S.W. Fairview Blvd.; 228–8732. Brochures are available at the Tree House Visitor Center.

Portland's floral centerpiece in the spring (April and May) is the *Crystal Springs Rhododendron Garden,* S.E. 28th near Woodstock, on the east side of the Willamette River near Reed College. This scenic garden, complete with lake and, yes, ducks, explodes with color when the azaleas and their rhododendron relations bloom. Some 2,000 plants are maintained there by the American Rhododendron Society's Portland Chapter.

Another east-side showplace is the *sunken rose garden* at Peninsula Park, N. Albina and Ainsworth in North Portland, 796–5193. The rose population here is larger than the one at the Rose Test Garden.

City gardens are generally closed from midnight to 5 A.M.

**PARTICIPANT SPORTS** are always in season in Portland. With year-round skiing only 90 minutes away, a downtown fishing dock, two first-rate municipal indoor tennis centers, and more than 50 miles of hiking trails within city limits, Portland is nirvana to the sports activist. **Bicycling.** If you're unfamiliar with the terrain, the best way to see Portland by bike is to sign on for a midweek or weekend tour sponsored by *Outdoor Recreation,* 426 N.E. 12th 97232 (248–4018), a service of the Portland Park Bureau, or *Portland Wheelmen Touring Club,* P.O. Box 40753, Portland, 97240 (282–7982). If you prefer to do it yourself, contact the Park Bureau for maps and guidance. Maps can also be obtained at the *Portland Convention and Visitors' Association* information center at S.W. Front Ave. and Salmon St. (222–2223), at bike shops, or at the offices of the *Portland Bicycle and Pedestrian Program,* 1120 S.W. 5th, Room 834, 97204; 248–4407. Two good bike maps are the *Portland Bicycle Map* ($2), published by the city's Bicycle and Pedestrian Program, and a regional map, *Getting There by Bike,* which is published by the Metropolitan Service District and sells for $3. A book of suggested cycling trips, *Portland by Bicycle,* by Virginia Church, Cheryl Low, and Anndy Wiselogle, is available in bookstores and bike shops or from Anndy Wiselogle, 914 S. Ankeny, 97214; 233–0564.

Among the most popular west-side bike rides are the Terwilliger Blvd. bike path, from Sam Jackson Park Rd. to Barbur Blvd.; and Fairmount Blvd., a winding road around the base of Council Crest Park in southwest Portland. A bike path in southeast Portland passes the Crystal Springs Rhododendron Test

Garden and skirts the Eastmoreland Golf Course. Sauvie Island, northwest of Portland, and Tryon State Park are also popular with cyclists.

Rent downtown at *The Bike Gallery,* 1201 S.W. Morrison; 222–3821. In the fair-weather months, this bike shop often rents to business travelers who prefer getting around by bike to renting a car. In the Beaverton area, *The Bike Route,* 301 N.W. Murray Rd. (641–4195) rents bikes and car racks.

**Boating, rafting.** While canoeing and sailing are the old standbys in the Columbia and Willamette marine ways, the "in" water sports for the 1980s are windsurfing and river rafting.

For **sailing** and **windsurfing** guidance and rentals, try *Yacht Services,* 7330 S.W. Macadam (245–4290) on the west side of the Willamette, south of the Johns Landing area. Across the river, at the foot of S.E. Marion, is the *Sailing Center;* 233–1218. At Vancouver Lake, four miles west of Vancouver on the Washington side of the Columbia River, sailboats, sailboards (for windsurfing), canoes, paddleboats, and rowboats are rented in season.

Thrill-seekers can get information about **raft** trips on the Deschutes, Sandy, and Clackamas rivers by calling *Ken Warren Outdoors,* 5200 S.E. McLoughlin, 97202 (232–4676) or *Whitewater Outfitters,* 5160 S.W. Beaverton-Hillsdale Hwy., 97221 (245–1358).

*Brown's Landing,* just off U.S. Hwy. 30 on the Multnomah Channel, northwest of Portland, rents **canoes** for outings in the Sauvie Island area. South of the city, in the scenic Oregon City area on the east side of the Willamette, is *Sportcraft Marina,* 1701 Clackamette Dr. (656–6484), which rents canoes, boats, motors, and car-top carriers.

The Portland Park Bureau's Outdoor Recreation program, 1120 S.W. 5th Ave. (248–4018), offers sailing, canoeing and rafting trips, and instruction.

**Fishing.** The Willamette River attracts its share of urban anglers. The floating dock at *Waterfront Park,* at the foot of Ankeny Street in downtown Portland, is used for fishing for warm-water fish as well as more glamourous species. So are other locations along the waterfront promenade. North Portland's *Cathedral Park* has a fishing dock with access for the handicapped. The Willamette is known for its run of spring chinook salmon in March, April, and early May; for sturgeon year-round; shad in June and July; and steelhead, January through April. It also hosts plenty of warm-water fish, as do the sloughs at *West Delta Park* in North Portland and the *Sauvie Island Wildlife Management Area* lakes and sloughs.

Check the Yellow Pages under "Guide Service" for names of fishing guides who will take you to the best trout, salmon, and steelhead water.

For up-to-date recorded fishing information call *Oregon Fish and Wildlife* (229–5222) or look for weekly fishing reports in *The Oregonian.*

Write *Oregon Fish and Wildlife,* 506 S.W. Mill, P.O. Box 3503, Portland, 97208, for Oregon sport-fishing regulations. For a recorded message of outdoor information, call 229–5222; ocean salmon sport-fishing information, 222–6632; general information, 229–5403. One-day angling licenses, required for persons 14 and older, can be purchased at sporting goods stores (listed in the Yellow

Pages). For sporting goods at a convenient downtown location, visit *Pacific Hardware and Electric Co.,* 221 S.W. Alder; 228–8844.

**Golf.** With 14 public golf courses and many fine private ones, the Portland metropolitan area is a year-round golf center. Greens fees are generally reasonable at the public courses. For a listing of both public and private clubs, check the Yellow Pages.

**Hiking.** For hikers, Portland offers 30 miles of trails in *Forest Park,* the largest urban wilderness within an American city. The 4,700-acre park in the northwest section of the city is all the more attractive because its trails connect with those of some of Portland's most beautiful parks, including showy Washington Park and the Hoyt Arboretum. A hike on the 23-mile Wildwood Trail, which begins near the Western Forestry Center of U.S. 26 (westbound), will take you past both as it winds to its end deep in Forest Park. Get a map and trail guide of Forest and Macleay Parks at the Park Bureau, 1120 S.W. 5th, 97204; 796–5193.

For general information about hiking in Oregon's national parks and forests, visit the Multnomah Building, 319 S.W. Pine, Portland, OR 97208 (221–2877), an old hotel that now houses federal offices. Here the *U.S. Forest Service* and the *National Park Service* dispense advice, maps, brochures, and litter bags. Call them at 221–2877. Some of the maps are free, some cost a nominal amount. A series of hiking guides by Don and Roberta Lowe, published by Touchstone and available in bookstores and mountain shops, are the best for the Oregon Cascades.

**Ice skating.** For pure recreational pleasure, the *Lloyd Center Ice Pavilion* (288–6073) offers skaters the convenience of a shopping center locale close to downtown. An audience of shoppers is always gathered around the balustrade above to watch the action. The Lloyd Center, Portland's first major covered shopping center, is on the east side of the Willamette and easily reached by bus or cab. Other ice rinks are listed in the Yellow Pages.

**Mountain climbing.** Oregon mountaineers support the *Mazama Club,* 909 N.W. 19th Ave., Portland, OR 97209; 227–2345. You must have climbed a mountain with a living glacier to become a member, but you don't have to be a member to take advantage of many Mazama beginner climbs designed to help you reach the top. Because Mt. Hood, Oregon's highest mountain, is so close, some tourists are tempted to climb it without proper equipment or guidance. Don't. And don't listen to natives who like to say grandmothers climb Mt. Hood in tennis shoes. It's not that easy. For additional information contact the Park Bureau at 1120 S.W. 5th Ave.; 248–4018.

**Road running, jogging.** Some of the best runs in Portland originate downtown, so bring your running shoes when you come to the Rose City. The Marriott Hotel is close to the waterfront promenade, where you can travel 1¼ miles north to the Broadway Bridge and back, viewing the city skyline to the west and the river traffic to the east. At the Red Lion Inn, in Portland Center, you are amidst the landscaped walkways of a pleasant urban renewal area with sculpture and fountains. From the Hilton, run west to the South Park Blocks, which merge with the Portland State University campus to the south. Guests at the Benson can ask for *Running from the Benson* leaflets and a handy matchbook-size map of the downtown area. From the Benson, poise yourself for a run east to the waterfront promenade or west to the Park Blocks.

A hilly two-mile jogging/bicycle and exercise path on Terwilliger Blvd., which takes the runner from Duniway Park near downtown up past many scenic viewpoints, is incorporated in one of Portland's most festive events—the Cascade Run-Off, a 15-kilometer road race. The race, with some of the nation's top runners competing, is run in late June.

Best runs are incorporated in *Running around Portland,* by John Perry and Buzz Willits, and *Running around Oregon,* by John Perry and Paul Christensen, both published by RAP Press, 2655 N.W. Overton, Portland, OR 97210, and available in book and running stores.

**Roller skating.** Look for roller skate rental vans near the *waterfront promenade* and at *Laurelhurst Park.* Both locations are popular with skaters in summer. The city's Park Bureau maintains a public roller rink at *Mt. Scott Community Center,* 5530 S.E. 72nd; 774–2215. Skates rent for $.25 an hour. You skate free. Other roller rinks are listed in the Yellow Pages.

**Skiing.** Skiing is big business in the Pacific Northwest and a ski trek to Oregon generally begins in Portland. Ski areas closest to the city are *Mt. Hood Meadows, Multorpor-Ski Bowl,* and *Timberline,* all on Mt. Hood, about a 90-minute drive away. Transportation to Mt. Hood ski areas from Portland International Airport is provided by Mt. Hood Limousine, Inc.; 646–1296. Make arrangements ahead for the service. The $27 round-trip fare includes a lift ticket. Best destination ski resort in the state is *Mt. Bachelor,* about 175 miles from Portland in Central Oregon, on the east side of the Cascades. Travel to Mt. Bachelor, 22 miles west of Bend, via Pacific Trailways Bus to Bend or Horizon Air or Pacific Express air service to the Redmond/Bend Airport, 15 miles from Bend. Airport limousine service is available to Bend. A shuttle service operates daily to Mt. Bachelor from Bend and several nearby motels and lodges. Portland skiers can also reach Mt. Bachelor via the AMTRAK Coast Starlight, which stops at Chemult, 60 miles south of Bend. Ground transportation meets all trains.

Rental equipment is available at all the major ski areas, as well as at many sports stores in Portland. The Yellow Pages lists them all. Some of the best are *Howell's Uptown Sport Center,* 21 N.W. 23rd Pl. (227–7910); the *Mountain Shop* at two locations, 628 N.E. Broadway (288–6768) and downtown (Cloud Cap Chalet) at 625 S.W. 12th (227–0579); *Oregon Mountain Community* in Old Town at 60 N.W. Davis (227–1038), for cross-country rentals; and *REI Co-op,* 1798 Jantzen Beach Center (283–1300), near the Interstate Bridge (I-5).

Oregon offers the **cross-country (Nordic) skier** easy access to scenic winter trekking. The Mt. Hood Meadows Nordic Touring Center provides instruction on its 16 miles of trails. Nordic rentals are available there and at most places where downhill equipment is rented. For the more adventuresome, the opportunities are unlimited. Call Outdoor Recreation (Portland Parks, 248–4018) or the Mazama Club (227–2345) for information about cross-country ski tours and instruction. Call the *Zigzag Ranger Station* (U.S. Forest Service, 1–224–5243) for current conditions and information about trails in the Mt. Hood area.

For information about transportation from Portland to Mt. Hood ski areas, call the areas, sporting goods stores, or Trailways (228–8571).

(Also see "Ski Resorts" in *Practical Information for Inland Areas of Interest.*) The Park Bureau also provides skiing information, (248–4018). Dial these numbers for information about local and regional snow and ski conditions: Mt. Hood Meadows, 227–7669; Mountain Shop, 281–8886; Multorpor-Ski Bowl, 224–9221; Timberline Lodge, 222–2211; state police road and weather report, 238–8400; U.S. Weather Bureau forecast, 255–6661.

**Swimming.** For public swimming, Portlanders generally visit one of the city's three public indoor and 11 outdoor pools. Call 796–5193 for swim hours. A nominal fee is charged. In outlying areas, favorite swimming holes are at *Blue Lake Park,* off I-84, 15 miles east of Portland; *Dabney State Park,* on the Columbia River Scenic Route, 19 miles east of Portland; *Rooster Rock State Park,* I-84, 22 miles east of Portland on the Columbia River; and *Scoggins Park,* 30 miles from Portland off Oregon 47, six miles southwest of Forest Grove on Henry Hagg Lake in Washington County.

**Tennis.** Two municipally owned indoor tennis centers and more than 100 outdoor tennis courts, including 60 with lights, make Portland a year-round, day-and-night tennis town. The indoor centers are *Portland Tennis Center,* 324 N.E. 12th (233–5959), with four indoor courts and eight outdoor, and *St. Johns Racquet Center,* 7519 N. Burlington in north Portland (248–4200), with three indoor courts. Reservations must be made for play at either center. Both have lounges, showers, and rest rooms. Portland Tennis Center has a pro shop. Private clubs, which attract national tennis play, are the *Eastmoreland Racquet Club,* 3015 S.E. Berkeley Pl. (653–0820) and the *Irvington Club,* 2131 N.E. Thompson (287–8749).

 **SPECTATOR SPORTS.** Portland is home to the Pacific Coast League's *Portland Beavers,* one of the oldest AAA **baseball** teams in the nation. Season runs from early April to early September at Portland Civic Stadium, 1844 S.W. Morrison; 248–4345. Tickets are available at the stadium.

The 1977 World Champion *Portland Trail Blazers* of the National **Basketball** Association play home games in the Memorial Coliseum, 1401 N. Wheeler; 235–8771. Tickets are available by mail only, from the Trail Blazer Ticket Office, 700 N.E. Multnomah, Suite 750, Portland, OR 97232. The season runs from October through March. The *Far West Classic,* held during Christmas season at Memorial Coliseum, is recognized as the finest college basketball tournament in existence. Pacific Athletic Conference (PAC-10) University of Oregon and Oregon State University host the annual event. Just prior to the classic is the *Al Guisti Women's Basketball Tournament,* which attracts the finest women's collegiate basketball teams from throughout the nation. Call the Coliseum for ticket information.

Professional **boxing** is presented monthly by McNally Sports Attractions (777–5516) in the ballroom of the Marriott Hotel, 1401 S.W. Front; 226–7600.

*Portland Winter Hawks* junior professional **hockey** team, in 1983 the first American team to win the International Memorial Cup, plays at Memorial Coliseum, October through March. Tickets are available through the Hawks office at the Coliseum (1401 N. Wheeler; 235–8771) or write to P.O. Box 3009, Portland, OR 97208.

**Racing** takes a number of forms: **Auto racing** enthusiasts meet at the *City of Roses Speedway,* 9727 N. Union (285–2269), for destruction derby and speed-stock racing, beginning in late March. Other competitions include dragsters, formula road racing, limited stock and open competition continuing into late fall.

*Portland Meadows Horse Race Track* is at 1001 N. Schmeer Rd., 285–9144. Season runs from early November–late April.

For **dog racing,** visit *Multnomah Kennel Club Dog Race Track,* N.E. 223rd between Halsey and Glisan, Fairview, about 15 miles from the city (665–2191). The season runs May–September.

**Tennis.** The *Louisiana-Pacific Invitational Tennis Tournament* is usually held in April. The event, at Eastmoreland Racquet Club, 3015 S.E. Berkeley Pl., Milwaukie, OR 97222, attracts the world's top players. Call the club, 653–0820, for information on times and tickets.

**Wrestling** can be seen weekly at the *Portland Sports Arena,* 8725 N. Chautauqua; 289–4222.

**HISTORIC SITES AND HOUSES.** Just across I-5 is *Aurora,* a pioneer colony founded by Dr. William Keil. The Aurora Ox Barn Museum is open for a small charge Wednesday–Sunday 1 P.M.–5 P.M., except January, and includes a tour that shows the lively remnants of the colony life, including brightly quilted coverlets and musical instruments, as well as examples of the fine wooden furniture that made the colony famous. Call 678–5754. The town of Aurora is peppered with antique shops.

*Champoeg Park,* just 15 minutes south of Portland on I-5, includes many of the same trees that sheltered Joe Meek, U.S. marshal and mountainman, who called upon the men to cross his line for the United States and set up a provisional government for Oregon. Among the historic sites in the park are the home of Dr. Robert Newell (small fee), the last remaining structure of the vast settlement of the area's Hudson's Bay Company retired employees, the Champoeg Pioneer Mother's Home (DAR) (small fee), and a visitors information center that contains sight-and-sound exhibits relating to early Oregon. The Visitor Center is closed weekends in winter; open seven days in summer; 8 A.M.–4:30 P.M. Call 1–678–1251.

*Covered bridges* are alive and well in Oregon. For a complete listing and self-guided map, visit the Oregon Historical Society, 1230 S.W. Park; 222–1741. Open Monday–Saturday, 10 A.M.–5 P.M.

*Fort Vancouver,* just across the Columbia River via the Interstate Bridge on the Washington State side, marks the center of the old Oregon country and is a National Historic Site. A replica of the old fort operated by Dr. John McLoughlin, physician and chief factor of the Hudson's Bay Company from 1824 to 1846, includes his home, a trading store, blacksmith shop, bakery, bastion, and dispensary. All are part of 165 acres administered by the National Park Service, which maintains a garden in the style of the fort outside the main gates. Admission is free. Open 9 A.M.–4 P.M., winters; to 5:30 P.M. in summer. Call the information center at (206) 696–7655.

Two streets up from the river is Officers Row on Evergreen Blvd. in Vancouver. The row dates from the days of Indian wars in the West and is believed to be one of three such rows remaining. The oldest house on the row, that of U. S. Grant ([206] 694–4002), built in 1849, is a museum open to the public for a small admission. Lunch and dinner are served daily in the John Marshall house just down the street. Reservations are necessary; (206) 693–3588.

(For accommodations and restaurants in Vancouver, Washington, see the Washington chapter.)

*John McLoughlin House,* 7th and Center streets, Oregon City; 656–5146. After leaving Ft. Vancouver, this northwest figure made his home on the banks of the Willamette River in Oregon City, the first territorial capital. He chose a mill site at the Willamette Falls and started his settlement with retired trappers and voyageurs of Hudson's Bay Company. In 1842 he gave the city its name and lived there until his death in 1857. The house, now restored (it once sheltered the city's prostitutes) has been moved to the third level of the city where it overlooks the river and shelters the grave sites of the McLoughlins. Furnished with McLoughlin furniture—some say his ghost as well—it is open to the public February–December, Tuesday–Saturday, 10 A.M.–4 P.M.; Sunday 1–4 P.M. Small admission charge. Next door is the *home of his chief surgeon, Dr. Forbes Barclay.* The house is used by the Oregon City Chamber of Commerce, but visitors may peek inside.

The *Old Church,* 1422 S.W. 11th, is the oldest standing church structure on its original site in Portland. Built in 1882, the church was a place of worship until the 1960s when the Baptist congregation moved to a new building. Now owned by the Old Church Society, it is a popular place for weddings, receptions, and music. Phone 222–2031 for a schedule, but the main sanctuary is generally open for public viewing.

*Pioneer Courthouse* (and Post Office), 555 S.W. Yamhill. Built between 1869 and 1873, this building in the city center was the first federal office building in the Pacific Northwest and is the oldest public building in the region. The first floor is now occupied by a postal station, but visitors can and should tour the restored Victorian courtroom on the second floor and judges' chambers on the third. The building is open daily from 8:30 A.M. to 5 P.M.; 221–0282.

The *Pittock Manson,* 3229 N.W. Pittock Dr. (248–4469), was built at the turn of the century by the founder of the newspaper *The Oregonian,* and now belongs to the city. This French Renaissance mansion with its fine marble, cast bronze, hardwood, and classic plaster work—much constructed by European labor—

and the 46 acres on which it stands are open to the public year-round. The rooms are decorated as they might have been in the period. Christmastime is a good season to visit—the house is bedecked from rooftop to cellar with Christmas past. Volunteers conduct tours and the Gate Lodge is being developed as a tea room and exhibit center. Take your camera; this is one of the best views of the city.

West of Portland is *Sauvie Island,* used by the historic figure of Hudson's Bay Company, John McLoughlin, to raise dairy herds. The island, now a residential and farming area, is the site of the *Bybee-Howell House,* a pre–Civil War farm house that is administered by the Oregon Historical Society. It is open to the public, who may view the rooms and stroll the grounds free of charge from June until the end of September.

*Skidmore Fountain,* set in a plaza of rounded cobblestones at S.W. 1st and Ankeny, was a gift to the city by Stephen Skidmore, who left funds for a fountain for "horses, men, and dogs of the city." Olin Warner designed the bronze fountain in 1888.

 **MUSEUMS.** *Georgia-Pacific Historical Museum,* 900 S.W. 5th. This small museum tells the history of logging in many popular exhibits, including a film about logging operations half a century ago. Accessible via an underground tunnel that connects the Georgia-Pacific building to the parking structure across the street. Open 10 A.M.–3 P.M. Tuesday–Friday; 248–7529. Free.

*Oregon Historical Society,* 1230 S.W. Park. Outstanding museum and research society displays rotating exhibits in its spacious first-floor exhibit area and an Indian-life exhibit and other collections relating to northwest history on the second floor (you'll find a real covered wagon there). A regional research library occupies the third floor. Open Monday–Saturday, 10 A.M.–5 P.M.; 222–1741. Free.

*Oregon Museum of Science and Industry,* clustered with the Washington Park Zoo and the Western Forestry Center on a site just off U.S. 26 (westbound), three miles from downtown. OMSI hums with the vibrations of exciting viewer-operated displays, including its whiz-bang "Computer Company." Disciplines from physiology to physics are equally well represented. Small children enjoy the live reptile exhibits and the hatching chicks, which they can pick up. Daily shows (except for Mondays in winter) are presented in OMSI's *Kendall Planetarium.* Open 9 A.M.–5 P.M. every day except Christmas. Summer hours longer; 222–2828. Admission charged. Members free.

*Oregon Preservation Resource Center,* Captain John Couch Square, N.W. 2nd and Couch in Old Town. The center contains architectural history exhibits and gives advice on historic home restoration. Call ahead for hours; 243–1923. Free.

*Portland Art Museum* facing the South Park Blocks at S.W. Park and Madison. Outstanding collection of modern sculpture is displayed in attractive multilevel court just inside the front entrance. Museum is known for its exhibit of Northwest Coast Indian Art. Other permanent collections represent a variety of periods and cultures. Gift shop. Operates Rental Sales Gallery across mall in a neighboring building. Open Tuesday–Sunday, noon–5 P.M.; Friday, noon–10 P.M. Closed Monday. 226–2811. Admission contribution suggested, except for Fridays after 4 P.M.

The *Ox Barn Museum*, in Aurora off I-5, exhibits remains of the lives of the early colonists. The admission price includes a tour. Open Wednesday–Sunday 1 P.M.–5 P.M., except January. Call 678–5754.

*Portland Police Museum*, Captain John Couch Square, N.W. 2nd and Couch. Collections of police equipment, uniforms and photographs dating from the 1870s are displayed in a setting that re-creates an old-fashioned police precinct. Open Wednesday–Sunday from 10 A.M.–3 P.M.; Saturday, until 4. 223–5771. Free.

*Western Forestry Center*, Zoo-OMSI-Forestry Center exit off U.S. 26 westbound. Oregon's Number One industry is described by a "Talking Tree." A dramatization of a forest fire and a simulated paper mill are among other elaborate exhibits. Excellent collection of wood specimens. Special offerings include a Christmas tree show and periodic woodworking deomonstrations. Open 9 A.M.–6 P.M., summer, and 10 A.M.–5 P.M., winter, seven days a week. 228–1367. Admission charged. Members free.

 **FILM.** The following theaters can be counted on to show unusual films: *Bagdad III*, 3702 S.E. Hawthorne Blvd. (232–2685); *Cinema 21*, 616 N.W. 21st (223–4722); *5th Avenue Cinema*, 510 S.W. Hall (224–6038); *Fine Arts*, 2021 S.E. Hawthorne Blvd. (232–7005); *The Guild*, 829 S.W. 9th (226–0044); *The Movie House*, 1220 S.W. Taylor (222–4595); *Roseway Theatre*, 7229 N.E. Sandy Blvd. (281–5713); *Sherwood Oriental*, 125 N.W. 1st, Sherwood (625–6887); *St. Johns Theatre*, 8704 N. Lombard (286–1768; information: 281–5772).

 **MUSIC.** Three major classical musical groups fill the air in Portland regularly. Tickets are available through their offices and all perform at the Civic Auditorium, 222 S.W. Clay; 248–4496. Tickets are also usually available at the door before concert time.

The *Oregon Symphony Orchestra*, 813 S.W. Alder (228–1353), was founded in 1896 and is one of the oldest symphonies west of St. Louis. The 85-member orchestra, under the direction of James DePreist, presents more than 100 performances annually in the Northwest, including 35 classical and 15 pops concerts in Portland, led by Norman Leyden.

*Portland Opera Association Inc.*, 922 S.W. Main (248–4741), offers four productions annually, fall and spring. Visiting artists of international stature join the Portland cast at the Civic Auditorium.

*Portland Youth Philharmonic*, 922 S.W. Main (223–5939) in 1983 celebrated its 60th anniversary with a European tour and joined the New York Philharmonic Orchestra for a concert in New York City. The musicians, none older than 21, are heard in four concerts a year at Portland's Civic Auditorium under the direction of Jacob Avshalomov.

In addition to the three large groups, local colleges and universities produce excellent musical programs open to the public. Among such programs is the *Mt. Hood Jazz Festival*, sponsored each summer by Mt. Hood Community College on its campus at 26000 S.E. Stark, Gresham; 667–7155. Nationally known jazz musicians present a two-day program, which ranges from traditional to contemporary. Portland restaurants offer booths for outdoor dining and concertgoers come prepared to spend the afternoon and much of the evening at the ongoing performance.

**DANCE.** Portland is the home of the *Keith Martin Ballet Company*, with headquarters at Northwest Dance Center, 918 S.W. Yamhill; 227–1927. Oregon's resident professional dance touring company performs at downtown theaters offering a wide range of styles from contemporary to ballet. Check local papers for touring companies that are appearing in town. *The Oregonian's* Leisure Section, published on Friday, contains a listing of the week's events. *Willamette Week* also gives current listings.

**THEATER.** Portland has many small theaters and theater groups that perform constantly. In addition, it attracts many road shows. For current information on live theater productions coming to Portland call: *Celebrity Attractions*, 1010 S.W. Morrison (226–4371), which books most road attractions, or *Portland Civic Auditorium*, 222 S.W. Clay (248–4496), the scene of major productions. Also check local newspapers for performances in the area. *The Oregonian's* Leisure Section, published on Friday, contains a week's listing of coming events. *Willamette Week* also gives current listings.

*New Rose Theatre*, 904 S.W. Main (222–2487), offers local artists in classic repertory. *Oregon Contemporary Theatre*, 133 S.W. 2nd Ave. (241–3770), performs at Fir Acres Theatre on the Lewis and Clark College campus during summer months. Equity actors and nationally recognized stage directors and designers are featured. *Portland Civic Theatre*, 1530 S.W. Yamhill (226–3048), is where mainstage productions and theater-in-the-round often play side-by-side, using capable local talent—and in summer some equity actors. Curtain time, year around, is 8 P.M. *Storefront Actors' Theatre*, 6 S.W. 3rd (224–4001), blends contemporary theater with some original drama. *Willamette Repertory Theatre*, S.W. Front at Salmon (224–4901), offers a full year of theater, including summer stock. This privately endowed theater gives four plays during the regular season with nationally known directors.

**GALLERIES.** *Blackfish Gallery*, 325 N.W. 6th (224–2634). Paintings, sculpture, drawings, and sometimes photographs are exhibited in this gallery, an artist-owned cooperative. Open Tuesday–Saturday, 11 A.M.–5 P.M. *Contemporary Crafts Gallery*, 3934 S.W. Corbett; 223–2654. Long-established, non-profit gallery which exhibits work in clay, glass, fiber, metal, wood, mixed media. Open Tuesday–Friday, 11 A.M.–5 P.M.; Saturday, noon–5 P.M.; Sunday, 1–5 P.M. *Fountain Gallery,* 117 N.W. 21st; 228–8476. One of Portland's most prestigious, displaying work by leading artists of the Pacific Northwest. Sculpture, paintings, prints, drawings are contemporary. Open Monday–Saturday, 11 A.M.–5 P.M. *Lawrence Gallery,* 913 S.W. Broadway; 224–9442. Spacious, bright exhibit area enhances diverse collection of paintings, sculpture, photographs, ceramics, jewelry, furniture. Open Monday–Friday, 10 A.M.–6 P.M.; Saturday and Sunday, noon–5 P.M. *Portland Art Museum Rental Sales Gallery,* S.W. Park and Madison; 226–2811. Across an outdoor sculpture mall from the museum. Paintings, sculpture by northwest artists are rented and sold. Open Tuesday–Saturday, noon–5 P.M.; Sunday 2 P.M.–4 P.M. *Portland Center for the Visual Arts* (PCVA), 117 N.W. 5th; 222–7107. Unusual gallery presents exhibitions of sculpture and paintings, graphics and mixed media as well as performance events in theater, dance, and music. Open Tuesday–Sunday, noon–5 P.M. (September–May).

 **SHOPPING.** Of note to the consumer is the fact that at press time no sales tax is charged on any merchandise, food, or entertainment found in the city. Shoppers are also attracted to the city because of the Portland-based manufacturers and outlets. For example, a New York television news executive makes Portland an annual stop to purchase his fishing vests from *Columbia Sportswear Co.,* located at 6600 N. Baltimore. Catalog enthusiasts enjoy visiting the main headquarters of *Norm Thompson Outfitters Inc.,* 1805 N.W. Thurman, for British shearling coats as well as innovative and luxurious outdoor wear. *Pendleton* also has headquarters in Portland and those with an eye for economy quickly learn that the firm operates a seconds store in nearby Washougal, Washington, just a half-hour drive across the I-205 bridge and east on the Washington shore of the Columbia River. Oregon wines are winning international awards. Saving some money by purchasing local wines by the case is appreciated by travelers who visit the Willamette Valley vineyards of the growers. The *Oregon Winegrowers Association,* P.O. Box 2134, Salem, OR 97310, will provide vineyard visitors a complete list of sources and visiting hours.

The best shopping is done on foot since a fast ride may take you too quickly past some of the best nooks and crannies in the city. *Morgan's Alley,* 515 S.W. Broadway, is an example of the city's determination to conserve old structures. The block is honeycombed with small boutiques and restaurants. *Old Town,* reaching from S.W. Ankeny to N.W. Everett, along 2nd Avenue, is filled with fine shops and galleries. Stop for a loaf of French bread at *Le Panier,* 71 S.W. 2nd. The ovens, in operation seven days a week, come from Paris, as do the bakers. Visit the recently renovated *New Market Street Theater,* 50 S.W. 2nd, a former market and theater of the 1800s that once entertained Ulysses S. Grant. The building now houses shops and food outlets and is directly adjacent to the city's famous *Saturday Market* (which operates Saturday and Sunday from April through December) where artists and craftsmen from all over the state meet on the street to sell their wares at low cost, rain or shine.

Just up the street on S.W. Yamhill at 4th is the *Yamhill Market,* an ingenious four-story structure tucked into a two-story building. It offers fresh fruit, vegetables, meats, and seafood (*Crane and Company* will even ship fish out for buyers) on the street, and everything from Indian art at *Chief Lelooska's* to locally made country willow furniture. The third level of this market, open seven days a week, is devoted to food outlets. Take your choice at the counters, which serve up French specials, James Beard's favorite hamburger, Mexican food, Chicago deli items, and Italian and South American foods.

City center remains devoted to the main branches of its major stores, and city planners intend to keep it that way. A four-block project on Morrison Street promises to bring Saks Fifth Avenue and Brooks Brothers to the Portland area within two years. Meanwhile, *I. Magnin* carries a full line of clothing for men and women at 930 S.W. 6th; *Meier & Frank,* the city's oldest department store, is at 621 S.W. 5th, with ten floors of merchandise, including an excellent boutique, Northwest Territory, on the main floor, which is especially for tourists. *Frederick & Nelson* is directly across Alder from Meier & Frank. *Nordstrom,* at 701 S.W. Broadway, is the city's largest fashion store and includes designer boutiques as well as a vast shoe department.

**Antiques.** *Antique Finder,* 7843 S.W. Capitol Hwy., which is in the center of a single street of fine antique shops offering English and French collectibles. (A good lunch stop here is Fat City Café, a trip back to the thirties complete with soda-fountain stools and grilled hamburgers.) *Sellwood Peddler Attic Goodies,* 8065 S.E. 13th, is just one of several dozen shops on this southeast neighborhood street, dealing mainly in primitives. (Go on up the road to Milwaukie Ave. to find a special lunch at Papa Haydns, renowned for its desserts.) *Quintana's Gallery of Indian Western Art,* 139 N.W. 3rd, offers museum-quality Indian baskets and blankets. *Kerr's Economy Jar,* 424 N.E. 22nd, raises funds for children's services with donated elegance from Portland's finest old homes, including complete services in Spode, sterling flatwear, and furniture, all at considerable savings.

**Flowers.** *Flowers by Dorcas,* 617 S.W. Washington, not only serves Portland but the nation's capital as well, since the wife of Oregon Senator Mark Hatfield hand-carried two centerpieces east to President and Mrs. Reagan. The downtown store also carries rare Chinese porcelains and fine gift items.

**Gifts.** *Kathleen Connolly, Irish Shop,* 725 S.W. 10th, offers fine linens and wool all from Ireland; *Kathleen Rockwell,* 803 S.W. Morrison, antiques and collectible china; *Lelooska Indian Art,* Yamhill Market, carvings, baskets, jewelry, all Indian—some old, some new—all the finest quality; *Omnibus,* 837 S.W. 1st, contemporary items for the home with a special flair.

**Seafood.** Many outlets will ship fresh seafood across the U.S. for customers. *Crane & Company,* 8610 S.W. Terwilliger Blvd. and at the Yamhill Market; *Green's Seafood Inc.,* 6767 S.W. Macadam; *Troy's Seafood Markets* at four locations: 11130 S.E. Powell Blvd., 3055 S.W. Cedar Hills Blvd., 816 N.E. Grand, and 15900 S.W. Boones Ferry Rd., are some of the best.

**Wines:** Oregon wines are winning national awards. Purchase by the case at the local Willamette Valley vineyards. For a complete list of vineyards and visiting hours, write the Oregon Winegrowers Association, P.O. Box 2134, Salem, OR 97310.

 **DINING OUT.** Following is a list of some of the best Portland restaurants, listed in alphabetical order according to price classifications. The ratings are based on the cost of a complete dinner for one person, not including beverages or tip. *Deluxe* is used for restaurants charging more than $20 per person (and $20 is just about the limit); *Expensive,* $15–$20; *Moderate,* $8–$12; *Inexpensive,* less than $8. An inexpensive meal in Portland can be a delightful experience, while a deluxe meal often equals—at a much lower price—the finest of tables set in eastern states. All but a very few restaurants take major credit cards. We note those establishments that do not take credit cards. Traveler's checks are cashed easily, and many restaurants will honor personal checks if the diner has a major credit card for identification.

Since the Pacific Coast is noted for its fresh seafood, we open the listing with some of the best seafood restaurants in the area.

## SEAFOOD

### Deluxe

**Couch Street Fish House.** 105 N.W. 3rd; 223–6173. One of Oregon's finest spots for elegant dining and fresh seafood. The neighborhood does not lend itself to night strolling, so take a cab (valet service for parking), but inside, diners will find an old-line San Francisco atmosphere, including impeccable waiters, fresh flowers, silver, and linens all complementing a wide array of seafoods—every one of them fresh and cooked according to Chef Horst Mager's special recipes. In addition to the Pacific's daily catches, the menu includes Hawaiian Mahi Mahi and New England lobsters flown in fresh daily. Open seven nights a week. Reservations a must. AE, MC, VISA.

**Jake's Famous Crawfish.** 401 S.W. 12th; 226–1419. This restaurant has been open at the same location in Portland since 1892. More than 25 fresh catches of the day are included on the menu, and lunch and dinner is served seven days a week. The Victorian bar is a favorite meeting place for more than one generation. The large dining room offers leisurely dining and elegant service. Reservations suggested. AE, CB, DC, MC, VISA.

### Expensive

**McCormick & Schmick's Oak St. Restaurant.** 235 S.W. 1st; 224–7522. If you sense a similarity to Jake's, it's because the ownership is the same. This old-world–atmosphere spot features the same fresh catch that Jake's does, as well as a regular selection that includes beef and veal. Seafood specials include deep-fried calamari and alder-roasted salmon. The main doors open onto a vast bar, which owners claim has standing room for 200; that is exactly where you will be if you don't make reservations. Open seven days for lunch and dinner. Live music. AE, CB, DC, MC, VISA.

**Rian's Eating Establishment.** 720 S.W. Alder; 222–9996. If it's Wednesday be sure to make reservations for John Rian's weekly seafood buffet. The entire side of the lanai room is lined with tables of imaginatively prepared seafood, beginning with chilled oysters on the half shell and running a full gamut of entrées. Fresh pastries are served for dessert at this fixed-price dinner, where the menu varies by the week according to the ocean's tides. There is no limit to the trips back to the buffet. Reservations a must. MC, VISA.

### Moderate

**Winterbourne.** 3520 N.E. 42nd; 249–8486. An all-fresh seafood menu is served imaginatively in an old Portland neighborhood at this spot, which has a loyal and regular following of diners. The menu varies with the catch of the day. Non-smokers receive a five-percent discount on the dinner tab. Wine. AE, MC, VISA.

### Inexpensive

**Dan and Louis Oyster Bar,** 208 S.W. Ankeny; 227–5906. A Portland institution. The Wachsmith family owns its own oyster beds on Yaquina Bay to insure an abundant supply for its customers. Here's the one spot in town where you can further cut your menu price by opening your own oysters—they provide instructions and equipment. The menu also includes crab, shrimp, scallops, calimari, and geoduck clams. Take the children; they'll love the décor. No liquor. Credit cards.

## MORE THAN SEAFOOD

### Deluxe

**Belinda's.** 112 S.W. 2nd; 222–6606. Pale grey velvet chairs, fresh flowers, white linen, and muted brick walls make this Old Town restaurant a romantic dining spot. Belinda's also has the largest wine list in the state to complement the continental cuisine, which is developed by the chefs around the freshest market buys of the day. Regular menu items that bring return customers include pork schnitzel and apricot duck. Dinner seven days a week. Reservations. AE, CB, DC, MC, VISA.

**L'Auberge.** 2601 N.W. Vaughn; 223–3302. Loosen your belt in this country French restaurant which offers a seven-course dinner with a choice of entrée and dessert. Lighter meals are served in the lounge, which attracts weekend diners with hamburgers and movies. All foods are from the freshest market selections, including seafood, veal, and chicken. Reservations for the dining room suggested. AE, MC, VISA.

**LeCuisinier.** 1308 W. Burnside; 224–4260. James Beard has knighted this out-of-the-way spot with his best wire whisk. A very small French restaurant where the emphasis is on food rather than atmosphere. A cab ride is suggested. Appetizers may include fresh steamed mussels and paper-thin slices of chilled leg of lamb with mustard sauce. Main courses may offer poached salmon, braised sweetbreads or duckling. Dinners only, Tuesday–Saturday. Wine.

Reservations are a must; leave yours with the recording service—the owner will call back to confirm. AE, MC, VISA.

**Fathers American Broiler and Nightclub.** 309 S.E. 3rd; 227–5492. This is the most fashionable of all Portland's restaurants, inspired by *Vogue* magazines of the 1930s, complete with banquettes, a cigarette girl, and exotic fresh flowers. The band begins to play at 9 P.M. so plan to stay to dance to the best in swing tempos. The menu is classically American, from Dungeness crab served atop fresh spinach leaves to steaks and an order of chocolate chip cookies, warm from the oven, for dessert. Reservations are a must for lunch (Monday–Friday) or dinner (seven nights). Late-night breakfasts are also served. Valet service evenings. AE, DC, MC, VISA.

**Genoa Restaurant.** 2832 S.E. Belmont; 238–1464. Forget about the atmosphere and concentrate on a seven-course northern Italian menu every evening except Sunday. Reservations are a must for this intimate restaurant, which has a large local following for its unique recipes. Set menu price. Wine. AE, MC, VISA.

## Expensive

**Bishop's House.** 223 S.W. Stark; 225–9009. Once the home of Oregon's first Catholic archbishop, this three-story Victorian Gothic landmark building now proves an inviting atmosphere for lunch and dinner Monday–Saturday. All menu items are strictly fresh, including excellent seafood entrées. Home-baked bread, warm from the oven, may take the edge off the elegant dessert tray passed at the end of the meal, so be forewarned. Reservations suggested. MC, VISA.

**Brasserie Montmartre.** 626 S.W. Park; 224–5552. The décor, black and white; the atmosphere, French. Full dinners with wonderful pastries and live jazz in the bar. Check to see when they're open for lunch. Reservations suggested. AE, MC, VISA.

**Cousins Cafe-Bar,** S.W. 3rd and Ankeny; 228–4277. Happy hour aficionados say this has one of the best free buffets. Otherwise plan for continental dining seven nights a week with live jazz on weekends. Reservations suggested. AE, MC, VISA.

**London Grill and Bar.** S.W. Broadway and Oak; 295–4410. Breakfast, lunch, and dinner are served seven days a week in this elegant oak-paneled lower level of the Westin Benson, many times internationally honored for its menu. Excellent service in a subdued atmosphere. Lunch and dinner reservations suggested. AE, CB, DC, MC, VISA.

**Trader Vic's.** 309 S.W. Broadway in the Westin Benson; 228–9611. Traditional Trader Vic's fare of South Sea Island-influenced seafood, pork, veal, and beef. Some of the best appetizers in town. Closed Sundays. AE, CB, DC, MC, VISA.

## Moderate

**Aldo's Ristorante/Trattoria.** 824 S.W. 1st; 241–2550. Pasta with elegance for lunch Monday–Friday, and dinner Monday–Saturday. The northern Italian menu includes veal, chicken, and seafood. Entertainment after hours in the Trattoria Lounge. Reservations suggested. AE, MC, VISA.

**Caro-Amico Pizzeria.** 3606 S.W. Barbur Blvd.; 223–6895. This is the godfather of all Portland's pizzerias. The menu includes no-nonsense ravioli, spaghetti, and veal. Children welcome. MC, VISA.

**Crêpe Faire.** 133 S.W. 2nd; 227–3365. A wonderful place for a leisurely meal—breakfast, lunch, or dinner. In addition to the special crêpes of the day, this innovative spot in one of the city's historic buildings serves smashing salads with a special flair as well as superb soups. Breakfast from 7 A.M., lunch, dinner, and bistro service until midnight. Reservations suggested for lunch and dinner. AE, MC, VISA.

**Harrington's Bar and Grill.** 1001 S.W. 5th; 243–2932. Lively, young gathering place in the Orbanco Building. A continental menu is served in the dining room; the long bar area includes a dance floor. Closed Sunday. Reservations for lunch suggested. AE, MC, VISA.

**Jazz De Opus** and **Opus Too Bar and Restaurant.** 33 N.W. 2nd; 222–6077. When the musical background matters, this is the gathering spot for musicians. Intimate bar and adjoining restaurant with mesquite charcoal broiler for seafood and steak. Sidewalk service on sunny afternoons. Lunches and dinners seven days. Reservations suggested for dinner. AE, MC, VISA.

**Norton House.** 53 S.W. 1st; 223–0743. Open, airy atmosphere that includes sunny patio dining in fair weather; opera at the table during the fall and winter months. On the menu: beef, veal, seafood, and pasta, all well prepared. AE, DC, CB, MC, VISA.

**Old Country Kitchen.** 10519 S.E. Stark; 252–4171; and corner of Griffith Dr. and Beaverton-Hillsdale Hwy., Beaverton; 644–1492. This is the home of the 72-ounce steak. Eat it all, including the trimmings, and the bill is picked up by the house. Open seven days a week. No reservations taken. MC, VISA.

**Remo's.** 1425 N.W. Glisan; 221–1150. Fine dining in a renovated firehouse, featuring an all-Italian menu with rotating daily specials at lunch and dinner. Spacious bar downstairs features live jazz seven nights a week with groups performing Thursday–Saturday. Dinner reservations suggested. AE, DC, MC, VISA.

**Ringside.** 2156 W. Burnside; 223–1513. There's a sportsmanlike atmosphere here and eating is taken seriously. Steaks, potatoes, and superlative onion rings have been served to more than three generations of beef lovers in the commodious wooden booths. Dinner seven days. No reservations until after 10 P.M. on weekends. AE, MC, VISA.

**Rodeo.** 915 S.W. 2nd; 227–6336. Mexican food in a cantina atmosphere with what some consider the best live music in town—acts rotating regularly, live shows every night. Lunch and dinner. AE, MC, VISA.

**Tivoli Garden.** 111 S.W. Columbia; 222–4898. Possibly the prettiest room in Portland during the day when the light from the greenhouse-style roof is matched by the hundreds of twinkling lights in the tall ficus trees around the tables. Varied menu with a Scandinavian influence. One of the best Sunday brunches in town. Open seven days, lunch and dinner. Reservations suggested. AE, MC, VISA.

*Inexpensive*

**Abou Karim.** 221 S.W. Pine; 223–5058. Lebanese food with weekday lunches and dinners, Monday–Saturday. Lebanese music Friday and Saturday. Roast lamb is the dinner favorite, with falafel sandwiches ranking first for lunch. MC, VISA.

**Alexis.** 215 W. Burnside; 224–8577. Join the crowd waiting for a table in this family-run restaurant serving homemade Greek food. Entrées include grape leaves stuffed with rice, souvlaki, and calamari. Retsina, by the bottle, washes down a wide variety of appetizers. Closed Sunday. No reservations. MC, VISA.

**Carnival.** 0102 S.W. Abernethy; 227–4244. Open from 11 A.M. through dinnertime, this superior hamburger spot has been broiling hamburgers to order for more than three generations of hungry children and adults. Wide selection of homemade desserts, highchairs with animal heads, outdoor seating by a waterfall in warm weather. Closed Sunday. No liquor. No credit cards.

**Fong Chong.** 301 N.W. 4th; 220–0235. This old, established restaurant and grocery store combination offers dim sum service for lunch. In addition to this Chinese smorgasbord on wheels, diners may select from a regular menu. Open for lunch and dinner seven days. No credit cards.

**Metro on Broadway.** S.W. Broadway at Taylor. A variety of small service-at-the-counter restaurants that vend crepes, Belgian waffles, espresso, pasta, sandwiches, salads, beer, and wine from morning through late evening. No reservations. No credit cards.

**Papa Haydn,** 5829 S.E. Milwaukie Ave.; 232–9440. Lunches and dinners topped off with the most luscious desserts in the city. At least 25 different caloric tempters fill the pastry counter. Regular menu items include sandwiches, pasta, and seafood entrées. Open until midnight on weekends. Wine. No reservations. AE, MC, VISA.

**Produce Row Café.** 204 S.E. Oak; 232–8355. Very casual tavern-style eating next to Portland's produce warehouses. A half sandwich is offered for those with average appetites. Largest beer assortment in state. Minors welcome from lunch through afternoon. Beer. No reservations. No credit cards.

**Red Robin Burger and Spirits Emporium.** S.W. 20th Pl. at W. Burnside; 222–4602. Of course, Father can have his martini while Junior gets a burger. Red Robin serves nearly 30 varieties of hamburgers, as well as steaks, salads, barbecued chicken, and ribs. Open for lunch and dinner seven days. AE, MC, VISA.

**Yamhill Market.** S.W. 2nd and Yamhill. Contains at least two dozen fast-service food outlets on the third floor, including beer and wine service. Open seven days a week.

**Yaw's Top Notch.** 2001 N.E. 40th; 281–1233. (Also at the Lloyd Center.) This spot for lunch and dinner built its reputation on a piece of meat and bun now immortalized as the "Founder Burger", including two kinds of pickle, fresh lettuce, mayo, and butter. The menu now has full dinners, homemade pies, and desserts. No reservations. AE, DC, MC, VISA.

**BARS AND NIGHT LIFE.** Many of Portland's restaurants have active bars and live music. See the "Dining Out" section above—especially *McCormick & Schmick's* (under *Seafood-Expensive*); *Fathers American* (under *Deluxe*); *Cousins Cafe-Bar* (under *Expensive*); *Harrington's* (*Moderate*); *Remo's* (*Moderate*); Rodeo (*Moderate*); *Goose Hollow Inn* and *Veritable Quandary* (both listed under *Inexpensive*).

Other, smaller lounges and taverns also entertain through the night. Some of the most entertaining include: *Cracklin' Rosie's,* 2757 E. Burnside, Gresham; 661–1991. A wide selection of musical entertainment. Call to be sure it's your style that week. *Darcelle XV,* 208 N.W. 3rd; 222–5338. A gay tavern that caters to straights with a lavish female impersonator show. *East Avenue Tavern,* 727 E. Burnside; 236–6900. A variety of folk artists. *East Bank Saloon,* 727 S.E. Grand; 231–1659. Jazz. *Horse Brass Pub,* 4522 S.E. Belmont; 232–2202. An English atmosphere that draws Portland's British crowd with darts and sing-alongs. *Jazz Quarry,* 1111 S.W. Jefferson; 222–2227. Live jazz. *Last Hurrah,* 555 S.W. Alder; 224–1336. Rock, blues, contemporary. *Main Place,* 101 S.W. Main; 228–4224. Soft jazz and comedy acts. *Orange Peel,* 6327 S.W. Capitol Hwy.; 246–1530. Rock. *Rafters,* 220 S.E. Spokane; 238–7067. A large restaurant with a good-sized singles bar and music for listening and dancing. *Starry Night,* 8 N.W. 6th; 221–0011. Headliners with touring shows weekly. *Village Jazz,* 500 S.W. 1st, Lake Oswego; 636–2024. Headliners at times; the best of local jazz artists in between.

# EXPLORING OREGON'S MAGNIFICENT COAST

Of all sections of Oregon, the coast is the most famous and the most visited. It has often been termed the most scenic marine border drive in the world, and for good reason none who sees it is disappointed.

Take hundreds of miles of shore fronting the Pacific, fill with rolling sand dunes, mouths of swift rivers, freshwater lakes, craggy cliffs, toppled mountainsides, battered headlands, hills bursting with greenery, secret coves, deep inlets, picturesque lighthouses, broad beaches, herds of sea lions, grassy state parks, millions of wildflowers, leaping waterfalls—and you have the Oregon Coast.

To the purple-shadowed range skirting the shore and the virgin stands of giant firs, add the unsurpassed vistas of surf and sea—and you have one of the nation's grandest terrains. Add to all of this a salubrious climate, fabulous fishing, the taste of world-famous cheese in the valley where it is produced, colorful seashore towns, and a wealth of recreational opportunities—and the pleasure is doubled.

Almost all of the tideland of the coast belongs to the people; only a few miles are privately owned. More than thirty state parks, including the choicest scenic spots, are reserved for public use. In addition, there are many national forest camps.

The coastal towns offer a mix of clientele. The rich do not go one place, the middle class another, the respectable poor somewhere else. There is no place on the coast where the "beautiful people," the senior citizens, the collegiates, or any other group congregate exclusively. Half-a-million dollar homes can be a few blocks—or a block—from a dingy shack. An expensive motel can look across the road to a mom-and-pop cabin court. People on the Oregon Coast dress so informally that in a restaurant or motel it is difficult to know who is the richer.

It is a bit ironic, perhaps, that the most scenic and historical route linking Portland to the coast should be the longest and most time-consuming; nevertheless, U.S. 30, which skirts the Columbia River, is a storybook way to reach Astoria (the northern terminal of the littoral). On the other hand, U.S. 26, the more popular route, is also the most crowded.

## "Williamsburg of the West?"

"Oldest American City West of the Missouri" is what Astoria calls itself. It possesses, in this respect, many firsts, including the first post office west of the "Big Muddy." Local historians claim that there has been "more history made within twenty miles of Astoria than in all the rest of Oregon put together." This claim is disputed by others elsewhere, but Astoria is so steeped in history that some citizens would like to turn the city into a "Williamsburg of the West."

Tongue Point, which overlooks the Columbia, was discovered and named by the British in 1792. On November 17, 1805, the Lewis and Clark party landed "on a beautiful shore of pebbles of various colors." Lewis named the place "Fort William," after Clark's given name. But the British name has survived.

Oregon's first custom house was located at 34th and Leif Erickson Drive (U.S. 30) and is marked by a state historical sign, on the south side of the road.

Astoria is dotted with mid- and late-nineteenth-century homes, all of them photogenic and most of them included on a walking tour.

For the 1.2-mile walking tours of the historic homes of Franklin and Grand avenues, begin at the Clatsop County Historical Museum, at 441 Eighth St. The house, also known as the Flavel Mansion, was built for sea captain George Flavel and his wife, Mary Lydia Christina Boelling. It is recognized as one of the finest examples of Victorian architecture in Oregon. From its fourth-story cupola, Captain Flavel, master of his own sailing fleet and one of the first bar pilots licensed by the Oregon territorial legislature (January 1852), could watch his

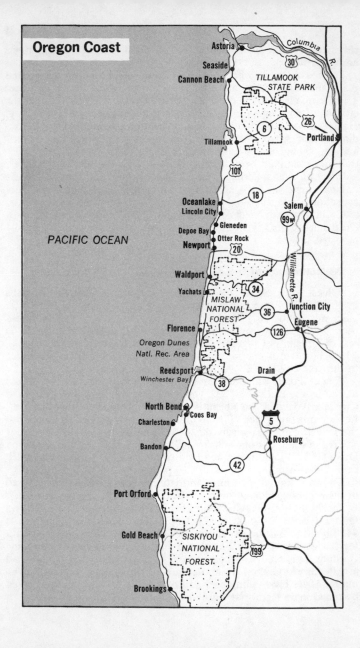

# Oregon Coast

PACIFIC OCEAN

Astoria
Seaside
Cannon Beach
TILLAMOOK STATE PARK
Columbia R.
30
Portland
6
26
Tillamook
101
18
Oceanlake
Lincoln City
Gleneden
Depoe Bay
Otter Rock
Newport
20
Salem
99w
Willamette R.
Waldport
34
Yachats
MISLAW NATIONAL FOREST
36
Junction City
Florence
126
Eugene
Oregon Dunes
Natl. Rec. Area
Reedsport
Winchester Bay
38
Drain
North Bend
Coos Bay
Charleston
Bandon
5
Roseburg
42
Port Orford
Gold Beach
SISKIYOU NATIONAL FOREST
199
Brookings

ships sail up the river and into port. President Rutherford B. Hayes was once a guest here.

Proceed to the southwest corner of Eighth and Exchange, to the 1863 Conrad Boelling residence (765 Exchange). The Boellings came from Cincinnati, Ohio, by covered wagon in 1846. In 1848 Conrad opened Astoria's first hotel. In 1851 he provided the building for Astoria's first school, located at Ninth and Exchange, near the site of the Boelling residence. Boelling's daughter Mary Lydia Christina, not quite fourteen, became Mrs. George C. Flavel on March 26, 1854.

Walk to Franklin Ave. At 960 Franklin is a house built in 1888 by Captain Eric Johnson, bar pilot. It was later the home of L. A. Larson, painting contractor, and also a talented organist and vocalist. He organized the Laerkin Male Chorus, a Scandinavian singing society whose *sangerfests* delighted Northwest audiences.

Francis Apartments, at 1030 Franklin Ave., was built in 1909 by Louis Franetovich, a wealthy restaurateur. The structure, named for his son, Francis, was once considered to be the most elite apartment house in Astoria.

One block north from Twelfth St., on the southeast corner of Twelfth and Exchange, is the YMCA building, put up in 1916. It survived the catastrophic fire of December 8, 1922, and was used as emergency relief headquarters. The fire leveled 40 square blocks of the downtown area.

As you walk along, notice the contours of bricks showing beneath the blacktop on the incline of Franklin Avenue. Tradition has it that traffic tempers flared when automobiles began to compete with horse-drawn vehicles for right-of-way on the graveled streets. The city fathers provided the diplomatic solution: they decreed that a brick strip should be laid down the center for the horses, with the paved strip on either side for the cars. Franklin Avenue was thus paved in 1916.

Astoria's oldest house is at 1337 Franklin. It was built in 1854 by Captain Hiram Brown, a river pilot who came to Astoria in 1850 and four years later built the west portion of this home in Adairville (East Astoria). In 1862 he barged the house down the river to Twelfth and Franklin, which was then a backwater of the Columbia, then had it drawn on log rollers by oxen to its present location, where the rollers remained as footing; the addition was attached to the portion already built. About the turn of the century the building became a boarding house. After several years of vacancy the house was authentically restored in 1964. The English holly tree here is as old as the house.

Grace Episcopal Church, at 1555 Franklin, built in 1885, is the oldest church building in Astoria in continuous use. The rectory was built in 1920. The original rectory is now the house at 637 16th St., first occupied in 1883.

The structure at the corner of 16th and Franklin was erected in 1885 and is the former home of Judge Frank J. Taylor. The Judge was the victim in one of Astoria's most famous murder cases when on September 14, 1913, he was shot while walking along Commercial Street. The assailant, the husband of a woman who had earlier been granted a divorce, was eventually hanged.

At 1687 Grand, the 1880 house was the home of John Henry Dix Gray, son of W. H. Gray, who came to Oregon in 1836 with pioneer missionary Dr. Marcus Whitman. J. H. D. Gray was born in Lapwai, Idaho, the second white boy born west of the Upper Missouri. He moved with his family to Clatsop Plains; later he became a riverboat captain, a state senator, and a county judge. He died in this house in 1902. The house, constructed largely of cedar, remains as it was built, except for the addition of a portion of the south wing.

Moving back downtown: 15th between Franklin and Exchange is the site of the first U.S. post office west of the Upper Missouri. In 1843, John H. Shively, first postmaster, operated the post office in his home. Postal rates were 40 cents per letter from Oregon Territory to "The States." The house, after a long period of vacancy, was demolished in the early 1900s.

At 15th and Exchange is the 1811 site of Fort Astoria. Log footings of the original buildings were unearthed in 1931 during excavation for the west wing of the hospital. Others were found at the present street intersection. The park area and replica of one of the Fort's bastions were developed in 1956.

The oldest gravestone in Oregon is found at the representation of Fort Astoria. It's the grave of Donald McTavish, a proprietor of the Northwest Company who came as governor to Fort George (the second name of Fort Astoria) in April 1814. In addition to some ale, cheese, and tinned prime English beef, he brought with him the first white woman in the Oregon country. Jane Barnes caused quite a stir, even receiving a marriage proposal from the son of the Chinook chief; she turned him down, eventually marrying a wealthy Englishman after McTavish was drowned in a boat accident in May 1814.

On the northeast corner of 15th and Exchange (where the newer wing of the Hospital stands), is the site of the Wells Fargo stagecoach station, located strategically between the first post office and Fort Astoria. The first hospital structure located on this site was built in 1889 by Providence Sisters of Charity. The east wing of the present structure was built in 1905, and miraculously escaped the 1922 fire.

In 1905 a structure on the northeast corner of 16th and Exchange streets was dedicated as the Astoria City Hall. During World War II it became U.S.O. headquarters. In 1962 it became the Columbia River

Maritime Museum. A few years ago a new museum building was constructed at the foot of 17th Street, near the lightship *Columbia.*

## Fort Clatsop

Four miles south of Astoria, and off U.S. 101, is the replica of Fort Clatsop, centerpiece of Fort Clatsop National Memorial. This replica was patterned after a sketch in the daybook of Captain William Clark. In the museum, graphic displays and audio-visual presentations dramatize the epic of the Lewis and Clark party. During the summer, young park rangers, dressed as the elkskin trail blazers, hew out canoes and carry out tasks as the men of the Lewis and Clark party did 180 years ago. The party built the original fort as shelter during the winter of 1805–06.

Clark's journals give some indication as to how his party felt about the Oregon coast. On November 22 he wrote, "O! how horriable is the day . . . waves brakeing with great violence against the Shore throwing the Water into our Camp&c. all wet and confind to our Shelters . . . " He wrote with a shiver of the "emence Seas and waves" and was troubled by the awesome noise: "this roaring has continued . . . Since we arrived in Sight of the Great Western; (for I cannot say Pacific) Ocian as I have not See one pacific day Since my arrival in its vicinity. . . . " Far different from the feelings of most of today's visitors to the area.

By the time the first white settlers arrived on Clatsop Plains, there was no vestige of the stockade.

Eight miles south of Astoria, on U.S. 101, stands Gray Memorial Chapel, better known as Clatsop Plains Pioneer Church, because the building is on the site of the first Presbyterian church, erected in 1850 as an outgrowth of Presbyterian Society organized in 1846. The congregation, whose early members included William H. Gray, a pioneer missionary and author of probably the most controversial history of Oregon, claims this to be the oldest continuing Presbyterian church west of the Upper Missouri.

Many Clatsop Plains pioneers are buried in the cemetery behind the church. Among them are Solomon Howard Smith, a New Hampshire native, and Helen Celiast Smith, princess daughter of Coboway, Supreme Chief of the Clatsops. The two were said to have fallen in love as soon as they met, ran off together, and later became the first schoolteachers in what is now Oregon.

Cullaby Lake Park near Astoria offers varied recreation, including waterskiing, swimming, and picnic facilities.

Gearhart, seven miles south, is a small town with a population of only about 1,000, but for a long time it was the convention center of the northern Oregon coast. Now there are too many convention centers to say that one is really dominant. But Gearhart is still a nice place to convene, because of its carefree, casual atmosphere and the golf course across from the convention site.

Gearhart is a town of condominiums, but there is no central agency to facilitate rentals. Realtors are helpful, but most transactions seem to be on a personal basis.

## Seaside

Seaside, two miles south of Gearhart, has the finest beach in the state. It also boasts an almost two-mile-long concrete promenade, which is the fashion walk of the town of 5,300 people. There are also more tourist facilities—and their variety is legion—than in any town twice its size. The "Miss Oregon" pageant is staged here, which some people think is appropriate, since for many years Seaside had a reputation of being a main-street, hurdy-gurdy, hustler town. But Seaside has cleaned up its act, and the old town is scarcely recognizable now. Gone is the carnival atmosphere; in its place Seaside has a sparkling shopping center and malls that bespeak propriety. The city is trying to regain its luster as the chief resort community in Oregon, but that hope seems dim, considering all the competition up and down the coast.

At the juncture of U.S. 101 and U.S. 26 you may want to turn east, or left, onto U.S. 26. In two miles you come to Klootchy Creek Park. Giant firs and spruce tower as hoary monsters of a dim age. Mammoth trees, with twined roots above ground, seem to belong in an ancient art museum. Here stands the world's tallest Sitka spruce, almost 200 feet high and about 16 feet in diameter. It was more than 300 years old when Columbus landed in the New World. There is a free campground here. Seven miles on east is the junction of Oregon 53. Turn right onto Oregon 53 and less than a mile down the road is Hamlet Junction. Turn left and drive six miles to Hamlet, so named because it was never more than a hamlet, a spread-out rural settlement now down to a faded community hall, once the schoolhouse, and a cemetery that hasn't seen a burial for almost two generations.

Returning to Hamlet Junction on this side trip, now turn left, or south. Drive 20 miles through a microcosm of a rain forest and then stump-ranch, dairy country to Wheeler, on U.S. 101. From the junction of Oregon 53, you may continue east a mile to the junction of Saddle Mountain State Park. Turn left, or north, and drive seven miles to the parking area. A four-mile-long trail leads to the top—elevation, 3283 feet. Inexperienced climbers require about four hours for the round trip. Along the trail you brush surges of wildflowers and are likely to encounter insects, birds, and some deer. You may also spot black bear.

## Ecola State Park and Cannon Beach

Back on the coast, from the junction of U.S. 101 and U.S. 26, continue south on U.S. 101. In three miles there is a turnoff for Ecola State Park and Cannon Beach. Take it, and follow the road for two miles to the picnic area of Ecola State Park.

The views from Tillamook Head dance before the startled eye. One is reminded of the observation made by the British mariner, Captain John Meares, in 1788: "Many beautiful spots, covered with verdure, solicited our attention: and the land rose in a very gradual ascent to the distant mountains, skirted by a white sand beach to the sea. . . . " Less than a mile offshore is a sea lion rookery. That dot far out at sea that looks like a lighthouse is, or was, one. The abandoned, crumbling structure rises 41 feet on an isolated rock, often swept in winter by gales of hurricane force. The base of the lighthouse (long ago abandoned and not accessible to tourists) is only 91 feet above the water, so the keeper must have had some chill moments in strong blows and lashing waves. Within the park, tame deer and elk roam freely.

At the base of the park is probably the site where Sacajawea watched members of the Lewis and Clark party purchase butchered meat cut from a beached whale. Sacajawea had prevailed upon William Clark to take her along because, she said, she had come so far and not yet seen the ocean. Later, she was to remember the "big fish" as one of the outstanding experiences of the long trek.

Ecola State Park is contiguous to Cannon Beach, the Carmel of the Oregon Coast. Until the renaissance of this small village (population 1,200), the town was best-known for its offshore, 235-foot Haystack Rock, one of the most photographed places in all of Oregon. Constantly presenting a changing face, this monolith seems tame in sunshine, eerie and forbidding in the fog. During low tide, the pools around the rock swarm with jellyfish, small crabs, starfish, sea anemones, and other marine specimens swept in by the tides. Do not try to climb the rock; there have been too many fatalities already. (Several other offshore rocks along the coast are also called "Haystack," but this is the famous one.)

Cannon Beach is a strolling town. Parking space is hard to find in the summer season, and walking is very pleasant here. No one hurries, everyone is casually dressed, and there is always an air of quiet bustling. There are lots of families visiting here, and numerous hotels and motels to accommodate their particular needs. The town is filled with intriguing shops and galleries.

Along the fine beach, surf, rock and bay fishing have become increasingly popular. People are finding that a day at the beach can pay extra dividends in surfperch, kelp greenling; lingcod, flounder, and rockfish.

The beach is also the site for the annual Cannon Beach Sand Castle Contest, attracting many participants and thousands of viewers who enjoy the temporary art that is soon erased by summer tides.

From U.S. 101, at the south end of the Beach Loop, it is two miles to Hug Point State Park. Here is a clean long beach with caves that tempt inquiry.

Hug Point is a literal description of an old road that hugs the point where the hill meets the sea. Early settlers used much of the beach along the coast for highways, but here at high tide there was no beach, and the slopes beside the water were too steep to be navigated. If there was to be a passage at high tide, a road had to be cut out of the hill. It was, and the road represented a great advance in coastal travel. You can picnic and surf fish here, too.

From Hug Point State Park it is only little more than a mile to Arch Cape, a rather inconspicuous wayside village, which has two bed-and-breakfast establishments. An antique shop here worth a pause is Cold Comfort Farm Antiques, Leach Ave. (436–2751), with a big stock of early American primitives.

Four miles on, through a canopied lane of trees, is Short Sands State Park, where you can picnic in a virgin forest or on a dazzling beach.

Oswald West State Park adjoins Short Sands and was named for a maverick governor who fought to preserve the coastal strip as a public heritage. Little wonder that this, and other progressive accomplishments, have earned him accolades as Oregon's greatest governor. Wooden wheelbarrows are available at the side of the road for lugging in gear. Parking is on the inland side of the road.

Soon the road leaves the rising flatland and climbs abruptly in sweeping quarter- and half-circles up Neahkahnie Mountain, which would be a small hill were it inland but at 1,661 feet seems a giant here. The road rides the cut-out shoulder of the mountain and affords an airy feeling, making visitors feel that they are much higher up than they are and that the ocean is closer than it is. There are numerous turnouts for clear, safe viewing, and at any one of them the heart rises to the drama of the pounding surf and headlands beset by vagrant winds.

The Tillamook Indians called Neahkahnie Mountain "the Place of the Fire Spirit" and showed it reverence—but whites have a different view. Since pioneer days, there have been frequent searches for a treasure supposedly buried on a slope by the crew of a wrecked Spanish galleon.

## Whale Watching from Neahkahnie Mountain

When there is clear weather in December, those in the know come here—as to other high vistas, such as Cape Lookout, Cape Kiwanda, or Cascade Head—with binoculars and telescopes to view the annual winter migration of the gray whale. In the spring the migration is repeated, this time northward, but December seems to be the better time for viewing.

Each year, thousands of huge, magnificent gray whales pass along the coast swimming at four or five knots, on their annual migration between the icy Arctic and sub-tropical Baja California. Protected by international agreement since 1937, when their population levels were so depleted by whalers that little chance was given for their survival as a species, the gray whales have managed an impressive recovery, now numbering abound 11,000.

The majority of these can be seen from high points along the Oregon coast as they swim this leg of their 14,000-mile journey. The lengthy sojourn through Pacific waters is the largest known annual migration of any mammal, and even more impressive is that they consume only tiny amounts of food during the eight months of swimming, mating, giving birth, and nursing a newborn member of the family. They subsist almost entirely on the energy stored in their thick blubber, which is laid down in thick, oily masses during four months of feeding in the plankton-rich summer seas of the Arctic.

Two miles south of Neahkahnie Mountain there is a turnoff for Neahkahnie Beach, a quiet, small beach with a high driftwood bank, one mile west of U.S. 101. Three-tenths of a mile from the turnoff to Neahkahnie Beach, there is another turnoff, this one to Manzanita, in the midst of seven miles of sand. Continue two miles to Nehalem Bay State Park, a sand spit between Nehalem Bay and the ocean.

Two miles below the Manzanita Junction on U.S. 101 is the sea-scoured town of Nehalem, one of the few towns on the Oregon Coast that has any resemblance to the days before big tourism. Still, it too is giving way to the artsy and touristy. The Nehalem River, which completes its journey here, is the first sizable salmon stream south of the Columbia. Fishing is all by trolling.

Rockaway, emerging from its long siesta as a sea bedroom of Portland, is scraping off the hills and felling the trees to make room for growth—houses and more houses. There is nothing to distinguish Rockaway—indeed, its beach is one of the less spectacular in Oregon—but from the beach Twin Rocks, clearly seen, looks like a Roman arch of antiquity, through which a seafaring Caeser would pass in triumph.

Three miles below Rockaway is Barview Jetty County Park. Here there is fishing from rocks at the north jetty of Tillamook Bay. Some fishers swear this is the best place for deep-sea jetty fishing in the state.

Another two miles south along U.S. 101 is Garibaldi, named for the Italian revolutionary hero. Garibaldi was a mill town, but when the mill closed, as has been common of late in Oregon, the town took a financial beating. Its prosaic looks are sharpened by the very nautical-looking Coast Guard station and by its pier and boat marina. Its fishing fleet at the basin is a romantic forest of masts. On the pier are two cafés that serve fine seafood meals, a fish cannery, and offices of charter boats. During the whaling migrations, in April and May and again in December and early January, charter boats are available for close-up looks at the gray whales.

Located within walking distance of downtown Garibaldi is the Old Mill Marina and RV Park, with shops, restaurants, and bars. The RV park has 165 RV sites on a daily, weekly, monthly, semi-yearly, or yearly basis.

Eight miles south of Garibaldi, on the east side of U.S. 101, stands the Tillamook Cheese Factory. Tillamook calls itself the land of cheese, trees, and ocean breeze, and this factory is reputed to be one of the largest cheese plants in the West. Large viewing windows and color exhibits permit visitors to observe the production process. Free samples permit them to taste the results. On the lawn outside the factory is the *Morning Star II,* a replica of a pioneer sailing vessel. It was moved here from the boat basin at Garibaldi.

Tillamook, a county seat of about 4,000 people, is another rather undistinguished coast town. But the town does possess the very fine Pioneer Museum, with the finest wildlife exhibits in the state, created by the late curator, Alex Walker. A quiet, gentle, devoted man of science and culture, Walker spent many a cold and wet day (and night) crouched on offshore rocks so that he could photograph birds and stayed put days at at time in a forest blind so that he could take pictures of wild animals.

Probably the most kaleidoscopic side trip on the Oregon Coast begins at Tillamook: Turn west on 3rd Street, go two miles to Cape Meares Junction, turn right. In 5½ miles, you reach the junction of 3 Capes Scenic Route. Continue straight less than a mile to a driftwood beach. This beach, with its fantastic driftwood, it is a ghost fort by the sea; one of the most unusual and spectral bits of beach on the Oregon Coast.

Backtrack to the junction of 3 Capes Scenic Route, turn right, and go another two miles to Cape Meares State Park. Turn right and go about half a mile to the parking area. A trail leads to Cape Meares Lighthouse, a restored structure with a photo mural display. Visitor hours vary. Another trail, through the woods, ends at the Octopus Tree, a giant Sitka spruce with a massive trunk that branches like a candelabra at the base. The tree was featured in *Ripley's Believe It or Not* as "Seven Trees in One." Beyond the tree, at the fence on the cliff, the views of sea and scalloped shoreline and offshore rocks are not to be missed.

Return to the road from the parking lot and turn right. Drive 2½ miles to Oceanside Junction. Turn right again. Almost immediately you are in Oceanside, a breeze-filtering hamlet facing out to Three Arch Rocks National Wildlife Refuge. During nesting season, the rocks are inhabited by swarms of sea birds—including murres, gulls, cormorants, puffins, petrels, and guillemots—and have become one of the largest "bird cities" on the continent. The rocks are also permanent home of a large herd of steller sea lions.

Oceanside boasts that it has "one of the finest bathing beaches of the Oregon coast with no crab holes assuring you the utmost safety in surf bathing." Also: "Excellent rock and surf fishing, scenery that will thrill the camera fan, agate and driftwood hunting, and at low tides you may explore ocean caves and natural marine gardens. You will enjoy smooth sandy beaches, the tunnel, sand dunes, more sun less wind." All this in an effort to lure visitors to a "one-stop vacation."

Return to Oceanside Junction. Continue straight for two miles to Netarts, which, like Oceanside, is a small beach village that seems more of an Eastern-cottage and family-vacation place than a West Coast village. There is a boat landing and a marina on Netarts Bay here, mostly used by folks who stay a while.

## Cape Lookout

Half a mile out of Netarts, turn toward Cape Lookout State Park. It is then six miles to the parking lot of the park. The park was named for Cape Lookout, a rocky headland which extends 1¾ miles into the ocean. The overnight camp is located in a typical coastal rain forest. A broad, gently sloping beach provides an ideal setting for ocean activities. North of the camp a four-mile sand spit and dune separates Netarts Bay from the Pacific. The Netart estuary provides an excellent habitat for many of the park's 154 species of birds.

The cape is geologically intriguing. Volcanic in origin, the basalt cliffs of Cape Lookout have resisted the attack of wind and sea for more than 20 million years. The northern face, in addition to being considerably lower than the southern side, is indented with several coves, contrasting with the nearly straight basaltic southern cliffs.

The vegetation of the cape and surrounding area is representative of a coastal rain forest. Sitka spruce, western hemlock, and western red cedar are the most commonly found trees, with red alder growing along clearings. The undergrowth of the area is a thick tangle of salal, box blueberry, salmonberry, and pacific waxmyrtle. Sword fern, skunk cabbage, and wildflowers, such as lily-of-the-valley and trillium, make up the ground cover of the moist, shady forest.

Hikers taking the Cape Lookout Trail to the tip of the cape will walk through a stand of Sitka spruce with no undergrowth but a blanket of sworn fern, into moist, shadowy glens where wildflowers abound, beneath giant trees toppled to the wind, and around corners that open onto spectacular views of the coastline and the cape. The trail is generally broad and easy to walk. In several places, however, it passes close to steep dropoffs, and hikers should exercise caution in these areas.

The parking area at the top of the cape allows easy access to the Cape Lookout Trail. If a longer walk is desired, a trail starts in the picnic area of the park and climbs to meet the cape section near the parking area. A half-mile, self-guiding nature trail begins near the registration booth at the entrance to the overnight camp.

Backtrack half a mile to Sand Lake Junction. Turn right and drive 1¼ miles to Anderson's View Point for a sweeping vista of Three Arch Rocks, miles of sunburst beach, Cape Meares, and the expansive Pacific.

Now the road winds through logged-off hills, thick banks of wild shrubbery, tall beach grass and dune ridges, and past overlooks, beaches, and camping and picnic grounds. The mood of this stretch of road extends from the gloomy moors of nineteenth-century British novelists to the barnyards of Iowa. The road swings around the east rim of Netarts Bay. The west side, Netarts Peninsula, reaches from the south end of the bay and has more than five miles of beach.

Ten miles from Anderson's View Point the road reaches Cape Kiwanda, a sculptured headland cave flanking a sprightly cove, shimmery beach, and (another) Haystack Rock. Cape Kiwanda is one of the few places in the world where boats are launched into the open surf from a sandy beach. This unique sport of dory fishing has been popular at the Cape for six decades. The Dory Fleet has grown to more than 1,000 boats and makes a major contribution to the economy of the area. Each week, crowds of spectators watch as the dories leave the beach and return with their catch. Once a year, usually early June, a dory derby is held, and thousands line the beach to watch the dories in action. Dory races around Haystack Rock, rowing exhibitions, skin diving, and surfing are only part of the weekend of ocean sports. A parade is held on Saturday, with the main events at the Cape on Sunday.

The majestic contours of Cape Kiwanda make calendar art at its best. Spectacular sand dunes rise from the Cape and provide a backdrop for amateur and professional artists. The cape itself is a literal jumping-off point for hang gliders. Miles of sandy beach extend to the south of the cape. Driftwood, glass balls, shells, and others treasures await the newcomer.

Beyond here lies Nestucca Spit, a "sand wall" for Nestucca Bay. Only in the northern part is there human habitation. The rest—3½ miles long—belongs to nature, and no part of the coast is so unspoiled. Dunes topped by waves of beach grass roll back from the sea to heights of 40 feet in the narrow part of the spit; in the widest part, a higher, naked "traveling dune" is pushed back and forth by fickle winds. Those who hike the beach in winter find Japanese glass floats, sand dollars, and bits of driftwood.

The Nestucca River, which flows into Nestucca Bay, is regarded by many fishers as the best fishing stream in the state. Nestucca and Little Nestucca are noted for excellent June and July chinook fishing in the tidewater areas.

Seven miles south of Tallamook on U.S. 101 is Munson Creek Falls County Park. A mile from the turnoff is the park and half a mile farther on, through a rain forest, is the parking area. There is a half-mile trail climb to Munson Falls, at 319 feet the highest falls in the Coast Range. The park—a darkling mass of old-growth firs, maples, alders, cedars, spruce, and hemlock—is a suggestion of what much of the Coast looked like before frenetic logging began.

From the turnoff to Munson Falls, continue for 7½ miles to Beaver, a wayside on U.S. 101. Here begins the Meadow Lake Road to Carlton, across the Coast Range in the Yamhill Valley. The 48-mile road does not pass a single settlement. The first half of the road, through the Siuslaw National Forest, follows the Nestucca River. Public campgrounds, about as primitive as is possible, dot the western portion of the road.

Few people pause at Neskowin, off 101. But those who do and hike out to the beach just south of the mouth of Neskowin Creek will find a sunken stump forest in the surf of the Pacific. Some time in the past there was a group of trees probably standing on low coastal land. Now all that is left of this forest are stark stumps protruding from the sand, some of them fairly well out beyond the line of breakers, some of them in the surf line, and some on the wet sand beach during low tide. What happened to this "forest" is at present a mystery.

At the south end of Neskowin, you can turn off left for an 11-mile scenic forest drive, ending at Oregon 18, near U.S. 101. If you have the time and love trees and plants, you will not mind the many crooks in the road.

Six miles south of the turnoff on U.S. 101 is Three Rocks Road. Turn right here for Cascade Head. At three miles there is a fork. Take the

Lower Salmon River branch to the end of the road, at Cascade Head Ranch. The southwestern-most portion of Cascade Head, a 1,400-foot promontory jutting out in the Pacific, was purchased in 1966 by the Nature Conservancy for preservation as a natural area. The preserve is bordered on the south by the Salmon River estuary and on the north by the Cascade Head Experimental Forest. It includes 1½ miles of shoreline and comprises 300 acres. Two-thirds of the preserve is in meadow, the rest being coastal rain forest, with Sitka spruce, lodgepole pine, and Western hemlock. There are nine species of fern, numerous grasses and rushes, and abundant wildflowers typical of the Pacific Coast, such as seaside daisy, silver cinquefoil, lupine, Indian paint-brush. Deer and elk frequent the area. Waterfalls plunge into the reaching sea from steep rocky cliffs. The magnificent view from the headland is perhaps the most striking aspect of this spot. The preserve is accessible only by trail.

### Twenty Miracle Miles

Three miles farther south is the Lincoln City Information Center, the beginning of Lincoln City and the "20 Miracle Miles." (The miracle will be if this area survives the excessive commercialization.) Nowhere in Oregon is there so much pressure on the land in a recreational area. The weight of all the motels alone would seem to sink Lincoln City into the sea. Nor is there any other area on the Coast where the pursuit of the buck is so hot. Where it comes to a choice between beauty and "progress," the latter always seems to win out. A bitter example is the 14-foot bronze statue, "Lincoln on the Prairie." The lank lawyer, in his saddle, reads pensively while his horse grazes. The statue occupied an appropriate place in the city park but "progress" stepped in and it was moved to an ugly spot on a paved lot.

Still, a lot of people go to Lincoln City, because it has a reputation of being glamorous, electric, "where the action is," and a "fun center." Wise travelers go to simpler, less-crowded, less tinsely communities.

From the Information Center, it is less than half a mile to Lacey's Doll and Antique Museum. Half a mile farther ahead, turn left, or east, and go one block for the Abraham Lincoln Statue. Back on U.S. 101, you can travel half a mile to Lincoln Art Galleries. Continue half a mile to the turnoff east for five-mile-long Devil's Lake, the centerpiece of a state park, and on whose waters the Speed Boat World Record Races are held in late summer. There is also excellent year-round fishing—for several varieties of trout, both large- and small-mouth bass, crappie, bluegill, and perch. Another half a mile brings the traveler to a turnoff east to East Devil's Lake Road. It loops Devil's Lake and East Devil's Lake, with boat launching and picnic facilities, Sand Point County

Park, with picnic facilities, swimming, and a beach, and returns to U.S. 101 north of Lincoln City. It is approximately two miles to Immomen Road. Mossy Creek Pottery and Galley and Alder House II are east on Immomen. About a mile and a half south of Immomen Road is Drift Creek Road. Turn left, drive 1½ miles, turn right, and half a mile farther on you'll come to the Drift Creek Covered Bridge, built in 1914, making it one of the oldest covered bridges in the state. It is typical of the flaring board-and-batten sides, curved portal, and shingled roofs of the covered spans in Lincoln County six decades ago.

Going south from Lincoln City on U.S. 101, it is 1½ miles from Immonen Road to the junction with Oregon 229. Oregon 229 is an extraordinarily lovely drive, through fair woods and sweet meadows, following the free-style countours of the serene, unbridled Siletz River. The road is little traveled, which makes it a good alternative to U.S. 101 when you want to go from Kernville to Lincoln City without pause and the highway is bumper-to-bumper traffic.

## Salishan

Little more than a mile south from the Oregon 229 junction on U.S. 101 at Gleneden Beach is the Taj Mahal of the Oregon Coast—Salishan, called by some "*The* Resort on the Oregon Coast." It has gracious hospitality, a magnificent setting, and distinctive flair. The exterior is opulent, yet people stroll about informally. Little wonder that people of modest income sometimes cut corners on their living cost throughout the year to save up enough money for a single weekend at Salishan.

Salishan is an environmentalist's dream come true. It is one of the few resorts anywhere that actually enhances its natural terrain. Everywhere here one feels the outdoors—even indoors. The resort was, in fact, developed and financed by a wealthy industrialist who is an ardent environmentalist.

Everything about Salishan is poetic. A westward view discloses an endless expanse of sea. A balcony vista shows the Salishan golf course meticulously sculpted into the surrounding landscape; the ducks in the golf course pond are one of the resort's fixtures. There is a Japanese feeling about the place, coming not only from the exquisite contours of the promontory and the delicate shrubs that grow everywhere, but, most of all, from the cedar-board-covered walkways that connect the 16 guest buildings, which house the 150 units of the lodge. You can walk half a mile here without leaving a walkway or go from any point in the lodge to any other point and be under cover all the way.

If you'd rather walk more, there are enough nature trails to keep you going day and night. Salishan is located on a 750-acre forest preserve by the sea, and if the resort isn't relaxing enough, you can be deep in the forest primeval within minutes. There are so many species of flora at Salishan that the lodge has prepared a *Botanical Guide,* put together by an Oregon State University professor and given free to askers.

The main lodge building holds no sleeping rooms; here are located the restaurants, the cocktail lounge, the Gallery Room, and the largest collection of original art on the Oregon Coast. The art gallery is one of Salishan's many contributions to the culture of the Oregon Coast and to the entire state. There is a constant schedule of exhibits by working Oregon artists. But it is the permanent collection, priced at more than $400,000, that is most intriguing. More than 300 works by several score of contemporary Oregon and other northwest artists blend, individually and collectively, with the native woods and stones that have been used extensively at the resort to convey the strength and beauty of the Pacific Northwest. It is alone worth a trip to Salishan to see the 13 bas relief panels in Thailand teak by Leroy Setziol, sculpted for the three-level, candlelit dining room. On the great doors of the adjacent Cedar Tree Room, Setziol's totem-spirit designs catch the mood of ancient Salish art.

Anyone can tour Salishan; and, of course, non-guests are welcome at the Gourmet Dining Room, the Cedar Tree, the lounge, or the Sun Room Coffee Shop.

## Depoe Bay

Depoe Bay is, geographically, the most exciting town on the Oregon seaboard. The rock-bound bay and colorful harbor have an amphitheaterlike setting. Through a restaurant window, above the cove, you can look down on deep-sea trollers. From a sidewalk adjoining U.S. 101 you can see over the seawall the Spouting Horn, a gap in the rocks through which the tide races upward in a geyser of spray.

The people of Depoe Bay call their snug little harbor the "Smallest Harbor in the World." True or not it is big enough to berth a good number of deep-sea fishing boats. These make several scheduled trips each day for salmon or the many deep-sea fish such as red snapper, bass, perch, and cod throughout the summer season.

It is obvious even at first glance that the business section of Depoe Bay is designed for tourists. The town lives off tourist trade. Along this U.S. 101 strip then are candy shops, restaurants, gift shops, and the Depoe Bay Aquarium, which specializes in clowning seals and has one of the best shell shops in Oregon.

## Otter Crest

Otter Crest, four miles south, is a must stop for anyone who truly wants to appreciate the glory of the Oregon Coast. From the parking area of the wayside on the promontory, miles of scalloped, battered coastline are visible. The lookout, 500 feet above the sea on Cape Foulweather, faces Oregon's most-photographed seascape.

The cape was given its dismal name by Captain James Cook, the celebrated British sea dog, on a nasty March day in 1778. Large observatory telescopes are available. Sea otters once dwelt on shallow rocks about half a mile offshore. Gone now, their place has been taken by a herd of gray sea lions and seals. The larger rock is a sea bird rookery.

One of the finest gift shops on the coast, The Lookout, is at Otter Crest. Its collections of Oregon books, shells, and myrtlewood products are outstanding.

Down the steep, curving cliff road from Otter Crest, then to the right, is Devil's Punch Bowl, a wave-worn, bowl-shaped rock where incoming tides pour through openings, seeming to boil up, then retreat. Devil's Punch Bowl is in the town of Otter Rock, best known as the home of The Inn at Otter Crest, which boasts that it has "all the warmth and intimacy of a secluded country inn with all of the amenities of a luxurious oceanfront resort."

Within the town of Otter Rock, the key delight is a branch of Mo's, a celebrated name in these parts. In Oregon, Mo's is synonymous with the tastiest in clam chowder. It won't take long to find Mo's; the entire business section is less than two blocks long. Lighthouse Road is at the north end of Agate Beach, off 101. Turn right onto the road and wheel a mile up the lopped-off slope of a hill to Yaquina Head Light Station. Its 96-foot tower is the highest of all coastal lighthouses. The station was built here by mistake, the designated site being Otter Crest.

Just beyond the lighthouse is a National Wildlife Refuge, comprising great dark and green-stained cliffs sheared from the mainland by the sea. A cacaphony of scoldings, calls, and announcements from a flight wheel of cormorants, murres, herring gulls, cliff swallows, and guillamots can be heard. The edges of the cliffs and the cliff trails that lead to the sea can be very dangerous, so beware. The sea seems never tranquil here, and for photography of raging waves, this is the place.

## Newport

Newport, three miles south of Agate Beach, was once the social lion of the Oregon Coast, with the affluent coming from San Francisco and Seattle by boat and by stagecoach and by train from Portland.

The city lives on two levels: the highway and Yaquina Bay. At the town's western edge, some of the most interesting regional houses will be found facing the sea. Along the highway is the main business district. Here are the Lincoln County Historical Museum, in a log structure in back of the Visitors' Information Center; the mid–nineteenth century Burrows House, once an opulent mansion and now an auxiliary of the Lincoln County Historical Museum; and, on the west side of U.S. 101, the Wax Museum.

The southern portion of Newport comes abruptly to an end at Yaquina Bay State Park; a lacy, iron bridge spans the bay.

Old Yaquina Bay Lighthouse—in the state park—was established in 1871. Near here Captain James Cook made the first recorded landfall of the Pacific Northwest on March 3, 1778. At noon he named this spot Cape Foulweather, a name inadvertently transferred later to a point northward. Because of the heavy weather Cook was compelled to stand out at sea at night, unable to approach land until the afternoon. It was another place along the Oregon Coast where he sought and failed to find a harbor.

The real charm of Newport is its Bay Front. It is a mixture of seafood restaurants, pubs, wharfside buildings and fishing boats. Sunset at Yaquina Bay, when the fishing fleet rides at anchor, is a symphony of vivid orange, yellow, red, and saffron, muted by a subtle range of pastels. A warning that on summer and early fall weekends it is often impossible to find a parking spot at Bay Front after 10 A.M.

In front of the Coast Guard Station along the bay front is a memorial park honoring those who have died at sea. The centerpiece of the park is a 36-foot motor lifeboat, veteran of many rescues on Yaquina Bay. Also on display is the fleet of lifeboats currently in use for rescue work. Visitors are welcome from 1 P.M. to 4 P.M. daily.

Between the Coast Guard Station and the Embarcadero is the natural, below-the-sea aquarium operated commercially as Undersea Gardens. From the underwater viewing chambers, visitors observe giant anemones, king-sized salmon, large sturgeon, ferocious wolf eels, octopi, and many other species.

With its excellent public moorages and extended jetties, Yaquina Bay plays host to many sports and commercial fishermen in search of salmon, bottom fish, and crabs. Several charter outfits offer one-day deep-sea fishing trips. Yaquina tide flats are a good source of clams, and Dungeness crabs are frequently caught off the piers or trapped in the bay. Fishing equipment is available for rent. There are no less than 14 boating facilities.

Some people come to Newport solely to search for fossils and agates on Newport beaches, one of the finest agate-hunting areas in the world.

During the fall and winter months, many species of ducks, geese, and sea birds not generally conspicuous during the spring and summer settle in the sheltered bays, such as Yaquina, to rest and feed. One of the more interesting is the California Brown Pelican, which defies convention and migrates to Oregon from Mexico and southern California when most birds are heading south. With a wingspread of almost five feet at full growth, the brown pelican is something to watch as it wheels and dives for food. Even more eye-filling is a formation of pelicans flying inches above the water or gliding down the slope of the sky. The adult pelican has a pure white head and neck, while the younger bird has a dark brown crown and neck.

Ten miles east of Bay Front the road reaches U.S. 20, at Toledo, a burly mill town built on hills. From Toledo, there a sleepier road yet another ten miles to Elk City, on the banks of Yaquina River. Elk City is today a backcountry flip of dwellings, about one street of them, with the homiest general store and bar one can imagine. For a ghost town and a "live" covered bridge, drive five miles from Elk City to U.S. 20, turn east, and continue 2½ miles to Chitwood.

Back on U.S. 101, cross the Yaquina Bridge, turn right, and go one mile farther to the Oregon State University Marine Science Center, a museum and acquarium designed to provide viewers with an awareness of the beauty and frailty of the ocean.

Waldport, at the mouth of Alsea River as it empties into Alsea Bay, is a picturesque little coast town of about 1,400. Trout, salmon, flounder, and dozens of other species of fish live around here, either in the ocean, the bay, or in Eckman Lake. An abundance of crabs, razor clams, and bay clams are here for the taking. December through March are particularly good for beachcombing, as the winter storms open agate beds and bring in exotic driftwood and Japanese glass floats.

From Waldport it is eight miles along the coastline to Yachats, passing three state parks: Beachside, for overnight camping at 20 improved sites, 60 tent sites, and 30 RV sites; Governor Patterson Memorial, with restrooms that are accessible to handicapped persons; and Yachats.

Yachats (Ya-hots), Indian for "at the foot of the mountain," is, for its size (approximately 500 population), quite well known along the central Oregon Coast. The town, on the namesake river, is a popular tourist resort for salmon fishermen, but surf fishing and clam digging also attract visitors.

Between May and September the mating season of the silver smelt brings hundreds of thousands of these delicious, sardinelike fish to the sandy coves of Yachats, where they are captured in special nets. Yachats claims to be one of the few places in the world where these sea-run smelt come into shore. The annual smelt run is celebrated with a community Smelt Fry in early July which attracts visitors from all over the West.

Yachats State Park, bordering the river as it enters the sea, is a scenic picnic spot. There is a boat landing on the Yachats River east of town.

Yachats's uncrowded beaches are especially promising territory for rockhounds, beachcombers, fishers, clamdiggers, and picnicking families. Its rocky promontories offer dramatic surf action, especially during the awesomely beautiful winter storms in December, January, and February.

Almost three miles below Yachats there is a turnoff west for Devil's Churn. The half-mile Trail of the Restless Waters leads through a variety of coastal vegetation and views of the many-splendored coastline, with tidepools etched in the rocky shelf. Devil's Churn is a deeply wrought fissure where the sea rushes in and spouts furiously. Volcanic action created a fracture in the earth's surface, and eons of water erosion have done the rest.

## Cape Perpetua

A tenth of a mile below the turnoff to Devil's Churn there is a turnoff east for Cape Perpetua Viewpoint. A tolerable road climbs two miles to the top of Cape Perpetua, 800 feet above the sea. The cape was named by Captain Cook for St. Perpetua on March 7, 1778. The view from here is truly spellbinding: a breathtaking vista of wave-fringed beaches broken by headlands and offshore rocks strewn below the green-clad hills.

The turnoff to the Cape Perpetua Visitor Center is a bit south of the turnoff for the Viewpoint. The Center is not a museum. Its purpose is to introduce the visitor to a living museum—the Oregon Coast.

The theme "Forces of Nature" tells a story of storm waves smashing rocky headlands, howling winter winds uprooting giant trees, the countless marine creatures competing for a place to live, and the unseen microorganisms turning fallen vegetation into soil. Nature trails connect points of interest near the visitor center. Many trails have signs pointing out botanical, marine, and geological features. Ask the receptionist for directions. This center is located in the 623,265-acre Siuslaw Forest.

Just below the Center stands the Prehistoric Life Museum, advertised as "A journey through 600 million years of time." Devoted to fossils, its exhibits are free.

Between Cape Perpetua and Heceta Head are four state parks and waysides, with a fifth state park, Devil's Elbow, embracing Heceta Head. Heceta (Heh-see-ta) Head Lighthouse, standing since 1894 on a spectacular headland rising sheer above the ocean and looking down on the spongy beach of Devil's Elbow State Park, is one of the most-photographed structures on the coast. Devil's Elbow Tunnel, within the state park, is a 600-foot bore through a jutting promontory. U.S. 101 swings around a cliff far above the Pacific, affording a startling view of land and sea.

A mile below the state park is Sea Lion Caves, one of the most popular commercial features on the coast. A modern elevator takes tourists down to sea level, 320 feet below the cave ticket office, where they can clearly and safely see the play of the 30- or 40-pound pups and the vigilance the 2,000-pound bulls display toward their harems. There are three cave openings: two face the sea and one faces the dry entrance to the north. A sea captain by the name of Cox first explored the caves in about 1880. He entered in a small skiff and it is said that he was marooned for several days until a storm passed.

The adjacent rocky ledge and the cave together form the only natural mainland sea lion home in the world. As a sea grotto, the cave has been compared in size and coloring to the more famous Blue Grotto of Capri. It has a floor area of about two acres and a vaulted rock dome about 125 feet high. Southward from the main chamber a low passage runs 1,000 feet to a sea-level opening.

The panoramas from the top, at road level, are majestic. Cape Blanco, far to the south, can be seen; so can ships as far out at sea as 30 miles. Heceta Head Lighthouse is clearly in view. And sometimes the air here seems filled with pigeon guillemots, tufted puffins, cormorants, and herring sea gulls.

Six miles south of Sea Lion Caves is one of the many oddities along the coast, Darlingtonia Wayside. A half-mile nature walk leads through bog clusters of the carnivorous, fly-catching pitcher plants, the Darlingtonia, also known as "cobra lily," perhaps because they look like cobras poised to strike. Insects that crawl into the hoodlike leaves are devoured. The plants need these minerals as their small root systems cannot supply them with necessary nutrients.

About half a mile below Darlingtonia Wayside stands Indian Forest, with authentic full-size Indian dwellings in natural surroundings. Among the types of Indian architecture displayed here are the Huron, Birch Bark, Mandan, Hogan, Hupa, and Earth Lodge. There is also a totem pole, a collection of buffalo, and some deer, as well as the Indian Trading Post gift shop, which sells Navajo, Papago, Acona and Zuni rugs, baskets, pottery, jewelry, sand paintings, beadwork, Indian dolls, and kachinas.

## Florence

Four miles on is the charming town of Florence (population: 4,400). Since its inception in 1895, Florence achieved prominence as a Siuslaw (Si-oos-law) River fishing town and a trading post for farmers in the narrow Siuslaw Valley. In spring and early summer, rhododendrons run riot over hills and lowlands and are celebrated in the showy Rhododendron Festival held the latter part of May. Sand dunes rise to heights of 100 feet between Florence and the ocean. Harbor Vista Park, on Rhododendron Drive, four miles from downtown, has a commanding view of the Siuslaw River.

In 1936, the bridge over the Siuslaw was completed. A gradual shift in emphasis from the waterfront business district to the new highway took place over some years. Eventually, the original part of Florence became known as a blighted area. In the 1970s, however, individuals began moving in and restoring some of the older buildings, living in them and operating stores along Bay Street. Today the area is now Old Town and is a tourist attraction.

To walk through Old Town, start with the Siuslaw River Bridge, one of 5 major bridges constructed on the Oregon Coast by the WPA in the 1930s. The bridge features huge Gothic columns and decorative concrete etchings on each arc. Steps at the west end of Bay Street guide visitors up to this Florence landmark.

From here it is a brief walk to the Mapleton Depot, reconstructed on this site in 1977 after being removed from its original location at Mapleton, 14 miles to the east. It was built in 1913 for use as a warehouse and was later sold to the Southern Pacific Railway and was used for the Mapleton Depot for several years.

Another skip along Bay Street brings you to the Kyle Building, put up in 1901 by local businessmen William Kyle and Michael Meyer and used as a general store until 1961. The lumber used to build it came from Kyle's own mill in Florence. The building is listed on the National Register of Historic Places.

Continue a block and turn left on Maple Street to the Florence Telephone Company. This building housed Florence's first telephone switchboards. The women who operated the boards lived upstairs.

Move up Maple Street to the end of the block, where stands Florence Rooms, one of the town's oldest buildings. It was apparently used as a boarding house originally and continues to be used in that capacity today.

Cross Second Street and come to the Johnson House, originally built in 1892 by the town's first physician. Today it takes in bed-and-breakfast guests.

While in Old Town, tourists may want to picnic at the Port of Siuslaw Park or at the Gazebo, surrounded by offbeat shops and restaurants in the heart of Florence's commercial district.

Little more than three miles south of Florence is what is probably Oregon's most-used state park, Jessie M. Honeyman. It has 316 campsites and 66 trailer spaces, electric stoves, showers, a laundry, boat ramp, and many other facilities, including an outdoor theater. Day-use facilities include picnic tables, toilets, and bathhouses. The 522-acre tract has a dense forest, swarms of rhododendrons, Cleawox Lake, and a part of Woahink Lake. Trails lead from the park into the cool forest or up to the undulating sand dunes.

## The Dunes

The dunes area, extending south about 50 miles to the Coos Bay country, is now the Oregon Sand Dunes National Recreation Area. The dunes, mutable and mysterious, rise to heights of more than 250 feet. Commercial sand buggies—motorized vehicles that can be as small as a Jeep or as big as a bus—grind across the dunes with absolute safety. Drivers halt frequently to permit passengers to take pictures. (See "National Parklands" in *Practical Information for the Oregon Coast*.)

Within the next twelve miles lie four beautiful coastal lakes: Siltcoos, the largest of the coastal lakes; Carter, gold-colored in the shadow of the dunes; Tahkenitch, a jewel in a cup of the emerald hills; and Elbow, which at sunset can be taken for a watercolor painting. All these lakes offer several varieties of trout, both large-mouth and small-mouth bass, crappie, bluegill, and perch. Siltcoos and Tahkenitch have become especially popular as bass waters. Popular with fisherfolk in this area is Westlake Resort (Westlake, OR 97493; [503] 997–3722) on Siltcoos Lake. The resort has cottages, a trailer park, boat rentals, tackle shop, moorage, and dock fishing.

Reedsport, eight miles below Elbow Lake, is entered by the Umpqua River Bridge. A pleasant town of 4,700, Reedsport is the gateway to Winchester Bay, a vigorous fishing village. Though Salmon Harbor, at Winchester Bay, is but a few blocks off U.S. 101, it seems miles removed from the highway. Motels are as close to the fishing boats as a single block—and the small cafés and grocery and other stores seem to belong to a down-to-the-sea coastal settlement a long way from big cities. Excursion salmon-fishing boats are numerous here—along with older, larger, and more colorful commercial craft. But if you don't want to go out to sea, you can sit on a bench overlooking the harbor and enjoy what can only be described as bustling serenity.

Mile-long McCullough Bridge, south of Reedsport, spans the channel of Coos Bay and leads into North Bend, a once-vital lumber town hard hit by the recession (here called a depression). This is a myrtlewood country, and by taking drives off the main roads, to the southeast, you will see the myrtle groves. They grow nowhere else in the nation. Millicoma Myrtle Grove State Park, 17 miles east of Coos Bay, via Eastside and Allegany, on a county road, affords a splendid opportunity to see these rare trees up close up.

## Coos Bay and North Bay

Coos County, embracing both North Bend and Coos Bay, is heaven-sent for bird watchers. The diverse geography and temperate marine climate provide a haven for a variety of pelagic birds, waterfowl, shorebirds, and passerines. A total of 264 listed species and 47 casual or accidental species belonging to 49 families have been sighted in the county.

Although there are artists and artisans, theater people and musicians, and romantics and dreamers burning in the night in both North Bend and Coos Bay, these are basically industrial, working-class cities.

The town of Coos Bay, contiguous to North Bend, is the largest city on the Oregon Coast, with about 13,000 people. It claims to be the world's largest lumber-shipping port, but the town has been badly hit by hard times, with unemployment well over 20 percent, and there has been an exodus of unemployed. Coos Bay has a picturesque waterfront, the House of Myrtlewood, Sun Museum, Coos Art Museum, and a downtown mall.

North Bend is generally considered the more prosaic of the two communities (and was for years regarded as Coos Bay's northern bedroom) but North Bend has developed independently and has consistently declined to be merged with Coos Bay. North Bend has the Coos County Historical Museum, Bayview Myrtlewood Shop, and the most architecturally unusual shopping center on the central Oregon Coast, Pony Village, where local wood products were used to create a shopping center with an atmosphere that combines the rural with the urban.

For two of the most enjoyable coastal scenic trips, turn right in Coos Bay on Commercial Avenue.

Charleston, nine miles west, is a salty fishing burg with a gutsy nautical atmosphere. Fishing and boating are the major activities here. Seven-tenths of a mile out of Charleston is one of the most important "discovery trip" junctions on the Oregon Coast. This is the Seven Devils Road-State Parks junction.

First, take Sunset Bay-Cape Arago Road toward the state parks. In 17 miles, turn right for Bastendorf County Park—campground, picnic ground, and beach. The beach is at the foot of Cape Arago, and Cape Arago Lighthouse perches on the promontory above the beach. From the turnoff it is a mile to Sunset Bay State Park. Wind-shorn and wave-battered cliffs and offshore rocks provide memorable photo views, especially at sunset.

A mile beyond Sunset Bay is Shore Acres State Park, with magnificent restored botanical gardens and an enclosed observation shelter at the edge of a rugged cliff popular among wave and storm watchers. The mansion built by the founder of the gardens is now the home of the parkkeeper.

Half a mile on, at Cape Arago, there are long, wide views of the ocean and the curving coastline and of ships entering and leaving the Coos Bay harbor. At Cape Arago State Park, bring out your field glasses to spot sea lions on Shell Island and Simpson Reef.

## Bandon

Bandon, which calls itself the "Cranberry Capital of Oregon," because of the many cranberry bogs in the area, has two business districts, one on the highway, which is rather prosaic, and one on the Coquille River; here Bandon resembles the calendar art setting of a New England fishing village.

"Old Town," on the waterfront, is the site of the original settlement and retains strong touches of the historic Bandon, with fresh-fish stores and the kinds of shops that were here early in the century. It also has some touristy nuances now, in the form of arts-and-crafts shops and the Cranberry Sweets candy factory. The Bandon Historical Society, at the south end of Second Street, changes its exhibits of bygone shipping, logging, pioneer, and Indian life four times each year.

Bandon Harbor is a scene of lumber barges, dredges, tugboats, commercial fishing vessels, sailboats, and other pleasure craft. Tourists can watch sport people pull in their catches of Dungeness crabs, or do it themselves, cooking their catches in salt water on a driftwood fire on the beach. Visitors can watch clammers dig for bay clams or razors—or do it themselves at low tide. In the summer evening hours, along about dusk, fishers who have been to sea bring their catches to market.

Bandon trumpets its virtues: "Play golf on our sporty nine-hole course right next to the ocean—hunt agates and driftwood on the beach. Rent a crab pot and go crabbing in the bay, fish from the jetty, or take a drive around the countryside and just enjoy the scenery where rhododendrons and azaleas grow brilliantly in the wild. Take a barbecue to the beach. Visit the craft shops. A hike through the woods or a romp down the beach is a great way to clear out the cobwebs!

"Low tide brings out the best along the ocean front. As the waves retreat westward, tide pools appear and reveal the beautiful anemone, a star fish, a mollusk, darting fishes and crabs. Enjoy the marine life— but please leave them behind on the beach for those who follow you."

The town also has the second largest cheese factory in Oregon— Coquille Valley Dairy Co-op, which welcomes visitors.

Its size (2,400 population) and its mix of people give Bandon a small-town ambiance that is heavily streaked with cosmopolitanism. Few of the residents are "natives"; many came here to get away from the rat race. Artisans have located in Bandon, making it a sort of Cannon Beach of the southern Oregon coast.

A pleasurable side trip out of Bandon is the Beach Loop, starting at Old Town. The high point on this drive is Face Rock Viewpoint, two miles south: one of the largest and oddest array of offshore rocks to be seen anywhere on the Oregon coast.

About eight miles south of Bandon on U.S. 101 is a truly delightful tourist attraction, West Coast Game Park Safari, inhabited by over 400 tame, exotic birds and animals. Visitors are permitted to feed and pet many of the animals, most of which would fear humans in the wilds but socialize easily here. Say hello up close to a friendly tiger, leopard, wolf, camel, bear, bison, llama, or deer.

Almost nine miles below Langlois is the turnoff to Cape Blanco Lighthouse, built in 1870 on the most westerly point of Oregon. The light station, standing almost six miles from the Cape Blanco junction at U.S. 101, is also the oldest and loftiest lighthouse in the state. Open in December 1874, its light has been shining nightly for more than 11 decades, though it is now automated. The cape was so named, because of its chalky appearance, by a Spanish sea captain. Cape Blanco offers unobstructed views of migrating gray whales in December and January, and again in May and June. A two-mile walk south on the beach may reward the visitor's efforts with the sight of rare brown pelicans feeding at the mouth of the Elk River from July to October.

Port Orford is a rather small town (population 1,100) and its main street is the highway, but it is a pretty place and quite popular in summer. Its key tourist attraction is Battle Rock State Park, a bulky extension of the coast on top of which nine white men, brought here in 1851 to start a supply depot for the mining camps in southern Oregon, held off an undetermined number of local—and furious— Indians.

Port Orford is the northernmost incorporated city in Curry County, probably the most politically conservative county in the state. But its coastline is without doubt the most spectacular in Oregon, and perhaps, along the entire U.S. Pacific coast.

Although U.S. 101 in these parts is fairly curvy, the curves are not sharp. Traffic along the highway seems scantier here than elsewhere. There is no commercial pollution of the environment, and the seascapes, with their offshore rock formations, are nothing less than breathtaking.

Six miles below Port Orford U.S. 101 crosses the turnoff to Humbug Mountain State Park, with 30 trailer sites and 75 tent sites. The park is a joy: myrtles, alders, and maples; an old apple orchard nearby; a trout stream at hand; and only a short stroll to sweeping sea views and breezy sand beach. A three-mile trail from the park reaches the top of 1,750-foot Humbug Mountain. The climb is not recommended for people who are not in good condition.

## Gold Beach

The seat of Curry County, Gold Beach has only about 1,500 residents but it is much more densely inhabited in summer. It is an airy town, with its great claim to fame being its location at the mouth of the Rogue River, one of the best fishing streams in the West. Sea lions and seals follow major fish runs into the Rogue River estuary from spring until fall. Peak months are April through July. These sea mammals are seen from the north and south jetties. Parking is best in the port areas of Gold Beach just south of the bridge.

The most popular tourist attraction associated with Gold Beach is jet-boating up the Rogue to Agness, a 64-mile round trip. Two lodges there serve lunch. More thrilling is the 104-mile round trip on the whitewater Rogue to Paradise Bar Lodge, where some people stay over for a night or more. Actually, the boat docks are in Wedderburn, but Gold Beach is always given as the address in guides.

Apart from the Rogue, Gold Beach is a typical coastal roadside community, pale in design to all the beauty around it.

Six miles south of Gold Beach, U.S. 101 meets the turnoff for Cape Sebastian State Park, a mile westward. The cape is a 700-foot-high precipitous headland. The Pacific is not pacific here—it is wild, wrathful, agitated.

## The Finest Scenery

The most fantastic part of the Oregon Coast is now ahead—from Cape Sebastian junction to Brookings, 21 miles. Among the sights and places along the way are incredible rock formations; Mack Arch, 2325-foot-high monolith; Arch Rock Point; Spruce Island; Natural Bridge; Thomas Creek Bridge, highest in Oregon; Indian Sands Trail Viewpoint, an abundant view of the forest plunging down to the sea; Whalehead Beach; Whalehead Trail Viewpoint; House Rock Viewpoint; Cape Ferrelo Viewpoint; and Lone Ranch Beach.

Brookings, a town of about 3,500, enjoys the most temperate climate of any city in Oregon. In deepest winter, when central Oregon is huddling against zero temperature and Portland has a wind chill factor of below zero, Brookings will be watching the thermometer rest comfortably in the mid-60s.

The town could call itself "Banana Belt of the North," but it prefers to be known as "Easter Lily Capital of the World." About 90 percent of the pot lilies used in the United States come from a 500-acre area here. Harbor, little more than a mile south, is surrounded by fields of commercially grown daffodil bulbs.

Brookings lies at the mouth of the Chetco River, the best-known salmon and steelhead stream south of the Rogue.

Brookings is the only city in Oregon to have two state parks within its corporate limits: Harris and Azalea. Harris has complete facilities; thick shrubs and firs provide privacy for each campsite. The vista from Harris Butte, near the registration booth, encompasses 24 miles of curving coastline, from Point St. George in California around Pelican Bay, and north to Cape Ferrelo. Goat Island, largest island off the Oregon Coast, is a bird refuge.

Azalea is a botanical glory. Spring pushes up wild strawberry blossoms, purple and red violets, and wild cherry and crabapple blooms, and, of course, the native azaleas. Swarms of butterflies, bees, and hummingbirds feed on the plants; fir and spruce house finch, robin, jay and kildeer colonies. Eat off hand-hewn myrtlewood tables, each weighing more than 200 pounds. The azaleas are celebrated in the colorful Azalea Festival in May.

# PRACTICAL INFORMATION FOR THE OREGON COAST

**HOW TO GET THERE AND HOW TO GET AROUND. By air:** Your gateway to the coast will probably be Portland (see "How to Get There" in *Practical Information for Portland*). *Horizon Airlines* flies three flights daily, except Saturday, to North Bend. **By bus:** *Greyhound* serves many coastal towns, but at press time is planning to eliminate some services, so check ahead. **By car.** This is probably the best way to see the coastal areas, and the only way that will give you the freedom to stop and appreciate some of the magnificent scenery or to detour along scenic stretches of road. Some of the major car rental agencies in Portland are: *Avis* (800–331–1212); *Budget* (800–527–0700); *Dollar* (800–421–6868); *Hertz* (800–654–3131); *National* (800–328–4567); and *Thrifty* (800–367–2277). All have counters at the Portland International Airport. Hertz also has a rental office in Astoria. Astoria, at the northern end of the coast, is reached from Portland by U.S. 30, or U.S. 26 to 101. U.S. 101 is the major north-south route.

**By cab:** Newport has a cab company: *Yaquina Cab Co.*, 334 S.E. 1st; 265–6313.

 **HOTELS AND MOTELS.** Most of the accommodations listed are air-conditioned. Some, though not all, accept major credit cards; it would be wise to ask in advance. Rates, based on double occupancy, are classified as follows: *Expensive* $50 and up; *Moderate* $36–$49; *Inexpensive* below $36. Informality rather than elegance, is a fact of life in Oregon.

## ASTORIA

Accommodations in and near Astoria are basically motels. For information on condominium units for rent, phone the Chambers of Commerce (see "Tourist Information," below). There are no hostels in the area and no tourist homes, but there is ample camping (see below).

**Thunderbird Motor Inn.** *Expensive.* 400 Industry St.; (503) 325–7373. Large motel affording fine views of the Columbia River and marina. Seafood restaurant and bar on premises. Only Astoria motel to take American Express cards.

**Crest Motel.** *Moderate.* 5366 Leif Erickson Dr.; (503) 325–3141. Located on a hilltop at the edge of town on U.S. 30, this small, well-maintained motel affords magnificent views of the Columbia River from a quiet location designed for relaxation. Seasonal rates.

**Dunes Motel.** *Moderate.* 288 W. Marine Dr.; (503) 325–7111. Medium-sized motel, two and three levels, with well-equipped units.

**Lamplighter Motel.** *Moderate.* 131 W. Marine Dr.; (503) 325–4051. Smaller, attractive motel on U.S. 30. Restaurant adjacent. Seasonal rates.

**Rosebriar Inn.** *Moderate.* 636 14th; (503) 325–7427. Opened in summer of 1983; eight units; very homey.

**Sunset Motel.** *Inexpensive to moderate.* Beach Loop Rd., Box 373; (503) 347–2453. 28 units; three two-bedroom; one three-bedroom; nine kitchens. On beach. Pets OK. Reservation deposit required.

**Bandon Beach Motel.** *Inexpensive.* 1110 11th St. S.W.; (503) 347–2103. A 27-unit facility with kitchens and a restaurant. Repeat trade is its trademark.

**Bandon Wayside Motel.** *Inexpensive.* Rt. 1, Box 16; (503) 347–3208. Smallest (10 units) of Bandon motels, but for some this is an advantage. Comfortable, quiet.

**Caprice Motel.** *Inexpensive.* Rt. 1, Box 530; (503) 347–3208. Two two-bedroom units; two kitchens ($4 extra). Reservation deposit required. 15 units, all of high quality.

**La Kris Motel.** *Inexpensive.* PO Box 252; (503) 347–3610. A well kept, 12–unit accommodation.

**Table Rock Motel.** *Inexpensive.* Beach Loop Road; (503) 347–2700. Sparkling 16-unit facility, with restaurant adjacent; kitchens. Ocean and jetty views.

## BROOKINGS

**Bonn Motel.** *Moderate.* 1216 Chetco; (503) 469–2161. 37 units with indoor heated pool, two large saunas, ocean views, movie channel. Very pleasant rooms.

**Spindrift Motor Inn.** *Inexpensive to Moderate.* 1215 Chetco; (503) 469–5345. 34 sparkling rooms. Reservation deposit required. Restaurant adjacent.

**Brookings Inn.** *Inexpensive.* Box 1139; (503) 469–2173. 41 units, all fresh-looking. Four two-bedroom units. Restaurant and lounge. Near ocean beaches and river.

**Econo Lodge.** *Inexpensive.* 1144 Chetco; (503) 469–2141. 41 units; two two-bedroom units; three efficiencies. Restaurant opposite. Rated very high by travelers.

## CANNON BEACH/TOLVANA PARK

**Land's End Resort Motel.** *Expensive.* 263 W. 2nd; (503) 436–2264. Medium-sized motel with ocean front, fireplaces, kitchens. Near store. A metropolitan touch on the sea.

**Surfsand Resort Motel.** *Expensive.* Gower and Oceanfront; (503) 436–2274. Large (39 units), with elegant touches. Covered swimming pool, play area, kitchens, fireplaces, and ocean views. Also, one- and two-bedroom housekeeping apartments with three-day minimum stay from June 15 to September 15; two-day weekends from September 16 to June 14. Reservation deposit required; three-day refund notice.

**Tolovana Inn.** *Expensive.* S. Hemlock and Warren Rd., Tolovana Park; (503) 436–2211. Largest motel in Cannon Beach area, with 96 units, and the swankiest. In keeping with kind of people who come to the area, Tolovana Inn has kitchens, an oddity in luxury facilities. It also has covered swimming pool, sauna, therapy pool, and some glitter mixed with a lot of western informality.

**Bell Harbor.** *Moderate.* Hwy. 101 Alternate at Elk Creek, P.O. Box 562; (503) 436–2776. Near ocean. Kitchens, play area, fireplaces.

**Blue Gull Motel.** *Moderate.* 632 S. Hemlock; (503) 436–2714. Near ocean. Kitchens, water beds.

**Cannon Village Motel.** *Moderate.* 3215 S. Hemlock, Tolovana Park; (503) 436–2317. Good ocean views. Good for families. Kitchens, play area, children welcome, charge for pets, near store. Small motel (seven units) with fine local reputation.

**Major Motel.** *Moderate.* Chisana St. and Oceanfront; (503) 436–2241. 20 units with ocean view.

**Sea Sprite Motel.** *Moderate.* Nebesena St. and Oceanfront, Tolovana Park; (503) 436–2266. Another small motel, with six units, including family units. Well tended, with the usual amenities, including play area.

**Viking Motel.** *Moderate.* Matanuska St. and Oceanfront; (503) 436–2269. Medium-size, with all the attractions and comforts offered by other medium-size motels.

**Waves Motel.** *Moderate.* Second and Larch St.; (503) 436–2205. Twenty oceanfront cottages in old-time style, before Cannon Beach became the Carmel of Oregon. No pets, but otherwise a fine place to spend a week. Watch the ocean at night beside warmth of a fireplace.

**Coach Inn.** *Inexpensive.* 164 Kenai St., Tolovana Park; (503) 436–2848. Only four units, but they are quite nice. Kitchens, fireplaces. No phone reservations.

**The Cove.** *Inexpensive.* Larch St. off 2nd and Oceanfront; (503) 436–2300. Ocean views, play area. Twelve clean units.

**The McBee.** *Inexpensive.* 888 S. Hemlock; (503) 436–2569. Eleven-unit facility with kitchens, play area, and fireplace. Near the ocean.

**Schmitz's Oceanfront Cottages.** *Inexpensive.* Umpqua St. and Oceanfront; (503) 436–2218. A five-unit facility operated family-style by a caring couple.

**Webb's Scenic Surf.** *Inexpensive.* Larch St. north of 2nd; (503) 436–2706. Each of the 13 units is up to snuff, with all the amenities of other motels of the same size.

## CHARLESTON

**Capt. John's Motel.** *Inexpensive.* Boat Basin; (503) 888–4041. Interesting 40-unit facility that gives one the feeling of being at sea. Good food and cocktails, too.

## COOS BAY/NORTH BEND

**Thunderbird Motor Inn.** *Expensive.* 1313 N. Bayshore Dr.; (503) 267–4141. Largest motel—168 units—in Coos County. Restaurant, lounge, air conditioning, pool, a touch of lavishness, and a high degree of reliability.

**Bay Bridge Motel.** *Moderate.* 33 Coast Hwy., North Bend; (503) 756–5818. Located at the north end of the Coos Bay Bridge, this small motel (16 units) offers comfortable units, lovely harbor views, and an adjoining restaurant.

**Bayshore Motel.** *Moderate.* 1685 N. Bayshore Dr.; (503) 267–4138. Medium-size facility (34 units) maintained energetically by cordial management.

**Best Western Holiday Motel.** *Moderate.* 411 Bayshore Dr.; (503) 269–5111. Few frills in this 68-unit enterprise, but what is there is good and cozy. A 24-hour restaurant adjacent.

**Pony Village Lodge.** *Moderate.* Virginia Ave., at Pony Village Shopping Center, North Bend; (503) 756–3191. Large (119 units), two-level motel with comfortable units. Coffee shop, restaurant, cocktail lounge. A distinctive motel near a distinctive shopping center.

**City Center Motel.** *Inexpensive.* 750 Connecticut, North Bend; (503) 756–5118. In town and evidently designed for the commercial traveler, but others will also find it to their satisfaction, because of the quality of the rooms.

**Lazy J. Motel.** *Inexpensive.* 1143 Hill St.; (503) 269–9666. Small—11 units—with cozy feeling. All the basics, nicely put together.

**Royal Dunes Motor Inn.** *Inexpensive.* 1445 N. Bayshore Dr.; (503) 269–9371. One of the best motel bargains in these parts. The 87-unit facility doesn't offer any more amenities than kitchens and the usual, but it is comfortable and well planned.

**Southsider Motel.** *Inexpensive.* 1004 S. Broadway; (503) 267–2438. Another 11-unit motel that is friendly without encroaching on your privacy. Tidy, well kept rooms.

**Timberlodge Motel.** *Inexpensive.* Box 578; (503) 267–7066. Medium-sized motel on U.S. 101. Free morning coffee delivered. 47 units. Restaurant open 24 hours. Seasonal rates.

## DEPOE BAY

**Holiday Surf Lodge,** *Inexpensive to expensive.* 939 N.W. Hwy. 101; (503) 765–2710. Large—84 units—with kitchens, honeymoon suite, conference room. Ocean front, with grand views.

**Channel House.** *Moderate.* At the entrance to Depoe Bay on the south side of channel, one block off U.S. 101 (foot Ellingson St.), Box 49; (503) 765–2140. A member of Unique Northwest Inns. Solidly perched on rocky ocean front, this establishment affords ideal views of ocean storms and whales. Sport fishing; kitchens available; movie channels. Restaurant.

**Whale Cove Inn.** *Moderate.* On U.S. 101 south of Depoe Bay; (503) 765–2255. Ten-unit motel with excellent restaurant, lounge, kitchens. With a "hideaway" atmosphere, the Whale Cove is tucked away in a romantic curve at the highway's edge close to the sea.

**Arch Rock Motel.** *Inexpensive.* Box 251; (503) 765–2560. An eight-unit, very clean facility that lends the guest the impression that he or she is part of a close-knit family.

**Siltcoos Lake Resort/Motel.** *Inexpensive.* Six miles south of U.S. 101 at West Lake; (503) 997–3741. Resort cabins, motel; all kitchen units; family rates; year-round fishing; boats; moorage, RV spaces. A catchall recreation facility that sometimes looks like the wagons have drawn up from the Oregon Trail. But comfortable.

## FLORENCE

**Driftwood Shores and Surfside Resort.** *Moderate.* 88416 First Ave., four miles northwest of Florence along Heceta Beach Road; (503) 997–8263. The largest facility—136 units—in the Florence area. Balconies facing ocean. Twenty-five three-bedroom apartments with fireplaces. Twenty-one two-bedroom units. 88 kitchens. Coin laundry. Reservation deposit required. Dining room. The only complete resort on the beach in and near Florence.

**Pier Point Inn.** *Moderate.* 85625 Hwy. 101 S.; (503) 997–7191. Most of the 44 units have balconies and views of Siuslaw Bay. Dining room and coffeeshop. Highly recommended.

**Silver Sands Motel.** *Moderate.* 1443 Hwy. 101 N.; (503) 997–3459. Kitchens, movie channel. Heated pool. Restaurants nearby. Pets welcome. The services at this medium-size motel are above average.

**Americana Motel.** *Inexpensive.* 3829 Hwy. 101; (503) 997–2274. Kitchens, pool, spa and indoor heated pool; close to the heart of town.

**Le Chateau Motel.** *Inexpensive.* Hwy. 101 at 10th St.; (503) 997–3481. Free coffee all day, heated swimming pool, sauna, water beds, movie channel. Restaurants nearby, pets welcome. A pleasant facility, well laid-out and attractively furnished.

**Fish Mill Lodge.** *Inexpensive.* Six miles south of Florence, ½ mile east of U.S. 101; (503) 997–2511. Furnished cottages with kitchens; trailer spaces; full hookups; fishing; boats; motors and tackle. A rustic place for a family get-away-from-it-all.

**Money Saver Motel.** *Inexpensive.* 170 Hwy. 101; (503) 997–7131. A highly regarded 40-unit motel that continues to win praise for its appointments and service.

**Park Motel.** *Inexpensive.* 85034 Hwy. 101; (503) 997–2634. One of the smallest of the Florence inns, this 14-unit facility operates with the class and style of a place four times larger. Three two-bedroom units. Restaurant adjacent. Reservation deposit required.

**Villa West Motel.** *Inexpensive.* Hwy. 101 at 9th St.; (503) 997–3457. The smallest of the Florence motels, with 22 units. Free morning coffee; restaurants nearby. Close to center of town, at junction. A favorite place for commercial travelers.

**Westlake Resort on Siltcoos Lake.** *Inexpensive.* Six miles south of Florence, ¼ mile east of U.S. 101; (503) 997–3722. Housekeeping units on the lake. Boat and motor rentals. Tackle shop. Moorage for guests. Neat and well attended.

## GLENEDEN BEACH

**Salishan Lodge.** *Expensive.* Hwy. 101; (503) 764–2371. One of the most luxurious resorts in the state—and the rates may be the highest. Located on a driftwood beach, the resort offers an indoor pool; hydrotherapy pool and saunas; ladies' and men's gyms; an 18-hole golf course; indoor and outdoor tennis courts; a fireplace in every room; an imaginative children's playground; and an unhindered view of greenery. Dining in the *Gourmet Dining Room,* the *Cedar Tree,* or the *Sun Room Coffee Shop.* Candlelight dancing and lounge. It all seems very private, with paths laid out so that no one passes by your window. The visitor may well feel that he or she has one foot in the Pacific wilderness, the other in a rural Japanese garden—and both feet in Paradise. Three-day minimum stay July 1–September 30. Reservation deposit required. Pets extra charge. (See the description of Salishan in *Exploring the Oregon Coast,* earlier in this chapter.)

## GOLD BEACH

**Jot's Resort.** *Moderate to Expensive.* North end of Rogue River Bridge on North Bank Rd., Box J-A; (503) 247–6676. 61 units, two two-bedroom units; 25 efficiencies. Coin laundry, heated pool, rental boats and motors, marina, fishing. Fee for use of dock and for fishing supplies. Daily river excursion leaves from here. Pets OK. Restaurant; cocktails. A repeat couple called Jot's "elegance down to earth." They may be right.

**Tu Tu Tun Lodge.** *Expensive.* 96550 N. Bank Rd.; (503) 247–6664. Open May 1–November 1. Member of Unique Northwest Country Inns. Quiet accommodations seven miles up Rogue River. Balconies and patios overlook Rogue. Only 18 units, giving an uncrowded feeling. Heated pool, boat dock and ramp, fishing, daily river excursions. Dining. Pets extra. Reservation deposit required. Having lodged at Tu Tu Tun is a status symbol for many.

**Inn at Gold Beach.** *Moderate.* 1435 S. Ellensburg; (503) 247–6606. Relatively large—43 units—with kitchens and beach access. Highly rated for efficiency and amenities.

**Inn of the Beachcomber.** *Moderate.* 1250 S. Hwy. 101; (503) 247–6691. Indoor pool, ocean view, restaurant and lounge adjacent; emphasis here on comfort in all 40 attractive units.

**Ireland's Rustic Lodge.** *Moderate.* 1120 S. Ellensburg; (503) 247–7718. Sited on magnificently landscaped grounds. 16 units; cottages and motel units, with fireplaces. Three two-bedroom units. Reservation deposit required.

**Lucas Pioneer Ranch and Lodge.** *Moderate.* Agness; (503) 247–7443. A 200-plus–acre homestead at junction of Rogue and Illinois rivers. Old-time inn still giving guests good lodging, food, and company. Fishing for trout, salmon, and steelhead. River guides available. Hiking and backpacking on river and mountain trails.

**Nimrod Motel.** *Moderate.* 775 S. Ellensburg; (503) 247–6635. 17 nice units lovingly tended.

**Singing Springs Resort.** *Moderate.* On Rogue River, Agness; (503) 247–6162. A backcountry inn with six units, kitchens, restaurant.

**Western Village Motel.** *Moderate.* 975 Ellensburg, Box 793; (503) 247–6611. Medium-size—27 units—with some rooms facing ocean. Pets OK. Restaurant adjacent. Reservation deposit required.

**Drift In Motel.** *Inexpensive.* 715 N. Ellsensburg; (503) 247–6020. Kitchens in the 23 units. Restaurant. Neatly maintained. At mouth of Rogue.

## LINCOLN CITY

**The Inn at Spanish Head.** *Expensive.* 4009 S. Hwy. 101; (503) 996–2161. Self-termed "the most breathtaking resort on the Oregon coast," it is certainly the best-known, perhaps because of its romantic name. Some geologists find fault with the location of the motel, saying it could be swept into the sea, and the motel has suffered from unusual tides. Rising 10 stories above the pounding surf, the Inn is quite a sight, and so are its individually decorated condominium-style suites and rooms. In addition to a long sandy beach, there are saunas, a heated outdoor pool, rec room, and great dining.

**Coho Inn.** *Moderate.* 1635 N.W. Harbor; (503) 994–3684. 50 units, many with balconies or patios overlooking ocean. 20 two-bedroom units, 25 efficiencies. Some fireplaces. Pets extra.

**Cozy Cove Motel.** *Moderate.* 515 N.W. Inlet Ave.; (503) 994–2950. The "No Vacancy" sign is usually up here in summer after the sun goes down. Reputation for cleanliness. Long ocean front; sundecks; woodburning fireplaces, kitchens. Phone for reservations.

**D-Sands Motel.** *Moderate.* 171 S.W. Hwy. 101; (503) 994–5244. 63 units, most with balconies, some fireplaces. 42 two-bedroom units with kitchens, 21 efficiencies. On the beach. Heated indoor pool. Reservation deposit required.

**Edgecliff Motel.** *Moderate.* 3733 S. Hwy. 101; (503) 996–2055. At 16 units this is regarded as small in Lincoln City. The large amount of repeat business says something about the quality.

**International Dunes Ocean Front Resort.** *Moderate.* 1501 N.W. 40th; (503) 994–3655. The largest hostelry in the Lincoln City area, with 190 units, all neat and glistening. A pool, of course, and, to make life more agreeable, a lounge; and for the kids, a playground. Because of its size there is more of a resort atmosphere here than in many of the folksy places along the Oregon Coast.

**Nordic Motel.** *Moderate.* 2133 N.W. Inlet Ave.; (503) 994–8145. Right on the ocean front, this 52-unit motel is highly respected by keen-eyed travelers. Kitchens, pools, saunas, fireplaces.

**Sailor Jack's Oceanfront Motel.** *Moderate.* 1035 N.W. Harbor Ave.; (503) 994–3696. Another medium-size motel (41 units) with king-size reputation. Overlooking ocean; well-maintained rooms, 28 with refrigerators, 17 efficiencies, five two-bedroom units with fireplaces. Reservation deposit required.

**Surftides Beach Resort.** *Moderate.* 2945 N.W. Jetty; (503) 994–2191. Another large (91 units), classy place that is washed by Pacific breezes. Restaurant, lounge, kitchens, pool, sauna, indoor tennis, all in a casual, properly informal atmosphere.

**Sea Gull Motel.** *Inexpensive to Moderate.* 1511 N.W. Harbor Ave.; (503) 994–2948. Kitchens, in-room movies, water beds in this 25-unit facility. Basically oriented to folks who want a small fling at a small price.

**Beachcliff Motel.** *Inexpensive.* 1301 N.W. 21st; (503) 994–5262. On the oceanfront. Kitchens, game room, TV movie channel. Medium-size hotel with repeat clientele.

**Seahorse Oceanfront Motel.** *Inexpensive.* 2039 N. Harbor Dr.; (503) 994–2101. All units with oceanfront views. A lot here for the price at this 21-unit motel. Kitchens, indoor pool, easy beach access.

**Travelers Budget Motel.** *Inexpensive.* 1713 N.W. 21st; (503) 994–5281. Senior rates, which brings a lot of senior citizens here as well as young folks who've saved up for a night at the coast. Some nights, all 50 units are filled up.

## NEWPORT

**Embarcadero.** *Expensive.* Box 1067; (800) 547–4779. Stunning in design, overlooking Yaquina Bay and Bay Front. Luxurious one- and two-bedroom kitchen condominiums as well as overnight sleeping units. Indoor pool, saunas, and whirlpool. Restaurant, lounge, entertainment. Full-service private marina. Fishing, crabbing, clamming year round.

**Newport Hilton.** *Expensive.* 3019 N. Coast Hwy.; (503) 265–9411. Its former name, the Agate Beach Hilton, tells where this facility is really located. The largest motel on this part of the coast—146 units—the Hilton has everything for comfort, in addition to superlative sea views and a beach that was made in a dream.

**Jolly Knight Motel.** *Moderate.* 606 SW Coast Hwy.; (503) 265–7723. Some ocean-view rooms and one- and two-bedroom units; restaurant opposite. One of the best medium-size motels.

**Moolack Shores Motel.** *Moderate.* SRN Box 420; (503) 265–2326. Halfway between Newport and Agate Beach, with fine beach access, kitchens, fireplaces. Small—13 units—but lovingly cared for by its owners.

**Newport Aladdin Motor Inn.** *Moderate.* 536 S.W. Elizabeth; (503) 265–7701. A large facility—117 units. Clean and efficient.

**The Vikings Motel.** *Moderate.* 729 NW Coast St.; (503) 265–2477. Small—12 units—and sparkling. Ocean vistas, kitchens, family appeal.

**West Wind Motel.** *Moderate.* 747 S.W. Coast Hwy. 101; (503) 265–5388. Kitchens, indoor heated pool, whirlpools. The managers go out of their way to please at this 23-unit facility.

**Whaler Motel.** *Moderate.* 155 S.W. Elizabeth; (503) 265–9261. An excellent middle-size (61 units) motel. Some ocean views, nearby beach access, some fireplaces. Reservation deposit required. Four blocks off the highway, at this place you'll hear little but the wind.

**Windjammer Motel.** *Moderate.* 744 S.W. Elizabeth; (503) 265–8853. Ocean-front location for the 72 units here. Kitchens. A lot of families come here.

**El Rancho Motel.** *Inexpensive.* 1435 N. Coast Hwy. 101; (503) 265–5192. One of the smaller motels in the Newport area, with 20 units. Families seem to like it here.

**Sands Motor Lodge.** *Inexpensive.* 206 N. Coast Hwy. 101; (503) 265–5321. Another strip motel of medium size, with kitchens and sauna. The usual Newport cheeriness.

**7 Seas Motel.** *Inexpensive.* 861 SW Coast Hwy. 101; (503) 265–2277. Kitchens, coin laundry, prompt service.

**Surf 'n Sand Motel.** *Inexpensive.* Star Route, Box 390; (503) 265–2215. Quiet reigns in this relatively small, 17-unit, facility. A good place to relax.

**Willer's Motel.** *Inexpensive.* 745 S.W. Coast Hwy. 101; (503) 265–2241. This 33-unit facility has kitchens and garages. On the highway, but set back to screen off excessive noise.

## NORTH BEND
### (See Coos Bay/North Bend)

## OTTER ROCK

**The Inn at Otter Crest.** *Moderate to Expensive.* Box 50; toll-free in Oregon; (800) 452–2101; elsewhere in the United States, (800) 547–2181. 250 deluxe rooms and suites with all amenities. Direct access to a secluded beach; 40 acres of lush forest; jogging path; a Walden-like pond. Dining in the gourmet *Flying Dutchman* restaurant; live entertainment and dancing in the *Wardroom Lounge.* Supervised children's summer recreation program; complimentary in-room movies.

## PORT ORFORD

**Neptune Motel.** *Moderate.* 545 W. 5th; (503) 332–4502. Ocean, mountain, and harbor views. Restaurant adjacent; kitchens, fireplaces in the 13 units.

**Sea Crest Motel.** *Inexpensive to Moderate.* Box C; (503) 332–3040. Quiet location, overlooking ocean. Well-tended grounds. 18 units; eight two-bedroom units. Pets OK.

**Battle Rock Motel.** *Inexpensive.* Hwy. 101 S.; (503) 332–7331. Small—seven units—with beach access; restaurant/lounge adjacent. If cleanliness is virtue, the place reeks with virtue.

**Port Orford Motel.** *Inexpensive.* 1035 Oregon; (503) 332–7081. 12 units, with kitchens and the usual—in these parts—color cable TV.

**Shoreline Motel.** *Inexpensive.* Hwy. 101 at Battle Rock; (503) 332–2903. 12 units; kitchens; great view of Battle Rock; within easy stroll of downtown.

## REEDSPORT/WINCHESTER BAY

**Seacoast Inn.** *Inexpensive.* Hwy. 101, Winchester Bay; (503) 271–2607. A 24-unit facility with kitchens and restaurant. Close to Salmon Harbor and its sights, sounds, and smells.

**Tropicana Motel.** *Inexpensive.* 1593 Hwy. 101; (503) 271–3671. Restaurant, lounge, pool are bonuses to the neatness and efficiency of this 41-unit motel. Reservation deposit required.

**Western Hills Motel.** *Moderate.* 1821 Winchester Ave.; (503) 271–2149. One two-bedroom unit; four efficiencies ($4 extra). Pets OK. This 21-unit motel offers the usual amenities well cared for by an interested management.

## SEASIDE

**Ebb Tide Motel.** *Expensive.* 300 N. Prom; (503) 738–8371. Oceanfront, with splendid views of beach and sea. Most units have fireplaces. Heated indoor pool, saunas, whirlpool. Reservation deposit required.

**The Tides.** *Expensive.* 2316 Beach Dr.; (503) 738–6317. On the ocean front with, naturally, ocean view. One of Seaside's larger and more luxurious motels, with kitchens, pool, fireplaces.

**Hi-Tide Motel.** *Moderate.* 30 Ave. G.; (503) 738–8414. On ocean front. Gas-burning fireplaces, refrigerators, movies, heated indoor pool. Reservation deposit required.

**Lanai Motel.** *Moderate.* 3140 Sunset Blvd.; (503) 738–6343. Medium-size (24 units) with good reputation for hospitality and service.

**Landmark Motor Inn.** *Moderate.* 441 2nd Ave.; (503) 738–9581. Across street from Convention Center. Sauna, indoor pool, Jacuzzi hot tub, kitchens, in-room movies, laundromat. Easy walk to beach. Efficiently managed.

**Midtown Motel.** *Inexpensive.* 55 N. Columbia St.; (503) 738–6542. Another small (11 units) motel that is in keeping with the time when Seaside was the summer playground of the northern Oregon coast and almost every home took in boarders.

**Royale Motel.** *Moderate.* 531 Ave. A; (503) 738–9541. Medium-size but large in heart. Kitchens, in-room coffee, water beds, fresh-smelling rooms.

**Seashore Resort Motel.** *Moderate.* 60 N. Prom; (503) 738–6368. Open to invigorating ocean breezes and lovely seascapes. Prompt service, rendered with a smile.

**Sundowner Motor Inn.** *Moderate.* 125 Oceanway; (503) 738–8301. Sauna, small heated indoor pool, in-room movies, some kitchens. A very short stroll from the beach.

**Surf Motel.** *Moderate.* 561 S. Prom; (503) 738–5613. Smallest of Seaside motels, with only six units. Family-style ambiance. More like an oceanfront rooming house of yore than stereotypical motel of today.

**Ambassador by the Sea.** *Inexpensive.* 40 Ave. U; (503) 738–6382. 63 units. Pool, tidy, good mix of clientele.

**City Center Motel.** *Inexpensive.* 250 1st Ave. (503) 738–6377. 33 units. An airy spot with cheerful management. Private sundeck, kitchens.

**Driftwood Motel.** *Inexpensive.* 815 N. Holladay; (503) 738–5597. Intimate atmosphere, with only seven units. Rooming-house feeling.

**Four Winds Motel.** *Inexpensive.* 820 N. Prom; (503) 738–9524. A typical Promenade lodging, more characteristic of old Seaside than the new. Friendly, family management.

**Hillcrest Motel.** *Inexpensive.* 118 N. Columbia; (503) 738–6273. Kitchens, pool, sauna, laundromat. 13 units. Close to Convention Center and beach. Designed for more than stay-a-night customers.

**Holladay Motel.** *Inexpensive.* 426 S. Holladay; (503) 738–6529. Small motel (10 units) that has lots of repeat customers. Tidy and well-managed.

## TILLAMOOK

**El Rancho Motel.** *Moderate.* Between the city center and the Tillamook Cheese Factory, 1810 Hwy. 101 N.; (503) 842–4413. Medium-size, it is basically a transient point for tourists, since Tillamook is not a beach or resort area.

**Mar-Clair Motel.** *Moderate.* 11 Main Ave.; (503) 842–7571. The largest and fanciest of all Tillamook motels, with 47 units. It has a pool, spa, and restaurant, as well as six one-bedroom apartments and six two-bedroom units. Rooms and apartments are well furnished and service is good. Reservation deposit required May 15 to October 1.

**Coastway Motel and Restaurant.** *Inexpensive.* 1910 Hwy. 101 N.; (503) 842–6651. Pool, in-room movies, not far from downtown Tillamook, as are all the motels.

**El Rey Sands Motel.** *Inexpensive.* 815 Main Ave.; (503) 842–7511. Another utilitarian, middle-size motel just off the highway.

## WALDPORT

**Terry-A-While Motel.** *Moderate.* Box 8700, Hwy. 101; (503) 563–3377. 14 units; kitchens, fireplaces. Fine décor and firm beds.

**Alsea Manor Motel.** *Inexpensive.* Box 446; (503) 563–2349. A clean 16-unit facility one block from Alsea Bay. Color cable TV, in-room movies and coffee; restaurant adjoining.

**Bayshore Inn.** *Inexpensive.* 500 Bayshore Dr.; (503) 563–3202. On the north shore of Alsea Bay, looking out to miles of beach. Well off the road and far from traffic, the inn has a certain solitude. All the 90 units are comfortable, and tides and waves will lull you to sleep. Cheery dining room.

**Deane's Oceanside Lodge.** *Inexpensive.* 8800 Hwy. 101 S.; (503) 547–3321. Kitchens and fireplaces make this 17-unit facility take on a touch of home. It has the feel of an old-time beach accommodation.

**Sea Stones Cottages.** *Inexpensive.* 8935 Hwy. 101 S.; (503) 547–3118. Only six units, some with fireplaces. Rates are weekly, which means that more vacationers than day transients come here. Family atmosphere.

**Waldport Motel.** *Inexpensive.* Hwy. 101; (503) 563–3035. Down-to-earth, with few fancy touches, but neat and quiet.

## YACHATS

**The Adobe.** *Moderate.* Box 219; (503) 547–3141. Well appointed, bright, with a solid feeling of comfort. Overlooking ocean; some fireplaces; three two-bedroom units. Pets extra. 38 units.

**Fireside Motel.** *Moderate.* Box 648; (503) 547–3636. Well off the highway, with many units overlooking Pacific. Another sterling 38-unit facility. Fine beach.

**Shamrock Lodgettes.** *Moderate.* Box 346; (503) 547–3312. This 19-unit motel is well off the highway and on lovingly landscaped grounds. To add another romantic touch, 12 of the units have balconies; all have fireplaces. Five two-bedroom units, two three-bedroom units. Beach, sauna, whirlpool, exercise room. Obviously, a motel for those who want to stay longer than overnight. Pets in cottages only, extra charge. Weekly rates available. Reservation deposit required.

**Holiday Inn Market-Motel.** *Inexpensive.* Box 830; (503) 547–3120. Only seven units, all with kitchens and fireplaces. Daily and weekly rates. Cozy, like living in an old-time boarding house.

**Jacqueline's See Vue Motel.** *Inexpensive.* 95590 Hwy. 101; (503) 547–3227. Another small facility—this one with 11 units—that tries to convey a homey feeling. Near the beach and not too far from town.

**Oregon House Motel.** *Inexpensive.* 94288 Hwy. 101; (503) 547–3329. The smallest facility of its kind in town—only five units; all have kitchens and fireplaces. Delightful place for small families.

**Yatel Motel.** *Inexpensive.* Box 266; (503) 547–3227. A seven-unit motel with a family ambiance.

 **BED-AND-BREAKFASTS.** There are a number of homes along the Oregon coast that provide such accommodations. For a complete listing contact *Northwest Bed and Breakfast,* 7707 S.W. Locust, Portland, OR 97223; (503) 246–8366. Prices vary, but most seem to be in the *Inexpensive* range, as categorized in "Hotels and Motels," above. In **Astoria,** a 1916 house high on a hill overlooking the harbor is a b-and-b. In **Bandon,** homes sit high above the pounding surf; in **Tolvana Park** an art-collector host rents out rooms in a comfortable home back from the beach; in **Depoe Bay** a b-and-b is perched on a hillside above the town with a panoramic view of the Bay and the Pacific. **Newport** b-and-b's include a large, modern house in a wooded setting and an older home high on a bluff overlooking the ocean and Yaquina Head. A cheery house in **Port Orford** affords great views of the ocean from three directions and is only a few hundred feet from the beach, and some educators in **Seaside** offer separate guest quarters in thir contemporary hilltop home.

In **Florence** the Johnson House *(Inexpensive)* is a b-and-b. 216 Maple St., Box 1892; (503) 997–8000. It's an 1892 house in historic Old Town.

 **YOUTH HOSTELS. Cannon Beach:** *Cannon Beach Youth Hostel,* N. Hemlock and 3rd St.; (503) 436–2603. Open summer season only.

**CAMPING AND RV PARKS.** Campsites for public use are spread throughout the state. 13 state parks allow for reservations for the period between Memorial and Labor days; after the second Monday in January to Labor Day, contact the particular park you're interested in. No phone reservations are accepted, and an advance deposit is required. (See "State Parks," below.) The U.S. Forest Service also operates campgrounds. Contact them through the U.S. Department of Agriculture, Washington, D.C. 20250.

The Bureau of Land Management also operates a small number of campsites for small fees. For a list of their sites write BLM, Box 2965, Portland, OR 97208.

Listed below are some of the private campgrounds and RV parks along the coast:

**Brookings:** *Chetco Travel Trailer Resort,* 16117 Hwy. 101 S.; (503) 469–3863. *Driftwood Travel Trailer Retreat,* 1611 Lower Harbor Dr., Harbor; (503) 469–3213. *River Bend Park,* 98203 South Bank Chetco Rd.; (503) 469–3356. RVs. 55 spaces; full hookup, showers.

**Cannon Beach:** *Wright's for Camping.* E. Elliot at Hwy. 101 Underpass; (503) 436–2347. 16 spaces, fireplace, tables, hot showers, wood available for a fee. Memorial weekend through September. (Spring and October—weekends only.)

**Charleston:** *Charleston Travel Park,* Boat Basin; (503) 888–4139.

**Coos Bay:** *Lawnridge Mobile Home Park.* RVs. 2550 Ocean Blvd.; (503) 267–2804. 10 spaces; full hookup, showers, store.

**Depoe Bay:** *Holiday R.V. Park.* Hwy. 101; (503) 765–2302. Very popular in summer and on weekends, when all 110 spaces are generally occupied. Full hookup, showers, store.

**Florence:** *Waterland R.V. Park & Marina.* Harbor and 1st St.; (503) 997–3040. 78 RV spaces on the Siuslaw River. Showers, tables, barbecue, water, electric and sewers; dump station; laundry; groceries; crabbing and clamming rentals; complete fishing needs; salmon charters daily. Also RV spaces at some lodges in Florence; see "Hotels and Motels," above.

**Gold Beach:** *Anglers Trailer Village,* 95706 Jerry's Flat; (503) 247–7922. *Indian Creek Recreational Park.* Trailers. 94680 Jerry's Flat Rd.; (503) 247–7704. *Kimball Creek Bend RV Resort.* 32051 Watson Ln.; (503) 247–7580.

**Newport:** *Harbor Village Mobile Home Park.* 923 Bay Blvd.; (503) 265–5088. 135 spaces; full hookup, showers, on Bay Front. *Sportsman's Trailer Park.* Marine Science Dr.; (503) 867–9588. Near Oregon State University Marine Science Center. 30 spaces; full hookup, showers, store nearby.

**Port Orford:** *Arizona Beach Resort.* Hwy. 101 S.; (503) 322–4491.

 **TOURIST INFORMATION.** For general information about the state contact *Oregon Travel Information Section,* Box 595, Cottage St. N.E., Salem, OR 97310; (503) 378–6309; or (800) 547–7482. The *Oregon Coast Association* can be reached at Box 670, Newport, OR 97365.

The *Astoria Area Chamber of Commerce,* Box 176, Port of Astoria Building, Astoria, OR 97103; (503) 325–6311, maintains an active tourist information service. It is open from 8:30 A.M. – 5 P.M. weekdays. Visitors coming to the Chamber of Commerce office receive a gift and complete packet of information.

**Bandon** *Chamber of Commerce,* 1280 Beach Loop Dr., Box 1515, Bandon, OR 97411; (503) 347–9616, is open 9 A.M. – 5 P.M. weekdays.

**Brookings-Harbor** *Chamber of Commerce* is on Hwy. 101 S., P.O. Box 940, Brookings, OR 97415; (503) 469–2213. Open 9 A.M. – 5 P.M. weekdays. The *Chetco Ranger Station,* 446 Oak St., Chetco, OR 97415; (503) 469–2196, offers forest and trail maps and other recreational information about the Brookings area. Open Monday–Friday, 7:30 A.M. – 4:30 P.M.; closed holidays.

**Cannon Beach** *Chamber of Commerce,* 201 E. Second St., Box 64, Cannon Beach, OR 97110; (503) 436–2623. Hours are 9 A.M. to 5 P.M., weekdays.

**Coos Bay** *Chamber of Commerce,* 502 E. Central Ave., Coos Bay, OR 97420; (503) 269–0215 is open daily 9 A.M.–7 P.M., June 1–Labor Day, 9 A.M.–5 P.M. weekdays rest of year; **North Bend** *Chamber of Commerce,* 1380 Sherman, North Bend, OR 97459; (503) 756–4613. Open business hours.

**Florence** *Area Chamber of Commerce,* Box 712, Florence, OR 97439; (503) 997–3128. Open business hours.

**Gold Beach** *Chamber of Commerce,* Box 55, City Hall, S. Ellensburg; (503) 247–7526. Open business hours.

**Lincoln City** *Chamber of Commerce,* Box 787, 3939 Northwest Hwy. 101, Lincoln City, OR 97367; (503) 994–3070. Open business hours.

**Newport** *Chamber of Commerce,* 555 S.W. Coast Hwy., Newport, OR 97365; (503) 262–2462. Open 9 A.M.–5 P.M. Monday–Friday; daily June–Sept.

You can write the **Port Orford** *Chamber of Commerce,* Box 637, Hwy. 101 S., Port Orford, OR 97465.

The **Reedsport** *Chamber of Commerce* can be contacted during business hours at (503) 271–3495; 805 Highway Ave., Reedsport, OR 97467.

**Seaside** *Chamber of Commerce,* 7 N. Roosevelt, Box 7, Seaside, OR 97138; (503) 738–8700 is open weekdays 9 A.M.–5 P.M.

**Tillamook** *County Chamber of Commerce* is located at 2105 First St., Tillamook, OR 97141; (503) 842–7525. Open 8:30 A.M.–5 P.M. weekdays.

For information on **Yachats** contact *Yachats Chamber of Commerce,* Box 174, Yachats, OR 97498; (503) 547–3392, during business hours.

For information on **Waldport** activities, write: *Waldport Chamber of Commerce,* Box 419, Waldport, OR 97394; (503) 563–2133. Open business hours.

 **SEASONAL EVENTS.** All coastal small-town festivals are basically the same: parade, fireworks, booths of crafts and foods, flurry of boats in harbor or out to sea within sight of shore, etc. Because of location, there are sometimes variations on themes: Seaside holds its Beachcomber Festival on beach as well as in town; Astoria's Maritime Week is promoted along water as well as in town; Brookings and Florence pray that their festivals coincide with the full bloom of flowers, so they can have pretty floral displays. But we here have come to expect very little difference in activities and moods. **February:** *Newport:* Seafood and Wine Festival. **March:** *Newport:* Blessing of the Fleet. *Yachats:* Arts and Crafts Fair, featuring the works of local and regional craftspeople. **April:** *Seaside* hosts an arts-and-crafts festival and its Beachcomber Festival. **May:** *Astoria* celebrates Maritime Week, followed by the Six-Pac Sailboat Races from Portland down the Columbia. *Brookings* has its annual Azalia Festival. In *Depoe Bay* the Fleet of Flowers Memorial Servie is a moving tribute to fishermen who did not return from the sea. *Florence:* Rhododendron Festival. *Newport* celebrates Loyalty Days. In **early summer** *Cannon Beach* holds its Annual Sandcastle Contest. **June:** *Astoria's* annual Scandinavian Mid-summer Festival celebrates Astoria's heritage with a colorul parade, arts-and-crafts demonstrations, delicious Scandinavian foods, and dancing. **July:** Early in the month *Yachats* holds its Community Smelt Fry to celebrate the end of the annual smelt run. The Lincoln County Fair is held in *Newport. Seaside* hosts the Miss Oregon pageant. The big event in *Waldport* is Beachcomber Days; prize floats are dropped by planes on incoming tides; other highlights usually include waterskiing on the bay front, dog-sled races on the beaches, teen dances, and motorboat racing on nearby Eckman Lake. **August:** *Astoria:* The 50-year-old Astoria Regatta is an annual tradition that includes a carnival, a salmon barbecue, water shows, hydroplane racing, seafood booths, and ship tours. *Depoe Bay* holds a very popular Indian-style salmon bake. *Lincoln City* hosts the Speed Boat World Record Races on Devil's Lake. *Seaside* has an arts-and-crafts show. **September:** *Bandon* holds its Cranberry Festival. **November:** ARTSgiving, a show of local artists and craftspeople, is held during Thanksgiving weekend in *Cannon Beach.* **December:** *Cannon Beach* holds a Dickens Festival, with music and plays.

**TOURS.** Many of the fishing boat charters are happy to take along non-fishing passengers for the ride. See "Fishing," below. For information on whale-watching water trips see "Wildlife Watching," below.

*Out & About Adventures,* Box 372, North Bend, OR 97459 (756–5945) offers "European-style tours" to interesting places in **Coos County.** The guide goes with you in your car at $2 per person per hour. For a luxury-style tour, the operators drive while you enjoy the scenery; $4 per person per hour. This entrepeneur also provides "trouble-free picnics", convention services, industrial tours, and charter fishing arrangements.

River charters on the Siuslaw are available out of **Florence.** Call the Chamber of Commerce for further information, 997–3128.

Rogue River boat trips are the most popular tourist activity in the **Gold Beach** area. Because there is such an interest in these trips, reservations are encouraged. *Court's White Water Trips,* Box 1045, Gold Beach, OR 97444; 247–6504. A six-hour, 64-mile round trip to Agness leave daily from Jot's Resort at 8:30 A.M., April 1–October 31; Adults, $20; ages 4–11, $8; over 65, $15. An eight-hour, 104-mile round trip leaves daily at 8 A.M., April 1–October 31; adults, $40; ages 4–11, $15. A two-hour scenic wildlife cruise on Lower Rogue leaves daily at 10 A.M., November 1–April 30; adults, $15; ages 4–11, $7.50. *Jerry's Rogue River Jet Boats and Wild River Trips,* Box 1011, Gold Beach, OR 97444; 247–7601. Leaves from boat basin at Port of Gold Beach, on south side of river. Round trips to Agness depart daily at 8:30 A.M., May 1–October 31; also at 2:30 P.M., July 1–Labor Day. Adults, $20; ages 4–11, $7. Trip to Paradise Bar (104 miles round trip) leaves daily at 8 A.M., May 1–October 31. Adults, $40; ages 4–11, $15. Two-hour scenic wildlife cruise leaves daily at 10 A.M., November 1–April 30. Adults, $15; ages 4–11, $7.50. *Rogue River Mail Boat Trips,* Box 1165, Gold Beach, OR 97444; 247–6225. Leave from mail boat dock, ¼ mile upstream from north end of Rogue River Bridge, across the river from Gold Beach. Jet boats for the round trip to Agness leave daily 8:30 A.M. May 1–October 31 and also at 2:30 P.M. July 1–Labor Day. Adults, $20; ages 4–11, $8. Departure time for 104-mile trip is 8 A.M. daily May 15–October 15; boats return at 3:30 P.M. Adults, $40; ages 4–11, $15. A few things to remember: parking at docks is free; all trips to Agness are the same length and take the same time. All boats stop at Agness for two hours for lunch. The 104-mile trip takes 7½ or 8 hours. Luncheon is two hours. Reservations for meals on both the 64- and 104-mile trip must made at dock. Fares do not include the price of meals. Overnight arrangements can be made at boat offices for stays at wilderness lodges. (See "Gold Beach Hotels and Motels.") Though there may be competition between the boat companies, their prices are the same, and so are their services and what they show passengers.

**STATE PARKS.** The State Parks and Recreation Section of the Oregon Department of Transportation maintains almost 250 Parks, Waysides, Recreation Areas and historic sites totaling more than 92,000 acres. These areas provide over 6,000 picnic sites, 5,500 campsites, and an unlimited variety of outdoor recreation activities. The parks—54 of which have overnight camping facilities—are found in every part of Oregon; some, in the remote areas, are sparsely occupied, while parks on the coast and at popular lakes are sometimes filled up weeks in advance. (Many parks have restrooms that are accessible to handicapped persons). With a minimum of common-sense planning one can travel slowly through Oregon and put up at a state park every night. Every major city is within easy driving distance of at least one state park. For further information, contact *State Parks and Recreation Division,* 525 Trade St. S.E., Salem, OR 97310; (503) 378–6305.

There is no charge for the use of picnic, boat-launching, or other day-use facilities in state parks. There is a charge for firewood of $.50 cents per 2 cubic feet.

Overnight camping is permitted in state parks in areas designated for camping, with length of stay at any one park limited to 10 days in any 14-day period from mid-May through Labor Day; also limited to 14 out of every 18 days from September 15 through May 14. The main season for overnight camping is mid-April–October. Those parks that are open year-round on the coast are noted as such here. At parks with camper registration booths, campsites are assigned by attendant. Check-out time is 2:30 P.M.

Thirteen Oregon state-park campgrounds operate on a reservation system from Memorial Day weekend through Labor Day weekend. Beginning the second Monday in January to Labor Day weekend, reservation requests may be sent directly to the park where the reservation is desired. Campsite reservation applications are available from all state park, state police, and motor vehicle offices, and from many chambers of commerce. An advance deposit must accompany each reservation request.

Oregon State Parks operates a *Campsite Information Center* from the first Monday in March to Labor Day weekend. Staff are on duty 8 A.M.–5 P.M., Monday–Friday, to provide current information on campsite availability in state parks and other recreation information. Campsite reservations cannot be made through the center, but the center does accept campsite reservation cancellations. Toll-free calls can be made to the Center from anywhere within Oregon but Portland. The number is (800) 452–5687. Portland and out-of-state residents should call (503) 238–7488.

Although camping rates change, as of press time the following rates apply:

Trailer campsite: $8 per night; full hookup. Facilities include hookups for water, electricity, and sewage disposal at each site, with a table, stove, and access to a modern utility building containing toilets, showers, and laundry facilities.

Improved campsite: $7 per night. Facilities include water supply and electric hookups at each site, plus a table, stove, and access to a modern restroom or a utility building with toilets, showers, and laundry facilities.

Tent campsite: $6 per night. Facilities include a tent site with a table, stove, water, and access to a nearby rest station with flush toilets.

Primitive campsite: $5 per night. Facilities include a table and stove but water and sanitary facilities may be some distance from the site.

(At all overnight parks, $2 charge per extra vehicle per night.)

Coastal state parks have a non-resident additional fee of $2 per night.

*Beachside* and *Beverly Beach State Parks,* both in **Newport,** take campsite reservations from Memorial Day–Labor Day. Second Monday in January–Labor Day write (with deposit) for reservations to Beachside, Box 1350, Newport, OR 97365; (503) 563–3023; to Beverly Beach, Star Route North, Box 864, Newport, OR 97365; (503) 265–7655. Beverly Beach is open year-round.

*Cape Lookout State Park* in **Tillamook** is lush with vegetation; hiking trails help the visitor to experience it all. A sea-bird rookery with thousands of California murres in nesting season can be viewed. The park has 245 campsites, which can be reserved for the period from Memorial Day weekend through Labor Day weekend. Reservations cannot be made by phone. Second Monday in January–Labor Day, write Cape Lookout State Park, 13000 Whiskey Creek Rd. W., Tillamook, OR 97141; (503) 842–4981. Advance deposit required. The park is open all year.

*Fort Stevens State Park* is ten miles west of **Astoria.** In 1863, the U.S. Army began construction of Fort Stevens with the objective of defending the mouth of the Columbia River from a Confederate invasion. Battery Russell, which in 1904 became the fort's seventh battery, eventually received the dubious distinction of being the only fortification in the continental United States to be fired upon by an enemy since the War of 1812: during World War II it was shelled by a Japanese submarine but could not return fire because its guns lacked range.

Battery Russell and the rusting skeleton of the *Peter Iredale,* a four-masted British ship, are only two of the many attractions at Fort Stevens.

Fifteen miles of ocean beach are available for clam digging, surf bathing, and beachcombing. The south jetty provides an excellent place for surf fishing for salmon and boom fish. Freshwater fishing for bass, perch, and trout in Coffenbury Lake is a popular activity at the park. The lake has two swimming areas, a fishing pier, and a boat ramp.

A 2½-mile hiking trail circles the lake and is ideal for nature study. Fort Stevens is the northern trail head for the Oregon Coast Trail. The Pioneer Nature Trail has over 20 plants and animal signs identified on a half-mile loop.

A naturalist is on duty during the summer to assist in the understanding of the Park's ecosystems and to provide local history and information through evening programs and organized walks.

For the bicycle enthusiast, seven miles of paved trail wind casually through the park. The trail goes past Battery Russell, extends into the sand-dune stabilization area, and returns close to the *Peter Iredale* and Coffenbury Lake.

The campground of the 3,670-acre park contains 260 campsites, 120 improved sites, 223 trailer sites, and 225 picnic sites; hot showers, laundry room, trailer dumping station, outdoor theater, and group camp facilities. Reservations can be made for Memorial Day–Labor Day from the second Monday in January–Labor Day by writing the park, Hammond, OR 07121; (503) 861-1671. No phone reservations. Advance deposit required. Open year-round.

*Harris Beach State Park* in **Brookings** offers magnificent coastal scenery. It is one of the 13 campgrounds operating on a reservation system from Memorial Day weekend–Labor Day weekend. Beginning the second Monday in January–Labor Day weekend, reservation requests may be sent directly to the park. An advance deposit must accompany each reservation request. Write the park at 1655 Hwy. 101, Brookings, OR 97415; (503) 469–4774. 34 trailer sites, 51 improved sites, 66 tent sites. Restrooms accessible to the handicapped. Open year-round.

*Honeyman State Park* just south of **Florence** is probably Oregon's most popular state park. It is one of 11 campgrounds which remain open year round. It is also one of 13 campgrounds that operate on a reservation system from Memorial Day weekend–Labor Day weekend. Beginning the second Monday in January–Labor Day weekend, reservation requests may be sent directly to the park. An advance deposit must accompany each reservation request. Reservations cannot be made by telephone. Write: Honeyman State Park, 84505 Hwy. 101, Florence, OR 97439; (503) 997–8484.

*Humbug Mountain State Park,* 6 miles south of **Port Orford** on U.S. 101, has a virgin forest, trout streams, sandy beach, swimming, fishing, electric stoves, and 32 picnic sites. The overnight camp has 75 tent campsites, 30 trailer sites, showers, and laundry rooms. Humbug Mountain, climbed by a winding trail, rises to an elevation of 1,750 feet, and the seascapes from the top are spectacular. (The state park is at the foot of the mountain.)

Between **Newport** and Waldport, 16 miles away, U.S. 101 adheres to the sea, and in the process touches five state parks, one of which, *South Beach,* near Newport, has 257 improved camp sites and 53 sites for RVs. South Beach also has an area for bikers and hikers and restrooms that are accessible to handicapped persons. South Beach is one of 13 state parks that operate on a reservation system from Memorial Day weekend through Labor Day weekend. Reservations cannot be made by telephone: Contact, South Beach State Park, Box 1350, Newport, OR 97365; (503) 867–6611.

*Sunset Bay State Park,* with its wave-battered cliffs and picturesque offshore rocks, is one of 13 campgrounds that operate on a reservation system from Memorial Day weekend to Labor Day weekend. Beginning the second Monday in January to Labor Day weekend, reservation requests may be sent directly to the park. A deposit must accompany the reservation request. Reservations cannot be made by telephone. Write: Sunset Bay State Park, 13030 Cape Arago Hwy., **Coos Bay,** OR 97420; (503) 888–9200. Sunset Bay has 29 trailer and 108 tent sites. It has restrooms that are accessible to handicapped persons. Nearby are a number of other state parks including *Cape Arago* (sea lions can be spotted off the coast on Shell Island and Simpson Reef) and *Shore Acres,* with its magnificent botanical gardens.

 **NATIONAL PARKLANDS.** The *Suislaw National Forest,* divided into two major areas along the coast, contains the *Oregon Dunes National Recreation Area,* which was established in 1972 with 32,237 acres. The undulating dunes cover everything in their path, even forest, but conservationists are attempting stabilization with beachgrass and broom. (Contact Oregon Sand Dunes National Recreation Area, 855 Highway Ave., Reedsport, OR 97467, (503) 271–3611, for a guide to hiking or riding through the dunes. *Sand Dunes Frontier,* 83960 Hwy. 101 S., Florence, OR 97439, (503) 997–3544, gives sand-buggy tours of this area. There's also a miniature golf course and a private trout lake, which can be used for a fee.) The Forest Service's *Cape Perpetua Visitor Center* offers a free color motion picture, "Forces of Nature," which describes the geologic life of the coast and the effect of waves, wind, and weather on her rugged beauty. Exhibits, nature trails, and camping and picnicking facilities round out Perpetua's offering. From here the vacationer can travel north, south, east—and a few feet west—to enjoy the approximately 40 campgrounds and picnic areas of the Siuslaw National Forest. For more information write District Ranger, Waldport Ranger Station, Waldport, OR 97394.

Located in the southwest corner of Oregon, the *Siskiyou National Forest* embraces rugged terrain, heavily timbered mountainside and bold, rocky cliffs that rise abruptly from the sea. The famous Rogue River (one of a handful of National Wild and Scenic Rivers in the United States) and Illinois River systems bisect the National Forest and offer unparalleled fly fishing for native trout, including the fighting sea-run steelhead. There are about 30 campgrounds and picnic areas in the Siskiyou National Forest. Write Box 440, Grants Pass, OR 97526; (503) 479–5301.

 **ZOOS AND AQUARIUMS.** Small fees are charged at the following establishments. Eight miles south of **Bandon** is the *West Coast Game Park Safari.* Over 400 tame, exotic birds and animals. Visitors can feed and pet many animals they would *never* be able to get close to ordinarily. On U.S. 101; (503) 347–3106. Open daily 9 A.M.–dusk, March 1–October 31, Monday–Friday; 9 A.M.–dusk the rest of the year.

A mile below **Devil's Elbow State Park** is *Sea Lion Caves,* where visitors descend to sea level to view adult and young sea lions. It's open daily, 9 A.M.–6 P.M.; 547–3415.

**Seaside Aquarium,** 200 N. Prom. Although the aquarium has Oregon Dungeness, spider, decorator, kelp, box, and hermit crab; Pacific and Atlantic lobster, wolf fish, moray eel, and seal turtles, as well as an octopus, leopard shark, and sand shark, the big attraction is the group of seals—the clowns of the ocean. Of interest, too, are the sea anemones—rainbow-colored, plantlike creatures that are actually fed salmon. Call 738–6211 for more information.

 **WILDLIFE WATCHING.** Do, by all means, bring your field glasses; there's much to observe. All along the Oregon Coast there is a plethora of shorebirds. The birds are migratory, moving up and down the coast, but one or more species of bird specially adapted to the shoreline can be seen almost anywhere.

In December, gray whales are migrating south; in the spring, north, moving between the Artic and Baja California. Many can be seen from high points along the coast and some communities have tour boats to give visitors a closer look.

April–May and December–January, migrating gray whales can be seen off the coast of **Garibaldi.** Charter boats are available. Business phones of Garibaldi charter boat operators are: Dave Haas, 322–3285; Dale Walers, 322–3395; Ed Boucher, 322–3666; John Brown, 355–2439; Don Johnson, 322–3395; Morrie Barackman, 322–3285; and Joe Gierga, 322–3285.

Tours in the **Gold Beach** area often include wildlife cruises. See "Tours," earlier in this *Practical Information* section.

Excursions to watch the whales off **Depoe Bay** happen during May and December and last 40 minutes. Contact *Tradewinds,* Box 123, Depoe Bay, OR 97341; 765–2345.

See also "Zoos and Aquariums."

 **BEACHES.** Except for where the seawall meets the Pacific, the Oregon coast is all beach, and practically all of it is accessible to the public. The list below does not include all the beaches—some are handkerchief size, some are quite difficult to find, some lack room for parking; all of these are nameless on maps. But there are a sufficient number of named beaches for the traveler to pause often to visit the sandy littoral of Oregon. North-to-south these are: **Ft. Stevens State Park.** Waders frolic around the diminishing remains of the *Peter Iredale,* a British bark stranded on the beach during a heavy storm in the autumn of 1902. **Gearhart.** Back of the condominiums and motels is a beach that always looks untrammeled, even in its most crowded hour. **Seaside.** The state's most populated beach, looking inland to the state's longest boardwalk. The warmest part of the Pacific off the Oregon Coast is here, which may be why the Miss Oregon contest is held in this resort town. **Cannon Beach.** At the foot of Haystack Rock, a monolith that is the Oregon Coast's most photographed seamark. Driftwood seems to have a propensity for piling up on this beach, and the wood provides the fuel for cheery fires, which are the scene of weenie and marshmallow roasts. The beach is also used by joggers, walkers, kite flyers, horseriders, shell collectors, and sunbathers. Within the corporate limits of Cannon Beach is Ecola State Park. A trail leads from the park to **Indian** and **Ecola** beaches, small and secretive. A lot of people think the coves at these beaches ideal places to picnic. **Hug Point State Park.** A long, clean beach with caves and the ruts of a wagon (and later auto) road cut across a seawall. **Oswald West State Park.** You have to go through a forest to get to the beach but the hike is worth the effort. **Manzanita.** The town is in the midst of seven miles of sand. A typical airy, broad, seashell, driftwood beach that seems to attract what ought to be more than its share of seagulls. A good road leads little more than a mile to Nehalem Bay State Park, where the wind cuts like rawhide and the sea gets churly. **Rockaway.** A long, wide foreshore, with plenty of space since Rockaway is not an exotic beach town. But the beach is marvelous for hiking, jogging, riding, building fires, and watching the sun go down. **Cape Lookout State Park.** Golden sands below a headland projecting 1½ miles into the sea make a fine place to sunbathe, beachcomb, and just feel free as the wind. **Cape Kiwanda.** Not too many people come to use the beach; most journey here to take their dories to sea, watch the boats and the hanggliders take off from Cape Kiwanda Head. But the beach is used for more conventional purposes too. **Fogarty Creek State Park.** This well-trod beach below seagrass bluffs is split by a sheltered creek trickling into the sea, and the result is a photogenic setting. **Beverly Beach State Park.** The broad, sandy beach is lovely for casual strolling or vigorous hiking or any kind of running you wish. Marine fossils, including the bones of whales and sea lions, have been found in the cliffs of the park. **South Beach State Park.** For sweeping vistas of the ocean, climb atop a sand dune. **Lost Creek State Park.** Below a picnic ground the beach seems to drift in the cool Pacific breeze. **Ona Beach State Park.** A well-equipped, little-known day-use facility. A boat ramp leads to Beaver Creek. In summer, the beach is host to fishers and waders. **Driftwood Beach Wayside.** The name was well chosen. Driftwood piles up here as though the ocean had been clear cut. **Waldport.** The finest beach in the area is on the north side of Alsea Bay. The beach is wild and thinly populated. Sunsets are gorgeous. **Governor Patterson State Park.** The sandy beach is as trim as the landscaped area above it. **Beachside State Park.** This smooth foreshore was once part of the only road between Newport and Yachats. It was abandoned after the building of U.S. 101. **Yachats State Park.** The uniqueness of this beach consists of heaps of shells, cemented together by time and salt air, that were deposited by Indians for at least several centuries. **Washburne State Park.** A pleasant place to picnic, browse, wade in the ocean surf, romp on the beach, or shore fish. **Devil's Elbow State Park.** The spongy beach has most of the attributes of the other beaches—with one addition. On a rugged headland rising sheer above the ocean, and clearly seen from the beach, is Heceta Head Lighthouse. **Heceta Beach.** A secluded nook on the littoral. It is a favorite journeying point for sophisticated driftwood collectors. **Umpqua Lighthouse State Park.** Below the lighthouse road lie ocean-rim scablands and driftwood beaches. This is not an area for sunbathing or wading but it has a raw, vigorous look that appeals to the poetic.

The beaches off the Seven Devils Road between Charleston and Bandon—**Sacchi, Agate, Merchant's** and **Whiskey Run**—are not "pretty" but they contain agates, agatized myrtlewood, and jasper and are rich in clams. Amateur prospectors come to Whiskey Run hoping to find bits of gold not scooped up during the Coos County gold rush of 1853–55. **Bandon.** The beach south of Bandon looks out to the largest and oddest array of offshore rocks to be seen anywhere on the Oregon Coast. **Humbug Mountain State Park.** The sands here comprise a beachcomber's paradise: Japanese glass floats, driftwood, petrified wood, beeswax, rare shells, bamboos, bottles—and lots more. **Whalehead Beach.** Better known for viewing than anything else. Cameras are out to photograph the offshore rock formation resembling a whale spouting. **Harris Beach State Park.** Open all year, the state park has complete facilities. The beach is not long, by Oregon coastal standards, but is heavily used, for all the usual things. From atop Harris Butte there is a vista encompassing 24 miles of curving coastline.

 **SPORTS. Boating.** For information on boating throughout the state contact the *Oregon State Marine Board,* 3000 Market St. N.E., Salem, OR (503) 378–8587 or toll-free (800) 452–7813. Inquire locally at sporting goods stores, marine businesses, chambers of commerce. The facilities are numerous.

**Bicycling. Astoria** is the start of the *Oregon Coast Bike Route,* which extends the length of the coast. A brochure with strip maps of the route and safety rest areas and their facilities is available free of charge by writing to *Bicycle Route Engineer,* Oregon Department of Transportation, Salem, OR 97310. Space has been set aside near existing utilities for use by bikers and hikers at a cost of $1 per night.

**Hunting.** Although the big game seasons vary from year to year, it is generally as follows for the Oregon Coast: *deer*—early October to the first week of November; *Roosevelt elk*—mid-November; *bear*—late August to the end of November. *Bow-hunting* is from late August to the last week in September. Tags, in addition to a license, are required, and there are deadline dates for each species. Juveniles from ages 12 through 17 must have a Hunter Education Certificate, in addition to the license, while hunting. A nonresident hunter's license is $75, and a nonresident bear tag is also $75. A nonresident deer tag (rifle or bow) is $50, and a nonresident elk tag (rifle or bow) is $105. Licenses and tags are obtainable at sporting goods stores, hardware stores, some supermarkets, and at some chambers of commerce. Inquire at chambers of commerce or contact *Oregon Department of Fish and Wildlife,* 506 S.W. Mill St., Portland, OR 97208; (503) 229–5403, or *U.S. Fish and Wildlife Service,* 500 N.E. Multnomah, Portland, OR 97232; (503) 221–6021.

*Saddle Mountain State Park* near **Seaside** is one of the more popular hunting areas for black bear. The most successful method of hunting bear is with the use of trained dogs to track down and tree the animal. Bear may be hunted with rifles or shotguns using rifled slugs. Archers also find the black bear a fine challenge. Numerous black bear are taken by hunters during the general deer and elk seasons.

For **Fishing,** see below.

**Hiking.** The state and national parklands are perfect spots for just walking. The *Exploring the Oregon Coast* section, above, also describes trails that lead visitors to awesome natural sites. For information on more elaborate hikes, including those that require guides, contact *Oregon Guides and Packers Association,* Box 3797, Portland, OR 97208; (503) 234–2173.

**Horseback riding.** In **Cannon Beach,** *Sea Ranch Stables,* Beach Loop and Ecola Creek, rents horses in the summer for trail and beach rides, 436–2815.

**Golf.** There are golf courses up and down the coast. Some specific courses are listed below. The *Astoria Golf and Country Club* between **Seaside** and **Astoria** has a beautiful 18-hole course and offers guest privileges. 861–2211. In **Bandon** the *Face Rock Golf Course* is at 3225 Beach Loop; 347–3818. In the **Coos Bay/North Bend** area: *Coos Bay Golf Course,* 6905 Cottrell Lane, Coos Bay, 888–9301 and *Kentuck Golf Course,* Kentuck Inlet, North Bend, 756–4464. The **Florence** *Golf Course* (997–3232) is on Munsel Lake Rd. In **Gold Beach,** the *Cedar Bend Golf Course* is on Hwy. 101 N.; 247–6911. One mile north of the **Lincoln City** Chamber of Commerce on N.W. Hwy. 101 is *Devil's Lake Golf Course,* 997–8442. **Waldport** has a year-round, nine-hole golf course: *Crestview Hills Golf Course,* 1401 Crestline Dr., 563–3020.

**FISHING.** For up-to-date information of fishing, contact the *Oregon Department of Fish and Wildlife,* 506 S.W. Mill St., Portland, OR 97208, (503) 229–5403, or *U.S. Fish and Wildlife Service,* 500 N.E. Multnomah, Portland, OR 97232, (503) 221–6021.

A valid angling license is required to be in possession of all persons 14 years or over who angle for or take game fish for personal use. The only exception is Oregon residents fishing on their own land or on land owned by a member of their immediate family and upon which they reside. When angling for salmon or steelhead, all anglers regardless of age, except for daily angler license holders, must have a salmon-steelhead tag in possession. Only one salmon-steelhead tag may be purchased per year. Upon landing an adult salmon or steelhead that is to be retained, the angler must immediately fill out the catch record on the tag or daily license.

A nonresident license is as follows: Annual angling, $30; ten-day angling, $18; daily angling, $3.50 (salmon-steelhead tag not required); annual salmon-steelhead tag, $5. Licenses are obtainable in every community on the coast at sporting-goods stores, fish markets, supermarkets, hardware stores, and a number of other retail outlets.

No license is required for taking shellfish for personal use. All of Oregon's coastal bays are open year-round for crabbing.

There is excellent fishing of all kinds along the Oregon coast. Highlights are as follows:

**Astoria** proper and surrounding **Clatsop County** offer the entire range of northwest fishing, and lots of it. Charter boats are readily available for those after the big chinook, silvers, tuna, sturgeon, and other whitefish. Pier fishing and surf casting produce good results at a number of locations. Clatsop County's 22 lakes, rivers, and streams are some of the Northwest's best for cutthroat, rainbow trout, and the hard-hitting steelhead. For a slower-moving quarry, try the excellent razor-clamming on a minus tide south of the Columbia River jetty. Clatsop Spit, due west of Astoria at the mouth of the Columbia, is one of the best spots in Oregon to catch the delicious Dungeness crab. Charters are available. Charter boats in the Astoria area are: Astoria: *Cheyenne, Irish, Kingfisher, Lin-Dee, Shamrock,* and *Silver Fox,* at 325–7990. Warrenton: *Aquarius* and *Pacific Salmon,* at 861–3705; *Dark Rock* at 861–1445; *Executive* at 648–7616; *Naughtyless* at 228–6607; *Okie* at 253–5186; and *Rochelle* at 861–1008; Hammond: *Doll-Fin* at 861–2698; *Donrimick* at 289–9578; *Howdy Do* at 861–1201; *Lite Rock* at 777–2204; *Marta* at 861–1867; *Rockin' C* at 861–1814; *Time Out* at 861–1008; and *Zoea* at 861–1211.

The mouth of the Chetco River is at **Brookings.** It's a great place for salmon and steelhead. The offshore chinook fishing begins in July, while the best coho fishing is in August and September. *Leta "J"* takes fishers and sightseers out on the Pacific; (503) 469–3452. Five-hour salmon and bottom-fishing trips may be arranged through Leo's Sporthaven Marina, Box 2215, Harbor, OR 97415; (503) 469–3301.

Surf, rock, and bay fishing for surf perch, kelp greenling, ling cod, flounder, and rock fish is becoming increasingly popular in **Cannon Beach.**

**Cape Kiwanda** is the site of much dory fishing, with the annual dory derby taking place in early June. The Nestucca River, in the Cape Kiwanda area, is regarded by many anglers as the best fishing stream in the state. The Nestucca and Little Nestucca are noted for excellent June and July chinook fishing in the tidewater areas. The main fall run begins about the first of August and continues through September. Coho salmon normally enter the river about September 20 and the run continues until the winter freshets, about December 1. Spinners are generally used, although some fishers use wobblers. For information on guides who work the Nestucca, write Oregon Guides and Packers Assoc., Box 3797, Portland 97208; (503) 234–2173.

Deep-sea fishing from **Pacific City** starts in late June or early July and continues throughout the summer. Sport tackle is used with plugs and wobblers; mooching is popular. Some fishers use a fly rod and streamer fly. The catch is predominantly coho salmon although a few chinooks are taken. Boats and guides are available for fishing on the river or at sea.

In the **Coos Bay** area chinook and coho are abundant offshore from early June–early September. Charter boats, guides, tackle, food and lodging are available at the Charleston Boat Basin, 888–4041, or for charters for fishing or sightseeing call *B & B Charters* at the Boat Basin, 888–4139; *Charleston Charter Service,* 888–4846; or *Hanson's Charters,* 888–3855. *Out & About Adventures,* Box 372, North Bend 97459, 756–5945 also offers fishing charters.

In **Depoe Bay,** excursion cruises for sightseeing and fishing are available aboard the *Kingfisher* and *Sunrise.* Five-hour trips for salmon run daily, starting at dawn, mid-morning, and mid-afternoon, commencing in May and continuing into September. Fishing license required—season and one-day permits may be purchased at *Tradewinds* office. Bottom-fishing cruises year-round; five-hour trips leave the docks daily, weather permitting. Catch ling cod, red snapper, sea bass, and much more; no license required. Tuna cruises mid-July through September. Trips leave at dawn on a twelve-hour tuna adventure; albacore may be spotted and caught as close as 15 miles offshore. Gloves and sack lunches recommended. Poles, tackle, bait, hot coffee, and raingear are furnished for all trips. Fish cleaning available at the dock. Non-fishing passes are available for half fare. During whale migrations in May and December, there are 40-minute trips to watch the great mammals of the deep. Contact Tradewinds, Box 123, Depoe Bay, OR 97341; 765-2345.

Other charter boats at Depoe Bay are operated by *Jimco Sportfishing,* 765-2382.

In and around **Florence** there are 21 kinds of freshwater fish and good opportunities for shore, boat, and jetty ocean fishing. (For information on boat charters call the Chamber of Commerce, 997-3128). Crabbing and clamming are also good here. There are a number of fishing lodges; see "Hotels and Motels," above.

The Rogue River, its mouth at **Gold Beach,** is considered to be one of the best fishing streams in the West. For fishing charters out of Gold Beach contact *Bansee Charters,* waterfront, 247-2112.

Tenmile Creek and Tenmile Lake, around **Lakeside,** are noted for trolling. Any questions can be directed to the Lakeside Chamber of Commerce, Lakeside, OR 97449.

Around **Lincoln City** the Siletz River is a known salmon stream: chinooks in August and September, silvers in October and November. Devil's Lake is a good spot for trout, large-and small-mouth bass, crappie, bluegill, and perch.

The first sizable salmon stream south of the Columbia is the Nehalem River.

In **Newport,** charter boats, basically designed for anglers, also carry people who just come on board for the sightseeing, which includes trips around Yaquina Bay and along the coast near Newport. *Johnny's Sportfishing Co.* has a fleet of boats anchored at Neptune's Wharf, on Bay Front, 325 S.W. Bay Blvd.; and arranges excursion trips on request. 265-2411. *South Beach Charters,* located at the South Beach Marina, on the south side of the Yaquina Bay Bridge, offers salmon, bay crabbing, tuna, year-round bottom fishing, and ocean-bay and river excursions—five- and seven-hour trips. Fishing licenses and box lunches are available. P.O. Box 1446; 867-7200. Other charters in Newport are the *Allegra,* 265-7558; *Blue Shark,* 265-2101; *Cheyenne,* 265-2101; *Chiloquin,* 265-7558; *Kai-Aku,* 265-7558; *Sea Pirate,* 265-2101; *Sea Venture I,* 265-2101; *Super Star,* 265-2101; *Sweet Betsy,* 265-7558; and *Taku,* 265-7558.

Everything in **Reedsport** revolves around fishing, because of the fame of Winchester Bay. Both cohos and chinooks are caught by trolling (mostly herring), June–September. Salmon Harbor is like many of Oregon's coastal river outlets, with excellent facilties to accommodate fishermen. Boats, guides, and tackle are available to those who wish to fish in the bay and "across the bar" at sea. Charter boats make regular trips and may also be reserved for special fishing groups. Charter boats at Winchester Bay are: *Becky Lynn,* 271–3017; *Bikini,* 271–3133; *Holiday Too,* 271–3702; *Ladies Choice,* 271–3800; *Shamrock II,* 271–3232; and *Marsadon,* 271–3122.

Some say the best place in the state for deep-sea jetty fishing is at Barview Jetty County Park, just south of **Rockaway.**

There is active fishing in the rivers near **Tillamook.** The Wilson River, reached by Oregon 6, which is the direct route to Portland, is highly used by winter steelhead and fall chinook fisherfolk who play its waters in driftboats or plunk from the bank. A public access by the Oregon Department of Fish and Wildlife is located at Sollie Smith Bridge about a mile from downtown Tillamook. The Trask and Tillamook rivers, both entering Tillamook Bay near its southernmost point, are outstanding streams for the various salmon species and for cutthroat trout. The Trask has good wild runs of spring and fall chinook, winter steelhead, and some summer steelhead. It also has good runs of coho, including many fish produced at the Trask River Hatchery at Gold Creek. The Tillamook River supports runs of coho, fall chinook, chum salmon, cutthroat, some stray summer steelhead, and a good run of winter steelhead. Tillamook Bay is open all year for all fishing. Bay angling for salmon is considered best during July and August. Sea perch and flounder enter the bays in the spring.

 **HISTORIC SITES AND HOUSES.** Astoria is very proud of the large number of century-old Victorian homes that grace its streets. The elegant cupolas, verandas, and ornate window work testify to Astoria's heyday as a major coastal port beginning in the 1850s, whem most of these structures were built. A walking tour past some of the homes on Franklin and Grand streets is outlined above in the Astoria section of *Exploring the Oregon Coast.* The oldest house in Astoria, built in 1854 by Hiram Brown, a river pilot, is at 1337 Franklin. The house was restored in 1964.

The lightship *Columbia,* a restored Columbia River ship, is berthed at the foot of 17th St. For information contact the Maritime Museum at 325–2323. Open daily 9 A.M.–6 P.M.

The *Flavell Mansion* was built in 1883 by a sea captain and is one of Oregon's finest examples of Victorian architecture. It now houses the Clatsop County Historical Museum. On 8th St., between Duane and Exchange; 325–2203. Open Monday–Friday, 9 A.M.–5 P.M.

**Newport:** *Burrows House,* 545 S.W. 9th St., is furnished as a late nineteenth-century house would be. It's part of the Lincoln County Historical Society, 265–7509. Open 11 A.M.–4 P.M.; closed Monday.

Visitors can wander through the *Old Yaquina Bay Lighthouse* in Yaquina Bay State Park, June–September, Thursday–Monday, 12:30 P.M.–5 P.M.

**Seaside:** The *Levi Coffman House,* 616 N. Holladay, was built in 1853. It is the oldest in Seaside and, while it may not be architecturally exciting, it deserves respect for its vintage. A private residence, it can be viewed from the outside only.

Just south of **Tillamook** are two reminders of World War II, now being used as a lumber mill—"blimp" hangers, each of them 1,080 feet long by 300 feet wide by 190 feet high. The Chamber of Commerce calls them the "world's largest wooden structures."

 **MUSEUMS.** Some of the museums listed below charge a small fee; others request a donation. **Astoria:** *Clatsop County Historical Museum,* on 8th St. between Duane and Exchange, 325–2203. Open Monday–Friday 9 A.M. –5 P.M. This museum is in the Flavell Mansion, built in 1883 by a sea captain and one of the finest examples of Victorian architecture in Oregon. The museum houses an important collection of period exhibits.

*Columbia River Maritime Museum,* at foot of 17th St., 325–2323. One of the country's finest displays of nautical artifacts, ship models, fishing implements, and dioramas of early history, all housed in an impressive 37,000 square-foot structure. Open daily, 9 A.M.–6 P.M.

**Bandon:** *Bandon Historical Society Museum,* south end of 2nd St.; (503) 347–2164. Contains memorabilia of the early days of settlement. Open daily, 9 A.M.–5 P.M.

**Brookings:** *Chetco Museum,* 15461 Museum Rd.; 469–6651. The life of Chetco Valley pioneers told through artifacts and graphics. Open 9 A.M.–5 P.M., May 1–October 31.

**Coos Bay/North Bend:** *Coos Art Museum,* 515 Market St.; 267–3901. Generally regarded as the finest art museum on the coast. Exhibits displayed at high professional level.

*Coos County Historical Museum,* Simpson Park, North Bend; 756–6320. Implements, garments, firearms, photos, and a lot more from pioneer days in Coos County.

**Florence:** *Indian Forest* displays full-size Indian dwellings in natural surroundings. There's also a gift shop selling Indian crafts and artwork. 88493 Hwy. 101 N.; 997–3677. Open May 1–October 15; June, July, August, 8 A.M. –dusk; May, September, October, 10 A.M.–4 P.M.

*Siuslaw Pioneer Museum,* 85290 Hwy. 101, south of Bridge; no phone. Memorabilia of early days along Siuslaw Bay and the Siuslaw Valley. Indeterminate hours. Contact Chamber of Commerce for further information; 997–3128.

**Gold Beach:** North of Gold Beach on U.S. 101 S. is *Prehistoric Gardens,* a "lost world" of life-size replicas of dinosaurs and other prehistoric animals that may have roamed these parts. Open daily 9 A.M.–6 P.M.; 332–4463.

**Lincoln City:** *Lacey's Doll and Antique Museum,* 3400 N.E. Hwy. 101; 994–2392, open 8:30 A.M.–6 P.M. daily. One of the largest private collections of dolls in the West. The largest doll is 48-inches-tall Linda Susan, a black-haired China doll that's over 100 years old and wears a dress of the 1860s. There are also exquisite reproductions of Jenny Lind, the Gibson Girl, Will Rogers, and many more. Home of one of the old hurdy-gurdys used on the streets of Portland from

1895 to 1905; it still plays. Old furniture, dolls, and firearms from out of the past.

**Newport:** (Hours are subject to change; contact Chamber of Commerce for more information, 262–2462.) *Burrows House,* 545 S.W. 9th St. What a mercantile prince–dowager home looked like back a hundred years ago. Furnished in period style. Part of the *Lincoln County Historical Museum;* 265–7509. Both are closed Mondays; open 11 A.M.–4 P.M. Museum, in log structure, has Lincoln County artifacts from pioneer days.

*Old Yaquina Bay Lighthouse,* in Yaquina Bay State Park, at south end of Newport. Open June–September, Thursday–Monday, 12:30 P.M.–5 P.M.

*Royal Pacific Wax Museum,* 550 S.W. Coast Hwy.; 265–2062. Life-size wax figures from Josephine Tussaud. Lighted for photography. Open daily, 10 A.M.–5 P.M.

*Undersea Gardens,* 267 S.W. Bay Blvd.; 265–7541. A below-sea walk through corridors of dramatic exhibits. Open daily, 10 A.M.–5 P.M.

*Oregon State University Marine Science Center;* 867–3011. Exhibits, lectures, movies—all for free. Well-planned living museum, augmented by fine bookshop. Open daily, 10 A.M.–5 P.M.

**Tillamook:** *Tillamook County Pioneer Museum,* 2016 2nd St.; 842–4553. In addition to its marvelous wildlife exhibits, the museum has fine logging, Indian, and historical displays, as well as a military room and a mineral collection. Open 10 A.M.–6 P.M. daily.

**Yachats:** The *Prehistoric Life Museum* is a free museum devoted to fossils. It also sells equipment for rockhounds, semi-precious jewelry, and gifts. It's located just below the Cape Perpetua Visitor Center in the Siuslaw National Forest. For details call 547–3836.

**THEATER. Cannon Beach:** *Coaster Theatre,* a playhouse, presents family entertainment from July through August by Portland University Players, 436–1242. A year-round director brings visual and dramatic events, highlighted by the special Dickens program in December. Contact Chamber of Commerce, 436–2623, for more information.

**SHOPPING. Bandon:** *Harbor Vista Gift Shop & Tea Room,* 755½ 2nd; 347–4122. A delightful place to browse, sip tea, and watch the harbor activities. *Oregon Myrtlewood Factory at Candlewood,* Hwy. 101 S.; 347–2500. Retail selling of fine wares of this unique wood. *Out of the Woods— Myrtlewood,* Hwy. 101, Box 1325; 347–2721. Noted for expressive designs. *Pacific Myrtlewood Products,* Hwy. 101; 347–2200. Another fine display of myrtlewood giftware. *Zumwalt's Myrtlewood Factory,* Rte. 1, Box 1222; 347–3654. Retail trade of well-crafted myrtlewood products.

**Brookings:** *The Gray Whale,* 553 Chetco; 469–2024. Sea lore in the form of hand-wrought products. *Old Fashion Fantasy's,* 1007 Chetco; 469–6311. Odd things and square things in an enticing mileu.

**Cannon Beach: Antiques:** *Elaine's Attic,* 231 W. Coos; 436–2751. Antiques and collectibles. By appointment. *Heartwood Antiques,* 2432 S. Hemlock; 436–1260. Midwest and primitive collectibles and furniture. *Mariner Market,* 139 N. Hemlock; 436–2442. Nostalgic grocery containers, signs, and furnishings. **Food stores:** *Bruce's Candy Kitchen,* 256 N. Hemlock; 436–2641. Candy makers who ship anywhere. Delicious salt taffee. *Berger's Cannon Beach Bakery,* 144 N. Hemlock; 436–2592. Probably the most popular commercial place in Cannon Beach; it always seems crowded. The slogan here may be "Haystack Bread Our Specialty" but most customers come for the pastries. *The Ice Creamery,* 232 N. Hemlock St. Nostalgic and unique ice cream parlor; 16 flavors; hand-packed cartons. *Pat's Coffees and Baskets,* 255 N. Hemlock; 436–2920. Imported coffees, teas, baskets and gifts. *The Wine Shack,* 263 N. Hemlock; 436–1100. The boast here is that the business has the "finest selection of wine on the North Coast." **Specialty shops:** *The Bird and Beach,* Cannon Beach Mall. Hand-crafted jewelry, shells, and gifts.

**Coos Bay/North Bend: Coos Bay:** *Fiddlesticks Toys and Joys,* 345 Central; 267–6615. Joyful, well-stocked place. *Greater Things Import,* 180 Central; 269–7525. This could be the best import house on the coast. *Hilda's Chalet Antiques & Collectibles,* 818 S. Broadway; 269–5615. Homey place with ever-changing inventory. *House of Myrtlewood,* 1125 S. 1st; 267–7804. One of the really famous myrtlewood places in Oregon. More than 200 items provided. Tours. *Nature's Best Burl Products,* 1662 Ocean Blvd.; 888–4438. Wide variety of myrtlewood gifts. *The Oregon Shoppe,* 700 S. Broadway; 269–7032. Specializing in Oregon products. *The Velvet Teasel,* 198 S. 2nd; 267–5321. Cleverly displayed items.

**North Bend:** *Bayview Myrtlewood,* 3955 Coast Hwy. 101; 756–2582. Established in 1911 and still a leader in hand-crafted myrtlewood. *Classical Glass Stained Glass Studios,* 2269 Broadway; 756–7360. Everything that glitters. *G & B Myrtlewood Products,* 3862 Tremont; 756–5823. A strong stock of myrtlewood gifts. *Old World Antiques,* 2072 Sherman Ave. N.; 756–2121. Some "sleeper" bargains here for the discriminating. *Pony Village;* 756–3191. The largest and most unusual shopping center on the Oregon Coast. Few outstanding shops but the design, charm, and spirit of Pony Village makes it a travel experience. *Seadrift Flowers,* Public Square Shopping Center; 756–0531. Offbeat, avant-garde shop that is bright and crisp. *The Unicorn Castle,* 1058 Virginia; 756–2911. Smart shop that is well-stocked and fresh-looking. *The Buttery,* Sandpiper Square; 436–2723. Country-kitchen wares. *Elizabeth Boyer Interiors,* 192 N. Hemlock; 436–2601. Art in stitchery. *Fair Winds,* 120 N. Hemlock; 436–1201. Marine antiques, artifacts, and rare items. *Melo Cactus,* Haystack Square; 436–1367. Rare and exotic cacti. *Once Upon a Breeze,* 253 N. Hemlock. Kites of distinction.

**Florence:** *Catch the Wind,* Bay St. The place to buy your kites for fun on the beach. *The Bay Window,* Bay St. Unique, coast-crafted gifts.

**Gold Beach:** *By the Rogues,* Beach Mall; 247–2721. Gifts from the southern Oregon Coast. *The Silvertree,* 310 N. Ellensburg; 247–2714. A favorite with tourists who want to bring back mementos of their visit here.

**Port Orford:** *The Wooden Nickle,* 1205 Oregon: 332–5201. Fine myrtlewood products in decorative shop.

 **GALLERIES. Bandon:** *River's End Gallery,* 2nd and Baltimore. Paintings and crafts by local artists. Daily 9 A.M.–5 P.M., June 1–September 30; rest of year 10 A.M.–4 P.M.

**Cannon Beach:** *All This & Heaven Too,* 165 Second St.; 436–2504. Famed for its otter wood pottery. *Cannon Beach Stained Glass,* 987 S. Hemlock; 436–2761. Windows, lampshades, window hangings. *Den of Oz,* 216½ N. Hemlock. Working studio of artist Don Osborne and sales of fine art. *The Ingle-Nook,* Sandpiper Square; 436–2553. Weaving, jewelry, ceramics, imported baskets, and yarns. *Framian Gallery of Cannon Beach,* 187 S. Hemlock; 436–2964. Picture matting and framing. *Greaver Gallery,* S. Hemlock and E. Monroe; 436–1185. Paintings, drawings, and graphics by Hanne and Harry Greaver. *Haystack Gallery,* 183 N. Hemlock; 436–2547. Painting, sculpture, prints, fiber art, and photography. *The Lodestone,* Haystack Square; 436–2277. Sculpture and jewelry. *Ocean Pottery,* W. 2nd near Hemlock. Stoneware. *Puffin Gallery,* Coaster Theatre Square; 436–1142. Watercolors, oils, prints by recognized Northwest artists. Delft, porcelain, stoneware. *Steidel's Art,* Sandpiper Square; 436–2210. Paintings and prints by Bill Steidel. *Wavecrest,* S. Hemlock at Brallier Rd.; 436–2842. Custom hand-weaving. *The Weathervane,* 130 N. Hemlock; 436–2808. Metal sculpture and windows by David Louis and Jeff Hull. *The White Bird Gallery,* 251 N. Hemlock; 436–2681. Fine arts and crafts. *Worcester Glass Works,* Gower and Hemlock Sts. Glass blowing—art-glass sculpture.

**Charleston:** *Wood 'n' Things 'n' Wooden Things,* 4826 Boat Basin Dr.; 888–3491.

**Florence:** *River Roost Art Studio,* 129 Nopal St. Collection of central Oregon Coast artists. *Wind Drift Gallery,* 1250 Bay St. Features the works of local artists.

**Gold Beach:** *Gull Gallery,* 756 N. Ellensburg; 247–7513. A fine place for tourist browsing. *Pelican's Pouch Gallery,* 705 S. Ellensburg; 247–2311. Individualistic—covering a fascinating spectrum of style.

**Lincoln City:** *Alder House II,* one-half mile east of U.S. 101 on Immonen Rd. A glassblowing studio where the owner works in the traditional off-hand method, with each piece being completely individualized in design. *Lincoln Art Galleries,* 620 N.E. Hwy. 101; 994–5839. The best-known and most elaborate of the galleries in Lincoln City. Specializing in Western and marine art; fine gift shop. *Lincoln City Art Guild,* 1006 S.E. 51st.; 996–4111. Many of the artists in the area congregate here and show their works. An attractive building with an airy interior. *Mossy Creek Pottery and Gallery,* located in a wooded setting ½ mile off U.S. 101 on Immonen Rd.; 996–2415. A small pottery workshop emphasizing a limited production of fine handmade pottery by the owner, and a gallery featuring the work of other excellent artists and craftspeople. *Oceans West,* 30 S.E. Hwy. 101; 994–2755. One of the coast's largest galleries and gift shops. The works of more than 300 artists are on display. Sculptors working in metal seem to like this place. *Oceanside Galleries,* ½ mile northeast of Lincoln Plaza Shopping Center on U.S. 101; 994–5391. Upcoming artists find the galleries receptive to new talent and there is always an air of excitement here. *The Red Cock,* 1323 N.W. Hwy. 101; 994–2518. A variety of styles in this smaller and artier gallery. One feels the intimacy here of being in an artist's studio. *Thelma Pearson Gallery,* 446 S.E. Hwy. 101; 994–3276. A very respected name in Oregon art circles, with a tradition of displaying and selling only quality products. Tourists with a sharp eye and some knowledge of art will find themselves at home here.

**North Bend:** *Hauser Arts Village,* 4207 Coast Hwy.; 756–6717. Attracts coastal artists who are experimental in form and tone. *Seaborne Gallery,* 1656 Sherman; 756–3451. A wide range of subjects, styles, and prices.

**Port Orford:** *The Art Hatchery,* 832 N. Oregon; 332–4011. The works of southern and central coast artists on display. *Pacific Folk & Fine Art Guild,* 264 W. 6th; 332–2512. Handsome arrangements and frequent exhibits. *Quarles Fine Art Studios & Gallery,* 519 Jefferson; 332–9061. Discriminating in taste and highly selective in display.

 **DINING OUT.** Classifications are based on the price of a full dinner for one, excluding tip and alcoholic beverages. *Inexpensive,* less than $10; *Moderate,* $10–$15; *Expensive,* $15–$25. Many of these establishments accept credit cards, but it's best to check in advance.

## ASTORIA

**Thunderbird Seafare Restaurant.** *Moderate.* 400 Industry St., at Thunderbird Motor Inn; 325–3551. Attractively decorated in nautical theme, with view of marina. Good selection of seafoods and steaks.

**Sunset Empire Room.** *Inexpensive.* 2813 Marine Dr.; 325–3551. Popular with Astorians. Cocktails and lounge. Open evenings only; closed major holidays.

**Drop Anchor Restaurant.** *Inexpensive.* 11 W. Marine Dr.; 325–3031. Neat, compact place, with a cheery ambiance. Children's menu. Closed Mondays.

## BANDON

**Andrea's Old Town Café.** *Inexpensive.* 160 Baltimore; 347–3022. Fine country cuisine; excellent homemade soup.

**Bandon Boatworks Restaurant.** *Inexpensive.* South Jetty Rd.; 347–2111. Fine dining with an ocean view.

**The Inn at Face Rock.** *Moderate.* 3225 Beach Loop Rd.; 347–9441. Exquisite cuisine.

## BROOKINGS

**Flying Gull.** *Inexpensive.* 1153 Chetco; 469–5700. One of the largest seafood menus on southern Oregon Coast.

## CANNON BEACH/TOLVANA PARK

**Tolovana Inn Restaurant.** *Moderate.* S. Hemlock and Warren Rd., Tolovana Park; 436–2211. Elegantly furnished, with tasty lunches and dinners.

**Lemon Tree Inn.** *Inexpensive.* 140 N. Hemlock; 436–2918. In the heart of Cannon Beach. A favorite with tourists. Omelet and seafood specialties.

**Morris' Rathskeller West Tavern.** *Inexpensive.* 224 N. Hemlock; 436–2870. A unique tavern in appearance and style. In addition to the potables, the charcoal-broiled hamburgers and steaks are delicious.

**Round Table Restaurant.** *Inexpensive.* 163 N. Hemlock; 436–2746. Great for early risers: opens at 6 A.M. Home cooking.

## CHARLESTON

**Portside.** *Moderate.* Boat Basin; 888–5544. French and Polynesian cuisine. Daily fresh seafood from dock.

## COOS BAY

### (See Also North Bend)

**Timber Inn Restaurant.** *Moderate.* Box 578; 267–4622. All-around good restaurant.

**Benetti's Italian Restaurant.** *Inexpensive.* 260 S. Broadway; 267–6066. Enjoy Italian hospitality and the veal scaloppini and lasagna.

**Hurry Back: The Good-Food Restaurant.** *Inexpensive.* 100 Commercial; 267–3933. Wholesome, homemade, and hearty food in a sidewalk café atmosphere. Lunch offers big deli sandwiches on seven different homemade breads. Dinners include fresh local seafood (nothing deep-fried), quiches, fondues, and homemade pastries.

**Knight of Cupse.** *Inexpensive.* 1740 Ocean Blvd. N.W.; 888–9531. Homemade pastries, espresso, cappucino—and good cheer.

## DEPOE BAY

**Whale Cove Inn.** *Moderate.* South of Depoe Bay on U.S. 101; 765–2255. Food equal to the scenic seaward views. Appetizing menu with family warmth.

**Channel House Restaurant.** *Inexpensive.* One block from Hwy. 101 at foot of Ellington St.; 765–2140. Good food and great views.

**The Sea Hag.** *Inexpensive.* On U.S. 101 in "mid-town"; 765–7901. Huge salad bar. Fish-and-chips buffet Monday. Lavish seafood buffet Friday. Prime rib special Saturday. Champagne brunch on Sundays. The hospitality is as good as the food.

## FLORENCE

**Driftwood Shores.** *Moderate.* Heceta Beach Rd.; 997–8544. Lively seafood menu; scampi a specialty. Well furnished; natty.

**Pier Point Inn.** *Moderate.* South of bridge on Hwy. 101; 997–7191. Fine food in dining room overlooking the Siuslaw River. Sunday brunch, 9 A.M.–3 P.M., is a winner.

**Windward Inn.** *Moderate* Hwy. 101 at 37th St. N.; 997–8243. Fanciest and best-known restaurant in town, featuring local seafoods, broiled steaks, and homemade pastries. Superb wine list.

**Charl's Pancake Haven.** *Inexpensive.* 1310 Hwy. 101; 997–2490. Family dining, featuring sourdough pancakes and homemade rolls.

**Lam's Sand & Sea.** *Inexpensive.* Hwy. 101 at 12th St.; 997–3813. Chinese and American menu; teriyaki steak a specialty. Orders to go. Congenial place with rapid and pleasant service.

**Mo's Restaurant.** *Inexpensive.* 1436 Bay St.; 997–2185. Good old Mo's, which got its start in Newport. Open seven days a week, 11 A.M.–9 P.M., for best clam chowder in these parts.

## GLENEDEN BEACH

**Salishan Lodge.** Hwy 101; 764–2371. **Gourmet Dining Room.** *Expensive.* Outstanding dining-room staff and careful attention to detail make a meal here a memorable experience. **Sun Room Coffee Shop.** *Moderate.* More casual dining offered in pleasant surroundings with the outdoors everywhere you look.

## GOLD BEACH

**Tu Tu Tun Lodge.** *Expensive.* 96550 N. Bank Rd.; 247–6664. Superb cuisine at a famous resort seven miles upstream on the Rogue River.

**Adventure on the Rogue.** *Moderate.* Jerry's Flat Rd.; 247–6626. Lounge and river-view dining are bonuses to gourmet prime ribs, seafood, and steaks.

**Rod 'n Reel.** *Moderate.* West of U.S. 101 off end of bridge; 247–6823. Full menu range in pleasurable surroundings.

**Sea, Earth & Sky.** *Inexpensive.* 1020 S. Ellensburg; 247–2322. Sumptuous sandwiches and lunches at this deli.

**The Golden Egg.** *Inexpensive.* 710 S. Ellensburg; 247–7528. Omelettes a specialty.

**Jot's Resort.** *Moderate.* North end of Rogue River Bridge on North Bank Rd.; 247–6676. Watch the Rogue ripple by as you enjoy fresh river and ocean fish.

**Perico's.** *Inexpensive.* 811 Ellensburg; 247–2033. Mexican food and pizza draw the locals here.

## LINCOLN CITY

**Inn at Spanish Head.** *Expensive.* 409 So. Hwy. 101; 996–2161. Luxurious dining in elegant surroundings. Sumptuous menu; immaculate service.

**International Dunes.** *Expensive.* 1501 N.W. 40th; 994–3655. Justly famous for its cuisine.

**Surftides Beach Resort.** *Expensive.* 2945 N.W. Jetty Ave.; 994–2191. Elegant fare and a romantic setting.

**Bay House.** *Moderate.* 5911 S.W. Hwy. 101; 996–3222. Charming view of Siletz Bay combines with such exquisite dishes as Bay House Oysters Sauté for a visual and palatable experience. This small, family-owned establishment prepares every request to order. Reservations essential.

**Road's End Dory Cove Restaurant.** *Moderate.* 5819 Logan Rd.; 994–5180. Chowder, fish and chips, oysters, clam strips, salmon, steak—this place has all the goodies, served in a soft-tone "roadside inn" atmosphere.

**Mo's.** *Inexpensive.* 860 S.W. 51st; 996–2535. Seafood at Mo's—their clam chowder is famous as far away as New York—is the best part of a trip to Lincoln City for some people.

## NESKOWIN

**Golden Cove Restaurant.** *Moderate to expensive.* At Neskowin Lodge, off Hwy. 101; 392–3191. Ocean view adds to fresh fish and seafood—or filet mignon. At sunset the captain's room becomes a hot nightspot.

## NEWPORT

**The Moorage at Embarcadero.** *Expensive.* On Bay Front; 547–4779. Nautical setting overlooking Yaquina Bay. Fantastic dining. Best single bargain on the coast may be the Friday-night seafood buffet. Everything—and more—for a fair price.

**Neptune's Wharf Restaurant.** *Moderate.* 325 S.W. Bay Blvd.; 265–2532. View the harbor, Yaquina Bay Bridge, seagulls, (and maybe) sunsets as you dine from a fine menu of seafood.

**Mo's.** *Inexpensive to moderate.* 622 S.W. Bay Blvd; 265–2979. This is the original home of this famous seafood spot, and it now has two—the original and an "annex." Some folks love Mo's so much that they just follow it along the coast, Lincoln City to Otter Rock to Newport. Frequently there's a long line to get in—particularly for Mo's famous clam chowder—so don't wait until you're starved. Sawdust floors, rough-hewn tables, and benches makes Mo's all the more charming.

## NORTH BEND
### (See Also Coos Bay)

**Kuni's Express.** *Moderate.* 1577 Sherman; 756–1612. Delicious Japanese cuisine.

**Manni's Hilltop House.** *Moderate.* 166 N. Bay Dr.; 756–6515. Candlelight-atmosphere dining room with clear view of bay.

**Fisherman's Grotto.** *Inexpensive.* Pony Village; 756–6341. Fish and chips, shrimp, scallops, clams, chowder: delicious in all respects.

**Gino's Pizza Inn.** *Inexpensive.* 1324 Virginia; 756–5000. 25 varieties—and all good.

**The Greek Gyro.** *Inexpensive.* Pony Village; 756–7811. Beef, seasoned with Greek herbs and spices, served in warm pita bread.

## OTTER ROCK

**Mo's West.** *Inexpensive.* 765–2442. Small, colorful restaurant a few yards from the rocky coast. Wonderful seafood.

## REEDSPORT

**Sarratt's Seacoast Restaurant.** *Inexpensive.* Route 4W; 271–5715. Full menu and pleasant service. Menu varies but you can always count on good seafood.

**Sugar Shack Bakery.** *Inexpensive.* 145 N. 3rd; 271–3514. Appetizing light meals in sunny surroundings.

## SEASIDE

**Crab Broiler.** *Moderate.* Three miles south of town at junction of U.S. 101 and U.S. 26; 738–5313. One of the best-known restaurants on the coast, with exquisite interior and lovely gardens lighted at night. Seaside folks go here regularly, and so do people from towns much farther away. Word-of-mouth has made it famous beyond the borders of Oregon. Excellent selection of seafood steaks; also salads and sandwiches. Reservations advised.

## TILLAMOOK

**The Victory House.** *Moderate.* 2015 1st St.; 842–4111. Attractive dining room. Emphasis on seafoods and steaks but the entire menu is well prepared. Cocktails and lounge. Reservations advised.

**The Hadley House.** *Inexpensive.* 2203 3rd St.; 842–2101. Cozy family-type restaurant, with full menu and homemade pastries. From the minute you walk in you feel at home.

## WALDPORT

**Bayshore Restaurant and Lounge.** *Moderate.* 500 Bayshore Dr.; 563–3202. Superior food and service. The lounge is a popular local nightspot.

## YACHATS

**The Adobe.** *Moderate.* Hwy. 101. A good seafood restaurant in the motel.
**Beulah's Sea View Inn.** *Moderate.* Hwy. 101; 547–3215. Fine view of bay; good menu of seafood and other popular dishes. Reservations advised.
**La Serre.** *Moderate.* Off U.S. 101 at 2nd and Beach; 547–3420. Attractive dining room; specialties here are shellfish. Reservations advised.

 **BARS AND NIGHT LIFE. Bandon:** *The Bandon Boatworks Restaurant* (see "Dining Out," above) is a popular night spot. Intimate lounge and entertainment attract locals and visitors.

**Brookings:** *Bob's One on One Tavern,* Hwy. 101; 469–2419. A pleasant place to meet the local folks. The *Myrtlewood Lounge* in the *Flying Gull* restaurant (see "Dining Out") is the main magnet in Brookings after the sun goes down.

**Cannon Beach/Tolvana Park:** *Bill's Tavern,* 188 N. Hemlock, 436–2202, is where the locals hang out and swap stories about the tourists, who, of course, swap stories about them. *Driftwood Inn,* 179 N. Hemlock; 436–2439, livens up in the cocktail lounge when the stars come out. *Tolovana Inn* (see "Dining Out") bids welcome to warm-hearted folks in search of cocktails. *Whaler Restaurant,* 200 N. Hemlock, 436–2821, serves up live music in the Harpoon Room Lounge come evening. And there is dancing in the Hatch Room.

**Coos Bay** (see also North Bend): *Balboa Bay Club,* 1125 Empire Blvd.; 888–4774. One of the favorite cocktail lounges in the area. *Belle Bee Tavern,* 702 Newmark; 888–5231. Small-town sociability. *Blue Moon Tavern,* 871 S. Broadway; 269–7514. Gusty and warm-hearted place with no frills. *The El Toro,* 3290 Ocean Blvd.; 267–3632. No bull and all bull; storytellers and good times. *Fran's Tavern,* 365 S. Broadway; 269–0641. A trademark among tavern goers. *Goodfellows Tavern,* 143 Hall. Aptly named by old-timers and newcomers. *The Silver Dollar,* 479 Newmark; 888–9723. Tops to the many faithful clientele. *Thunderbird Motor Inn,* 1313 N. Bayshore; 267–4141. A pleasant watering hole when day is done. *Timber Inn Restaurant,* 1001 N. Bayshore; 267–4622. Live music at the DJ Bar.

**Depoe Bay:** (see "Dining Out,") At the *Channel House Restaurant,* folks gather after sundown at the *Oyster Bar and Inn* for cocktails and gossip. At the *Sea Hag,* cocktails come with live music in an upbeat atmosphere. For the Humphrey-Bogart-and-Ingrid-Bergman-in-spirit souls, the *Whale Cove Inn* is a retreat in mood as well as an off-the-beaten place geographically.

**Florence:** Live music Wednesday, Friday, Saturday, and Sunday nights at the *Pirate's Cove* at *Driftwood Shores* (see "Dining Out," above); dancing, too. Town folks gather at *Sea Gull Tavern,* 1161 Hwy. 101 N., 997–3883; *Fisherman's*

*Wharf,* 1341 Bay St., 997-2613; and *Woahink Landing,* 83693 Hwy. 101 S., 997-2721. At the *Seawall,* in *Pier Point Inn* (also see "Dining Out," above), there is the bubble of merriment; the *Windward Inn* attracts a rather subdued, dressed-up crowd.

**Gold Beach:** *Chowderhead Restaurant,* 910 S. Ellensburg; 247-7174. There's always local color and charm here, joined in by tourists. *Cork's,* Nesika Beach; 247-7782. A tavern where good times flow along with the river. *Hunters Creek Tavern,* 28773 Hunter Creek Loop; 247-7509. *O J's Tavern,* Beach Loop Rd.; 247-2342. "There are no strangers here," say the patrons. *P. J. Catlocks Arcade,* 230 N. Ellensburg; 247-7393. Laughs and tall stories here to while the night away.

**Lincoln City** (see "Dining Out"): *Inn at Spanish Head.* Cocktails and entertainment in the most striking setting in or around Lincoln City. *International Dunes Ocean Front Resort.* Dancing nightly at *Henry Thiele at the Dunes*— a most romantic setting. *Surftides Beach Resort.* "Over-the-waves" dancing and entertainment, year-round, at Robert Dumond's restaurant here.

**Newport:** Many gather after sundown at the *Newport Hilton* (see "Hotels and Motels"), at the lounge of the *Embarcadero* (see "Dining Out"), and in the *Dolphin Room* of *Neptune's Wharf* (see "Dining Out"). At the Dolphin Room, there is live music Friday and Saturday nights; at the Embarcadero a piano bar adds a romantic touch to the evening. Locals in the know let the out-of-towners trek off to the motels listed above for night life, but they make their way to the *Pit Tide,* 836 S.W. Bay Blvd., 265-7030, down on Bay Front. The house guard says the Pit Tide is not only the swingingest place in town, it's the only place. And they add that the real fisherfolk spirit of Newport is here.

**North Bend** (see also Coos Bay): *The Hook Tender,* 2043 Sherman; 756-2175. A tavern popular with longshoremen and loggers. *Humboldt Club.* 2056 Sherman; 756-6314. Always a relaxing atmosphere. *Manni's Hilltop House.* 166 N. Bay; 756-6314. The fun place for the "beautiful people" of the area. *Ron's Tap & Bottle,* 5815 Wildwood; 759-3701. A bar that reflects the breeziness of the area. *Sawmill Restaurant and Lounge.* 3491 Broadway; 756-0575. Dancing, entertainment, and a big-screen TV.

**Port Orford:** *Peg Leg Saloon,* Hwy. 101; 332-9461. A bright spot for local fisherfolks and ranchers come in from the hills. *Pitch's Tavern,* 6th and Washington; 332-8841. For people in the know, this is where the good night life takes place in Port Orford.

In **Waldport** the *Bayshore Restaurant and Lounge* livens up at night. (See "Dining Out".)

# INLAND AREAS OF INTEREST

## CRATER LAKE

The unknown scribe who wrote of Crater Lake in *Oregon: End of the Trail* 45 years ago, reflected, perhaps without knowing it, the effect the lake has upon those who pause to really see it:

> Chaliced in the crater of an extinct volcano, walled by majestic cliffs, and miraculously blue, it is one of Earth's most beautiful lakes. No one can stand without reverence in the presence of this sublime creation. A beholder becomes silent as the sea at his feet.
>
> Not only the beauty of the lake and its utterly blue color, but its crater within a crater makes it unique among the world's great scenic features. Crater Lake has been named with the Grand Canyon of the Colorado and Victoria Falls of Africa as one of the three greatest scenic marvels of the globe. Set high in Mount Mazama's shattered crest, its rugged cliffs rise to imposing heights. These implacable walls of volcanic rock send their reflected color into the deep, still water, so blended that the reality and the image are one. The two perfectly mirrored islands that seem but illusion add to the mystical effect.

Geologists believe that glacier-covered, prehistoric Mount Mazama towered 15,000 feet, surpassing any of the existing peaks of the Cascade Range. In all likelihood, no human being ever beheld Mazama. The lake was formed eons ago when Mazama exploded, in a sort of volcanic suicide, forming the great crater, 4,000 feet deep. Seepage and precipitation filled the caldera with water, and as it rose precipitation and seepage were eventually balanced by evaporation. The result is a lake that is 6-miles long and 4½-miles wide, is 1,932 feet deep, and has a 20-mile shoreline that is encircled by 500- to 2,000-feet-high cliffs. The elevation of the lake's surface is 6,177 feet.

Until 1888 it was believed the lake had no fish. Steel, thinking so too, gently slipped 37 fingerlings into the lake—survivors of the 600 he scooped from the Rogue River and hauled in a bucket all the way, pausing at streams to freshen the water. Over the roughest terrain he carried the bucket in his hand. He regarded it as something of a miracle that the few survivors had sufficient life to swim away, even feebly. More fish were added over the years and the lake now has a fish population numbering in the thousands.

Within the lake the outstanding feature is without question Wizard Island, a symmetrical cinder cone rising about 760 feet above the surface of the lake. It has a crater 400 feet in diameter and approximately 80 feet deep. Wizard Island is reached by regular boat trips during the summer. A 1½-mile trail leads from the landing to the crater. The launch trip starts from Cleetwood Cove, at the foot of mile-long Cleetwood Trail, which begins along Rim Drive eleven miles from Rim Village.

A lesser volcanic island, but attractive and photogenic, is the Phantom Ship, resembling an old double-masted sailing ship. The sharp pinnacles are the masts, 175 feet tall, and the pine and fir trees blend into ropes and rigging. The best views are from the launches and from Kerr Notch on Rim Drive.

Crater Lake Lodge, at the rim of the lake, is the starting point of daily ranger-guided and bus tours around the lake. There is no charge for joining the caravan of cars that gather at the lodge for the guided tours.

Rim Drive, 35 miles in length, is one-way, because of its narrowness, and almost encircles the caldera. Numerous lookout points along the road reveal the lake in varied forms and moods, all spellbinding. Rim Drive is open from about July 4 to September 25, depending on snow conditions.

A ¾-mile paved spur road off Rim Drive, on the east rim, leads to Cloudcap, about 1,770 feet above the lake, providing one of the finest views of the phenomenon.

Another place from which to view the lake without exerting yourself is the parapet of Sinnott Memorial Overlook, a picturesque stone building below the visitor center. Inside, a large relief map locates landmarks and other significant features of the park. The history of the lake is explained in pictures, and the walls are covered with pictures and paintings of the lake. Park rangers give lectures daily, on the half-hour. Open July 1 to September 15, weather permitting.

Llao Rock, a lava flow that inundated an ancient crater, and was named for Llao, Indian god of the underworld, is on the north rim of the lake. Long before the first whites showed up here, the Indians, particularly the Klamaths, had woven a body of mythology to explain the various characteristics of the lake and its environs. Young Indians tested their courage by descending to the water, and medicine men of ancient tribes journeyed here to seek the knowledge and the secrets of the gods.

The Watchman, a rock formation 1,800 feet above the lake and directly west of Wizard Island, is the focal point for an extraordinary view of the park. It is reached via a good trail, and is approximately a 20-minute hike from Rim Drive.

Hillman Peak, directly to the north of the Watchman, at 8,156 feet, is the highest point on the rim. It was named for the first white to look upon Crater Lake.

Mount Scott, at 8,926 feet, is the "roof" of the park, and the views from the top are panoramic, as might be expected. A 2½-mile trail from Rim Drive to an abandoned lookout station at the summit can be negotiated without trouble by people in good condition.

Garfield Peak, at 8,060 feet, is the most-climbed of the mountains along the rim. It is reached by a 1¾-mile trail from the lodge and is worth the trip, for the views from the summit are superb.

Much of the activity at Crater Lake starts in, at, or from the visitor center. In addition to providing information on almost every phase of park life, it has exhibits on the geology, fauna, and flora of the park. In summer, evening programs are given by park rangers. The visitor center is open only in summer.

The beautiful Castle Crest Wildflower Garden is near park headquarters.

The National Park is more than the lake, yet not many people venture away from the lake area. Few see the Pinnacles, slender spires of cemented pumice and scoria that rise to a height of up to 200 feet above the floor of Wheeler Creek Canyon, near the east boundary of the park. Fluted columns that have eroded from soft volcanic material are prominent in Sand Creek Canyon. There are also, away from the lake, velvety meadows and dreamy marshes, more than 500 species of flowering plants and ferns, and birds galore. More than 70 species of birds make the park their habitat and another 130 species have been identified here. In the park's three zones of vegetation live many animals, including deer and bear.

The park and administration building are open all year. Oregon 62, which is theoretically an all-weather road, is the shortest road to the park—Rim Drive is only 74 miles from Medford, southern Oregon's largest city, via this route. In actuality, 62—the only winter road into the park—has not infrequently been closed because of heavy snows.

The northern entrance road (reached by Oregon 138, 15 miles west of U.S. 97), traditionally opens about June 15, but intemperate weather can delay that date.

With winter—meaning snow, which can come long before calendar winter—come snowmobiles. They are permitted to operate only on the north entrance road. Cross-country skiers and snowshoers also arrive on the heels of the first good snow. Those planning overnight trips are required to register at park headquarters. Snowshoe hikes led by park rangers are offered on Saturdays and Sundays. The park does not possess ski tows, ski equipment, or snomobile facilities. If weather permits, a lunch counter at the lodge is open, but snow activists should not count on it. Most people taking to the snow at Crater Lake are day-users, returning in the late afternoon to Medford and other towns in the lowlands.

Pets do not have a happy time at Crater Lake. They are not permitted to enter public buildings or be taken on hikes. They are, for the most part, confined to vehicles or walked on leashes in restricted areas.

## SUNRIVER

Oregon's largest resort, Sunriver, is 175 miles from Portland and 15 miles south of Bend, the second-largest city in the state east of the Cascades. The 3,300-acre Sunriver, started in 1969 principally as a resort, is in a natural forest setting on the banks of the Deschutes River. It is now a community with municipal services and has a zip code of its own (97702). All electrical and telephone lines are underground at Sunriver, eliminating the unsightly network of wires often found in suburban developments. The current developed area consists of approximately 1,100 homes. In addition, there are now over 590 condominiums constructed at various locations throughout the property. The community has some 800 year-round residents.

For visitors, there is Sunriver Lodge with its condominium units, and about 150 private resort homes and condominiums available through the Sunriver rental program.

Sunriver Lodge houses dining and lounge facilities (see below) and also provides meeting and banquet rooms to accommodate convention groups of up to 350.

Recreation facilities at Sunriver include two 18-hole golf courses; 18 tennis courts—three indoor; 20 miles of paved bike paths, two swimming pools, a wading pool, racquetball club, stables, marina, jogging course, nature center, arts-and-crafts center, gameroom, and a bike/cross-country ski pavilion. It also has canoes and inflatable rafts for paddling the Deschutes River. And then there is fishing. The Deschutes is noted for its brookies, rainbows, and German browns. When Sun River, a stream near the Lodge, freezes, ice skating is allowed and the Lodge area is lit for night skating.

The Sunriver Country Mall includes varied stores and a variety of professional services. Near the mall are a pizza parlor, Mexican restaurant, light eating establishments, book store, service station, and a family physician.

Mt. Bachelor, 18 miles northwest, offers Alpine and Nordic skiers superb skiing, with the season usually extending from late August through late May, depending on the available snow. Completion of a chair lift to the 9,060-foot summit of Mt. Bachelor permits all-year operation, accommodating sightseers when the snow is gone. Cross-country skiing at Mt. Bachelor is on 32 kilometers (18 miles) of groomed trail; on the many miles of unmarked and marked trails in the Deschutes National Forest, which surrounds Sunriver; and at Sunriver itself, with 3,300 acres of woods and meadows. Trekking on the two snow-covered golf courses is popular. The area surrounding the lodge is lit for night skiing. Trails are laid for guests when snowfall permits.

### SKI RESORTS

Oregon snow sports are basically located on four independent mountain ranges; the Cascades, the Siskiyous, the Blue, and the Wallowas. The Siskiyous are shared with California; the others are completely in Oregon. Most snow areas are found on the Cascade Range, which traverses the state north to south.

More than a third of the state's downhill areas—five out of 14—are on Mt. Hood. The Mt. Hood areas profit from the mountain's proximity to Portland and its metropolitan suburbs; except for extremely bad weather, it should be no more than a 90-minute drive from downtown Portland to Government Camp, at the base of the Mt. Hood ski areas. Detailed information about the major resorts is given under "Skiing," in the *Practical Information* section that follows.

# PRACTICAL INFORMATION FOR INLAND AREAS
# OF INTEREST

(Note: All information on ski resorts is detailed under "Ski Resorts," below.)

**HOW TO GET THERE: Crater Lake National Park:** **By bus:** There is daily bus service from Klamath Falls, June 15–September 15. Buses leave from the Greyhound Depot at 1200 Klamath St.; call 882–4616. Buses also make daily trips around Rim Drive. They leave from Rim Drive; 594–2511. **By car:** Oregon 62 enters the park from the west and south; Oregon 138 enters from north and east. Oregon 62 is an all-weather road, although is has been known—not infrequently—to be closed because of heavy snows. Oregon 138 opens about June 15. Rim Drive, which circles Crater Lake is open around July 4–September 25.

**Sunriver: By air:** *Horizon Airways* from Portland to Redmond, 16 miles north of Bend. Cars can be rented at the airport in Redmond; see "By car," below. Sunriver's airport is for private craft only. **By train:** *Amtrak* from Portland to Chemult, where buses run to Sunriver. See "By bus," below. **By bus:** *Pacific Trailways* runs from Portland to Bend, where cars can be rented. *Resort Buslines* meets the train at Chemult and runs to Sunriver; call (503) 389–7755. **By car:** From Portland take U.S. 26 to U.S. 97 at Madra and continue down 97, through Bend to Sunriver Junction. Turn west; in two miles you'll reach Sunriver. *Hertz* has cars for rent at the the Sunriver Airport, (503) 593–1221, ext. 419; Redmond Airport, (503) 923–1411; and at Bend; (503) 382–1711; or call Hertz toll-free nationwide, (800) 654–3131.

**HOTELS AND MOTELS.** Price categories for double rooms are as follows: *Expensive,* $50 and up; *Moderate,* $36–$49; *Inexpensive,* below $36.

## CRATER LAKE

**Crater Lake Lodge.** *Moderate.* Crater Lake National Park; (503) 594–2511. At Rim Village. Open June 15–September 9. 80 units. Some rustic cottages. No pets. Not the best there could be but that's all there is.

## SUNRIVER

**Sunriver Lodge.** *Expensive.* Sunriver; (503) 593–1246 (call collect); toll free (800) 547–3922; Oregon toll free (800) 452–6874. 336 units. Housekeeping suites, houses, fireplaces, and porches. Seventy two-bedroom units; 55 three-bedroom units. Coin laundry; two heated pools; wading pool; saunas; whirlpool. Dock; fishing; golf; tennis courts; recreational program; rental bicycles; playground; exercise rooms; riding. Airstrip. No pets. Reservation deposit required; seven days refund notice. Dining room, coffee shop, cocktails, entertainment.

**CAMPING:** Crater Lake **National Park** has overnight camping. Nights are chilly even in summer. No reservations.

**TOURIST INFORMATION. Crater Lake:** Superintendent, Crater Lake National Park, Box 7, Crater Lake, OR 97604; (503) 594–2211. Mon.–Fri. 9 A.M.–5 P.M. Or contact the Visitors Center at (503) 594–2511. Open only in summer.

**Sunriver:** Sunriver Media Communication Department, Administration Office, Sunriver, OR 97702; (503) 593–1221, ext. 285.

**SEASONAL EVENTS.** Sunriver: **February 4–18:** *Sunriver Annual Juried Exhibit of Oregon Art.* Open to all Oregon artists. **December 3–January 27:** *Sunriver Owner-Resident Exhibit.* An art exhibit of the works of Sunriver residents.

**TOURS. Crater Lake:** Two-hour boat trips daily, 9 A.M.–3 P.M., mid-June–early September from Cleetwood Cove. Adults, $6.75; under 12, $3.75. Naturalists explain geologic and natural history of area. Cruises touch Wizard Island and the Phantom Ship. There are also daily ranger-guides driving tours that leave from Crater Lake Lodge.

For ski tours of the central Cascades, see "Winter Sports," below.

**SUMMER SPORTS. Crater Lake:** There is **fishing** and **hiking** throughout the park. **Sunriver** has **golf, tennis, bike** paths, **swimming** pools, **stables,** a **marina,** a **jogging** course, and **canoes** and **rafts** for paddling the Deschutes River. There is also **fishing** (notably for brook, rainbow, and German brown trout) on the Deschutes, **hiking, climbing,** and **bird watching.** Anyone can use the facilities for a user fee. Call the Sunriver number listed under "Hotels and Motels." Equipment for rent.

**WINTER SPORTS.** (See also "Ski Resorts," below.) Crater Lake: The lodge isn't open, but those interested in daytrips can **cross-country ski** and **snowshoe.** No equipment available. (Register at park headquarters if planning an overnight trip.) **Snowmobiles** are permitted only on the north entrance road.

**Sunriver: Skating, cross-country skiing, racquetball.** Equipment can be rented; user fee required. Call the lodge for more information. (see "Hotels and Motels.") There is twice-daily shuttle bus service to Mt. Bachelor—at 8:15 A.M. and noon. (See "Ski Resorts" below.)

**Cross-country ski tours** of the **central Cascades** are offered by *Oregon Trek,* Box 15230, Portland, 97215; (503) 238–1001.

For maps and details on Nordic terrain and the brochure, *Oregon Marked Cross-Country Trails,* write *USDA Forest Service,* Pacific Northwest Region, P.O. Box 3623, Portland, OR 97208; (503) 221–2971. For a catalog on skiing in Oregon, write *Tourism Division/Oregon Economic Development Department,* 595 Cottage St. N.E., Salem, OR 97310.

**SKI RESORTS.** *Anthony Lakes,* high in the Elkhorn Range of the Blue Mountains, lies in a magnificent Alpine lakes basin, where a backdrop of towering ridges thrusts up into the sky, catching ample amounts of fine, dry snow on the slopes. Here Anthony Lakes Ski Area offers all types of skiers the opportunity to enjoy miles of open powder, 10 kilometers (6 miles) of groomed cross-country trails, and a variety of packed runs descending from the 8,100-foot crest of the main lift. Throughout the season, daily sun and nightly snow dustings prevail, providing ideal snow pack and powder conditions.

Anthony Lakes is located 42 miles southeast of La Grande and 40 miles northwest of Baker. The season begins the end of November and extends through April.

The longest run is 1½ miles; there are 11 groomed runs, plus open powder. Lifts are one chair and one poma.

For cross-country, there are 10 kilometers (6 miles) of groomed trails; Alpine lakes area for touring; lessons; and equipment rentals.

Facilities include a day lodge, at 7,100 feet. It contains a cafeteria, lounge, ski school, and ski shop. Accommodations are available at North Powder (22 miles), La Grande, and Baker. Amtrak goes to La Grande and Greyhound goes to La Grande and Baker.

Contact Anthony Lakes Corporation, P.O. Box 3040, La Grande, OR 97850; (503) 963–8282.

*Cooper Spur,* 24 miles south of the Hood River, and about an hour's drive from the Government Camp-Timberline area, is reached from Portland via I-84 to Hood River (61 miles), then south on Oregon 35 (24 miles).

The season is from mid-December–mid-April.

Base altitude is 4,000 feet. Lifts are comprised of one rope tow and one T-bar. Facilities include a day lodge and fast food. Instruction is available for cross-country skiing. The nearest accommodations are at Hood River.

Cooper Spur is about one-third of the way up the mountainside to Cloud Cap, which confronts Eliot Glacier on Mt. Hood. But in the winter the road above Cooper Spur is closed; return in summer for some fantastic views.

Contact Cooper Spur Ski Area, 1850 Country Club Rd., Hood River, OR 97031; (503) 386–3381.

*High Wallowas Ski Area,* six miles south of Joseph, is in the Wallowa Mountains. The gondola that in summer carries tourists to the summit of 8,256-foot Mt. Howard is used for skiers on weekends December–May.

Below, in chutes, bowls, and trails, unspoiled powder skiing abounds. Above, craggy limestone and granite peaks soar to 10,000 feet, earning the area its title, "Switzerland of America." The longest run is 3½ miles, with a vertical drop of 3,700 feet; plus powder.

Cross-country skiers find trails at the summit of Mt. Howard, as well as Nordic touring in nearby wilderness terrain. Snowcat skiing is available for those seeking an unusual wilderness experience.

Day facilities include a summit warming hut and snack bar.

Lodging units equipped with fireplaces and kitchens are offered right at the base of the lift, on the south shore of beautiful, morainal Wallowa Lake. But there is a caveat: the resort is open by reservation only. Groups must call in advance—$200 minimum to open doors.

Accommodations without reservations are at Joseph, a colorful leathery village six miles from the gondola station, and Enterprise, the seat of Wallowa County, six miles away.

High Wallowas is the most difficult ski area to reach, though good roads connect to it. La Grande, 71 miles southwest, is reached by Amtrak and Greyhound. By car from Portland, take Interstate 84 to La Grande and Oregon 82 to Joseph.

Contact High Wallowas, Inc., Box 128, Joseph, OR 97846; (503) 432–5331 (call before you plan your trip).

*Hoodoo Ski Bowl,* 88 miles southeast of Salem and 43 miles northwest of Bend, is located in the Central Oregon Cascades and has been operating for more than 40 years.

Hoodoo is not a large mountain ski resort but its services and programs are designed to provide excellent winter recreation for the mid-Willamette Valley.

The season extends from December through April 15 and the area open daily. Night skiing is 4 P.M.–10 P.M. on Friday. The longest run is one mile, with vertical drop of 1,000 feet. There are 16 runs. Lifts are comprised of three double chairs and one rope tow.

For cross-country skiing, trails are close by and maintained by the area. There are adjacent Forest Service trails for experienced skiers. There is a ski school, a ski shop, and rentals.

Hoodoo has two day lodges, *The Deli,* serving assorted sandwiches and salads, and a bar. Overnight camper parking is welcome.

Accommodations are at Camp Sherman (15 miles) and at Sisters (20 miles.) Both are calendar-art locations. Camp Sherman, in a pine forest, is on the Metolius River. Sisters, a false-fronted "Old West" town, looks up to stunning panoramas of the white-blazing Three Sisters mountain range.

To reach Hoodoo Ski Bowl from Portland, take Interstate 5 to Oregon 22, at the south end of Salem, and follow to Hoodoo. Contact Hoodoo Ski Bowl, Box 20, Highway 20, Sisters, OR 97759.

*Mt. Ashland,* a Siskiyou Mountain resort in southwestern Oregon, is nine miles off Interstate 5 at the Oregon-California border. Its operating schedule is daily from the first skiable snowfall (generally late November–May 1).

The longest run here is ¾ mile, with a vertical drop of 1,150 feet; there are 23 runs. Top elevation is 7,500 feet and lodge elevation is at 6,600 feet. Bottom elevation is 6,350 feet. Lifts comprise two double chairs, one rope tow, one poma lift (weekdays and holidays only), and one T-bar.

Facilities include a day lodge, dining, lounge, ski shop, and rental concession.

Lodging is at Ashland (18 miles) and at Medford (33 miles). Horizon Air, United Airlines, and Greyhound go to Medford. By car from Portland or California, Interstate 5 to Ashland. Contact Ski Ashland, Box 220, Ashland, OR 97520; (503) 482–2987.

*Mt. Bachelor,* 22 miles from Bend and 18 miles from Sunriver, is the most famous ski area in Central Oregon and the largest ski complex in the state.

The season generally begins in early November and runs through August (one of the longest in North America).

From Mt. Bachelor, all the high peaks of the Oregon Cascades swim into view and one has the feeling here of being on top of the world.

In 1983 Bachelor celebrated its 25th anniversary with the addition of a new chairlift to the mountain's 9,060-foot summit. The "lift to the top" provides for 3,100 vertical feet of terrain and 360-degree skiing off the top. The chair is used for sightseeing purposes when the snow is gone.

The longest run is approximately two miles, with a vertical drop of 3,100 feet. There are more than 40 runs. The area has five triple and five double chair lifts; 25 kilometers (15 miles) of groomed, double-tracked trails; a Nordic sports center, with lessons; and guided picnic tours.

Facilities include four day lodges, dining, live music and entertainment, a ski school, recreational race department, ski and rental shop, and state-licensed day-care center for children six weeks to six years.

Accommodations are available at Sunriver Lodge, Inn of the Seventh Mountain at the foot of Mt. Bachelor *(Expensive;* call (503) 382–8711 for more information), and Bend. Resort Bus Lines provides shuttle service between these points and the ski area. Contact Mt. Bachelor, Inc., Box 1031, Bend, OR 97709; (503) 382–2442.

*Mt. Bailey,* on the crest of the Cascades in south-central Oregon, near Diamond Lake Resort (and only a short drive from Crater Lake National Park), is called "the ultimate backcountry ski experience." The mountain rises to a height of 8,363 feet, providing a drop of over 2,800 vertical feet.

There are no lifts, no fancy lodges, and very few people. Instead, there is a Pisten Bully snowcat and a rustic cabin. Being transported in the enclosed snowcat, receiving personal attention and an alpine lunch, finds favor with practically every one of the small number of skiers here. Fewer than 20 people each day try the challenging bowls, chutes, and glades on Mt. Bailey. An experienced mountain guide takes skiers where the mountain is best.

Each day begins at 7 A.M. in the lobby of the Diamond Lake Resort. The parking area is 9 miles from the lodge. After the skiers arrive, the guides load the gear aboard the snowcat; packs and cameras are encouraged. Coffee is provided on the initial one-hour ride. After the skiers complete the runs and the catch-line traverse, the snowcat gives skiers a quick ride back to the top.

Around 1 P.M. an alpine lunch of breads, meats, cheese, vegetables, and homemade pies is served. By 4 P.M., each skier has completed about 15,000 vertical feet of skiing, the sun is setting on Mt. Bailey, and the snowcat is heading home.

The season extends December–April; Wednesday–Sunday. Reservations are required for snowcat skiing and lodging. A deposit for the first day of skiing and for lodging is required at the time of booking, with full payment upon arrival.

Fine dining and overnight lodging are available at Diamond Lake Resort *(Inexpensive)* and at Steamboat Inn ( *Moderate,* 40 miles from Mt. Bailey).

Diamond Lake Resort has a choice of three restaurants and accommodations include cabins and motels. Steamboat Inn offers good dining and secluded cabins. Transportation is provided by the Inn to Mt. Bailey.

Rates at Mt. Bailey are $55 per day and include a full day of skiing, personal attention, alpine lunch, the use of avalanche beacons, and, weather permitting, the use of video equipment. A season pass is $600.

A word of caution: snowcat skiing on Mt. Bailey is not for everyone. The visitor should be able to ski different types of terrain and snow conditions. In addition, the skier should be physically fit since there is steep terrain as well as the difficult catch-line traverse.

Amtrak and bus lines stop at Chemult. Air service and rental cars are available to and at Eugene, Klamath Falls, Medford, and Redmond.

By car from Portland: Interstate 5 to Roseburg and then Oregon 138 to Steamboat Inn and Diamond Lake Resort. The resort is 80 miles east of Roseburg. The drive from Portland to the resort should take about 5½ hours. Contact Mt. Bailey, Diamond Lake Resort, Diamond Lake, OR 97731; (503) 793-3333.

*Mt. Hood Meadows,* 11 miles east of Government Camp, has its season from November until May. The mountain is met face-on here. The longest run is three miles, with a vertical drop of 2,777 feet; and there are over 50 trails and slopes, divided as follows: beginners—30 percent; intermediate—40 percent; advanced —20 percent; expert—10 percent.

Lifts are comprised of seven double chairs, including a beginner's chair, and one complimentary rope tow.

Heather Canyon is a three-mile outback downhill adventure.

Hours of operation are 9 A.M.–4:30 P.M., Monday and Tuesday; 9 A.M.–10:30 P.M., Wednesday–Friday; 9 A.M.–10 P.M., Saturday; 9 A.M.–7 P.M., Sunday.

For cross-country skiing there is the Nordic Touring Center; equipment rentals; lessons; 26 kilometers (16 miles) of trails; ski school; and ski shop.

Facilities include a large day lodge, dining, fast food, lounge, entertainment, dancing Wednesday–Sunday; in-lodge video system.

Nearby accommodations are at Government Camp (11 miles) and Welches, 23 miles.

From Portland, take US 26 to Oregon 35 and turn north.

Contact Mt. Hood Meadows, Box 47, Mt. Hood, OR 97041; (503) 337-2222.

The twin mountains of *Multorpor Ski Bowl* offer the closest skiing to Portland. The site is lovely: nestled in a wooded alpine setting with numerous crossover trails.

Multorpor Ski Bowl opens early in December and closes in mid-April. It is closed Mondays except Christmas and Spring vacations.

Its longest run is 1½ miles, with a vertical drop of 1,400 feet; and has 12 groomed runs, plus open slopes. There are 4 double chairlifts and 7 rope tows. Night skiing is Tue–Sun. to 10 P.M. on all 4 lifts.

For cross-country skiing there are lessons and equipment rentals adjacent to the area.

A relatively new addition to Multorpor is the 2-tracked Alpine Slide (1 for fast folks, 1 for slow folks), with the season from May 30–Oct. 31.

Facilities are comprised of 2 day lodges, lounge, ski school, and rental shop. Accommodations are at Government Camp (0.5 miles) and Welches, 13 miles.

Contact Multorpor Ski Bowl, Box 87, Government Camp, OR 97208; (503) 272-3522.

*Spout Springs,* in the Blue Mountains above the great wheat fields of Oregon, is 44 miles from Pendleton and 40 miles from Walla Walla, WA.

It is localized in clientele, although the beauty of the Blue Mountains attracts some outsiders.

The season traditionally begins on Thanksgiving and continues Wednesday–Sunday through March. There is skiing every night except Sunday.

The longest run is one mile, with a vertical drop of 550 feet; there are ten runs. Spout Springs has two double chairs, a rope tow, and a T-bar lift.

Cross-country enthusiasts find a 16 kilometer (10 mile) trail system through the peaceful mountain woods that lives up to this place's reputation as a fine touring area.

Facilities include two day lodges, a café, snack bar, and lounge, serving skiers day and evening throughout the season. Base facilities also include a ski shop with rentals and a ski school.

Lodgings in Elgine (18 miles), with other accommodations found in Milton-Freewater (30 miles), Walla Walla (40 miles), and Pendleton (44 miles). Horizan Air, Amtrak and Greyhound go to Pendleton. Hertz has a rental agency in Pendleton. Contact Spout Springs, Inc., Rt. 1, Weston, OR 97886; (503) 566-2015.

*Summit Ski Area,* a half-mile east of Government Camp, has a rather short season: December–March 31.

It has a base altitude of 4,000 feet and a vertical drop of 400 feet; one double chairlift and one rope tow.

Facilities include day lodge, food service, equipment rental for downhill, cross country, tubing, or discing, lessons, and a ski shop.

Accommodations are at Government Camp and at Welches. Contact Summit Ski Resort, P.O. Box 385, Government Camp, OR 97028; (503) 272-3351.

*Timberline,* on 11,235-foot Mt. Hood, is the oldest and most popular of ski areas in Oregon, probably because of its Timberline Lodge, built by the W.P.A. and dedicated in 1937 by President Franklin Roosevelt.

Located on the south face of Mt. Hood, Timberline calls itself the "only year-round ski area in America" as well as "North America's first summer ski area."

The longest run is 2½ to 5 miles long, depending on the weather, with a vertical drop of up to 3,700 feet; there are 23 runs. Summer skiing is made possible by the Palmer chairlift, while in winter five double chairs and one rope tow carry visitors to snowfields of wide-open runs, trails, and chutes.

Cross-country skiing is available, with numerous trails and a new Nordic center offering tours, track and downhill telemark lessons, and events.

There are two lodges at the site. The most famous by far is Timberline Lodge, which is open all year and has lodging, dining, a lounge, year-round heated outdoor pool, and a sauna. The Lodge is a huge stone castle built by hand from native materials: for the exterior, stone from nearby quarries; for the interior, hand-hewn timbers from the forests below. Details in iron, wood, fabric, and watercolors give the lodge, including each guest room, a unique identity.

Accommodations at the Lodge, which has 56 units, range from *moderate* to *expensive*. Two-day minimum stay on weekends. Reservation deposit required.

As dusk sets, the *Cascade Dining Room* beckons with candlelight and sparkling fireplace. Cuisine is American and Continental; prices range from *moderate* to *expensive*.

The *Ram's Head Bar* overlooking the main lobby provides after-dark entertainment. Paul Bunyan smiles from the murals in the *Blue Ox Bar,* the favorite for storytellers.

Timberline Lodge now has a neighbor—the Wy'east Day Lodge, built across the parking lot. The attractive 44,000-square-foot building houses rental and ticket facilities, ski shop, gift shop, ski school. It also has a broad food menu (with quick service), beverage service, and live evening entertainment in the lounge.

For those who cannot find overnight space at Timberline Lodge or who would prefer to stay elsewhere—though that is hard to imagine—there are accommodations at Government Camp (six miles from Timberline) and Welches, 18 miles west. However, to reach Government Camp means driving down the hill from Timberline; and to come to Welches means climbing down the steep and curvy west slope of the Cascades—and on a foggy winter night both can present problems, though the roads are plowed.

Timberline Lodge is reached from Portland by U.S. 26 to Government Camp and then six miles up the mountainside.

Contact Timberline Lodge, Timberline, OR 97028; (503) 272-3311; toll-free in OR (800) 452-1335; in Washington, (800) 547-1406.

*Willamette Pass,* on Oregon 58 atop the Cascades here, is the closest ski resort to the upper Willamette Valley; it is 65 miles from Eugene.

The season is from late November–May; closed Monday and Tuesday except for holidays. The longest run is 2½ miles, with a vertical run of 1,525 feet; there are 17 runs. In 1983 the area added a mile-long Summit double chairlift to the top of 6,666-foot Eagle Peak, starting operation with the then-distinction of being the greatest vertical-drop chairlift in the nation. There is also a trip chair and a rope tow.

Night skiing is Friday and Saturday, 5 P.M.–10 P.M.

An area adjacent to Willamette Pass is for experienced cross-country skiers; equipment rentals are available. Facilities include the Cascade Summit Day Lodge, built in 1982. Inside the spacious facility are ski and rental shops, a day-care center for children, restaurant, lounge, and lift-ticket windows.

Overnight lodgings are available at Crescent Lake (10 miles) and Oakridge (27 miles).

Horizon and United fly to Eugene; Amtrak and Greyhound go there as well. Hertz and Avis have car rental agencies in Eugene. From Portland by car, take Interstate 5 to Eugene and Oregon 58 to Willamette Pass. Contact Willamette Pass Ski Corp., 1872 Willamette St., Eugene, OR 97401; (503) 484–5030.

*Warner Canyon,* in southeastern Oregon, ten miles northeast of Lakeview, and the gateway to Hart Mountain National Wildlife Refuge, is mostly a local skier area.

The season begins in late December and continues to mid-April. The area operates weekends, Thursday and Friday afternoons, legal holidays, and Christmas and Spring vacations.

Base altitude is 5,270 feet, with a vertical drop of 730 feet. For lifts, there is one T-bar.

Facilities include a day lodge with a fine restaurant. Accommodations are at Lakeview.

To get to Lakeview from California, take U.S. 395; from Portland, fly to Klamath Falls via Horizon or take Amtrak or Trailways there. Red Ball Stages goes to Lakeview from Klamath Falls. Contact Warner Canyon Ski Area, P.O. Box 1204, Lakeview, OR 97630; (503) 947–2379.

**CHILDREN'S ACTIVITIES. Sunriver:** This is not just a place for the grown-ups. In the arts and crafts center of the Lodge, kids can play table tennis, paint rocks, watch movies, and enjoy the soda fountain. They can meet Hooter the owl in the Nature Center and learn a lot about nature from the resident naturalists. In winter, the frozen pond in the meadows is a popular place to slip 'n' slide 'n' skate. Horseback riding, bicycling, swimming, and wading are also available.

**THEATER.** The *Oregon Shakespeare Festival Association,* in **Ashland,** provides the state's outstanding theatrical venture with three theaters and two seasons, which include some Shakespearean productions. Contact the Ashland office direct, (503) 482–4331, or write to the theater, Box 158, Ashland, OR 97520, for information.

**ART GALLERIES. Sunriver:** *Lodge Upper Gallery.* Exhibits by Oregon artists, particularly those residing at Sunriver.

**DINING OUT.** For a full dinner, excluding drinks and tips, restaurants are categorized as follows: *Expensive,* $15–$25; *Moderate,* $10–$15; *Inexpensive,* under $10.

## CRATER LAKE

**Crater Lake Lodge.** *Moderate.* 594–2511. The food isn't gourmet, but it's a long way to the next restaurant.

## SUNRIVER

**Sunriver Lodge Restaurants. Meadows Dining Room.** *Expensive.* 593–1221. Great food in a delightful setting.

**Casa de Ricardo.** *Moderate.* South Country Mall; 593–8860. Mexican dining in traditional "South of the border" atmosphere. Fruit margaritas and fruit daquiris at $1.50 during Fiesta Hour, 5 P.M.–6 P.M., with your meal.

**The Kitchen Store and More.** *Moderate.* Country Mall; 593–1637. Step in anytime for a free cup of freshly ground gourmet coffee of the day.

**Marcello's Pizzeria.** *Moderate.* Next to service station; 593–8300. Italian cuisine and pizzeria.

**"The" Restaurant.** *Moderate.* Near Great Hall; 593–8117. Casual family dining featuring steaks and seafood as well as daily chef's specials. Tuesday spaghetti diners are terrific.

**SunDown South Restaurant.** *Moderate.* At Sunriver Business Park Plaza, ¼ mile south of Sunriver; 593–2853. Continental cuisine well prepared.

**Afternoon Delights.** *Inexpensive.* North Country Mall; 593–1904. Everything from ice cream to sandwiches to croissants. Always fresh and tasy.

**The Chuck Wagon.** *Inexpensive.* Country Mall; 593–1100. Full menu, with lobster and snapper the Friday specialties.

**The Deschutes River Trout House Restaurant.** *Moderate.* Sunriver Marina; 593–8880. Waterfront setting. Serving great sunrise breakfast, fine seafood dishes, salads, and daily house specials.

**The Dough Factory.** *Inexpensive.* Country Mall; 593–8296. Espresso and cappuccino. Continental breakfasts. Famous for its hot bagels with cream cheese.

**Hook, Wine & Chedder.** *Inexpensive.* South Country Mall; 593–1633. Sandwiches and box lunches to go.

**The Sunspot Restaurant.** *Inexpensive.* Next to Great Hall; 593–1988. Hamburgers, fries, sandwiches—the usually plebian fare.

 **NIGHT LIFE.** Sunriver: *Owl's Nest Lounge,* Sunriver Lodge; 593–1221. Live entertainment nightly, and it's the best money can buy in Central Oregon.

# WASHINGTON

*The Remote, Wild Coast*

### by
### ARCHIE SATTERFIELD

*Archie Satterfield has written extensively about Washington. He is currently the editor of* Northwest Edition, *and his books include* The Seattle GuideBook.

Of the three contiguous West Coast states, Washington's coast is the wildest and most undeveloped. Miles and miles are untouched by highway and building, and accessible only by foot from the thin scattering of small towns and trails that penetrate the virgin forests of the Olympic National Park strip of land, which protects the coastline for all time from logging and developments.

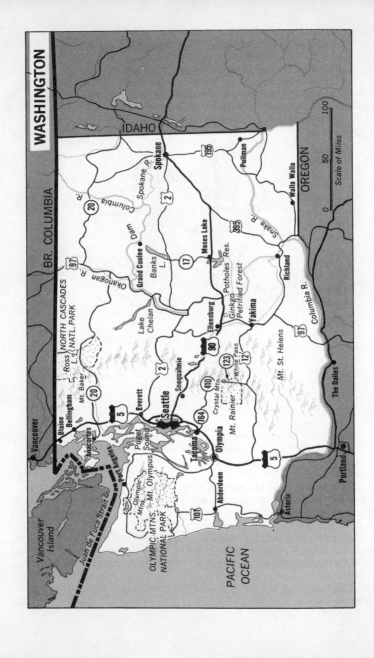

## Long Beach Peninsula

The only really accessible stretch of Washington coastline is from the Columbia River, at Washington's southern border, northward to a short distance north of Grays Harbor. This part of the coast includes the popular Long Beach Peninsula, a narrow ribbon of sand that fronts on the Pacific and has the broad, shallow Willapa Bay at its back door. The Washington coast proper really begins at Cape Disappointment on the northern side of the Columbia River estuary, one of the most rugged and wild pieces of real estate anywhere along the Pacific coastline. It is here that the Coast Guard established its school for small-boat coxswains because they routinely have rougher water to trail in here than at any other place in the 48 contiguous states.

Perched high on the cliffs above the Cape, with stunning views across the open Pacific and headlands, is the state's Lewis and Clark Interpretative Center, with its glass walls and exhibits showing the explorers' route from St. Louis to the Pacific in 1805–06, and explaining their accomplishments. Virtually beneath the headlands of Cape Disappointment is Fort Columbia State Park, an abandoned military outpost dating back to the Spanish-American War of 1898, when gun emplacements were built on either side of the Columbia River's estuary for protection against an enemy that never appeared. The 554-acre area includes old buildings and gun batteries. The museum contains Indian and pioneer relics, pictures, dioramas, and ship relics relating to the explorations of the region. The park has no campground but has tables and stoves for picnicking. Included in the park is the D.A.R. House Museum, home of a former commanding officer.

Residents of the towns in this area—Ilwaco, Seaview, Long Beach—all are dependent on the sea for much of their income. Fishing has always been the major source of income for people in this area: salmon (both commercial and charter fishing), crab, tuna, albacore, and bottom fish. Over on the Willapa Bay side, oyster farming is an important industry, as you will see when driving past the stacks of oyster shells piled outside processing plants.

This is also an important area for cranberries, and most of those grown in the Northwest come from bogs created for that purpose in the Long Beach Peninsula area. Visitors during the autumn months of September and October frequently see the flat, flooded fields with machines that look like eggbeaters knocking the brilliant red berries off the bushes into the water, where they float until scooped up into waiting trucks.

The Long Beach Peninsula has long been a favorite place for families on vacation or weekends because the beach is so long and so broad that it can absorb thousands of people without becoming crowded. Rolling sand dunes march inland from the sea, and more and more motels have been built well out onto the dunes so guests will have the sight, as well as the sound, of the surf to lull them to sleep at night and to wake them in the morning.

## Willapa Bay

The opposite side of the peninsula, which fronts on Willapa Bay, offers a totally different kind of scenery. The towns along the beach-front have a driftwood, seascape appearance to them, while the bay towns and homes still bear a striking resemblance to the small New England towns from which most original settlers came.

Oysterville, the farthest north of the Long Beach Peninsula towns, is an excellent example. In fact, it has survived so well and with such loving care by homeowners that the entire town has been set aside as a registered National Landmark. But rather than getting cute about it, as so many such towns feel compelled to do, Oysterville has stayed essentially what it has always been—a small town where ordinary people live and work.

The only other town of any size on the broad mudflats of Willapa Bay is Nahcotta, which is mostly an oyster-processing town with one or two nice restaurants. Bed-and-breakfast establishments have grown in this area to offset the more standard motels and hotels along the ocean strip.

Across Willapa Bay is the Willapa National Wildlife Refuge. You'll have to walk a bit to get to the shore of the Refuge to see the migratory birds and waterfowl. Part of the refuge is on Long Island, which is reached by boat or a ferry that operates during peak seasons for hunters or birdwatchers.

This type of town and scenery continues on northward from the Willapa River to Grays Harbor. Small resort and retirement settlements line the beach from Tokeland to Westport. Westport is known as the salmon-chartering capital of the state, and through the summer and fall the harbor is filled in the afternoons and evenings with charter fishing boats. Then it's virtually empty from dawn until noon or shortly afterward as the boats leave the harbor, diesel engines humming their baritone tunes, for the good salmon fishing a few miles offshore. During the past few years, the charter boat owners have become more versatile as salmon have become more scarce. Now they offer bottom-fishing charters, and when the great gray whales begin their northward migrations late each winter, many boat owners take people out to cruise alongside these gentle giants.

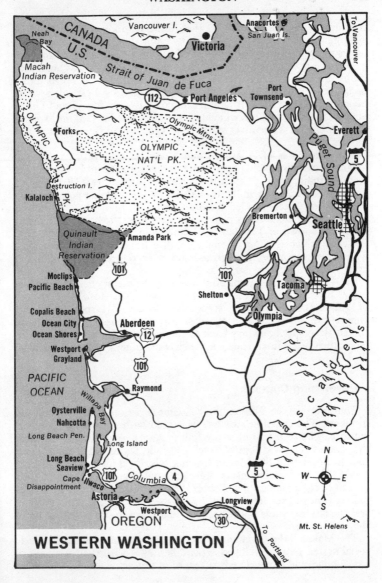

**WESTERN WASHINGTON**

The largest resort-residential development along the Washington coastline is at Ocean Shores, at the southern shore of Grays Harbor. This area hasn't grown as rapidly as its original backers had hoped, but no resort-residential area ever does. Most of the hotels offer rooms with great views across the beach and surf, and amenities such as horseback riding are available. The local chamber of commerce is noted for its imaginative methods of attracting visitors: the Fog Festival, because other resorts don't like to admit the coast is ever foggy; and Ocean Shores Undiscovery Day, which is supposedly the day that the explorer Captain George Vancouver sailed past what is now Ocean Shores and did *not* discover it.

The twin cities of Aberdeen and Hoquiam are two of the oldest logging, sawmilling, and paper-manufacturing towns in the Northwest. Here the major paper producers, such as Weyerhaeuser, ITT Rayonier, and others, have their mills. It is also a major shipping point for logs and wood products headed for the Orient.

After a few more miles of small coastal resort towns, the highway ends at the town of Taholah inside the Quinault Indian Reservation. Few visitors go this far, though, because travel is severly restricted within the reservation, and permission is needed to use the beaches. For most visitors, Moclips is the last stop.

Most of the travel is along Highway 101, the major coastal route that begins in California and follows the Oregon Coast to Astoria. North of Willapa Bay, the highway stays inland to Grays Harbor, then heads almost due north through the vast forests, bypassing the Quinault Indian Reservation, swings back to the coastline for a very short distance, then heads inland again and skirts the edge of Olympic National Park.

### Developing Cultures

Thus, most of the Washington coastline is remote and available only to hikers. The coastline's history is dotted with shipwrecks, some of which can be seen rusting away today. And it is along this coastline that one of the most highly developed cultures of Northern Coastal Indians flourished. The Makah Indians, who lived toward the northern end of the Olympic Peninsula, were great whalers and continued their pursuit of the giants until well after the turn of this century. Going out in long canoes, they harpooned the beasts and attached floats made of seal and sea lion skins to the harpoon lines to support the whales when they finally died.

The Makahs, the Quinaults, Ozettes, and Quillayutes had intricate social systems and developed artistic heritages with their carvings of wood, bone, and stone. The best record of this achievement was found in a village repeatedly buried by mudslides at Cape Alava, where the Ozettes lived. The three-mile hike from Lake Ozette to the cape and excavated village is one of the favorite walks for visitors who want to see the coast and the village without having to camp overnight. The trail is "paved" with a boardwalk. However, the major artifacts are moved to an important tribal museum in Neah Bay as soon as they are unearthed.

Since the weather is so rough, and the natural harbors so few along the coastline, it is no surprise that Puget Sound has attracted more commerce and a greater population than the coast has. For a short time in the nineteenth century, it appeared that Port Townsend, situated where the Strait of Juan de Fuca and Puget Sound meet, would be the major city of the protected inland waters. But after the city had grown rapidly and some magnificent homes were built, all the international railroads ended at Seattle and Tacoma and attempts to extend them to Port Townsend came to naught. That put an end to Port Townsend's dream of dominance, and the city languished for decades until the revival of the 1960s brought the Victorian seaport back into its own as a tourism and cultural center. (For more details about Port Townsend see "Exploring Washington," which follows the section on Seattle.)

## EXPLORING SEATTLE

Seattle is a rarity among big cities—it grows more attractive with the years in spite of urban sprawl. In recent years, the "flight" to the suburbs has subsided. Instead, renovating old homes in the center of the city, or buying condominiums and co-ops in the heart of town, has become common. On the other hand, people still can buy pleasant homesites not far from town and become the first occupants of the land. The metropolitan-area population has increased steadily for decades, to a current 1,500,000, fortunately with neither boom nor bust.

Downtown Seattle's answer to the challenge of suburbs and their shopping centers has been a constant upgrading, with plantings, fountains, sculpture, malls, imaginative urban parks, and preservation-renewal of two historic areas and the waterfront. Bus drivers collect no fare in the downtown area—everyone rides free. One result has been that Seattleites repeatedly read national magazine articles describing their city as "the most liveable." They can't decide whether to be smug or alarmed that such praise will bring a crowd and less liveability.

The central skyline changes each year as 30-to-50-story buildings go up. The Space Needle, built for the World's Fair in 1962, was called

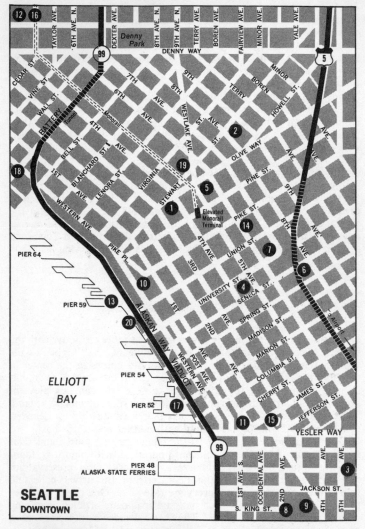

**SEATTLE**
DOWNTOWN

ELLIOTT BAY

PIER 64
PIER 59
PIER 54
PIER 52
PIER 48
ALASKA STATE FERRIES

**Points of Interest**
1) Bon Marché
2) Central Bus Terminal
3) Chinatown
4) Four Seasons Olympic Hotel
5) Frederick & Nelson
6) Freeway Park
7) Hilton Hotel
8) King Dome
9) King Street Station (Amtrack)
10) Pike Place Market
11) Pioneer Square
12) Seattle Center
13) Seattle Public Aquarium
14) Seattle Sheraton
15) Smith Tower
16) Space Needle
17) State Ferry Terminal
18) Waterfront Terminal
19) Westin Hotel
20) Waterfront Park

the tallest structure in town, but it was soon topped by the 50-story Sea-First Bank Building. The L.C. Smith Tower, correctly bragged about by two generations as "the tallest building west of the Mississippi," is now a quaint little spire peering up at its neighbors.

Skyscrapers with thousands of feet of new office space are visual proof that Seattle is indeed the paperwork capital of the Pacific Northwest. Their height also means that, as in San Francisco, the easiest way to go is up. The central city is narrow-waisted, squeezed in against hills by its Puget Sound harbor, Elliott Bay. Lake Union, the city's backdoor, freshwater harbor, lies just to north. South, the land was once a tideflat; now it is occupied by rail lines, warehouses, trucking companies, machinery manufacturers and, along the waterfront, the piers and giant cranes of the shipping business. Seattle's aerospace activities get the publicity locally and nationally, but the maritime industry accounts for more jobs. East lies Lake Washington, the other half of the water girdle that squeezes the city's waistline.

The best way to see this all at once and get oriented to the city's layout is from the observation platform at the 500-foot level of the Space Needle at the Seattle Center. If you are downtown you can get there in two minutes for a $.35 fare on the Monorail. (Its terminal is at the Westlake Mall.) The Space Needle (elevator fare) is not the only spectacular vantage point, but it is the only one that presents a 360-degree panorama.

The central business district lies to the south. To save later confusion, first note that downtown is different from the main pattern of avenues north-south, and streets east-west. The pioneers laid out the first avenues parallel to the waterfront, so downtown faces southwest toward the bay.

Ocean-going ships used to moor right downtown. Today you'll see the working port at the southern end of Elliott Bay, where the Duwamish River flows in. The residential area southwest across the water is West Seattle, and the extreme point at the entrance to the bay is Alki, where the first settlers landed in 1851. Early the next year they found the deeper harbor along the present waterfront and moved to it to start the city.

The state ferries coming and going to the west across Puget Sound are bound for Bremerton, back in a mainland channel of the Kitsap Peninsula, and to closer Bainbridge Island, where many commuters live. Backing the whole scene are the Olympic Mountains.

Queen Anne Hill, to the north of the city, blocks a view of what is down behind it, the ship canal whose locks connect salt water with Lake Union, seen to the right of the hill. Lake Washington, which forms the entire eastern boundary of the city, is over other hills.

Northeast, on the canal between the two lakes, is the University of Washington and its surrounding business district.

The backdrop on the east side is the Cascade Range, with Mount Rainier looming on the southerly horizon and, farther away, toward the north end, 10,778-foot Mount Baker.

Back to earth. Downtown Seattle has three built-in shows that run all year, most busily from mid-spring through October. They are the Pioneer Square Historic District, the Pike Place Public Market, and the waterfront. They can be reached by foot or by free city bus from the main hotels, and they cost nothing except what you may decide to pay for food, drink, a boat ride, or an aquarium admission.

## The Waterfront

The biggest circus is the waterfront. After the maritime trade moved down the harbor to modern facilities, people and fun moved in. Don't allow less than half a day on foot if you are really going to savor this section. It stretches some nineteen blocks, from Pier 51 at the foot of Yesler to Pier 70 at the end of Broad Street, and up to Pier 91 on a foot path.

Pier 51 is approximately where the city began, with Henry Yesler's pier and sawmill. Actually, as a result of landfills, that site is now a couple of blocks inland, near Pioneer Square and the totem pole. South of Pier 51 is an old-fashioned pergola marking the first city-owned dock for the Harbor Patrol; and the Alaska State Ferries pier. The ferries sail north once a week in the summer, twice in the winter, and since they are conditioned and repaired in Seattle, their blue funnels with the seven stars of the Big Dipper are often seen there.

At the street end of Pier 51 is the unusual, widely-known Ye Olde Curiosity Shop, a mixture of souvenir store and museum that has been in existence (with one move) since 1899.

State ferries load and unload at Pier 52, and its second-level open walkways on each side afford waterfront viewpoints. (For more about the ferries, see "How to Get There" in *Practical Information for Seattle*.) Pier 52's predecessor was Colman Dock, long the terminal for traffic up and down the Sound back when roads were few. Passengers and freight were carried by a "Mosquito Fleet" on small steamers that called at dozens of otherwise isolated villages and brought back farm produce.

North of 52 is Fire Station No. 5, a great curiosity to inlanders because it traditionally housed seagoing "firetrucks," boats designed to protect Seattle's many miles of shoreline buildings and capable of pouring thousands of gallons of seawater a minute through their "cannon" nozzles. The fireboats are now stationed closer to Harbor Island's shipping facilities but are periodically seen in the bay when they go out to test their equipment, or to greet Tall Ships, or the occasional cruise ship that calls on Seattle and other cities on the Sound.

In the blocks on north there are numerous seafood restaurants and snack bars opening on the street. Except in the worst weather there are people eating outside under heated canopies. One of the most famous is Ivar's Acres of Clams, because it was the pioneer seafood restaurant along the waterfront and the foundation for one of Seattle's most popular chains of restaurants. Large import shops display goods bazaar style. Sightseeing boats operate from here. (See "Tours" in *Practical Information for Seattle*.) Pier 57 offers public fishing. A city park has walkways built over the water, and observation platforms. Also novel is the aquarium featuring Pacific Northwest marine life. It has a sunken dome that allows spectators to walk around under the surface so fish outside can watch them through the glass. In other sections sea otters and seals lead as normal a life as is possible in captivity (no performances), and along with live specimens in tanks, there are educational exhibits.

The Schwabacher Wharf, Pier 58, is still remembered in a historical marker. The *Portland* landed here on July 17, 1897, with its "ton of gold"—news of which set off the Klondike rush, transformed Seattle, and made its name known around the world. The shops on this pier are all of the Klondike theme, and sourdough bread is a specialty. At this writing, plans are under way to make Pier 58 a cruise ship dock because only small cruise ships now can dock in Seattle; the large ones depart from either San Francisco or Vancouver, B.C.

Canadians have bought Pier 69, where their excursion ship *Princess Marguerite* docks for her runs to Victoria, B.C. (again, see "Tours"), and have turned part of it into another center for people who want to stroll on ships.

The Edgewater Inn (see "Hotels and Motels" in *Practical Information for Seattle* ) is on Pier 67, and if you have a bayside room and want to fish out the window, the hotel will go along with the gag by lending you a pole and tackle.

Pier 70's huge warehouse was converted into a self-contained bazaar. It runs the gamut of shops, galleries, eating and drinking places. Here you can find imported goods from all over the world with an emphasis on the Orient and Middle East, regional artwork, and one of the most tempting coffee shops (Starbucks) in the city. Parking is available at city meters, along the pier, and upstairs. Across the street is the popular, open-evenings-only, Old Spaghetti Factory. (See "Dining Out.")

Except for a small oil dock, waterfront buildings end at Pier 70, but a newly built trail leads on north along the shore, toward the monstrous grain elevators, which stand beside such deep water they can handle the largest tankers afloat.

The railroad tracks under the viaduct are not-much-used spurs left from days when they carried cargo to freighters. Trolley cars to run up and down the waterfront were purchased in Australia.

The viaduct between downtown buildings and the waterfront was an aesthetic mistake, Seattleites now admit, but there is no gainsaying it furnishes a fast-flowing freeway that bypasses the city center.

## Farmer's Market

A number of cities include a "farmer's market" in their list of attractions, but none has the historic background of Seattle's, nor the fervent, emotional support of citizens who went to the polls to vote money to preserve it.

The market began in 1907 when the city issued permits to farmers to sell their produce off wagons parked in Pike Place. As time went on, too many wagons showed up and the city built stalls which it allotted for a small fee on the basis of daily drawings.

Pike Place became a Seattle phenomenon, an amiable madhouse of vendors hawking their wares (including seafood) and willing to haggle over price—a quite unAmerican practice that astounded visitors.

The fading of nearby farmlands into subdivisions and commercial zoning, the addition of non-local produce (bananas, grapefruit, and California vegetables to keep counters in business during the winter), the leasing of otherwise unused space for the sale of nonagricultural products, and a city decision to subdue so much shouting and bargaining, somewhat changed the original character of the market.

The buildings had aged, so planners blithely wrote off the market in an urban renewal plan. That's when Seattle voters said "no" and decreed it to be a historical asset. Most of the buildings have been restored and the complex also is newly connected by stairs and elevator to the waterfront park. Some grocers, such as DeLaurenti's Delicatessen, have been here so long that they are Seattle institutions. The market continues as the place to find fresh octopus, bulk spices, every kind of cheese, arts and crafts, home brew supplies, old books and records, fresh vegetables, fruit, meat, seafood—you name it. Restaurants are here with menus from around the world, ranging from the Bolivian (Copacabana), to the French (Le Bistro), to the local seafood (Emmett Watson's Oyster Bar).

## Skid Road or the Pioneer District

The term "Skid Road" originated in Seattle for a logical reason. Oxen or horses dragged timber down off the hill to Yesler's mill and wharf at the village center. The skidroad consisted of small logs placed crossways to the path and greased, a method widely used in the woods before the advent of steam donkey engines and later diesel-powered skidders.

By the 1890s Victorian brick buildings had sprouted on the site; and with the Klondike gold rush, the area just to the south of them—a former tideflat whose fill included a lot of sawdust—became the saloon and red-light district. During the first decades of the century, city business gradually moved north into newer buildings, and the original center deteriorated. The old Skidroad became known for its dubious character and (with cheap rents) as the place where men went when they were down on their luck.

New buildings began creeping back down the streets, demolishing old structures in their path. As they approached Pioneer Square, Seattle arrived of an age to become interested in its heritage. The upshot was a preservation movement that progressed into an official declaration of a protected "Pioneer District" (sounds better than "Skidroad") whose landmark is the totem pole in Pioneer Square, a triangle at First and Yesler.

The district takes in eighteen blocks and by now includes pedestrian malls, arcades, shops of all descriptions, and some fashionable restaurants. You can't tell what's inside a building by its antique exterior; you have to explore.

One of the best ways to see Pioneer Square is to sign on for one of the daily Underground Tours offered by a firm owned by Bill Speidel, an irreverent Seattle historian and publisher of a guide found in hotel rooms throughout the city. (See "Tours" in *Practical Information for Seattle.*)

Pioneer Square Park is a broad cobbled plaza in the center of the historic district with a cast-iron pergola that was recently restored to its original grandeur. In the same small park (they call it a square but it is actually a triangle) is a giant totem pole with its own history. Back near the turn of the century, a group of Seattle businessmen were on a ship in Alaskan waters and found a large totem pole in an abandoned Indian village. They simply hauled it away and stationed it in Pioneer Square. Later it burned, and they wanted a replacement, so Tlingit Indian carvers were hired to produce another one. Local legend has it that the fee for the replacement was so high that the Indians got their revenge through the pocketbooks of Seattleites.

Pioneer Square is ringed with the historic buildings of the district, many with restaurants on the ground floor and galleries and professional offices on the upper floors. South one block is Occidental Park, much larger, also cobbled, and with trees giving shade in the summer for loungers and brown-baggers. More restored buildings surround the park, and across Main Street is the Klondike Gold Rush National Historical Park interpretative center. This is the southern unit of the park, established here because of Seattle's vital role in the 1897–98 gold rush. The headquarters are in Skagway, Alaska.

The district is alive with elegant restaurants, imported clothing stores, antique shops, art galleries, and fine furniture stores. Since it is adjacent to the Kingdome covered stadium, much of its success, especially that of the restaurants, is related to sporting events. Thus, it is best to plan your meals in the district when no sporting event is scheduled.

Adjoining the Pioneer District on the east is Chinatown. The Chinese are actually outnumbered by other races, so the area was renamed the "International District," but tradition keeps that name from sticking. What with Pioneer Square developments and the nearby Kingdome stadium, this district also is reviving. It contains the top Chinese and Japanese restaurants. Two colorful events are Chinese New Year and the Japanese Bon Odori street dances in August. Daily tours of the area (reservations required) begin at 622 S. Washington.

The domed stadium's name is from the local county, King, but it is also king-size, the building itself encompassing ten acres. It has the world's largest self-supporting roof (no posts to sit behind). Among the superlatives applied to the Kingdome is that "you could put the Roman Coliseum inside it, lions, Christians, chariots, and all." There are daily tours of the stadium, on which senior citizens are charged the same reduced rate as children.

The 1962 World's Fair never really ended in Seattle. Its legacy, two miles from Pioneer Square, is the former fairgrounds now called Seattle Center, has as many visitors as ever, to the Space Needle, theaters, Coliseum, exhibition halls, Seattle Art Museum's contemporary gallery, rides, shops, the old Food Circus renamed Center House, and the exhibits of Pacific Science Center.

The free show at Hiram Chittenden Locks, on N.W. 54th and Ballard, better known as the Ballard Locks, rates with the rest. Allow more time than you expected to spend watching boats go up and down between saltwater Shilshole Bay and the freshwater lakes. Or view the show while eating at the nearby restaurant, Hiram's at the Locks. You also can watch fish going up the ladder, through glass from a viewing room. There are neatly landscaped grounds, and a new interpretive center has been added. On the way to the locks you'll see the fishing fleet's marina on the south shore just west of the Ballard Bridge.

For the motorist there are four scenic drives called Trident Tours. Follow the street signs with Neptune's fork, and you will see all parts of the city.

# PRACTICAL INFORMATION FOR SEATTLE

 **HOW TO GET THERE. By air:** Seattle–Tacoma International Airport (recently renamed the Henry M. Jackson International Airport in honor of the late U.S. Senator), is 15 miles south of Seattle, roughly halfway to Tacoma. At presstime, it is served by 18 foreign and domestic lines, although the figure changes rapidly with the deregulation fallout. The airlines include *United, Northwest, Pan American, Western, Republic, Cascades, Eastern, Continental, Alaska, Scandinavian, Pacific Western, TWA, National, Wien, Reeve Aleutian, Mexicana, British Airways,* and *Thai.* For information on getting from the airport see "How to Get Around," below.

**By train:** *Amtrak* brings passengers to Seattle up the West Coast from San Diego, from the East Coast via Chicago, Minneapolis, North Dakota, and Montana, stopping in Spokane enroute, and from Vancouver, B.C.

**By bus:** *Greyhound* has extensive schedules within and to Washington, while *Trailways* (interstate only) swings into Seattle along I–5.

**By car:** About three-fourths of the 10 million tourists who visit Washington each year arrive by car. The major north-south route is I–5, which runs from Vancouver, B.C., to San Diego, and connects all the major population areas along the coastal region. I–90 runs east-west.

**By ferry:** *Washington State Ferries* are part of the state highway system. All but one route is across Puget Sound, which is not very wide but forms an efficient barrier to westbound roads for about 90 miles along I–5. The only bridge crossing Puget Sound itself (no toll) is at Tacoma.

South to north, the ferry route is Fauntleroy (southwest Seattle) to Vashon and on to Southworth on the Kitsap Peninsula; Pier 52 in downtown Seattle to Bremerton; and another route to Winslow on Bainbridge Island.

Crossing times vary; the ferries are relatively inexpensive. Ages 5–11 and 65-up ride half fare. There are round-trip excursion fares that allow time ashore before return. For ferry information call (206) 464–6400 or write *Washington State Ferry System,* State Ferry Terminal, Seattle, WA 98104.

Washington State ferries to the San Juan Islands and Sidney, B.C., run from Anacortes.

The *British Columbia Steamship Co.* operates one round trip daily in summer between Seattle and Victoria. For information call 623–5560 in Seattle; 386–6731 in Victoria.

Alaska Ferries connect Seattle with with southeast Alaska ports. Reservations are needed well in advance. Contact *Alaska Marine Hwy.*, Pier 48, Seattle, WA 98104; (206) 623–1970.

 **HOTELS AND MOTELS.** The half-century-old Olympic, with its aura of earlier-day elegance, recently reopened as the Four Seasons Olympic with most of the rooms remodeled, many enlarged to suites, and the entrance and lobby restored to their original opulence. All other hotels in the deluxe category are sleek and relatively new, both downtown and at the Seattle-Tacoma International Airport. A growing number are in Bellevue, separated from Seattle on the east by Lake Washington but easily reached by two floating bridges. (A semi-rural suburb 30 years ago, Bellevue is now an independent city of 70,000 population.) As elsewhere, hotels and motels are arranged alphabetically within price range (based on double occupancy). The price categories are: *Deluxe,* $75 up; *Expensive* $50–$75; *Moderate* $35–$50; *Inexpensive* under $35. Also remember the hostelries tend to change names overnight as they join or switch management chains. Those listed are typical but, especially in the less-expensive categories, represent only a fraction of the rooms available.

Since a single "Seattle" listing would lump together motels and restaurants up to 30 miles apart, they have been put into "central," "north," "south," and "east" categories. Through Seattle, "Motel Strip" is along old Highway 99—Aurora Avenue north of the city center and Pacific Highway South, toward the airport. Biggest suburban cities surrounding Seattle are Edmonds, Lynnwood, Mountlake Terrace, and Bothell to the north; Kirkland and Bellevue east across Lake Washington; Renton, Tukwila, unincorporated Burien, and Des Moines to the south, along with Kent, Auburn, and Federal Way. Most hotels accept major credit cards.

## CENTRAL SEATTLE

### Deluxe

**Camlin Hotel & Cabanas.** Pine St., between 8th & 9th; (206) 682–0100. This hotel–motor inn complex offers a wide range of rooms and suites. Pool. Dining room, coffeeshop, lounge, and entertainment.

**Edgewater Inn.** 2411 Alaskan Way on Pier 67; (206) 624–7000. Attractive four-story motor inn hanging over Puget Sound on a pier. Coffeeshop, dining rooms, cocktail lounges, and entertainment. Wide range of accommodations.

**Park Hilton.** 6th & Seneca; (206) 464–1980. This is one of Seattle's newest and finest, and one of the first built in the downtown area in decades. It is near virtually everything, and only two blocks from the grand old remodeled Olympic.

**Seattle Hilton.** 6th and University St.; (206) 624–0500. This large downtown hotel offers the convenience of inner-city location, attractive units with views, some suites, a pay garage, coffeeshop, a beautiful dining room called "Top of the Hilton," and cocktail lounge.

**Sorrento Hotel.** 900 Madison; (206) 622–6400. This small, intimate hotel was recently completely renovated to become one of Seattle's showplaces. Perched on a steep hill, it has the best views of Puget Sound and the Olympic Mountains of any Seattle hotel. Dining room, cocktail lounge, suites.

**University Tower.** 45th & Brooklyn; (206) 634–2000. In the University district, this large hotel offers 155 corner rooms with views of Lake Washington and mountains. Parking lot. Coffeeshop, dining room.

**Westin Hotel.** 5th & Westlake; (206) 624–7400. Seasonal rates. A very large, attractive hotel with twin circular towers that provide stunning views of the Puget Sound region. Some suites. Pay garage. Coffeeshop, dining rooms (*Trader Vic's* is located here), and cocktail lounge with entertainment.

### Expensive–Deluxe

**Continental Plaza Motel.** 2500 Aurora Ave. N. (Highway 99); (206) 284–1900. A motor inn of two- and four-story buildings comprising units of varying sizes, many with lake and mountain views. Some with refrigerators, a few with water beds and some with kitchens at extra charge. Pool. Coffeeshop. Seasonal rates.

**Downtown TraveLodge.** 2213 8th Ave.; (206) 624–6300. Attractive, convenient motel. Restaurant near. No pets.

**Roosevelt Motor Hotel.** 7th Ave. and Pine; (206) 624–1400. Wide choice of units. Some suites. Dining room, coffee shop, lounge, and entertainment.

### Expensive

**Mayflower Park.** 405 Olive Way; (206) 623–4750. Charming smaller hotel, downtown. Comfortable rooms; pleasant, low-key bar that attracts local people as well as hotel guests.

**TraveLodge by the Space Needle.** 200 6th Ave. No.; (206) 623–2600. As its name implies, this motel is handy to Seattle Center and all its attractions. Pool. Seasonal rates. No pets.

**University Inn.** 4140 Roosevelt Way N.E.; (206) 632–5055. Large motor inn near the U. of W. campus. Many kitchenettes. Laundry. Pool.

**The Warwick.** 4th Ave. and Lenora; (206) 625–6700. This recently refurbished hotel on the northern edge of the downtown district is modest on the outside, luxurious inside.

### Moderate

**City Center Motel.** 226 Aurora Ave. N.; (206) 682–0266. Comfortable, conveniently located between downtown and the Seattle Center. Some kitchenettes, some with two rooms. Coin laundry.

**Sherwood Inn.** 400 N.E. 45th, just off I–5; (206) 634–0100. Large motor inn near the University of Washington. Some suites. Some refrigerators. Dining room, lounge, and entertainment. Pool. Transportation to downtown air terminal.

**The Tropics.** 225 Aurora Ave. N. and John St., near Seattle Center; (206) 624–6789. Large, attractive four-story motor inn with some suites. Covered parking. Indoor pool. Dining room, lounge, and entertainment.

*Inexpensive*

**Bridge Motel.** 3650 Bridgeway N.; (206) 632–7835. A rather small motel situated a block east of the north end of the Aurora Bridge. Some units have a beautiful view of the city, Lake Union and mountains.

**Marco Polo Motel.** 4114 Aurora Ave. N.; (206) 633–4090. Two-story motel with one- and two-room units. Some with kitchen facilities at extra charge.

**Vance Motor Hotel.** 7th Ave. & Stewart St.; (206) 623–2700. Convenient, comfortable downtown hotel with garage. Popular grill and Cedar Room. Cocktail lounge.

## NORTH SEATTLE

*Expensive–Deluxe*

**Ramada Inn.** 2140 N. Northgate Way; (206) 365–0700. Large motel near the Northgate shopping mall. Pool. Restaurant and lounge adjacent.

**Rodeway Inn.** 12501 Aurora N.; (206) 364–7771. Large motor inn. Restaurant, lounge with entertainment. Pool, sauna and whirlpool.

*Expensive*

**Landmark Best Western Motor Inn.** 4300 200th, just off I–5 in Lynnwood; (206) 775–7447. Large motor inn with a variety of accommodations. Some rooms with steam baths. Very good restaurant, coffeeshop, lounge with entertainment. Indoor pool and whirlpool.

*Moderate*

**Black Angus Motor Inn.** 125th and Aurora; (206) 363–3035. Part of the extensive Black Angus restaurant chain founded in Seattle. The motel offers comfortable rooms, on-site restaurant and usual amenities.

**Geisha Inn.** 9613 Aurora Ave. N.; (206) 524–8880. Medium-size motel with a variety of accommodations (some have a sunken bath in the room!). All units are beautifully decorated in oriental style. Some kitchenettes. Whirlpool. Coin laundry. Gift shop. Restaurants near.

*Inexpensive–Moderate*

**Thunderbird Motel.** 4251 Aurora Ave. N.; (206) 634–1213. An attractive, smaller motel, very accessible to downtown area. Some two-bedroom units with kitchenettes (extra charge).

## SOUTH SEATTLE (AIRPORT)

*Deluxe*

**Airport Hilton.** 17620 Pacific Highway S.; (206) 244–4800. One of the two Hiltons in the Seattle area, this also has the amenities expected of its name. Dining room, coffeeshop, lounge, and entertainment. Swimming and wading pools. Pets allowed. Courtesy car to airport.

**Doubletree Inn.** 205 Strander Blvd., just off I–5; (206) 246–8220. Large motor inn in the Southcenter Shopping Complex. Wide choice of units—some with refrigerators, some with steam baths, and there are several suites. Dining room, coffee shop, lounge with entertainment. Playground, pool. Pets (extra charge).

**Holiday Inn of Sea-Tac.** 17338 Pacific Highway S.; (206) 248–1000. Large hotel with a friendly atmosphere. Revolving restaurant on top of building serving excellent dinners. Young waiters/waitresses furnish the entertainment. Coffeeshop, lounge with entertainment. Pool. Car to airport.

**Hyatt House.** 17001 Pacific Highway S.; (206) 244–6000. A very large motor inn. A broad choice of accommodations. Some suites with refrigerators. Pool and saunas. Coffeeshop and dining room. The lounge is popular with local people for its entertainment and dancing. Car to airport.

**Jet Inn.** 3000 S. 176th St.; (206) 246–9110. Large three-level motor inn. Restaurant, cocktail lounge with dancing and entertainment. Indoor and outdoor pools, an exercise room, whirlpool, and sauna. Courtesy car to airport.

**Marriott.** 3201 S. 176th at 32nd.; (206) 241–2000. The newest Sea-Tac hotel, and one of the finest in the area. Many rooms have views of Mt. Rainier (on clear days, that is).

### Expensive-Deluxe

**Sandstone Motel.** 19225 Pacific Highway S.; (206) 824–1350. A 2-level motor inn with units of one and two rooms, several with kitchenettes. Lounge and an excellent 24-hour restaurant. Pets allowed. Free parking for "fly-away" guests. Airport transportation.

**Vance Airport Inn.** 18220 Pacific Highway S.; (206) 246–5535. Large 5-story motor inn. Attractively furnished rooms. Restaurant, lounge with dancing and entertainment. Pool, sauna and whirlpool.

### Expensive

**Imperial 400 Motel.** 17108 Pacific Highway S.; (206) 244–1230. Medium-size motel. Some units have kitchenettes. Pool. Car to airport. Pets allowed. Restaurant next door.

### Moderate-Expensive

**West Wind Motel.** 110 Rainier Ave. S.; (206) 226–5060. In Renton city center. Several units with kitchenettes (extra charge). Adjacent restaurant.

**YOUTH HOSTELS.** The *SeaHaven Hostel,* 1431 Minor Ave., (206) 524–2844, is a member of the American Youth Hostels Association. It has 150 beds and a cooperative kitchen. It is a pleasant, well-managed place. Persons of any age are welcome, but must have their A.Y.H. pass. An adjacent restaurant is under the same management.

**TRAILER TIPS.** For information on keeping your trailer just outside the city, see *Practical Information for Washington.*

**HOW TO GET AROUND. From the airport:** The best way to get from the airport to downtown is by the *Airporter* buses that run roughly every half hour to major downtown hotels. Price is $8. The *Suburban Airporter* vans run less frequently and cover the entire region from Tacoma north to Everett. *Taxis* are available, but their fares have been deregulated. *Caveat emptor:* the trip downtown may cost as much as $20, while the usual rate is between $12 and $15.

**By bus:** *Metro Transit* runs not only city buses but routes all over the county. It is one of the best transit systems in the United States. Most schedules are frequent. The no-fare zone in the downtown area is from Sixth Avenue to the waterfront, and from South Jackson to Battery Streets. Beyond, to the city limits, fare is $.50, with transfers, during off-peak hours; during rush hours it's $.60. A two-zone fare is $.75; $.90 during rush hour. (A Metro line goes to and from Tacoma, stopping at Sea-Tac Airport.) Heading away from town, pay when you get off; toward downtown, when you board.

You must have exact change. With a pass from the Metro office (Exchange Bldg., Second & Marion), senior citizens (65 or older) can ride anywhere for $.10.

**By monorail:** The *Monorail* runs from Westlake Mall to Seattle Center, non-stop Sunday–Thursday, 10 A.M.–midnight; Friday, Saturday, 10 A.M.–12:30 A.M. Fare is $.50. For information on both city and county destinations call Metro at 447–4800.

**By trolley:** Vintage streetcars from Australia run along the waterfront between Broad St. and S. Main St., at 30 min. intervals, 7 days a week. Fare is $.60; Metro bus passes and transfers honored.

**By car:** *Hertz* (800–654–3131), *Avis* (800–331–1212), and *National* (800–328–4567) are the most popular rental agencies.

**TOURIST INFORMATION.** The *Seattle Visitor's Bureau* is located at 1815 7th Ave. on the main floor of Tower Bldg., between Olive Way and Stewart St., downtown. Open Monday–Friday, 8:30 A.M.–5 P.M.; (206) 447–7273.

**SEASONAL EVENTS. May:** First Saturday—opening day of yachting season, parade of boats. **July:** Seafair and Seafair Grand Parade. **August:** Seafair continues into August, ending with hydroplane races on Lake Washington; the Japanese Festival of Bon Odori in the International Settlement. **September:** Bumbershoot Festival, music, craft, arts, at Seattle Center; Milk Fund Salmon Derby. **December:** Christmas Around the World.

**TOURS.** A ferry ride may not have a guide, but it gives a good perspective on the city and environs. Food and drink (including beer) are available and you can either catch the wind in your hair or sit indoors, protected from the elements. See "How to Get There," above. *Seattle Harbor Tours* (623–1445) runs a one-hour, narrated trip around Elliott Bay, Seattle's waterfront, leaving from Pier 56 on the downtown waterfront, mid-April to October.

*Canadian Pacific* has a summertime daily cruise from Seattle to Victoria, B.C. The *Princess Marguerite* (623–5560) leaves Pier 69 at 8 A.M., arrives in Victoria at noon. Five hours ashore. Reboard at 5 P.M. and reach Seattle at twilight. Dine aboard if you wish. While in Victoria there is the choice of two sightseeing tours—world-famous "Butchart Gardens" or "Sealand of the Pacific"—with afternoon tea at the Empress Hotel. Mid-May through mid-September.

A trip to Tillicum Village on Blake Island runs May to September, twice a day. You go by sightseeing boat from Pier 56 on Seattle's downtown waterfront. The captain points out points of interest on the 45-minute trip. Tour Tillicum Village longhouse, with its Indian carvings and totem poles. Indian-made handicrafts available at the curio shop. Salmon is barbecued the way the Indians did it centuries ago on five-foot cedar stakes over an open alder fire. Menu includes Tillicum hot bread and wild blackberry cream tarts. Interpretative North Coast Indian songs and dances performed after dinner. For reservations, call 329–5700.

*Gray Line of Seattle* (343–2000) offers a wide variety of tours in and around Seattle. Its 2½-hour "Discovery City Tour of Seattle" takes in Chinatown; the world's first concrete floating bridge; the arboretum; the University campus; and the Metropolitan Tract, new glass-and-steel downtown skyline. Year-round. The "Adventure Water Tour," a 2¼-hour cruise aboard Gray Line's double-decked *Sightseer* boat, includes a cruise through Seattle's busy harbor, from saltwater to freshwater, via Government Locks to Fisherman's Terminal and Lake Union. May through Sept. A combination of the "Discovery" and "Adventure Water" tours takes 4½ hours.

*Underground Tour* (682–1511) is an off-beat 2½-hour guided walking tour of five blocks, both above and below ground, in the Pioneer Square area. A fire in 1889 destroyed much of Seattle, and the city took the opportunity to improve the waterfront and rebuild streets ten to eighteen feet higher than they had been. Blocks of stores and sidewalks became subterranean, and eventually were forgotten for several decades. No children under 5, or under 17 on evening tours. Wear walking shoes.

*Chinatown Tours* also go afoot. Call 624–6220 for required reservations. Starting point is 622 South Washington St.

The *Kingdome* has three daily tours except when some event is in progress; call 628–3331.

The self-guiding, drive-yourself *Trident Tours* provide the easiest and most inexpensive method of seeing the Seattle area for visitors with cars.

Probably the most popular surface tour out of Seattle is Gray Line's *Mt. Rainier National Park Tour.* "The Around the Mountain Sightseeing Tour," as it is called, completely encircles the mountain, with two hours for passengers to explore along the trails, take in the Visitor Center, and enjoy the lunch at Paradise Inn. Tour starts at 9 A.M.; completes at 6 P.M. May through Sept.

 **ZOOS AND AQUARIUMS.** *The Aquarium.* Pier 59; 625–5030. This is the only aquarium in the world that is connected directly to the ocean. It features a viewing area several feet beneath the surface of Elliott Bay, where fish native to Puget Sound swim by. At water level are crabs, starfish, and other bottom creatures in native habitats. It has a false tide that raises and lowers every three hours to show the life on the bottom and the tidal effects on it. Open daily 10 A.M.–5 P.M. winter; 10 A.M.–9 P.M. summer. Adults $3.25; $1.25 ages 13–17; children $.75. *Woodland Park Zoo.* N. 59th Street and Aurora Avenue; 625–4550. Although the zoo has made great strides in making life as pleasant for the animals as for the human visitors, it still isn't a world-class zoo. Recent additions are the Nocturnal House where night creatures reside with their daily cycles reversed: they think it is night when outside it is really daytime, so they're moving around for visitors. The Swamp and Marsh is populated by birds, gorillas, monkeys, and other creatures. An African Savanna closely duplicates the native environment. The zoo opens every day of the year at 8:30 A.M. and closes from 4 P.M. to 6 P.M., depending on the season. Admission: $2.50 adults, $1 youths (13–17), children $.50.

 **GARDENS.** *U. of Washington Arboretum,* 543–8800 or 325–4510, along Lake Washington Blvd., south of the campus. Public roads wind through 250 acres of extraordinary plantings that have blooms throughout most of the year. The delicate *Japanese Tea Garden,* which encompasses four acres in the Arboretum, is the largest of its kind outside Japan. Open daily 10 A.M.–8 P.M. in summer; weekends 10 A.M.–sunset in spring and fall, depending upon the weather. *Woodland Park Zoological Gardens,* on N. 50th Street, cover about 95 acres and include an extensive rose garden. Seattle has 45 parks, each of which has a bit of garden. Picnicking is allowed at almost all of them; some even have stoves. There's an early-day conservatory at *Volunteer Park,* site of the Seattle Art Museum. At the *Carl S. English, Jr., Gardens* at Hiram Chittenden Locks on Seaview Avenue N.W. you can pick up a self-guiding tour brochure at the Interpretive Center. *Freeway Park,* in the center of town just off Sixth Ave. near Spring St., is a garden consisting of huge planter boxes and waters. It "lids" the I–5 freeway and is quite unusual. All of the gardens are open all the time.

**FOR SPECTACULAR VIEWS.** The *Space Needle,* Seattle Center; 447–3100. Built for the 1962 World's Fair, this Seattle landmark affords views from 500 feet above the city. Observation deck open seven days, 9 A.M.–5 P.M.; $3

adults; $1.50 for children under 12. Gourmet restaurant, *Emerald Suite,* and more informal *Space Needle* restaurant at the top.

 **SPECTATOR SPORTS.** Completion of the West's first domed stadium made Seattle eligible to have major league baseball and football teams. (For all sports schedules, consult the daily papers or the Seattle Visitors Center.) **Baseball:** *Seattle Mariners,* playing at the Kingdome in Pioneer Square, are in the American League. For tickets: Box 4100, Seattle 98104; 628–3300. **Basketball:** *Seattle Supersonics,* in National Basketball Association, play in the Coliseum in Seattle Center. For tickets: 221 W. Harrison St., Seattle 98109; 628–8448. Top college contests are at the *University of Washington's* Hec Edmundson Pavilion (call 543–2200 for all U. of W. ticket information), and *Seattle Pacific,* an independent, plays at Royal Brougham Pavilion on the SPC campus. **Football:** *Seattle Seahawks,* National Football League, play in the Kingdome. For tickets: 5303 Lake Washington Blvd., Kirkland; 827–9766. *University of Washington Huskies* often draw capacity crowds in 55,000-seat stadium. **Auto racing:** Three tracks in the region are *Seattle International Raceways,* 31001 144th S.E., Kent; 631–1550; *Evergreen Speedway,* at Monroe (call 776–2802); and the *Puyallup Raceway Park* (call 845–1771). **Horse racing:** Season at *Longacres,* in Renton, is from mid-May into latter part of September. **Hydroplane racing:** The big unlimiteds compete on Lake Washington in early August.

 **PARTICIPANT SPORTS.** Because of the mild winter climate, most outdoor recreations, including golf and even skin diving, go on the year-round in the lowlands, and determined skiers can find snow in the high mountains eight months of the year.

**Bicycle riding:** One popular place for this is the 2.8-mile public track around Green Lake, a short distance north of downtown on Aurora Ave. Rent bikes at Gregg's, 7007 Woodlawn N.E., 532–1822. And watch out for joggers. *Alki Beach* in west Seattle has a rental shop (call 938–3322) and miles of streets marked for cyclers. *Bicycle Centers* has outlets in the University District and Kenmore for riding the Burke-Gilman Trail. Call 523–8300 or 523–7008.

**Boating:** Canoes to yachts, motorized or for sailing; rented, chartered, or on tours; on Lake Union, Lake Washington, Green Lake, or in Puget Sound; with or without pilot—all are available. Some 30 charter, tour, and rental firms are listed in the yellow pages of the Seattle telephone directory. *Kelly's Landing* on Lake Union, for example, rents small sailboats and canoes; 1401 NE Boat St. At Green Lake, canoes, paddleboats, and windsurfers can be rented at the east end of the lake. *Northwest Marine Charters* at Shilshole Bay Marine on Puget Sound rents everything from small sailboats to sloops, small outboards to cabin cruisers.

**Fishing:** In parks, the Sound, Lake Washington, Lake Union, other lakes, or by designated public access to otherwise private lakes. Bass, perch and crappie, and cutthroat, silver, and rainbow trout are the principal species taken. A license is needed in freshwater, and for salmon and clams in saltwater; they are available at all sporting goods stores. Boathouses at Ballard, in West Seattle, and in suburban Puget Sound shore towns rent boats and gear. Pier 57 on the waterfront is a public fishing pier, as are the piers at Madison Park, Madrona Park, Baker Park, Seward Park, Leschi Moorage, and Hiram Chittendam Locks.

**Golf:** Seattle has three municipal courses, 18–27 holes: *Jackson Park,* 100 N.E. 135th, 363–4747; *Jefferson Park,* 4101 Beacon Ave. S., 762–4513; *West Seattle Golf Course,* 4470 35th S.W., 932–9792. There are a dozen 18-hole public courses in the immediate suburbs, plus some 9-hole courses and private clubs with exchange privileges for visiting members of other clubs.

**Hiking:** Many trails in and around the city. *Myrtle Edwards Park* is a two-mile path along Elliott Bay. *Foster Island Nature Walk* is on a paved trail over marshland beside Lake Washington, leading from the Museum of History and Industry to Foster Island. Other trails are in *Seward Park,* a small peninsula on the south end of Lake Washington; *Schmitz Park,* a small, wooded area in west Seattle; and *Discovery Park,* a former military base on the tip of Magnolia Bluff in Northwest Seattle. Burke-Gilman Trail runs 12½ miles from north side of Lake Union to Kenmore, north end of Lake Washington. *The Mountaineers* (300 Third Ave. W., Seattle 98119; 284–6310) publishes guides to hiking trails in the Northwest and offers guided trips for a range of outdoor activities.

**Swimming:** *Green Lake* is about the only place it gets warm enough. Almost nobody swims in the Sound; it hurts to even think of it. There are nine municipal pools and several commercial indoor pools, but in many cases the out-of-town visitor has a heated pool at his motel.

**Skiing:** The nearest area to Seattle is *Snoqualmie Summit,* 50 miles east on I–90. Three ski slopes are all under the same management there: Alpental, Snoqualmie Summit, and Ski Acres. Shuttle buses serve all three. Information: 434–6161.

**Tennis:** At *Green Lake, University of Washington, Alki Community Center.* The *Seattle Tennis Center,* on Martin Luther King, Jr. Way S., and S. Walker St. (324–2980) is a park department indoor center for tennis.

 **WHAT TO DO WITH THE CHILDREN.** There is an abundance of parks and beaches. The most unusual playground is the new *Gas Works Park,* north side of Lake Union. You'll never see another one like it, nor will you see children any happier as they clamber over and into what was once industrial equipment. Ferry rides and the Monorail appeal to youngsters. (See "How to Get There" and "How to Get Around," above.) There's *Green Lake,* on Aurora Avenue., with boats, bikes, and fishing gear to rent and with swimming both indoors and out; *Seattle Center,* with the *Space Needle* (open seven days 9 A.M.–midnight; $3 for adults; $1.50 children 6–12; under 5, free; 447–3100); the *Skyride,* which swings small passengers high over the ground; the *Pacific Science Center,* where a child can see more than 100 special exhibits, including laser shows and an amusement area (open seven days 10 A.M.–5 P.M., but to 6 P.M. on Friday and Saturday; small admission charge; 625–9333; for laser show info: 382–2887). Then, in another part of Seattle, there's *Lake Washington Ship Canal and Locks*—and *Woodland Park Zoo*, with its children's zoo. On the waterfront is the *Marine Aquarium*. See "Zoos and Aquariums," above. Tillicum Indian Village on Blake Island (see "Tours," above) is a family experience.

**MUSEUMS AND GALLERIES. Historical:** *Museum of History and Industry,* 2161 E. Hamlin; 324–1125. History of Pacific Northwest from time of the Indian, transportation and fire engines, aerospace exhibits, fashions, and furnishings. Maritime collection of figureheads, ships' bells, ship models; dioramas and specimens of wildlife. Closed Monday. Tuesday–Friday, 11 A.M. –5 P.M.; Sunday, noon–5 P.M. Free.

**Art:** *Charles and Emma Frye Art Museum,* 704 Terry; 622–9250. Large collection of Munich School paintings, 1850–1900; American School, 19th and 20th centuries. Open Monday–Saturday 10 A.M.–6 P.M. Free. *Seattle Art Museum,* Volunteer Park; 447–4710. Exceptional collections in all fields of Asian art; pre-Columbian collection; European and American paintings. Tuesday–Saturday 10 A.M.–5 P.M.; Thursday 7–10 P.M.; Sunday noon–5 P.M. Members free; others small charge; Thurs. are free. *Seattle Art Museum Pavilion, Seattle Center;* 447–4670. Rotating exhibits, generally contemporary art. Tuesday–Saturday 10 A.M.–5 P.M.; Thursday to 9 P.M.; Sunday and most holidays, noon–5 P.M. Admission charge but free on Thursday. *Henry Art Gallery,* U. of Washington, 15th Ave. NE and NE 41st St.; 543–2280. 19th- & 20th-century American and European paintings; contemporary prints and American ceramics; modern Japanese folk pottery. Tuesday–Wednesday, 10 A.M.–5 P.M.; Thursday–Friday to 7 P.M.; Saturday–Sunday, noon to 6 P.M. Free except for special events. Newest on the institution scene is the *Bellevue Art Museum,* Bellevue Square Mall, Bellevue. Permanent collection, rotated on exhibit, and juried shows as well. Tuesday–Friday, noon–8 P.M.; Saturday, 9:30 A.M.–6 P.M.; Sunday, 11 A.M.–5 P.M. Free on Tuesdays.

As elsewhere, private galleries and craft shops have been springing up faster than they fade away. You find them everywhere. Among those well established are *Linda Ferris,* 320 Second Ave. S., 623–1110; *Kirsten,* 5320 Roosevelt Way N.E., 522–2011; *Gordon Woodside,* 1101 Howell St., 622–7243 and those at *Frederick & Nelson,* 5th and Pine, and the *Bon Marché,* 4th and Pine. For others and what they present, see Friday editions of the newspapers, when more than 100 galleries are listed.

**Special Interest:** *Pacific Science Center,* Seattle Center; 625–9333; for laser show info: 382–2887. Exhibits primarily math, space, astronomy, and physical science, with developing programs in life science and Northwest Indians. *Flight,* 9404 E. Marginal Way S.; 747–7373. A world-class museum telling the whole story of flight with emphasis on the Pacific nations. *Thomas Burke Memorial Washington State Museum,* U. of Washington; 543–5590. Unique collection of

Northwest Coast Indian material; ethnology of the Pacific Rim; geology and paleontology of the Pacific Rim; zoology; human evolution. Closed Monday. Tuesday–Saturday, 10 A.M.–4:30 P.M., Thursday to 9 P.M.; Sunday, 1 P.M.–4:30 P.M. Free. *Wing Luke Memorial Museum,* 414 Eighth St. S.; 623–5124. Rotating exhibits emphasize Chinese history and culture.

 **MUSIC AND DANCE.** The *Seattle Symphony Orchestra* (447–4736) is among the best in the nation. It presents a long season at Seattle Center Opera House, in Seattle Center, and a number of special performances. The *Seattle Opera Association* (447–4711) has drawn raves from critics throughout the world, particularly for its presentation of Wagner's full Ring operas, which are presented each summer. There's a *Gilbert & Sullivan Society* (782–5033) and an outstanding *Seattle Youth Symphony* (623–2001). *Pacific Northwest Ballet* (447–4655) is a professional resident ballet company. Touring orchestras, singers, and dancers add to the full bill.

 **STAGE & REVUES.** A Seattle newspaper's list of stage events was chosen at random. It showed 12 theaters in action Fri.-Sun., and some all week. All companies were professional or semi-pro, based in the area and presenting a whole season. The two biggest are *Seattle Repertory Theater* in the new Bagley Wright Theatre in the Seattle Center; call 447–2222 for ticket information; and *A Contemporary Theater* (ACT) which uses its own theater, housed in the old repertory theater in Seattle Center; call 285–5110. Among others are the *Bellevue Playbarn, Empty Space,* (contemporary, off-Broadway and experimental theater; 919 E. Pike; 325–4443), *Intiman* (classical theater; 801 Pike St.; 624–2992), *City Stage* (experimental; 4th and Battery; 622–0251), *Puppet Power* (500 N. Aurora; 329–5534), and *Bathhouse* (children and adult programs; 7312 W. Greenlake Drive N.; 524–9110). Touring companies appear in several theaters. The University of Washington has three theaters: *Glenn Hughes* (Playhouse; 543–5636), *Penthouse* (an arena theater; 543–5636), and *Showboat* (also 543–5636).

The best way for a visitor to find out what is going on currently is to consult the Friday entertainment sections of the two Seattle dailies. The *Times's* section is called "Tempo" and the *Post-Intelligencer's* is "What's Happening." A third source is "Seattle Guide," a free weekly found at hotels, motels, Chamber of Commerce, and elsewhere.

This advice also applies to "Bars and Nightlife" and to "Museums and Galleries."

 **SHOPPING.** Seattle's central shopping district covers six blocks, from Seneca to Stewart streets, between First and Seventh avenues, and includes the Monorail Terminal and numerous good hotels. Browsers delight in its high-fashion shops, antique galleries, china shops, men's and women's specialty shops, pastry shops, and dozens of others. *Frederick & Nelson,* 5th and Pine, and the *Bon Marché,* 4th & Pine, are the best-known large department stores. Top quality is offered at plush *I. Magnin,* 6th & Pine. For fashions many Seattle women favor *Nordstroms,* 5th & Pine. *Eddie Bauer,* Rainier Concourse, is famous for its outdoor equipment for campers, hunters, fishermen, backpackers, and climbers. Long-established *Shorey Book Store,* 110 Union, specializes in old books and maps and in Northwest history. It also has a branch in the Pioneer Square area. The Pioneer Square area is, in fact, filled with small shops of every description, running strongly to handcrafts and imports. Nearby, at 4th and King, is the old *Union Station,* now the largest antique store in town.

Scattered throughout the downtown area and in the so-called *International District* are small shops specializing in ivory, furs, lacquerware, silver, silks, carpets, handmade furniture, glass, china, leather, and other imports. In the basement of Center House at Seattle Center is the *International Bazaar,* and nearby is *Hansen Baking Co.,* whose name is a non-sequitur. It used to be a bakery but is now a collection of restaurants and shops of all kinds. And, of course, the waterfront is filled with sellers of all kinds of foods and handcrafted items. See description of the waterfront under *Exploring Seattle.*

There are many sophisticated shops in the *University District* (University Way N.E. and N. 45th Ave. area), a living area reflecting the diversity of the more than 30,000 students from many countries who populate the campus. There is a genuinely cosmopolitan air on University Way, more familiarly known as "The Ave." Understandably, this district has a congregation of bookstores.

**DINING OUT.** During the past 20 years Seattle has moved its culinary rating up from "undistinguished" to "none better." There is fierce competition for a gourmet reputation among dozens of restaurants. There are hundreds of cafés and restaurants in the area and new ones are opening all the time. We have chosen but a few of them. Very good eating places are often to be found in the hotels and motels but have not usually been listed separately. Price categories for a complete dinner, excluding tax, tip, and drinks, are: *Deluxe,* $15–$20 and up; *Expensive,* $12–$15; *Moderate,* $9–$12; *Inexpensive,* under $9.

## Deluxe

**Brasserie Pittsbourg.** 602 First Ave., opposite the Totem Pole in Pioneer Square; 623–4167. One of Seattle's oldest restaurants, displaying the same old tables, marble counters, tile floors, and molded tin ceiling it had when it opened in 1893. Unexcelled French food, good wine and full bar.

**Canlis.** 2576 Aurora Ave.; 283–3313. A wonderfully friendly and relaxing restaurant. À la carte menu. Portions are large. The chef, presiding over a flaming pit, turns out steaks as ordered—also seafood and lamb. Sparkling view of the lights reflected in Lake Union. Piano bar.

**City Loan Pavilion.** Entrance is off Occidental Park in the Pioneer Square Area; 624–9937. The owners of this restaurant call their décor "Neapolitan Decadent"; you can call it anything you like. At best it is unusual—but looking at it will keep one busy while awaiting an order of distinctively prepared food. Full bar.

**Rossellini's Four-10.** 2515 Fourth Ave. (formerly at 410 Union, which gave it its name); 624–5464. This is where a lot of Seattleites go for an elegant, expensive dinner. There is no better service, food, or wine, and the new building is very attractive.

**Rossellini's Other Place.** 319 Union St.; 623-7340. The specialties in this popular restaurant are fresh trout, game, and vegetables raised on the owner's farms. The faultless service and quiet atmosphere make for a pleasant gourmet dining experience. Extensive wine list.

**Space Needle.** Seattle Center (you can't help but find this one—you can see it from all over town); 447–3100. Watch Seattle "revolve" around this 500-foot high restaurant. Of course it is the restaurant revolving, but it doesn't seem so. Just don't leave anything on the window sill because it will take one hour for it to get back to you. Good food and cocktails. Breakfast, lunch and dinner. The most formal and expensive of the Space Needle eating spots is called the Emerald Suite.

**Stuart's at Shilshole.** 4135 Seaview N.W.; 784–7974. Don't be fooled by the rustic exterior. This is a very formal dining place. The décor is nautical and diners are treated as though they were captains. A good view of lively yacht activities. Lunch and dinner served. Full bar.

**Le Tastevin.** 501 Queen Anne Ave. N.; 283–0991. Unexcelled French cuisine served by professionals. Exceptional wine cellar. Lunch and dinner, full bar. Accessible to wheelchairs. Reservations advised before 8 P.M.

### *Expensive*

**Benihana of Tokyo.** In the IBM Building, 1200 Fifth Ave.; 682–4686. This attractive place features the Japanese Steak Ceremony—at your table. Quite an experience. Lunch and dinner. Lounge and entertainment.

**Il Bistro.** Lower Post Alley, Pike Place Markets; 682–3049. Italian cuisine, but light. Pasta, braciole, crisp salads, rack of lamb. Good wine list and desserts that include homemade ice creams and sherberts and pecan pie.

**F.X. McRory's.** Occidental S. and S. King St.; 623–4800. A vast restaurant in Pioneer Square near the Kingdome. Will seat 350 at a time. Perhaps the loudest restaurant in town, but intentionally so. Premium meat and oyster bar; infinite number of liquor selections.

**Hiram's at the Locks.** 5300 34th N.W.; 784–1733. If one gets hungry while visiting the Hiram Chittenden Locks, this is a great place to eat. Try to get a table with a view of the constant activity in the locks. It will be an experience in both dining and viewing. Lunch and dinner. Wine list.

**Hong Kong.** 507 Maynard Ave.; 622–0366. Chinatown's oldest first-class restaurant. A real dining treat. À la carte and family-style lunch and dinner. Famous dim sum (tea pastries) served during luncheon hours. Lounge.

**Ivar's Captain's Table.** 333 Elliott Ave. W.; 284–7040. Seafood at its best, always fresh, and served in many ways. Large dining area with view of Elliott Bay. Lunch and dinner. Cocktails and entertainment.

**Mirabeau.** 5th and Madison; 624–4550. Top floor of the SeaFirst Building with excellent views of Puget Sound and city. Continental and Oriental cuisine.

**Ray's Boat House.** On Shilshole Bay, 6049 Seaview Ave. N.W.; 789–3770. The seafood is fresh. The décor is Scandinavian. Prime rib is also served. Saturday and Sunday lunches are served at the bar (no minors). Wine list.

**Maxmilien's.** A fine French restaurant in Pike Place Market; 682–7270. The chef shops there and food is fresh from the stalls and prepared with a special flair. Breakfast, lunch, and dinner. Watch the harbor activity as you dine. Small; dinner reservations advised.

## Moderate–Expensive

**13 Coins.** 125 Boren Ave. N.; 682–2513. This restaurant in the Furniture Mart Building has become a great favorite in spite of being so difficult to find. The only identification visible is a small sign over an unimpressive door on the street floor of the building. The food is well worth the search, however. Huge servings in categories from plain to exotic are available any hour of the day or night. Another *13 Coins* is at SeaTac at 18000 Pacific Highway S.; 243–9500.

## Moderate

**Ivar's Salmon House.** 401 N.E. Northlake Way; 632–0767. The building is a reproduction of an Indian longhouse; it houses artifacts collected by the owner. Old photographs and other memorabilia hang on the walls. Patrons enjoy full-course salmon dinners, prepared Indian-style over open alderwood fires. Children's portions. Buffet lunch. Cocktails.

**Jake O'Shaughnessey's.** 100 Mercer St.; 285–1897. Gold-Rush-days décor and a menu limited to that of the original Jake O'Shaughnessey who opened a restaurant in Seattle in 1897. The house specialty is "saloon beef," loin encased in salt and cooked for ten hours. An interesting bar—Irish coffee a specialty. A friendly, informal restaurant, not far from the Center in the old Hansen Baking Co. complex.

**The Phoenecia.** 4725 California Ave.; 935–8993. Mideast and Balkan menu, including lamb, seafood, curries and vegetarian dinners. A very interesting ethnic restaurant. No liquor served.

**Stuart Anderson's Black Angus.** At 12255 Aurora Ave. N.; 365–7600; and 208 Elliott Ave. W.; 282–1700. Top-quality beef. Excellent chefs who prepare it as ordered. A house specialty is steak and lobster. Lounge with entertainment and dancing.

**Andy's Diner.** 2963 Fourth Ave. S.; 624–4097. In a complex consisting of seven railroad passenger cars, guests can eat in an atmosphere which recalls the early years of dining on the rails. Choices are limited to prime quality beef.

## Inexpensive–Moderate

**The Wharf.** 1735 W. Thurman (off the south end of the Ballard Bridge); 283–6600. An interesting location on Fishermen's Wharf. Very fresh seafood, as well as other interesting dishes. Same meals served in coffee shop at lower prices than in the restaurant. Lounge and entertainment.

*Inexpensive*

**Copacabana.** Triangle Building, Pike Place Markets; 622–6359. Situated on a long, second-story veranda above the markets. The food is excellent: paella, shrimp soup, *saltena* (a meat-vegetable pie), *fritanga* (cubed pork with hominy) and other South American favorites. Hours are flexible, but it opens every day at 11:30. Monday, Tuesday and Wednesday it closes at 5 P.M.; Thursdays and Fridays at 9 P.M., and on Saturday it closes at 10 P.M. Closed Sundays.

**Emmett Watson's Oyster Bay.** Soames Dunn Building, Pike Place Markets; 622–7721. Raw oysters, clam chowder, gazpacho, and shrimp Orleans are the specialties, along with some 60 imported beers. The bar opens into a courtyard sheltered from the rain by awnings.

**Guadalajara Restaurants.** 1429 Fourth Ave.; 622–8722; 1718 N. 45th; 632–7858. Expertly prepared Mexican food. Imported and domestic wines and beer.

**The Lebanon Restaurant.** 112 5th N.; 624–6662. Middle Eastern cuisine with shish and chicken kebab and special Lebanese drinks. Belly dancing on Fridays and Saturdays.

**Old Spaghetti Factory.** At Alaskan Way and Broad St.; 623–3520. Family food and fun in a restored warehouse. Nineteenth-century décor, beautiful antiques in lobby and bar. Metal bedsteads form booths, and even an old Birney streetcar is used for seating space. Choice of sauces, plus salad, sourdough bread, beverage and spumoni for dessert. Dinners only. Expect to wait a while to be seated.

Restaurants large and small abound on the waterfront, ranging in price from inexpensive to deluxe. There is seafood, of course, but other specialties are also represented. This strip is best explored on foot. Places to look for are *Bruccio's* (682–3652) at the Ferry Terminal, *Ivar's Acres of Clams* (624–6852) on Pier 54, *Elliott Bay Fish & Oyster Co.* (623–4340) on Pier 56. Pier 57 has at least two restaurants, so has Pier 70. In between are numerous small cafes and snack bars.

While at the Seattle Center, a visit to the Center House's *Food Circus Court* offers a chance to sample a wide range of international snacks. Children have fun just trying to make up their minds on which one.

Chinatown is a great place to explore. There are numerous Chinese, Japanese and Filipino cafés and restaurants from inexpensive to deluxe. Some notable ones are *China Gate,* 516 Seventh Ave. S., 624–1730 (Cantonese); *Chiyoko,* 610 S. Jackson, 623–9347 (Japanese dishes, including tempura); *Tai Tung,* 655 S. King, 525–1060 (Cantonese). In the Pioneer Square Area are many snack shops and sidewalk cafes. The Pike Place Market has several ethnic cafés and restaurants as does the Broadway District on Capitol Hill.

In the University District one finds coffee shops and, always, kookie little cafes (that come and go). In the Ballard area (NW Seattle) one comes across home-style Scandinavian cafes.

**BARS AND NIGHT LIFE.** State law requires that any place licensed to pour liquor by the drink must also serve food—that is, to enough customers to prove its substantial business is being a restaurant or café. (The law is not applicable to taverns dispensing only beer and wine.) Therefore, there are no saloons as such, nor nightclubs devoted only to drinking, dancing, and floor-shows. However, that situation has not slowed activities very much. The restaurant side may close by 9 or 10 P.M.,but the bars are open until 2 A.M. More than 100 places in the Seattle area have live entertainment, ranging from a single pianist to floor shows.

The recently restored *Fifth Avenue Theater,* 1308 Fifth Ave., features road company productions of Broadway hits such as "Annie," and the gorgeous old theater is worth the admission price. The big hotels feature much the same thing in conjunction with their bars and lounges, both downtown and at the Airport Strip. Several downtown spots put on cabaret-style entertainment. In smaller nightspots, "entertainment" may mean featured soloists or an act during dancing intermissions.

Just drinking and listening to sometimes too-loud music can be done in any cocktail lounge, anywhere. Residents tend to take their guests—and visitors seek out—places that are distinctive to the area. (The same can be said for eating, but as noted above, all the lounges are in restaurants.) Half a dozen "sky rooms" on the top floors of buildings are popular. Numerous restaurants face Puget Sound, and more look out on Lake Union. The Wharf has a view of the fishing fleet, and half a dozen others are at marinas.

Best view bars are: *Hiram's at the Locks,* 5300 34th N.W. Great view of the activity in the Ballard (Hiram Chittenden) Locks with a grassy patio area outside. *The Lakeside,* 2501 N. Northlake Way. You can either tie up your boat at the Lake Union dock or drive in for a view across Lake Union toward the city. *Mirabeau,* 46th floor, Sea-First Building, 4th and Madison. The highest spot in the city for a drink. Stunning view across the Sound and of the Cascades. *The Space Needle* (of course), Seattle Center. This slowly revolving restaurant gives you the full 360-degree views of the region. Other good lounges are: *The Garden Court,* Four Seasons Olympic Hotel, 411 University. Dark wood and mellow lighting give this basement bar a plush atmosphere. *Labuznik,* 1924 First Ave. Probably the best spot in a part of town that is on the edge of the seedy First Avenue district. *Fitzgerald's,* Westin Hotel Lobby, Fifth and Virginia. A narrow alcove off the Westin lobby that is quiet and formal. *Blue Moon Tavern,* 712 N.E. 45th, in the University District. Has a reputation for attracting the Beatniks (Jack Kerouac and Allen Ginsberg), and later personalities of the same ilk (Tom Robbins and Darrel Bob Houston). Sort of cleaned up, but still has the best graffiti in the area. *J&M Café,* 201 First S. One of the most popular spots in the Pioneer Square area.

# EXPLORING WASHINGTON

## Excursions from Seattle

The ferry boats that connect the northwest Washington mainland with seven big islands and the Kitsap and Olympic peninsulas do more than provide essential commuter service; they are means of exploration. Capacity for automobiles ranges from 40 to 206. Hot meals and snacks are served at lunch counters on most runs.

The longest and most spectacular regular ferry run begins at Anacortes, about 75 miles northwest of Seattle, and weaves through the San Juan Islands to Sidney, above Victoria, B.C.

Anacortes is reached by I–5 to Mount Vernon and by Wash. 536. But a far more scenic, though slower, path to Anacortes traverses two islands, Whidbey and Fidalgo. The southern gateway to Whidbey is the ferry from Mukilteo to Columbia Beach, and the road north is Wash. 525, which becomes Wash. 20 midway up the island.

Approximately 50 miles long, Whidbey Island is the largest island in Puget Sound and is second only to Long Island, N.Y., in length. Here, rhododendrons, Washington's state flower, reach heights of 20 to 30 feet. Homes of early settlers dot the shores. Oak Harbor is the most important town. Ft. Casey is a former coast artillery post, whose long guns are now for tourist viewing.

Between Oak Harbor and Ft. Casey is Coupeville, where stands Alexander's Blockhouse, built as a defense against Indians. Actually, there is more: Coupeville is a museum piece, a restored 1875 town. One of the state's finest parks, Deception Pass, is on the northern tip of this island. Deception Pass Bridge spans a gorge notorious for its tidal currents, and links Whidbey and Fidalgo islands. From here it is a short distance to Anacortes and the San Juan ferry. Enroute, a short side trip leads to the top of the 1,270-foot Mt. Erie and a view of islands and mainland, all directions.

The ferry touches at Lopez, Shaw, Orcas, and San Juan Islands and skirts many more of the 172 isles that comprise this archipelago.

There are eight state parks with campgrounds (no trailer hookups) on the San Juan Islands, and the state owns 42 undeveloped islands, all but one of which are accessible by boat only. These are open for use by all who can get themselves there and want to camp. These isles range in size from 134 acres down to less than an acre. (If you use one of these islands, carry your garbage back with you.)

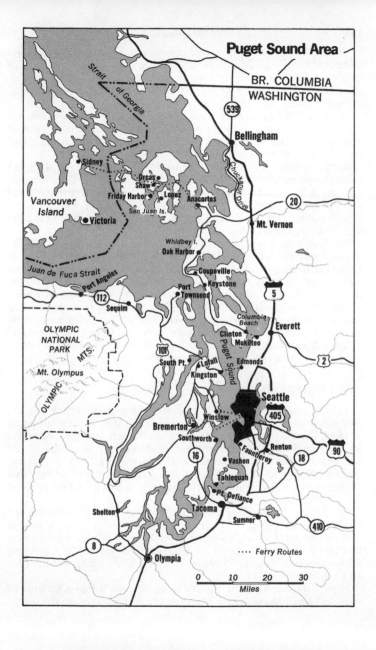

Orcas Island, in the San Juans, possesses the most vacation resorts and best beaches. Its Moran State Park contains picnic grounds, 124 campsites, four trout-stocked lakes, miles of foot paths cutting through thick stands of virgin forest, and an abundance of game and bird life, protected under state law.

Moran's Mt. Constitution rises 2,400 feet above sea level. From a 50-foot rock tower atop the butte, hundreds of miles of island-dotted waters are visible. To the east, Mt. Baker rears its white dome above the high Cascades.

San Juan was the site of the bloodless "Pig War" of 1859. It began when British settlers, claiming the island belonged to the Crown, wanted to try in Victoria an American farmer who had shot a British-owned pig. For twelve years the island was occupied by both American and British military forces. Finally the dispute was settled, sustaining the U.S. claim to the San Juans.

San Juan Island National Historic Park, in two sections, recalls the unnasty war, in which not a life was lost except that of the pig. English Camp lies 10 miles northwest of Friday Harbor. The blockhouse, commissary, and barracks still stand. American Camp is on the barren southeastern tip of the island, about five miles southwest of Friday Harbor. No buildings remain, but the vestiges of the principal American defense works are well preserved. The park is open daily from sunrise to sunset. Rangers are on duty from June through October and at the National Park Service office all year in Friday Harbor, the largest town in the group (population: about 800).

## The Olympic Peninsula

The "gateway" to Olympic Peninsula and the national park is wherever you start on the loop. If you do the whole U.S. 101 circle by way of Hood Canal, more than 400 miles, the longest but most complete way is from Seattle to Bremerton or Southworth by ferry, then down to the tidewater end of Hood Canal; or from Tacoma, across the Narrows Bridge to pick up the extreme end of the Canal at the same point. If you are in Olympia, you can start on U.S. 101 and get to Hood Canal much faster.

Hood Canal (Vancouver named it "Hood's Channel") separates the Kitsap Peninsula from the Olympic Peninsula and is actually an arm of Puget Sound. It stretches south from Admiralty Inlet, the entrance to Puget Sound, and ends in a fishhook curve back to the northeast, a total distance of some 75 miles. U.S. 101 winds along its shore for about 60 miles.

If you circle around the Peninsula on 101 you'll find a number of state parks with good fishing and camping. For instance, in the southeast corner of the Peninsula, moving north from Olympia, you'll reach Potlatch, Lake Cushman, and Dosewallips State Parks. Just north of Dosewallips you can turn off U.S. 101 onto a side road that leads five miles to Mt. Walker, for enormous vistas of the Olympics, the Cascades, and Hood Canal. A splendid time to come is in June, when rhododendrons sweep right up to the 2,804-foot summit of Mt. Walker.

Ferries or highways will bring you to Port Townsend, one of the most fascinating cities in the state. The town is in the northeast corner of the Olympic Peninsula. During the last decades of the nineteenth century it was one of the most posh cities on the West Coast. The people here claim that Port Townsend contains the best collection of Victorian architecture north of San Francisco—and they may be right. You can pick up at the Tourist Information Center, on Main Street by the Ferry Terminal, a city guide that will route you past all the points of historic and exotic interest, including a Chinese Tree of Heaven, which an emperor of China presented to the city more than 100 years ago. Rothschild House is a restored late-nineteenth-century house furnished in period. The Jefferson County Historical Society Museum and Library is housed in the 1891 City Hall building, on a hill overlooking the town, with pioneer exhibits, Indian artifacts, and one room devoted to Ft. Worden (a mile north of town).

The major downtown section of Port Townsend lies at sea level along the beach and has a variety of antique stores, restaurants, and small hotels. Up on the high bluff above town are gorgeous Victorian homes, many of which now are given over to bed-and-breakfast arrangements. One of the most unusual hotels is Manreesa Castle on a hill at the southern end of town. Built like a small French chateau, it now has a bath in every room—the movie "An Officer and a Gentleman" was filmed nearby and the film crew required rooms with baths; the hotel was advanced enough money to modernize it to meet Hollywood standards. Port Townsend is a rapidly growing center for art and culture, with a Summer School of the Arts and a Rhododendron Festival in mid-May. Point Wilson Lighthouse (1870) stands where the Straight of Juan de Fuca turns to form Admiralty Inlet, which leads into Puget Sound. Old Ft. Townsend State Park, three miles south of the city, has historical charm.

Not far from Port Townsend, off 101, lies Gardiner; more than 100 wolves of several species are kept at Loboland. The people running the place are very sincere about saving the only Lobo wolves left in the United States.

Dungeness on Juan de Fuca Strait, also off 101, is not far west of Port Townsend. This once-busy fishing village gave its name to the North Pacific coast's most delectable crabs. Near Dungeness is the Olympic Game Farm. You can tour it on foot, by car, or by sightseeing train.

(Half price for kids and senior citizens.) However, earnest believers in Walt Disney "true life" nature movies should be warned that they may be disillusioned. Here live all the creatures trained to perform for Disney and other TV and movie companies—Grizzly Adams' bear and all the rest who have ever appeared on a screen. Some 80 "nature" films have been made with these animals.

A pleasant stroll—or a long hike—can be made on Dungeness Spit, reportedly the longest such "spit" in the country. It curves along the edge of the strait and ends at a lighthouse on the tip, five miles out.

The largest city on the Olympic Peninsula, Port Angeles, is an important fishing town. Its Salmon Derby, held there every Labor Day weekend, is one of the big events of the Peninsula. At Ediz Hook, a natural sand spit forming the city harbor, there are places to picnic, and a boat launch. Visitors are welcome to tour the U.S. Coast Guard Air Rescue Station at Ediz Hook. Pioneer Memorial Museum, 2800 Hurricane Ridge Road, is at Olympic National Park Headquarters, where you can brief yourself about the park. There's a log cabin of the 1890s, a large relief model of Olympic National Park, and botanical, geological, and biological exhibits.

There is year-round ferry service from Port Angeles to Victoria, on Vancouver Island.

## The Olympic National Park

Port Angeles is also the gateway to Olympic National Park, a lush wilderness of thick rain forests (spruce, fir, and cedar), wildlife (65 species), alpine flower meadows, glaciers, lakes, and streams, all cradled in a rugged mountain fastness. Yearly rainfall on the western slopes of the park exceeds 140 inches and centuries of such heavy rains have promoted the growth of towering trees, many of them more than 200 feet high and more than ten feet in diameter. The park contains the largest known specimens of Douglas fir, red cedar, western hemlock, and Alaska cedar. Equally impressive are the mountains within the park's boundaries. Mt. Olympus, at nearly 8,000 feet, is the highest; many others rise above 7,000 feet. Just east of Port Angeles the Heart o' the Hills Highway leads to 5,228-foot Hurricane Ridge, where there are awesome views of Juan de Fuca Strait, Vancouver Island, and the Olympic peaks. A summit lodge is open daily after May 30 through the summer but has no overnight accommodations. Park naturalists give talks and lead nature walks throughout the day.

For other tremendous views, leave U.S. 101 about six miles east of Port Angeles and twist up a mountain road to 6,000-foot Deer Park.

Not well understood by out-of-state visitors is that relatively few miles of U.S. 101 are in the national park. Only nine dead-end roads enter the park elsewhere, and then just barely. The broad views of what is inside are from the two vantage points described above. (There is no entrance fee to the park.)

Under plans proposed by the National Park Service, 92 percent of the Olympic National Park will be designated wilderness area. The service proposes to take 834,890 of the park's nearly 900,000 acres and preserve them as "a pristine and undisturbed part of our natural inheritance." The wilderness designation would apply to three areas—two strips along the Pacific Ocean and the heart of the main park on the Olympic Peninsula. The federal Wilderness Act provides that the only facilities in wilderness areas will be "the minimum required for public enjoyment, health and safety, preservation, and protection of the features."

West of Port Townsend are three fine lakes, Aldwell, Sutherland, and Crescent. Lake Crescent is inside the national park and has one seasonal concession lodge and one all-year resort, Log Cabin, on private land. There are two campgrounds. From the Visitor Center, midway along the south shore, a nature trail leads to Marymere Falls, a 90-foot cascade.

A few miles beyond the lake a road takes off U.S. 101 and runs parallel to the Soleduck River to Sol Duc Hot Springs, a famous old early-century resort still in business but whose future seems threatened by Park Service plans to restore all the preserve to wilderness. (For more information about the resort see "Olympic National Park" under "Hotels and Motels" in *Practical Information for Washington.*)

Twelve miles beyond the Sol Duc turnoff, U.S. 101 arrives at Sappho, a former rough-and-tumble logging camp named, for some reason, for a poetess of ancient Greece. An interesting side trip can be made from Sappho to Clallam Bay, which lies 17 miles north via a county road. Clallam Bay is an old lumber town on the shore of Juan de Fuca Strait, but it is not the reason for detouring north. From Clallam Bay, Wash. 112 follows the coast 21 miles to the town of Neah Bay, on the Makah Indian Reservation, in the northwest corner of the Peninsula. The Makahs, whose canoe-building culture is closely related to that of the southeastern Alaska and Vancouver Island Indians, were once known for their fierceness and prowess as whale hunters. Today Neah Bay has quite a reputation among sports fishermen after salmon. The Makahs also derive some income from handicrafts, which are sold at local shops. There is a museum featuring the archaeological treasures from Ozette (see below).

From Neah Bay, intrepid sightseers can follow a quiet road out of town and through wooded terrain for about seven miles. From where the road ends, a path—perhaps a thousand yards long—snakes through a forest glade to a cliff. This is the tip of Cape Flattery, often called the most northwesterly point of the coterminous United States. (However, Cape Alava, 15 miles south, is the most western point by a few hundred feet.) From the cliff of Cape Flattery you see, across a trough of turbulent Pacific water, a large, high rock, on top of which is a lighthouse and several houses. This is Tatoosh Island, where until recently lighthouse keepers and their families lived. Now the light is automated.

On the way to Neah Bay there is really an unusual sidetrip from a sidetrip. Just west of Sekiu (another center for salmon fishing) a road leads off left, 20 miles to Lake Ozette and Cape Alava. You can't go any farther west in the continental United States than Alava, and Ozette was where the tide of immigration stopped in the 1890s. The Klondike gold rush of 1898 drew most of the homesteaders away, and the land went back to wilderness. Lake Ozette is in the Olympic National Park, and the coast north for 7-plus miles recently has been added to the park.

You have to hike three miles on a boardwalk to the cape, where archeologists made a very important find, an Indian village that had been buried beneath an air-tight clay slide which preserved artifacts that went back centuries to before the time white men arrived. Thousands of artifacts from the dig have gone on display at Neah Bay.

## The Rain Forest

On the main Olympic Loop road, U.S. 101 bends south to Forks, an important center in the logging industry of the Olympic Peninsula. Within 15 miles of Forks are six top rivers for rainbow trout, cutthroat, steelhead, and King salmon.

Two miles north of Forks a paved road takes off from U.S. 101 to wind west 14 miles to La Push, a rambling coastal village on the Quillayute Indian Reservation. La Push is a home for sports and commercial fishing boats, in a setting of offshore rocks, sandy beaches hemmed by wind-twisted trees, foaming surf, and far vistas. Driftwood and agates are found along the beach, and booming waves can bring in a lot of other things.

Return to Forks and follow U.S. 101 for 13 miles south to a turnoff east. This road, which runs for 18 miles following the Hoh River, is an entrance to Olympic National Park and is a good way to see the rain forest, where moss drapes the branches of trees and forms a thick carpet underfoot. Immense ferns also grow in the light dimly filtered through the overhead canopy. At the end of the paved road are camping facilities and self-guiding nature trails. Botanical, geological, and biological exhibits are on display at the Visitor Center.

Ten miles below the Hoh Valley turnoff, U.S. 101 enters a dozen miles of the Olympic National Park's Pacific Coast strip. About a mile south of Ruby Beach, a roadside viewpoint faces Destruction Island and a famous lighthouse. The lighthouse keeper once had to haul kerosene up the 90-foot tower every night. But today the lighthouse is completely automated—more efficiency, less strain, less romance.

This part of the Washington coast is strewn with grotesque rock formations. Between the Destruction Island viewpoint and Kalaloch, seven miles south along U.S. 101, there are more impressive seascapes. The driftwood-strewn beaches are only a short walk from the road, with trail entrances announced by signs on the highway. Camping and lodge accommodations are available at Kalaloch.

Six miles south of Queets a road leads 14 miles along the Queets River to another part of the rain forest, with camping at the end of the road.

On U.S. 101 you come to Lake Quinault. Roads on both sides of the lake, north and south, pass lake resort accommodations to penetrate more rain forest.

Now far inland, U.S. 101 turns south again. To reach the coastal towns of Moclips, Pacific Beach, Copalis Beach, and Ocean City, you have a choice of a wide, hard-packed gravel road that cuts right soon after you pass Neilton (south of Lake Quinault) or of a road that leaves 101 farther south at Humptulips. Moclips, Pacific Beach, Copalis Beach, and Ocean City date back to when they were resort towns way out on the Pacific coast. Some of their "resort" cabins are still in use, but scattered along the shore are also some new, very fancy layouts. Between Ocean City and Ocean Shores is a wonderful state park, Ocean City State Park.

Ocean Shores was a real-estate project that began some twenty years ago with full ballyhoo. Today you don't know whether to laugh or cry about it. It is laid out for miles with unused streets, lots, canals, and an occasional residence. At the same time it does have top-notch resort-type motels, a golf course, and a marina for charter fishing. It was recently incorporated as a city. Buses prowl its streets and connect to Hoquiam and Aberdeen. A passenger ferry runs several times a day, May 1 to Labor Day, over to Westport on the other side of Grays Harbor.

One last side trip to the sea from inland U.S. 101: At Aberdeen take Wash. 105 for 22 miles to Westport, near the southwest tip of Grays Harbor. (The bay was named for the first American to visit this part of the coast, Captain Robert Gray, a mariner out of Boston who sailed across the bar into the harbor in 1792—the same year, and on the same voyage, that he entered the Columbia River, becoming the first white person to find the Great River of the West.)

Westport is one of the great salmon-fishing ports of Washington, with a fishing fleet of more than 500 commercial, charter, and pleasure boats harbored in a sheltered cove. Clam digging is popular, and the beaches near Westport are perused for shells and driftwood. Twin Harbors State Park, two miles south of Westport, is the most popular ocean-front park on the Washington coast.

From Aberdeen, a 47-mile drive east via U.S. 12 and Washington 8 leads back to Olympia. The southwest coast section of Washington is discussed above, preceding "Exploring Seattle."

## The Capital

Olympia is the state capital. Lumber and shipping played a part in Olympia's development, too, but despite its fairly extensive role as a port and transshipment terminal, the city has remained basically a state governmental center. There are alternating periods of bustle and quiet, depending upon whether the legislature is in session. Incorporated in 1859, the city withstood several attempts by other localities to have the site of the capital shifted. Dominating the city's horizons to the northwest and east, respectively, are the peaks of the Olympic Mountains and Mt. Rainier.

On the meticulously landscaped Capitol grounds, Japanese cherry trees bloom about the third week in April. With summer comes the full color of the sunken rose garden. The Legislative Building, the central one in the Capitol group, is famed for its 287-foot dome, fourth highest of its kind in the world and resembling the dome of the nation's Capitol in Washington, D.C. Organ recitals are held here in summer. An incongruous and somewhat annoying aspect of visiting these public grounds is that you must pay to park on them.

Points of interest in Olympia include the State Capitol Museum, with its separate museums of history, natural history, and art; Washington State Museum of Pharmacy; and Crosby House, a furnished house built in 1860 by the grandparents of singer Bing Crosby.

Tumwater, three miles south of Olympia on I–5, is of interest for its history and type of industry. The first American settlement north of the Columbia River was established here in 1845. A granite marker on the west bank of the Deschutes River notes the spot where the first settlers, including a black family, put down roots. But Tumwater is better known these days for the Olympia Brewing Company, open for a nonguided look at beermaking. Adjacent to the brewery is Tumwater Falls Park. Self-guiding trails here take the visitor through springtime blooms of rhododendron and azalea. With playground and picnic facilities, the park is a very good place for a luncheon pause.

## Tacoma

Tacoma is 30 miles northwest of Olympia. Much of the mileage between the two cities is taken up, on both sides of I–5, by Fort Lewis and McChord Air Force Base. They are among the largest permanent military installations in the United States.

Lumber and shipping were, and continue to be, the major reasons for Tacoma's growth as a city. The first sawmill was built by a Swedish settler, Nichalas De Lin, in the early 1850s. Today industrial giants operate huge plants in Tacoma, and millions of board feet of lumber are used in the manufacture of pulp, paper, plywood, cartons, and furniture. The Tacoma Smelter at Ruston—visible for miles around because of its 570-foot stack, taller than the Washington Monument—refines about one-tenth of the nation's copper (but has long been threatening to leave because, it says, it cannot meet pollution control requirements).

The city's main business area overlooks Commencement Bay, a fine deep-water harbor that handles millions of tons of shipping annually. Along the bay and its tidal flats are several hundred industrial plants whose products range from chemicals to railroad cars. The bay, an extension of Puget Sound, is the city's eastern shoreline boundary. On the west is a body of water called The Narrows, and Tacoma is, in effect, a peninsula town jutting into these connecting waters. As a result, boating and fishing are highly popular.

The Tacoma Narrows Bridge, which carries Wash. 16 across the Narrows from the Kitsap Peninsula, had a famous predecessor. The original span swayed so much and so often that it earned the nickname "Galloping Gertie" before it collapsed in 1940. Gertie's trouble-free replacement was completed in 1950. It is 5,450 feet long, including its approaches, and its center span of 2,800 feet is one of the longest suspension spans in the country.

In common with many American cities, Tacoma was hard hit by the rise of suburban shopping centers, in this case to the east and south of town. Downtown was left with few department stores and only one first-class hotel. It has tried valiantly to make its main business streets more attractive, turning one into a pedestrian mall and connecting two hillside avenues with the first municipally owned escalators in the nation. Old City Hall, a distinctive landmark, has been converted into shops and eating places, and seeing how it was done is worth the visit. Restoration of other buildings is in progress.

A marked two-hour tourist trail affords visitors a convenient way to see Tacoma. The Kla-how-ya Trail (the word means "welcome" in the Chinook Indian language) starts at 9th and A streets in the heart of the downtown section. Marking the start of the trail is a 105-foot-high totem pole carved from a single cedar tree by Alaskan Indian artists.

Kla-how-ya points of interest include Wright Park, a botanical conservatory with more than 1,000 labeled trees of many varieties and a large collection of orchids and tropical plants, and the State Historical Society Museum, with its illuminated photographic murals and displays relating to Indian, pioneer, and Alaskan cultures.

The most interesting of Tacoma's 44 parks is also on the Kla-how-ya Trail. Point Defiance Park, at the northernmost extension of the city, has more than 600 acres of flower gardens, virgin forestland, a Children's Farm Animal Zoo, a bathing beach on Commencement Bay, a deep-sea aquarium, and a fine otter display. The Natural Habitat Aviary displays birds from all over the world. An ambitious plan is afoot to expand a small zoo into a major one.

There is also a lot of history at Point Defiance Park. Parts of the S.S. *Beaver,* first steamship on the Pacific Coast, are here for viewing. Camp Six is an outdoor museum of old-time logging equipment, with original bunkhouses, five steam donkey engines, a 110-foot spar tree, and a Lidgerwood skidder. The work-worn steam Shea locomotive gives passengers rides. The park is also the site of Ft. Nisqually. Built by Hudson's Bay Company in 1833 at a point south of the city, this old installation was moved to the park and restored in 1934. Two of the buildings (the factor's house and the granary) are original structures, and many original items, such as hand-forged hardware, were incorporated into the replicas of other structures.

Adjacent to the east entrance to Point Defiance Park is the ferry slip for the crossing to Tahlequah on the south end of Vashon Island.

For the artistically minded, Tacoma has Handforth Gallery, Tacoma Art Museum (founded in 1891), and the Kittredge and Hill Art Galleries, on the University of Puget Sound campus.

Recently Tacoma constructed its own domed stadium, similar to but smaller than Seattle's, to which it has successfully attracted sporting events and major exhibitions.

Puyallup Valley, with its renowned bulb farms, is only a 15-minute drive east of Tacoma on U.S. 410. The valley is a major center for the production of tulip, iris, and daffodil bulbs. Every April the Puyallup Valley Daffodil Festival is held jointly in Tacoma, Puyallup, Sumner, and Orting. Southwest of the city is Steilacoom, oldest incorporated city in the state (1853) and once the seat of Pierce County. A small county ferry runs to residential Anderson Island and to McNeil Island, formerly a federal penitentiary. There has been a real scramble among public agencies and private developers over who gets the island, or pieces of it. Nearby is Ft. Steilacoom, 1849–68, next door to Western Washington State Hospital.

Northwest from Tacoma, across the Narrows Bridge on Wash. 16, is Gig Harbor, a beautiful town devoted to fishing and pleasure boats, and arts-and-crafts studios. The town surrounds an enclosed bay, and has good restaurants, nice shops, and great views. Peacock Hill, to the north, affords a wide view of the setting and is also the site of Scandia Gaard, an old farm converted into a restaurant and a Scandinavian museum.

## North and East out of Seattle

A summer trip that draws Seattle residents who want to wander in the mountains by car, starts at Lake Stevens, five miles east and north of Everett. Continue north to Wash. 92 (which comes off Wash. 9), and then eight miles to Granite Falls. The road eastward meanders through the hamlets of Robe and Verlot, skirts 5,324-foot Mt. Pilchuck, eases into the massive Mt. Baker National Forest, and follows the Stillaguamish River toward 7,790-foot Sloan Peak (dwarfed by nearby 10,541-foot Glacier Peak) to arrive at Barlow Pass. Four miles up a dead-end road is Monte Cristo, a ghost mining town that started in 1889 but had petered out by 1909.

Going north from Everett, there's another alternative drive of interest. Fifteen miles north, turn off the freeway west onto Wash. 530 and in five miles you will reach Stanwood. A road takes you across a bridge to Camano Island, which has a large state park on the shores of Saratoga Passage.

Heading on from Stanwood to Mount Vernon, Wash. 530 rejoins I–5, the main route between Seattle and Vancouver, B.C. Mount Vernon is a pleasant city surrounded by the rich agricultural land of the lower Skagit River Valley. The highway west to Anacortes also gives access to Bayview State Park and, to the south, La Conner, a picturesque town on Skagit Bay next door to the Swinomish Indian Reservation. The Swinomish Tribal Celebration is held July 3–4.

Four miles north of Mount Vernon is Burlington, the turnoff point to Wash. 20, the North Cascades Highway. Wash. 11, north of Burlington, from Edison to the outskirts of Bellingham, was long known as the most spectacular marine drive on the state's inland coasts. People used to drive to Bellingham just to see this cliff-hanging stretch of highway known as Chuckanut Drive. It follows Sanich and Chuckanut Bays and passes Larrabee State Park seven miles south of the city.

Overlooking Puget Sound and the San Juan Islands, Bellingham is within view of both the Olympic Mountains and the Cascades, in which Mt. Baker is dominant—and, next to Mt. St. Helens, the hottest of the Cascade's volcanoes. Drive up Sehome Hill, on the campus of Western Washington College, for vistas of Bellingham Bay and the San Juan

Islands. (On a clear day you can see Vancouver Island.) For picnicking, there's Fairhaven Park, on Chuckanut Drive, at the southern entrance to the city. Bloedel-Donovan Park, three miles east of Lake Whatcom, has a picnic area, a playground, and a "swimming hole." Whatcom Museum of History and Art, in a former city hall built in 1892 (a good example of late Victorian civic architecture), has a large collection of regional exhibits; it's located at 121 Prospect Street.

Bellingham celebrates its reputation as a flower-area hub with a Blossomtime Festival in mid-May. (No one should come to Bellingham in the springtime without driving out to the tulip fields around Lynden and Everson.) From June to September a steam train runs weekends and Tuesdays from Bloedel-Donovan Park, at the southern end of Lake Whatcom, to Wickersham four miles away.

The city is close to the partly offshore Lummi Indian Reservation. The Lummi Stommish, held in June at the reservation village of Marietta, is highlighted by Indian canoe races, dancing, and a salmon bake.

Blaine, on Drayton Harbor, is best known (apart from being a port of entry for Canadians) for its Peace Arch State and Provincial Park—handsomely landscaped grounds, with a well-equipped picnic area. Birch Bay State Park, ten miles south of Blaine, on Birch Bay, is 172 acres, with a large campground and hookups for more than fifty trailers. Swimming, fishing, clamming, hiking.

Undoubtedly the most scenic trip out of Bellingham is to Mt. Baker, 58 miles east. Mt. Baker is seen much of the way, and you can understand why to the Indians it was the Great White Watcher and to Francisco Eliza it was La Montana de Carmelo (he saw in the long white slopes an imagery of the flowing robes of Carmelite nuns).

A mile past the village of Glacier, on Wash. 542, try Glacier Creek Road for superb views of Mt. Baker and the multihued face of Coleman Glacier. Turn onto Wells Creek Road, a few miles along; in half a mile you'll be at Nooksack Falls, whose thundering seems to shake the trees. Mt. Baker ski area, near the end of the road, offers nearly year-round skiing.

Although Baker is the drawing card, 9,127-foot Mt. Shuksan, just behind it at road's end, steals the scene for photographers.

## North Cascades

Washington's newest major road is the North Cascades Highway, which links the Puget Sound area to the north-central part of the state. Although Wash. 20 was primarily completed to provide a shorter route between these two sections of the state, it has become a prime tourist road because of its abundance of scenery.

From I–5 at Burlington, turn east on Wash. 20. The first few miles are pastoral, through the Skagit River Valley to Sedro Woolley. The next 23 miles to Concrete also pass through farmlands, but gradually forests and peaks come into view. At Concrete a lesser road north leads to Baker Lake, formed by Upper Baker Dam. (Lake Shannon, below, is formed by Lower Baker Dam.) Baker Lake is really away from it all, except for all the other people who are there to get away from it all. The lake is in Mt. Baker National Forest, and Mt. Baker covers a chunk of the skyline. Campsites are plentiful and good, and for those who don't have tents and campers and trailers, some cabins are available for rent. Trout fishing is good enough to attract a lot of anglers.

Wash 20 rolls on past Concrete for seven miles to Rockport, where there is a state park with a small campground. Rockport and nearby Marblemount are the largest settlements you will meet now for more than 100 miles. Fill up on gas and buy whatever groceries you need.

The dream of a road across the North Cascades began with a search for gold. Until the feverish prospectors arrived in 1858, the only white men to venture into the wilderness were a few hardy trappers. That gold activity lasted about a year. The country was too isolated, the terrain too rugged, the weather too fierce. For about twenty years the area was silent again. Then, in 1880, gold was "rediscovered" in the upper Skagit headwaters and the rush was on. But once again the rush was short-lived and once again, the lack of adequate transportation was blamed. Most of the year it was impossible to bring in supplies; the rest of the time it was difficult at best.

Continued agitation by the miners and cattlemen of the Okanogan Valley for the state to build a wagon road across the North Cascades resulted in several surveys. In 1893 the legislature appropriated all of $20,000 to build 200 miles of road from Bellingham Bay to the Okanogan Valley by way of the old gold country—$100 a mile for road through one of the wildest and most rugged sections of the entire United States.

Three years later a board of examiners judged Cascade Pass, to the south of Wash. 20, as the most feasible route, and work was started. But the next year slides and washouts ruined whatever construction had been done. Then, for more than thirty years, there was practically no activity.

Bits and pieces of road were worked on during the 1930s by the Public Works Administration and Civilian Conservation Corps. Using rudimentary equipment, compared to today's arsenal of machinery, they finally extended the Cascade River Road to its present terminus, still a long way from the Okanogan Valley. But the gravel road, southeast of Marblemount, leads to some very scenic country. From the end of the 25-mile-long road there is a trail that will take the hiker through Cascade Pass to Lake Chelan. Two campgrounds are along the road.

With the close of World War II, interest in a route across the North Cascades was revived. A route was settled upon, and in 1960 construction began. Ten years later it was possible to go from the Okanogan Valley to Puget Sound on a rather direct line, all things considered. There is a stretch of 75 miles where there are no facilities, and this section between Ross Dam and Mazama is closed in the winter.

Newhalem, east of Marblemount, is the gateway to the Ross Lake Recreation Area and is the point at which Seattle City Light begins its tours. (For information on the recreation area, see "National Parks" in *Practical Information for Washington;* for information on Seattle City Light tours, see "Tours.") There's also a lake-tour boat.

Places worth a pause are the roadside overlooks above Diablo Dam, with views of Ross Dam and Ross Lake. At Rainy Pass a 1.4-mile trail leads to Lake Ann, and the Pacific Crest National Scenic Trail crosses the highway. Whistler Basin Viewpoint, a couple of miles farther on, provides a view of alpine meadows and avalanche areas.

Washington Pass Overlook, at about 5,500 feet, is the most popular stop. A road leads half a mile from the highway to a parking and picnic area. The nearby viewpoint looks down to Early Winters Creek and up to the needle peaks of 8,876-foot Silver Star Mountain and Snagtooth Ridge; to Cooper Basin and Early Winters Spire and Liberty Bell Mountain. Lots of color film is shot here.

In the next 17 miles there are three Forest Service campgrounds: Lone Fir, Klipchuck, and Early Winters. All three accommodate some tents, and Klipchuck and Lone Fir have space for some trailers. On the west side of the highway there are only two camps, Goodell Creek and Colonial Creek, both operated by the National Park Service. A campground at Newhalem has just opened.

The first settlement on the east slope of the Cascades is Mazama, still an outpost hamlet, though it has grown since completion of the road.

## Mount Rainier

The state's most celebrated and highest (14,410 feet) mountain takes up all of Mt. Rainier National Park. (For details, see section on "National Parks" in *Practical Information for Washington.*)

From Seattle, drive to Enumclaw, then east on U.S. 410 up the western slope of the Cascades 41 miles to the Cayuse Pass "Y." (Shortly before you get to Cayuse Pass, a park road winds 19 miles to Sunrise, a 6,400-foot high campground "looking straight up the mountain." The dead-end road, usually not open until July, keeps Sunrise from being heavily visited, but its enthusiasts rate it as Rainier's most inspiring spot.) At Cayuse Pass it is worth driving several miles up the Chinook Pass highway for views of Mt. Rainier from its east side, and south along the Cascade Range. Return to the "Y" and drive south 15 miles to Stevens Canyon entrance. The park road goes 21 all-which-way miles to Paradise, whose inn is above the 5,400-feet level. This is the principal destination and stopping point for all tours, many of which turn around here after arriving from the other direction, through Sunshine Point (Nisqually), the longtime main entrance at the southwest corner of the park. From Nisqually it is about an hour and a half to Tacoma and two hours to Seattle via Eatonville and Puyallup.

### Mt. St. Helens

Mt. St. Helens blew its top in May, 1980, after being dormant for 123 years. The massive eruption killed 65 people and deposited ash nearly a foot deep in parts of eastern Washington. At press time there seems to be some evidence that the volcano is coming to life again. Approaches to the still-active volcano are closed, but interpretative centers are at the Ridgefield exit on I–5 just north of Vancouver, and near Chehalis. The best way to view the volcano is to take "flight-seeing" charters from the Kelso airport or from the small town of Toledo, just off I–5.

# PRACTICAL INFORMATION FOR WASHINGTON

**HOW TO GET THERE AND HOW TO GET AROUND. By air and by train:** Your gateway to Washington's coastal areas will most likely be Seattle or Portland, Oregon. See "How to Get There" in *Practical Information for Seattle* and in *Practical Information for Oregon.*

**By bus:** *Greyhound* runs to and within Washington; *Trailways* runs within the state. **By car:** The major route north-to-south is Interstate 5, running from Vancouver to San Diego. Hwy. 101 runs north along the coast to Astoria, Oregon, before turning inland to circle the Olympic Peninsula, finally ending in Olympic. I–90 and U.S. 2 are major east-west routes. The Hood Canal Floating Bridge carries traffic between the north end of Kitsap Peninsula and the Olympic Peninsula. The only bridge crossing Puget Sound is a free one at Tacoma.

**By ferry:** *Washington State Ferries* are part of the state highway system. Most routes are across Puget Sound. South to north, the ferry routes are: Tacoma to Tahlequah, Vashon Island; Edmonds, 15 miles north of Seattle, to Kingston at the north end of Kitsap Peninsula and to Port Townsend; Mukilteo, southwest of Everett, to Columbia Beach, Whidbey Island; and Keystone, Whidbey Island, to Port Townsend. Bainbridge and Whidbey islands are connected to the mainland by bridges, but not anywhere near their ferry landings.

From Anacortes, ferries run to the San Juan Islands, and one trip extends to Sidney, B.C., on Vancouver Island. For more details contact *Washington State Ferry System,* State Ferry Terminal, Seattle, WA 98104; (206) 464–6400. A Canadian ferry runs frequently to Vancouver Island from Tsawwassen, just north of the border and west of Blaine. Contact *B.C. Ferries,* 818 Broughton St., Victoria V8W 1EL; (604) 387–1401.

There's year-round ferry service from Port Angeles to Victoria. *Black Ball* runs daily in winter; twice daily spring and fall; four times each day in summer; call (206) 622–2222.

 **HOTELS AND MOTELS.** Accommodations equal to those of Seattle in comfort and facilities often cost less, giving you more for the dollar than you are likely to receive in the metropolitan area. Price ranges are based on double occupancy. *Deluxe,* $35 and up; *Expensive,* $30–$35; *Moderate,* $20–$30; *Inexpensive,* $20 and less. Resort areas often have off-season rates. Listings are in order of price category. Most of these establishments accept major credit cards.

## ABERDEEN

**Red Lion Motel.** *Expensive-Deluxe.* 521 W. Wishkah; (206) 532–5210. Medium-size motel, south end of town. Five kitchens, extra charge. Pool. Pets. Restaurant nearby. Seasonal rates.

**Nordic Inn.** *Moderate-Expensive.* 1700 S. Boone St.; (206) 533–0100. Medium-size motel at southern edge of town on Wash. 105. Two-story motel, units with in-room sauna, fine restaurant. Cocktail lounge and entertainment.

**Olympic Inn.** *Moderate.* 616 W. Heron St.; (206) 533–4200. Double-story motel with nicely furnished rooms. Some suites and efficiencies available. Restaurant nearby.

**TraveLure Motel.** *Inexpensive-Moderate.* 623 W. Wishkah; (206) 532–3280. Centrally located, smaller motel with one- and two-room units. Seasonal rates.

## ANACORTES

**Anacortes Inn.** *Moderate-Expensive.* 3006 Commercial; (206) 293–3153. Medium-size motel. Some kitchens, extra charge. Pool. Seasonal rates.

**Holiday Motel.** *Moderate-Expensive.* 2903 Commercial; (206) 293–6511. Two two-room units. Seasonal rates. Downtown area.

**San Juan Motel.** *Moderate-Expensive.* 1103 Sixth St.; (206) 293–5105. All 24 units have kitchens, some suites. Small pets.

**Island Motel.** *Inexpensive-Moderate.* 3401 Commercial; (206) 293–3622. Small motel with one- and two-room units, some with kitchenettes (extra). Pool. Car to airport and ferry landing. Seasonal rates.

## BELLINGHAM

**Leopold Hotel.** *Moderate-Expensive.* 1224 Cornwall; (206) 733-3500. Large, multistory downtown facility with nine-story hotel building, Inn wing, cabana units. Single rooms and larger suites available. Pool. Three dining rooms. Cocktail lounge with entertainment and dancing. Family rates.

**Pony Soldier Motor Inn.** *Moderate-Expensive.* 215 Samish Way; (206) 734-8830. Large, three-level motel with variety of accommodations, some units with refrigerators, some with balconies. Wide range of rates. Pool. Restaurant adjacent.

**Scottish Lodge Motel.** *Moderate.* 5671 Riverside Dr., Ferndale; (206) 384-4040. Large. 9 miles north of town. Pool, sauna, some refrigerators. Restaurant near.

**Motel Six.** *Inexpensive.* 3701 Byron St.; (206) 734-6940. Medium-size, no-frills member of well-known chain. Pool. 1½ miles from college.

## BREMERTON

**Hearthstone Inn.** *Expensive.* 4320 Kitsap Way; (206) 479-2132. Large, split-level motel overlooking bay, most units with balconies. Pool. No pets. Fine restaurant; cocktail lounge and entertainment. Some kitchenettes, extra.

**Westgate Motor Lodge.** *Moderate-Deluxe.* 4303 Kitsap Way; (206) 377-4402. Large, two-story motel with choice of one-, two-, and three-room units, many with kitchens at extra charge. Pool, playground. Pets, laundry, picnic tables and grill. Restaurant adjacent.

**Chieftain Motel.** *Moderate-Expensive.* 600 National Ave.; (206) 479-3111. Medium-size motel on three levels, units with electric fireplaces and balconies, a few with kitchen facilities at extra charge. Pool.

**Shorewood Motor Inn.** *Moderate-Expensive.* 500 Kitsap Way; (206) 373-2505. Medium-size two-story motel with one- and two-room units. Attractive grounds. Two efficiencies, laundry. Some rooms have refrigerators. Extra charge for pets.

## COPALIS BEACH

**Beachwood Resort.** *Expensive-Deluxe.* On Wash. 109, Copalis Beach; (206) 289-2177. Family-size units overlooking ocean, with fireplaces and kitchens featured at this small, attractive resort. Three-day minimum reservation required in season.

**Iron Springs Beach Resort.** *Expensive-Deluxe.* 3 mi. no. of Copalis Beach, Box 207, Copalis Beach; (206) 276-4230. This unique resort on the ocean front has individual cottages scattered upon a wooded hillside. Each has a fireplace, kitchen, livingroom, and bedrooms. Swimming pool (covered in winter), small grocery and delicatessen. Good spot for beachcombing. Reservations must be for at least three nights during season.

## COUPEVILLE
### (Whidbey Island)

**The Captain Whidbey Lodge & Motel.** *Deluxe.* 2072 W. Whidbey Island Inn Rd.; (206) 678–4097. Medium-size. Choice of lodgings: inn, motel units, and cabins, some with efficiencies. Private beach on Penn Cove. Boats available. Fishing, swimming, playground. Pets in cabins. Well-known restaurant adjoins.

## CRYSTAL MOUNTAIN

**Crystal House.** *Moderate.* Crystal Mountain; (206) 663–2265. Two-story ski lodge in village. Restaurant adjacent. No pets. Seasonal rates.

## ENUMCLAW

**King's Motel.** *Moderate.* 1334 Roosevelt Way E.; (206) 825–1626. Medium-size motel just a mile east of town and set well back from highway. Two-level, several units with kitchen facilities. Pool. Restaurant adjoining.

## EVERETT

**Holiday Inn of Everett.** *Deluxe.* 6030 Evergreen Way; (206) 355–3007. Large two-level motel, many conveniences. Pool and wading pool, coffee shop, dining room, cocktail lounge with entertainment. Pets.

**Imperial 400 Motel.** *Expensive.* 952 Hwy. 99; (206) 259–5177. Medium-size, two-story motel, a few units with kitchens at extra charge. Pool, restaurant adjacent.

**Topper Motel.** *Moderate-Expensive.* 1030 Broadway; (206) 259–3151. Medium-size motel with some kitchen units at extra charge. Several 2-room units. Restaurant near.

**Motel Six.** *Inexpensive.* 10006 Evergreen Way; (206) 355–1811. Large motel with the usual "6" accommodations. Pool. South of town on Highway 99.

## FORKS

**Kalaloch Lodge.** *Expensive.* Star Rte. 1, Box 1100; (206) 962–2271. Old-fashioned lodge atmosphere with beachcombing, wading lagoon. 56 units.

**Calawah Motel.** *Moderate.* Forks; (206) 374–5400. A short distance up the Calaway River from town. 30 units, some two-bedroom.

## FRIDAY HARBOR

**Imperial Gardens Motor Inn.** *Expensive-Deluxe.* 1016 Guard St.; (206) 378–2000. This three-level motel set in a Japanese garden affords convenience, relaxing atmosphere. Car to ferry landing and airport. Playground, dining room, bar. Seasonal rates.

## HOQUIAM

**Westwood Lodge.** *Expensive.* 910 Simpson Ave; (206) 562–0994. Large. Some kitchenettes, some suites and 2-room units.

**Sandstone.** *Moderate.* 2424 Aberdeen Ave.; (206) 532–4160. Small and pleasant, with pool.

**Stoken Motel.** *Moderate.* 2403 Simpson Ave.; (206) 532–7373. Small motel with pleasant, comfortable units, one- and 2-room units.

## ILWACO

**Captain Mike's Motel.** *Moderate-Expensive.* First & Main; (206) 642–3177. Small, 2-story motel, restaurant nearby. Charter boats available. Seasonal rates.

## LA PUSH

**La Push Ocean Park.** *Moderate-Expensive.* (206) 374–5267. Medium-size motel and cabins on the beach in Olympic National Park. The area is home to the Quillayute Indians. Modern units, all with complete kitchens. Beautiful scenery and great beachcombing. Surf fishing. Charter boats available. Off-season and senior-citizen rates.

**Shoreline Resort.** *Moderate-Expensive.* (206) 374–6488. Fully equipped modern cottages facing the ocean beach. Prices vary according to size of unit. Trailer park with some hookups. Seasonal rates.

## LONG BEACH

**Chumaree by the Sea.** *Deluxe.* Boulevard Ave; (206) 642–2434. Wide choice of one- to three-room units in individual cottages or three-level motel. Many units with ocean view, some with fireplaces, most with kitchens. Indoor pool. Seasonal rates. Fee for pets.

**Chatauqua Lodge.** *Expensive-Deluxe.* 205 W. 14th St. N.; (206) 642–2244. Large motel one mile north on beach. Many units with fireplaces and efficiencies. Indoor pool, whirlpool, and sauna. Recreation room with ping-pong and pool tables. Dining room, cocktails. Pets extra.

**Shaman Motel.** *Expensive.* 3rd S. and Pacific; (206) 642–3714. Medium-size, city-center, two-story motel. Ocean view from many units, several fireplaces, kitchen facilities in many units, with dish kits at extra charge. Pool, restaurant nearby. Seasonal rates. Wheelchair ramps.

## LOPEZ ISLAND

**The Islander Lopez.** *Expensive-Deluxe.* On Fisherman Bay, west side of island. Box 197, Lopez; 468–2233. Medium-size motel, 2 levels, some units with kitchen facilities. Pool, therapeutic pool, marina with boats and motors available, fishing. Coffee shop, dining room, bar. Seasonal rates. Reservations advised.

## MOCLIPS

**Ocean Crest Resort.** *Deluxe.* (206) 276–4465. Medium-size resort motel situated on a bluff overlooking the Pacific. Accommodations available in three cottages or motel. Some rooms have balconies and fireplaces. Restaurant, bar. Indoor pool (heated), saunas. On weekends minimum reservation is two days; holidays, three days.

**Hi-Tide.** *Expensive-Deluxe.* (206) 276–4142. Modern, fully equipped suites with kitchens, private lanais. Panoramic ocean view. Pets extra. (Must have approval by office.)

**Tradewinds Lodge.** *Expensive-Deluxe.* Two miles north of Pacific Beach bypass, junction Wash. 109; (206) 276–4453. Smaller motel on a bluff overlooking the ocean, units decorated in Polynesian motif, magnificent ocean view. Hiking, beach, fishing. Dining room, bar. Dining room operates on limited schedule during winter and spring. Seasonal rates.

**Moonstone Beach Motel.** *Expensive.* (206) 276–4346. Small motel right on the beach. Every unit has beach view. One–two bedrooms units with kitchens. Pets extra.

**Moclips Motel.** *Moderate-Expensive.* (206) 276–4228. Medium-size motel with wide range of prices and facilities. Completely furnished housekeeping units. 200 ft. from the beach. Good beachcombing. Ocean view. Seasonal rates.

## MT. RAINIER NATIONAL PARK
### (See Also "National Parklands," Below)

**Gateway Inn.** *Moderate-Expensive.* Ashford, S.W. entrance to Park; (206) 596–2506. Small cottages, some with fireplaces. Restaurant, cocktails. Pets. Reservations required during season.

**The Lodge.** *Moderate–Expensive.* Ashford, 1/4 mi. Mt. Rainier; (206) 569–2312. Lodges and cottages, 20 rooms, 78 beds. No credit cards.

**Paradise Inn.** *Moderate-Expensive.* Call or write Mt. Rainier Natl. Park Hospitality Service, Tacoma, WA 98409; (206) 569–2275. Large, older mountain lodge, within the park. No pets. Dining room, coffee shop, bar. Guided hikes and naturalist. Reservations.

## MT. VERNON

**West Winds Motel.** *Moderate.* 2020 Riverside Dr.; (206) 424–4224. Medium-size motel, very well kept, some steam baths, many units with refrigerators. Restaurant nearby Seasonal rates.

## NEWHALEM

**Diablo Lake Resort.** *Moderate-Expensive.* Dial operator and ask for Newhalem 5578. Lakeshore housekeeping cottages of two, three, or four rooms each. Snackbar, groceries. Boat ramp, dock, boats, fishing. Cruise boat, extra charge. One mile off Wash. 20, across Diablo Dam. Restaurant on premises. Seasonal rates.

## OAK HARBOR
### (Whidbey Island)

**Queen Anne Motel.** *Moderate-Expensive.* 1204 W. Pioneer; (206) 675–2209. Downtown motel with indoor pool, restaurant, bar. A few kitchens at extra charge. Seasonal rates.

**Alpen Haus Motel.** *Inexpensive-Moderate.* 1175 Midway Blvd.; (206) 675–5911. Most units have two rooms, refrigerators, some with kitchenettes (extra). Seasonal rates.

## OCEAN CITY

**Pacific Sands Motel.** *Moderate-Expensive.* Wash. 109, about ½ mi. north of town; (206) 289–3588. Small motel, direct access to beach. Some units with fireplaces, most have kitchens. Pool, playground. Extra charge for pets. Seasonal rates.

## OCEAN SHORES

**Canterbury Inn.** *Deluxe.* Ocean Shores Blvd., Box 310; (206) 289–3317. 3-story motel on beach, one- to three-room housekeeping units overlooking ocean. Many with fireplaces, some with balconies. Indoor heated pool. Seasonal rates.

**Ocean Shores Inn.** *Deluxe.* Box 639; (206) 289–2249. Two-story hotel and convention center overlooking ocean. Seasonal rates.

**Discovery Inn.** *Expensive-Deluxe.* Box 344; (206) 289–3386. Medium-size motel opposite marina and ferry landing. (Ferry to Westport, pedestrians only.) Over half of units have kitchens. Some units with fireplaces. Recreation room, barbeque grill, pool. Pets. Café nearby. Charter boats available at marina.

**Grey Gull Motel.** *Expensive-Deluxe.* Box 1417; (206) 289–3381. Three-level motel with kitchen units, fireplaces. Restaurant nearby. Pool (heated), sauna. Seasonal rates.

**Polynesian Motel.** *Expensive-Deluxe.* 291 Ocean Shores Blvd.; (206) 289–3361. Large, three-story motel overlooking ocean, some units with fireplaces, some balconies, most with kitchens. Indoor pool. Restaurant and bar. Seasonal rates.

## OLYMPIA

**Governor House.** *Expensive-Deluxe.* 621 Capitol Way; (206) 352–7700. Six-story downtown motor inn. Parking lot. Pool, coffee shop, dining room, cocktail lounge, entertainment.

**Olympia-Aladdin Motor Inn.** *Expensive-Deluxe.* 900 Capitol Way; (206) 352–7200. Large motor inn halfway between the capitol and downtown. Pool.

Some units have refrigerators. Dining room, cocktails. Pets. Under-building parking if desired. (Best Western)

**Vance Tyee Motor Inn.** *Expensive-Deluxe.* 3¾ mi. s. of town, in Tumwater, 500 Tyee Dr.; (206) 352–0511. Large motor inn with pleasant decor. Some private therapeutic pools available in cabana suites. Pool (heated). Restaurant, bar and entertainment.

**Westwater of Olympia.** *Expensive-Deluxe.* 2300 Evergreen Park Dr.; (206) 943–4000. Large motor inn overlooking state capitol and lake. Many units with balconies, some suites with refrigerators and whirlpool baths. Pool, dining room, coffee shop, cocktail lounge, and entertainment. (Best Western)

**Carriage Inn Motel.** *Moderate.* 1211 S. Quince; (206) 943–4710. Two-story motel with pool, five blocks from state Capitol, six blocks from city center. Restaurant nearby. No pets.

**Golden Gavel Motor Hotel.** *Moderate.* 909 Capitol Way; (206) 352–8533. Medium-size, 2-story, downtown motel, just 3 blocks north of capitol. Restaurant nearby. No pets.

## OLYMPIC NATIONAL PARK

**Lake Crescent Lodge.** *Expensive-Deluxe.* Twenty miles west of Port Angeles on U.S. 101; Rte. 1, Box 11, Port Angeles; (206) 928–3211. Two-story motor inn with cottage units. Lovely, quiet spot on lakeshore. Some lodge rooms with central bath. Some fireplaces. Swimming, hiking, fishing, boats available. Naturalist. Dining room, bar.

**Lake Crescent Log Cabin Resort.** *Moderate-Expensive.* (206) 928–3325. Smaller rustic resort on sunny side of the lake. Variety of accommodations including housekeeping units. Beautiful setting. Lodge has snack bar and dining room, cocktails. Playground, fishing, swimming. Boats, motors, canoes. Fee for use. Seasonal rates.

**Sol Duc Resort.** *Inexpensive.* Contact Park Headquarters, (206) 452–4501. Long established, rustic resort, 16 miles from US 101 in hot springs area. On trailheads leading into the Olympics. Units vary from primitive to comfortable. Pools, mineral baths. Coffee shop, cocktail lounge. Small store. Seasonal. Check at Park Headquarters in Port Angeles to find out if it is open.

## ORCAS ISLAND

**Rosario Resort Hotel.** *Expensive-Deluxe.* Eastsound; (206) 376–2222. Huge resort occupying 1,300-acre historic estate, wide range of accommodations, single rooms to spacious suites, most rooms with bay view, some with garden view. Heated pools, indoor and outdoor adult pools, therapy pool, children's pool, sauna. Tennis, lawn games, boating, boat dock, boat and motor rentals, fishing, water skiing. Coffee shop, dining room, cocktail lounge, entertainment. Seasonal rates. Reservations required.

**Captain Cook's Resort.** *Expensive.* Box 1040; (206) 376–2242. Small, two-story motor inn plus cottages with housekeeping facilities. Pool, playground, tennis, boat dock, boat and motor rentals, fishing. Seasonal rates. Two miles north of Eastsound on north shore of island. Reservations required.

## PACIFIC BEACH

**Sandpiper Beach Resort.** *Moderate-Expensive.* (206 276–4580. This medium-size motel has units right on the beach. All units are nicely furnished and have kitchens. Some have fireplaces. Almost all are set up for large families or groups. Advance reservations advisable. Seasonal rates.

## PORT ANGELES
### (See Also Olympic National Park)

**Red Lion Bayshore.** *Deluxe.* 221 N. Lincoln St.; (206) 452–9215. Large waterfront inn with lovely view of harbor and Juan de Fuca Strait. Pool. Fine *Haguewood* restaurant, bar. Seasonal rates.

**Aggie's Inn.** *Moderate-Deluxe.* 602 Front St.; (206) 457–0471. Large motor inn. Some suites, some kitchenettes. Indoor pool, sauna. Good restaurant, bar, entertainment. Pets. Seasonal rates.

**Uptown Motel.** *Moderate-Deluxe.* 2nd & Laurel; (206) 457–9434. Medium-size, multilevel motel, one- and two-room units, away from highway. Some units with kitchen facilities, extra charge. Seasonal rates.

**Aircrest Motel.** *Moderate-Expensive.* 1006 E. Front St.; (206) 732–1243. Smaller motel, comfortable units, east side of town.

**Hill Haus Motel.** *Moderate-Expensive.* 111 E. 2nd St.; (206) 452–9285. Medium-size, three-story, on bluff overlooking harbor. Some suites with kitchens. Café nearby.

## PORT LUDLOW

**The Admiralty Resort.** *Deluxe.* Rte. 1, Box 75; (206) 437–2222. Large resort and motor inn. Wide range of units, most affording view of bay. Pool, sauna, playground. Squash and tennis courts, water skiing, fishing. Full-service marina, boat and motor rentals. *Harbormaster* restaurant, offering boat moorage, entertainment, varied menu. Seasonal rates.

## PORT TOWNSEND

(Port Townsend is a regional leader in the bed-and-breakfast industry with at least half a dozen private homes offering rooms and breakfasts. Check with the Chamber of Commerce for listings, 2139 Sims Way, Port Townsend 98368.)

**Manresa Castle.** *Deluxe.* 7th & Sheridan; (206) 385–5750. An 1890 mansion converted to a medium-size hotel. Furnished with turn-of-the-century antiques. National historic site. Café, cocktails. Reservations required.

**Port Townsend Motel.** *Moderate.* 2020 Washington St.; (206) 385–2211. Small motel situated away from highway, comfortable one- and two-room units offering view of mountains and waterway. Seasonal rates.

## PUYALLUP

**Tamarak Motel.** *Moderate.* 403 W. Meeker; (206) 845–0466. Small two-story motel. Most units have kitchen facilities. Pool. Laundry. Pets (fee).

## QUINAULT

**Lake Quinault Lodge.** *Deluxe.* Two miles east of U.S. 101, south shore Lake Quinault, Box 7; (206) 288–7571. Medium-size, lakeshore motel. Some units with fireplaces. Indoor pool, therapy pool, health spa, saunas. Swimming in lake, boat dock, boat and motor rentals, fishing, putting green. Dining room, cocktail lounge, entertainment. Seasonal rates.

**Rain Forest Resort.** *Moderate-Expensive.* South Shore Rd.; (206) 288–2535. A complete resort: motel, fully equipped cabins, restaurant, trailer camp, general store and laundry facilities. Boat and fishing tackle rentals. A beautiful spot for nature lovers. Indian fishing license required on lake and lower river.

## RAYMOND

**Mountcastle Motel.** *Moderate.* 524 3rd St.; (206) 942–5571. Medium-size, downtown motel with 1- and 2-room units. A few kitchens, extra charge. Reservations required in season.

## RENTON
### (See "Hotels and Motels—South Seattle" in Practical Information for Seattle.)

## SEDRO WOOLLEY

**Skagit Motel.** *Moderate.* 1977 Hwy. 20; (206) 856–6001 Medium-size motel with both one- and two-room units, some with kitchen facilities at extra charge. Restaurant nearby.

## SEQUIM

**Sequim West Motel.** *Moderate.* 740 Washington; (206) 683–4144. Two-story motel, one- and two-room units, some suites. Units with kitchenettes at extra charge. Restaurant on premises. Seasonal rates.

## SHELTON

**City Center Motel.** *Inexpensive-Moderate.* 128 E. Alder; (206) 426–3397. Small but comfortable downtown motel.

## SILVERDALE

**Poplars Motel.** *Moderate.* 9800 Silverdale Way; (206) 692–6126 Medium-size motel on two levels, pool. Restaurant with bar, entertainment, dancing. No pets.

## SNOHOMISH

**Snohomish Motor Inn.** *Moderate.* 723 Ave. D.; (206) 568–6522. Small motel, 1- and 2-room units, some with kitchens at extra charge.

## TACOMA

**Lakewood Motor Inn.** *Expensive-Deluxe.* 6125 Motor Ave. SW; (206) 584–2212 Large, 2-story motel, fine accommodations, suites. Pool, putting green, restaurant, cocktail lounge with piano bar.

**Tacoma TraveLodge.** *Expensive-Deluxe.* 2512 Pacific Ave., near new domed stadium; (206) 383–3557. Medium-size motel with comfortable one- and two-room units.

**Holiday Inn of Tacoma.** *Expensive.* 3518 Pacific Hwy. E, near Port of Tacoma; (206) 922–0550. Large, two-story motel. Pool, coffee shop, dining room, cocktail lounge with entertainment.

**Doric Tacoma Motor Hotel.** *Moderate-Expensive.* 242 St. Helens Ave.; (206) 572–9572. Large, downtown hotel with two-story annex, some suites. Pool, coffee shop, dining room and lounge. Gift shop. Limousine to airport.

**Rodeway Inn.** *Moderate-Expensive.* 6802 S. Sprague Ave., So. Tacoma, off I–5; (206) 475–5900. Large, two-story motel with excellent facilities. Some units with steam baths, some large suites. Pool, dining room, cocktail lounge with entertainment.

**Sherwood Inn.** *Moderate-Expensive.* 8402 S. Hosmer St. Off I–5; (206) 535–2800. Large, three-story motel just a few minutes from Tacoma Mall. Pool, wading pool, coffee shop, restaurant, bar, entertainment.

**Nendel's.** *Moderate.* 8702 S. Hosmer, off I–5; (206) 535–3100. Very comfortable rooms, singles, and suites. Dining room and lounge. Adjacent to a golf course. Pool.

**Oakwood Motor Lodge.** *Moderate.* 9920 S. Tacoma Way; (206) 588–5241. Two-level motel with units of one and two rooms. Coffee shop, dining room. Some kitchens, extra charge for utensils.

**Motel Six.** *Inexpensive.* 5201 20th St. E., Fife; (206) 922–6612. Large two-story. Pool. Adjacent cafe. North, off I–5.

## UNION

**Alderbrook Inn.** *Deluxe.* E. 7101 Hwy. 106; (206) 898–2200. Large resort on Hood Canal. Units include nicely furnished family-sized cottages with kitchens. Dock, swimming, boats, water bicycles, golf, tennis. Dining at the Inn. Reservations required. No pets.

## VANCOUVER

**Thunderbird Inn at the Quay.** *Deluxe.* Foot of Columbia St.; (206) 694–8341. Large motel at the waterfront, many units offering dramatic view of Interstate

Bridge and Columbia River. Pool, three-level inn with coffee shop, dining room, bar, entertainment. Pool. Extra charge for pets. Boat dock.

**Vancouver TraveLodge.** *Expensive-Deluxe.* 601 Broadway; (206) 693–3668. Medium-size downtown motel. Some two-room units. No pets.

**Shilo Inn–Hazeldell.** *Expensive.* 13206 Hwy. 99; (206) 573–0511. Large motel. Some kitchenettes and suites. Coin laundry, pool, whirlpool, sauna, and steamroom. Pets extra. Restaurant near.

**Shilo Inn–Vancouver.** *Expensive.* 401 E. 13th St.; (206) 696–0411. Much the same accommodations as above, though larger.

**Aloha Motel.** *Moderate.* 708 N.E. 78th St.; (206) 574–2345. Large, two-story motel three miles north of town. Pool, playground, restaurant nearby. Pets.

**Fort Motel.** *Moderate.* 500 E. 13th St.; (206) 694–3327. Two-story motel, east side of town. Pool, parking.

## WESTPORT

**Islander Motel.** *Deluxe.* Westhaven Dr.; (206) 268–9166. At northeast edge of town, on jetty overlooking harbor. Medium-size motel. Pool, wading pool, charter boats. Coffee shop, dining room, cocktail lounge, entertainment. Seasonal rates. No pets.

**Canterbury West Motel.** *Expensive-Deluxe.* Wash. 105, three blocks south of Coast Guard Lighthouse, Box 349; (206) 268–0101. Large, four-story motel, small units, suites, some units with kitchen facilities, some with balconies and fireplaces. Heated indoor pool, charter boats. $3 extra charge for pets. Seasonal rates.

**Coho Motel.** *Expensive.* 2501 Nyhus; (206) 268–0111. Medium-size motel. Runs a large fleet of charter boats. Units include one- and two-bedroom suites. Restaurants near. Ask manager about best beachcombing spots. Seasonal rates.

**Shipwreck Motel.** *Expensive.* Box 494; (206) 268–1515. Medium-size, unique motel. All units have kitchens and are cheerfully decorated. Large recreation room with fireplace, kitchenette, ping-pong table, music, view of boat basin and ocean. Seasonal rates.

**Ocean Gate Resort.** *Inexpensive.* 1939 Hwy. 105; (206) 267–1956. Cabins and RV spaces, four miles south of town. No pets.

## WHITE PASS

**Game Ridge Motel.** *Inexpensive.* (509) 672–2212. Small motel in wooded area on Tieton River. 1- and 2-room units, some with kitchens, extra charge. Restaurant near. Hunting and fishing. U.S. 12, 20 miles east of White Pass. Pets.

 **YOUTH HOSTELS.** The establishment of youth hostels is a comparatively recent event in Washington State. American Youth Hostels can be found at *Evergreen Hostel* at Carnation; *Fort Columbia Youth Hostel* at Chinook; *Mike's Beach Resort,* Hood Canal at Lilliwaup; *The Lodge,* Ashford at the Nisqually Gate entrance to Mt. Rainier Natl. Park; *Fort Worden State Park,*

Port Townsend; *Fort Flagler State Park,* on Marrowstone Island. For information on all Washington hostels write *Seahaven Hostel,* 1431 Minor Ave., Seattle, WA 98101; (206) 524-2844.

 **CAMPING OUT.** There are campgrounds all through the state. See information under "National Parklands" and "State Parks," below. For detailed information on state parks, write to Travel Development Division, 101 General Administration Bldg., Olympia, WA 98504. KOA Kampgrounds are located at Anacortes, Bay Center, Gig Harbor (near Tacoma), Mossyrock, Olympia, and Bothell (near Seattle).

 **TRAILER TIPS.** The term "RV" now lumps together travel trailers, moter homes, and campers. Many state and national parks have spaces set aside for them, with hookups. Forest Service campgrounds also are open for their use but generally do not provide any special facilities. Most small towns, particularly along the ocean coast and other resort areas, have trailer parks for overnighters, where even short stays are welcomed.

It is tougher for transients in the vicinity of large cities, where "mobile" homes cluster in residential "parks" and never move. Those listed here for the Seattle-Tacoma area are some that specifically state "overnight space."

Holiday Resort & Trailer Park, 19250 Aurora N.; Jensen Trailer Court, 937 N. 97th; Orchard Trailer Park, 4011 S. 146th; Lake Shore Mobile Park, 11488 Rainier S.; Seattle North KOA, Bothell; Willo Vista Trailer Village, East Valley Highway, Kent.

 **TOURIST INFORMATION.** A Visitor Information Center is open all year on I-5, near the interstate bridge in Vancouver. Centers are open in summer during business hours on I-5 at Blaine, just south of the customs station on the Canadian border; at Megler, on U.S. 101, at the north end of the Astoria Bridge; and at Port Angeles on Hwy. 101 in the center of town. Questions and requests regarding tourist attractions and facilities are handled quickly by the Travel Department Division, General Administration Building, Olympia, WA 98504; (800) 562-4570. Local maps, guides, information on resorts, etc. may be obtained from the local Chamber of Commerce in the area you plan to visit. The U.S. Forest Service, Regional Office, P.O. Box 3623, Portland, OR 97208 ([206] 442-0170), supplies a directory of campgrounds, trails, etc. in National Forests. For camping on state lands with limited facilities write Washington State Dept. of Natural Resources, Public Lands Building, Olympia, WA 98501 ([206] 753-5330). For information on Mt. Rainier National Park contact the Superintendent, Mt. Rainier National Park, Longmire, WA 98397, (206) 569-2211; on Olympic National Park, Superintendent, Olympic National Park, Port Angeles, WA 98362, (206) 452-4501; on North Cascades National Park, Superintendent, North Cascades National Park, Sedro

Woolley, WA 98284, (206) 855–1331; Washington State Parks, State Parks and Recreation Commission, P.O. Box 1128, Olympia, WA 98504, (800) 562–0990. Hunting and fishing regulations are supplied by the Washington State Game Dept., 600 N. Capitol Way, Olympia, WA 98504, (206) 753–5700.

 **SEASONAL EVENTS.** Because of the mild weather, the festival season starts early in Washington as the state's many flowers break into full bloom. Most of the best-known festivals are built around the blossoms—daffodils in early April, apple blossoms in late April, rhododendrons and lilacs in May. The most popular parades are flecked with flowers—daffodils at Tacoma, Puyallup, and Sumner.

Here are samples of these and numerous other excuses for holding a festival:

**March:** Driftwood Show, Grayland.

**April:** Puyallup Valley Daffodil Festival, at Puyallup, Tacoma, Sumner, and Orting; Holland Happening (flower celebration), Oak Harbor; International Plowing Match, Lynden.

**May:** Blossomtime Festival, Bellingham; Rhododendron Festival, Port Townsend; Mason County Forest Festival, Shelton; Norwegian festivals in Ballard, Poulsbo, and other towns.

**June:** Salty Sea Days, Everett; Logging Show, Deming; Lummi Stommish Water Festival, with salmon barbecue and water sports, Lummi reservation.

**July:** Loggerodeo, Sedro Woolley; Swinomish Tribal Celebration, La Conner; 4th of July celebrations in most cities, big or little, throughout the state. Pacific Northwest Arts and Crafts Fair, Bellevue; Bear Festival, McCleary.

**August:** Logger's Jubilee, Morton; Salmon Derby Days, Port Angeles; Makah Days (Indian), with canoe races and tribal crafts, Neah Bay.

**September:** Western Washington Fair, Puyallup.

**October:** Scandinavian Festival, Tacoma.

County and regional fairs are held from late July through September. Rodeos are held in conjunction with most east-side county fairs and some western Washington fairs.

Arts-and-crafts shows are held from late March into early September.

 **TOURS.** From June 11 through September 5, *Seattle City Light* runs tours of its Skagit hydroelectric project, including a boat trip on Diablo Lake, a ride on an incline life (sort of a slanted elevator), and a family-style chicken dinner. Tours last about four hours. You provide your own transportation to Diablo, 140 miles from Seattle. Tours at 11 A.M., 1 P.M., and 3 P.M. (the latter July 17 through August 21 only). Adults, $15; Children 4–11 and senior citizens, $11. Children under 3, free. Information: Skagit Tours, 1015 Third Ave., Seattle, WA 98104; 625–3030. For tours out of the Seattle Area see "Tours" in *Practical Information for Seattle*.

**NATIONAL PARKLANDS.** Washington has three, including the fourth-oldest one to be set aside (1899), *Mount Rainier National Park.* Rising to 14,410 feet, most of it from sea level, Rainier keeps everyone within 100 miles mindful of its presence. Residents speak reverently of it as "The Mountain." In sheer aloof majesty, The Mountain chooses when to show itself, remaining invisible while sunshine falls on lesser areas, and looming awesomely in the sky on otherwise cloudy days. If, when you visit The Mountain benignly reveals itself to you, you have been favored.

An ice-clad, dormant volcano, Rainer stands on the western edge of the Cascade Range. Its gleaming mantle of ice is composed of more glaciers than there are on any other single mountain in the United States south of Alaska. The national park is the best-known tourist attraction in Washington (though not the most visited). More than 300 miles of hiking trails encircle the mountain.

During the summer, the wildflower fields provide a striking contrast to the mountain's glaciers. Wildlife includes mountain goats, bear, deer, and elk. Many of them are seen in the flower belt, which is above the 5,000-foot forest elevation. (Don't regard any of these animals as harmless.) Visitor centers are located at Longmire Park Headquarters, in the southwest corner (569–2211); at Ohanapecosh, at the southeast entrance; at Sunrise, on the northeast side of the mountain; and at Paradise, due south of the mountain. The *National Park Inn,* at Longmire, is open from early May to mid-October; *Paradise Inn,* mid-June until Labor Day. For rates and reservations, write: Rainier National Park Hospitality Service, 4820 S. Washington, Tacoma, WA 98409. There are no overnight accommodations at Sunrise or Ohanapecosh, but they are available near the park at Ashford, Packwood, White Pass, Crystal Mountain, and Enumclaw. Park activity includes mountain climbing with guide service, riding, hiking, fishing, and guided nature tours. Climbing information can be obtained through Rainier Mountaineering; call 475–7755. Camping, tenting, and trailering allowed in designated sites. Cats and dogs on leash only. Campgrounds are open throughout the park in summer on a first-come, first-serve basis. Stays are limited to 14 days a season. Sunshine Point Campground at the Nisqually Entrance is the only one open all year. There are no trailer utility hookups in the park, but there is a trailer dumping station at Cougar Rock Campground. All camping areas have water and toilet facilities. The use of the park is free.

*Olympic National Park* is a 1,400-square-mile jumble of glacier-studded mountains, coniferous rain forests, lakes and streams. Roosevelt elk, black-tailed deer, bear, raccoon, and skunk roam their feeding grounds, and about 140 species of birds have been identified in a variety of habitats. There are only a few peaks above 7,000 feet, with Mt. Olympus the highest at 7,965 feet. These figures, though, are deceiving—the mountains rise from near sea level. The park, pristine and rugged, has about 60 glaciers. Most of the lakes, however charming, are small, the largest (Crescent), being only 10 miles long and 1½ miles wide.

The park also includes a 60-mile-long, primitive strip of Pacific Ocean coastline, with rocky headlands and beaches. Seals are frequently seen in the water or on the offshore rocks. (Between the main part of the park and the coastal strip is the *Olympic National Forest* and a rich agricultural valley.) The Quinault Indian Reservation is to the south of the coastal strip. The rain forests are on the west side of the Olympic Peninsula and chiefly along the Hoh, Queets, and Quinault rivers. A yearly rainfall of 140 inches is not uncommon here. (In contrast, the northeast side of the Olympic Peninsula is one of the driest on the Pacific Coast outside of southern California.) Within the rain forests, some Douglas fir and Sitka spruce attain a height of nearly 300 feet and a diameter of eight feet or more. Western hemlocks also attain heights and diameters greater than in areas of less precipitation.

More than 600 miles of trails lead through the park and provide hikes of from a few minutes to several weeks. Probably no other national park offers such contrasts in hiking—from glaciers and blizzard-ridden mountain peaks to dense, perpetually shaded jungles. Mountain climbers must check in with the rangers at headquarters in Port Angeles and at various ranger stations within the park; only the experienced should attempt the peaks. Points of special interest include trails leading to beach adventure along the Ocean Strip and the spectacular view from Hurricane Ridge, reached by a fine highway off U.S. 101, near Port Angeles. There are concession-operated cabins, lodges, and trailer parks at Sol Duc Hot Springs (check first, this oldtimer is on the endangered species list), Lake Crescent, La Push, and Kalaloch. (See "Hotels and Motels," above.) For information, write: Superintendent, Olympic National Park, 600 E. Park Ave., Port Angeles, WA 98362; 452–4501.

All campsites are on a first-come, first-serve basis. Some campgrounds at lower elevations are open all year, but high-elevation areas are covered by snow from early November to early July. The park has three visitor centers—Pioneer Memorial Museum, near Port Angeles (open all year); Storm King Visitor Center, at Lake Crescent; and Hoh Rain Forest Visitor Center, southeast of Forks. Lectures, campfire talks, exhibits, and tours are provided by the National Park Service. Check visitor centers for details, interpretive publications, and maps. There is no park entrance fee.

*North Cascades National Park,* established by Congress in 1968, has four distinct units—North and South Units of the Park, and Ross Lake and Lake Chelan National Recreation Areas. The 1,053-square-mile area, designed to conserve an exceptionally wild and beautiful part of the extensive North Cascades mountain range near the Canadian border, has alpine scenery unmatched in the coterminous 48 states; deep-glaciated canyons, more than 300 glaciers, hundreds of jagged peaks, hanging valleys, waterfalls and icefalls, skyblue lakes nestled in glacial cirques, frigid streams that vein the wilderness, and vegetation regions that range from rain forest to dry shrubland. Ross Lake NRA also contains three dams—Ross, Diablo, and Gorge Lakes—which provide electrical power for Seattle. Ross Lake is 24 miles long and 2 miles across at its greatest width. Diablo Lake and Gorge Lake are much smaller.

Camping is not of the luxury type. It is available on a first-come, first-serve basis. Colonial Grounds and Goodell are developed, drive-in campgrounds off Wash. 20 in Ross Lake NRA, but a number of small ones are reached only by boat. There are no campgrounds in the North Unit of the national park, and only two in the South Unit. Lake Chelan NRA has about five campgrounds. In addition to the named lakes, there are many small mountain and valley lakes, and so many streams that no count has been made of them. The principal game fish are rainbow, eastern brook, Dolly Varden, and cutthroat trout. Swimming is not suggested—the waters of the lakes and rivers are quite chilly. Even in August, water activities are mainly confined to boating and fishing. For further information, write: Superintendent, North Cascades National Park, Sedro Woolley, WA 98284; 855–1331.

**National Heritage Parks:** *San Juan Island National Historic Park.* Site of the comic-opera "Pig War" between the U.S. and the British. Both countries claimed possession of the island following the Treaty of 1846. The British set up camp on the north end of the island, and the Americans established a base at the south end. The dispute, which was more serious in Washington and London than on the island, where the officers invited each other to dinner, was finally resolved by Kaiser Wilhelm I of Germany in 1872. Mementos of the almost-war everyone avoided form the basis of this national historic park. The island is reached by autoferry from Anacortes, about 75 miles north of Seattle. Open daily sunrise–sunset. Free.

**National Forests:** Washington had completely within its boundaries seven national forests—until Mt. Baker and Snoqualmie were combined—and parts of two other national forests, comprising more than 9 million acres. They hold more than a million acres of land designated as National Forest Wilderness. There are five such Wilderness Areas. *Glacier Peak,* in Mt. Baker and Wenatchee National Forests; *Goat Rocks,* in Gifford Pinchot and Snoqualmie; *Mt. Adams,* in Gifford Pinchot; *Pasayten,* in Mt. Baker and Okanogan. *Alpine Lakes Wilderness,* some 392,000 acres mostly in the Wenatchee National Forest, was added in 1976. All national forests have campgrounds, hundreds of miles of trails, and a great variety of lakes, streams and wildlife. Some charge a nominal fee for camping. Call 442–0170 for general national forest information.

*Gifford Pinchot National Forest* stretches from the Columbia River on the south, along the Cascade Range, to the edge of Mount Rainier National Park on the north. Near the western edge of the forest is 9,677-foot Mt. St. Helens; and near the eastern border is 12,307-foot Mt. Adams. Roads leading to the forest region are U.S. 12 and Wash. 504, branching off I–5, and Wash. 141 up from White Salmon on the Columbia. The Cascade Crest Trail extends through this national forest. Attractions are many lakes; the remains of Mt. St. Helens; Wind River Nursery; lake and stream trout fishing; huckleberry fields (stay out of Yakima Indian Reservation); saddle and pack trips; and mountain climbing.

*Mt. Baker-Snoqualmie National Forest* borders on British Columbia, includes Mt. Baker, Mt. Shuksan, and Glacier Peak, and extends south to Mt. Rainier. A big chunk of land was taken from the Baker region to create North Cascades National Park. Roads approaching the northern part from I–5 are Wash. 542, 20, 530 and 92. Wash. 542 goes from Bellingham to Mt. Baker and 9,127-foot Mt. Shuksan. The Cascade Crest Trail passes through the length of this forest (and on through Gifford Pinchot into Oregon). The Snoqualmie section is the national forest closest to Seattle and Tacoma. From I–5 it is reached by U.S.

2, U.S. 12, I–90 and Wash. 410. Attractions include the scenic Chinook and White Pass highways, and views of Mt. Rainier from various angles. The summit of the Cascades is the general eastern boundary of this forest, and there are winter sports areas at three of the passes.

*Olympic National Forest* borders Olympic National Park on the east, south, and northwest. Only one main highway approaches either the forest or the park: U.S. 101. Nearby towns are Aberdeen, Forks, Olympia, Port Angeles, and Shelton. Attractions include dense rain forests, giant trees, snow peaks, a myriad of lakes and streams, salmon and steelhead fishing, scenic drives, and deer, bear, cougar, and elk.

 **STATE PARKS.** Washington has more than 70 state parks where camping is allowed (generally including RV's and trailers). Largest along the coastal region are: *Twin Harbor,* three miles south of Westport (Wash. 105); *Deception Pass,* north end of Whidbey Island (Wash. 20); *Millersylvania,* 11 miles south of Olympia, off I–5; *Lake Chelan,* nine miles west of Chelan (U.S. 97) and *Moran State Park,* Orcas Island, is the largest state park in the San Juans.

The big ones are most likely to be full on summer weekends, while the lesser-known parks are uncrowded. No reservations, but you can check campsite availability by calling the Parks & Recreation Commission toll free. Dial 1 (800) 562–8200. (The service is in operation only during the busy summer season.) You can also obtain parks information by writing to Washington State Parks, State Parks and Recreation Commission, Box 1128, Olympia, WA 98504; (800) 562–0990.

Don't plan an arrival after 10 P.M. or before 6:30 A.M. in the summer. Gates close.

*Twanoh,* 15 miles northeast of Shelton (U.S. 101), is near the south end of Hood Canal. Dock and boat-launching for saltwater waterway. Swimming in sun-warmed water. Fills up on summer weekends. *Fort Worden State Park,* on the northwestern edge of Port Townsend, is an old military base now used as an arts center—drama, writing, dance, painting, sculpture (one of the few foundries for bronze statuary is here). Several year-round classes, plus jazz and classical music festivals, are held. There is camping on the beach near an old shore battery implacement and working lighthouse.

Because of its inland waters and islands—and forethought—Washington has more marine parks (56) than all the other states put together, which fits in with its highest-per-capita ownership of boats. Most of the marine parks are not developed, but they are reserved for seagoing explorers who want to put ashore and camp.

**ZOOS.** **Seattle** has the largest; see *Practical Information for Seattle.* **Eatonville** is the site of *Northwest Trek* where animals roam freely; visitors ride in motor trams. It is six miles north of Eatonville on Wash. 161. Open daily 10 A.M.–one hour before sundown, April–October; Wednesday–Sunday, November–March. Admission: adults, $4; children and senior citizens, $2. 832–6116. Near **Sequim** is *Loboland,* where numerous species of wolf are kept. Also near Sequim: *Olympic Game Farm* is the home of famous TV and Disney animals, and endangered species. Walk through on a guided tour, or drive yourself around. Five miles northwest on Ward Road. Open daily 9 A.M.–7 P.M., Memorial–Labor Day; 10 A.M.–4 P.M. rest of the year. Adults, $3; children, $1.50. 683–4295. *Tacoma Zoo* is part of the Point Defiance Park complex that includes a respected aquarium with more than 2,000 species of Puget Sound marine life.

**GARDENS.** **Bellingham:** *Fairhaven Park,* on Chuckanut Dr. at southern entrance to town, has lovely rose gardens. Open 8 A.M.–6 P.M. Free. **Blaine:** *Peace Arch State Park,* at Canadian border, between lanes of I-5. No hours; no admission. Highlighted by rare flowers and shrubs. **Olympia:** *State Capitol* grounds and conservatory. **Tacoma:** *Wright Park* has botanical conservatory; *Point Defiance Park* has rose gardens.

**SUMMER SPORTS.** Facilities for family activities are found throughout the state, especially in the larger towns, though even towns of 2,000 people have tennis courts, bowling alleys, swimming pools (or nearby facilities), and plenty of places for bicycling.

**Golf:** In all, there are nearly 200 courses. Since all chambers of commerce list them among tourist attractions, the state has discontinued its golf brochure.

**Fishing:** In rivers that run into saltwater, the great game fish is the steelhead, a large seagoing trout, for which a license is required. It is caught in winter, but trout fishing goes on from mid-April to the end of October. There are 8,000 lakes in the state, with trout, bass, and other whitefish. In saltwater, salmon fishing is at its peak in summer. Westport (Grays Harbor; call 268–8122), Ilwaco (mouth of the Columbia River), and Neah Bay and Sekiu (outer end of the Strait of Juan de Fuca) are the most popular centers for charter boats and equipment. However, Port Angeles and many other coastal towns have boathouses. A beach sport at Long Beach Peninsula and on the coast north of Grays Harbor is digging for the delicate-shelled razor clam. It is rated as "game," with a limit of 15 a day per person. License required; no clamming July through September. Clamming and fishing licenses are available at any sporting goods store. Note: At press time (early 1984) all Washington clam beaches have been closed indefinitely; the clam population has been decimated by disease, but clams are expected to return after 1984.

For license fees and regulations, write Dept. of Fisheries, Room 115, Administration Bldg., Olympia, WA 98504 (no license needed in national parks).

**Hiking:** You can set foot on a trail within an hour's drive of any city in the state, and the only limit to how far you go is time and endurance. The mountain trails vary from easy three-mile walks to rugged backpack trips not recommended for beginners. The lengthiest routes are the Cascade Crest Trail along the summit of the range from British Columbia to Oregon (230 miles, airline), and the crossing of the Olympic Peninsula by Olympic National Park trails. (Also see "National Parklands," above.)

**Horseback riding:** Available at dude ranches and in various National Forest areas, where packers still contract some work for the Forest Service. These are hard to keep track of, year to year, because helicopters may have displaced them. Call 442–0170 for information. On the other hand, horses for rent pop up around developing resort areas each season. Make local inquiry.

**Hunting:** The big game animals are deer, elk, black bear, cougar, and mountain goats. Hunters annually harvest about 75,000 deer and 10,500 elk. The 300 goats taken are on permits issued by public drawings. In five counties bears are considered predators and the season is always open on them. Between 5,000 and 9,000 are killed each year. Principal game birds are pheasants, ducks, geese, grouse, quail, and partridge, and among them they furnish an annual bag of well more than a million birds. Rabbit hunting averages an annual harvest of about 200,000. Hunting season on one game or another is open all year somewhere in the state, although fall and winter are the busiest. Age limit for a license is 18 unless the youngster has completed a firearms-training course. Licenses are purchased from sport stores, or request an application from the Washington State Game Department, 600 N. Capitol Way, Olympia, WA 98504.

**Mountain-climbing:** Mountains stand on fully half the area of the state, and vary from 2,000-foot hills to 14,410-foot Mt. Rainier—which you must climb with a guide unless you can give convincing proof of mountaineering experience. There are peaks with trails to the top and some that never have been scaled. Stick to trails unless you are fully equipped and know what you are doing. The high ones have glaciers on them, and a few climbers die every summer from overconfidence. Call Rainier Mountaineering, 475–7755, for details.

 **SKIING.** *Crystal Mountain.* A ski area 76 miles southeast of Seattle on Hwy. 410. Daily and night skiing with T-bars, ropetows, and chairs. No accommodations for overnight visitors. 634–3771. *Mt. Baker* is 60 miles east of Bellingham on Wash. 542. 599–2714. *Snoqualmie Summit.* The closest area to Seattle—50 miles on I-90—has three ski areas under the same management: Snoqualmie Summit, Ski Acres, and Alpental. Shuttle-bus service among the three. One lift ticket for all. Skiing both day and night. T-bars, rope tows, and lifts. 434–6161. *Stevens Pass.* 70 miles northeast of Seattle on Hwy. 2. Open Wednesday–Sunday both day and night. No overnight facilities. 937–2500. *White Pass.* 105 miles southeast of Seattle on Hwy. 12. Open daily. Chairs, poma and free rope tow for children under 12. Condo rentals available. 453–8731.

**SPECTATOR SPORTS. Baseball:** Tacoma has teams in the Pacific Coast League. Bellingham and Grays Harbor have teams in the Northwest League.

**Logger sports:** These are western Washington's equivalent of the rodeo, and they, too, come in all sizes from small-town events to major competitions at Shelton, Sedro Woolley, and Morton. (See "Seasonal Events.") As in a rodeo, "loggerodeo" is based on jobs that traditionally went with the work—sawing, chopping, tree topping, log rolling—even if modern methods have replaced them.

**WHAT TO DO WITH THE CHILDREN.** Even most of the small cities have parks and playgrounds for rest stops. With 3,000 miles of saltwater coast, Washington is a great place for beachcombing and peering at the creatures in tidal pools. At Mt. Baker and Mt. Rainier, nothing excites youngsters more than getting to throw a snowball in July. There are many rodeos and Indian celebrations. Boating goes on in lakes, rivers, Puget Sound, and around ocean harbors—the simplest form of it being to take a ferry ride to Victoria, B.C., the San Juan Islands, or round-trip on Puget South. (See "How to Get There and How to Get Around," above.)

Tacoma's *Point Defiance Park* has a "Never-Never Land" and a farm animal zoo for children. On summer weekends there are old-fashioned train rides there. The *Puget Sound and Snoqualmie Valley Railroad* is a seven-mile railroad with steam engine and streetcars. In **Snoqualmie.** Open Saturday–Sunday, 11 A.M.–5 P.M., June 1–August 31; Sunday only, May 31–September 30. Adults $4; children $2. 888–0373.

*Northwest Trek* at **Eatonville** is a branch of the Tacoma zoo. Animals roam freely, viewed from quiet motor trams. Near **Sequim** is *Loboland* with several species of wolf, and *Olympic Game Farm* where famous animal characters are kept and filmed for TV and Disney nature movies. (See "Zoos," above.) And of course with all the state's mountains, forests and open rangeland, there is always a chance of seeing bears, deer and smaller animals in the wild.

**HISTORIC SITES. Hoquiam:** *Hoquiam's "Castle"* has been declared a state and national historic site. The beautifully restored 20-room mansion is an antique fancier's delight. 515 Chenault St.; 533–2005.

**Port Angeles:** *Clallam Indian Longhouse,* in Lincoln Park.

**Port Gamble:** The town itself, established in 1863, is registered as a National Historic Landmark.

**Port Townsend:** Site of *Old Fort Townsend,* three miles south of town.

**Suquamish:** Site of *Old Man House* (Ol-e-man in Chinook jargon). A longhouse for communal living. *Chief Seattle's grave* in cemetery adjoining St. Peter's Church: a very old cemetery where both whites and Indians were buried.

**San Juan Islands:** *San Juan Island National Historic Park* has mementoes from the "Pig War" between the United States and Britain. See "National Parks," earlier in this *Practical Information* section.

**Vancouver:** See "Historic Sites" in *Practical Information for Portland, Oregon.*

 **MUSEUMS AND GALLERIES. Historical: Anacortes:** *Museum of History and Art,* 1305 E. 8th St.

**Auburn:** *White River Valley Historical Society Museum,* 918 H St. S.E.

**Bellingham:** *Whatcom Museum of History and Art,* 121 Prospect St.; 676–6981.

**Bremerton:** *Kitsap County Historical Society Museum,* 837 Fourth St.; 377–3546. Located in old telephone building put up in 1910. *Naval Shipyard Museum.* Ferry Building.

**Eastsound, Orcas Island:** *Orcas Island Historical Society Museum,* in buildings of six original homestead cabins.

**Fort Lewis:** *Fort Lewis Military Museum.* Just west of I–5. History of the military in the Northwest. Closed Mon.

**Friday Harbor:** *San Juan Historical Society Museum,* Price St. In pioneer residence.

**Neah Bay:** *Makah Museum,* P.O. Box 95; 645–2711. Artifacts from the archaeological dig at Cape Ozette are housed here, including a replica of a longhouse found in the Ozette site and replicas of canoes used in the Ozette village. Most important artifacts, such as tools, pottery, and cedar-bark mats, were unearthed from the village that had been buried for centuries under massive mudslides. Hours: September 16–May 31, 10 A.M.–5 P.M., Wednesday–Sunday. June 1–September 15, 10 A.M.–5 P.M., seven days a week. Admission: $2 adults, $1 students and senior citizens.

**North Bend:** *Snoqualmie Valley Historical Society Museum,* Fourth and N. Ballarat. Indian baskets and artifacts.

**Olympia:** *Washington State Board of Pharmacy,* 319 E. 7th. Restoration of 1860 pharmacy.

**Port Angeles:** *Pioneer Memorial Museum,* 2800 Hurricane Ridge Rd. at the Olympic National Park headquarters.

**Port Townsend:** *Jefferson County Historical Society Museum,* in old 1892 City Hall; 385–1001. *Rothschild House,* Rte. 1; 385–2722. Furnished nineteenth-century house.

**Puyallup:** *Ezra Meeker Mansion,* 321 E. Pioneer. Seventeen-room Victorian home. *Frontier Museum,* 23rd Ave. N.E. Indian artifacts, pioneer displays.

**Snoqualmie:** *Puget Sound Railway Historical Association.* Railroad museum.

**Tacoma:** *Museum of Natural History* in Thompson Science Hall at the University of Puget Sound. *Washington State Historical Society & Museum,* 315 N. Stadium Way; 593–2830. Collection of pioneer relics, large archives, frequent special exhibits and lecture series. Hours: Tuesday–Saturday, 9 A.M.–5 P.M.; closed Sunday and Monday.

Art: Port Townsend: *Jean Sprague Gallery,* Fillmore & Clay. Tacoma: *Hand-forth Gallery,* Tacoma Public Library, 1102 S. Tacoma; 572–2000. Exhibits change monthly. Monday–Thursday, 9 A.M.–9 P.M.; Friday–Saturday, 9 A.M.–6 P.M. *Tacoma Art Museum,* 12th & Pacific Ave. 272–4258. Permanent collection of American and European paintings, exhibitions of national and international art; children's gallery; Sara Little Center for Design Research. Hours: Monday–Saturday, 10 A.M.–4 P.M.; Sunday, noon–5 P.M. *Kittredge & Hill Art Galleries,* University of Puget Sound, 15th & N. Lawrence; 758–3348. Several shows of regional and national artists each year. Monday–Friday, 9 A.M.–4 P.M.; Sunday, 1–4 P.M. *Allied Art Center,* 621 Pacific. *Mortvedt Library Gallery,* Pacific Lutheran University.

 **DINING OUT.** As is true everywhere, the best hotels have one or more restaurants and so do the expensive motor inns. Quality is expected and prices are commensurate. Since restaurants of this type are run in connection with lodging, no attempt to list them has been made here or in the Seattle section. Those suggested below are only a few whose main business is food, and that have kept customers pleased for a number of years. Price ranges for dinner are: *Expensive,* $15 up; *Moderate,* $9–$15; *Inexpensive,* less than $9. However, in all categories dessert usually is extra, and often coffee or tea. Also add sales tax and the usual tip. Major credit cards are accepted at many of the establishments listed here, but you may want to double-check in advance.

## ABERDEEN

**Bridges Restaurant.** *Moderate–Expensive.* Island G; 532–6563. A very nice downtown restaurant with a children's menu. Lounge.

**Nordic Inn Restaurant.** *Inexpensive–Moderate.* 1700 S. Boone St.; 533–0100. Wide variety, with commensurate range in prices. Pleasant decor emphasizing the Viking theme. Children's menu. Entertainment in the lounge.

## BELLINGHAM

**Chuckanut Manor.** *Moderate–Expensive.* 302 Chuckanut Dr.; 799–6191. Specializing in prime ribs, steaks, seafood, and home baking. Sit at windows overlooking the bay. Bar, entertainment, and dancing some evenings.

**Johnson's Fine Foods.** *Moderate.* 5659 Barrett Rd., Ferndale; 384–1601. View of Mt. Baker and nearby farmlands from the dining room of this excellent family restaurant. Extra-large portions. Lounge.

**Stuart Anderson's Black Angus.** *Moderate.* 165 S. Samish Way; 354–3607. Specialty is steak done "as you like it." Bar, entertainment, dancing.

**La Creperie.** *Inexpensive–Moderate.* 1200 Harris; 676–1284. An interesting restaurant in Fairhaven Village, a restored section of old Bellingham. Taproom serving beer and wines.

**Royal Fork.** *Inexpensive.* 1530 Ellis; 676–8288. One-price buffet (small children eat for less). Large selection of salads, entrées and desserts.

## BREMERTON

**Hearthstone.** *Expensive.* 4312 Kitsap Way; 377–5531. Excellent view of the waterfront from paneled dining room. Specialties are fresh salmon in season, seafood, and steak. Cocktail lounge with entertainment and dancing.

## COUPEVILLE
### (Whidbey Island)

**The Captain Whidbey.** *Moderate.* Three miles north on Penn Cove, overlooking the water and docks; 678–4097. Building is unique turn-of-the-century structure of madrona logs. Decorated with antiques. Crabs, oysters, clams are specialties, also prime ribs.

## EVERETT

**Village Inn.** *Moderate.* 8525 Evergreen Way; 355–2525. Family restaurant with children's plates. Steaks, trout.

## OCEAN SHORES

**Marina View Restaurant.** *Moderate.* 1020 Discovery Ave.; 289–3393. This is an interesting place, situated next to the marina and "people ferry" to Westport landing. Excellent seafood dinners as well as steaks and sandwiches. Cocktails. Breakfast and lunch too.

## OLYMPIA

**Tumwater Valley Inn.** *Expensive.* 4611 Tumwater Valley Dr.; 753–9939. A la carte. This restaurant adjoins the Tumwater Valley Golf Club. Quality dining in pleasant surroundings. Varied menu with seafood dominating. Children's and senior citizens' portions. South of Olympia in Tumwater.

**Craig's Olympia Oyster House.** *Moderate-Expensive.* 320 W. 4th St.; 943–8020. Waterfront restaurant noted for seafood, but also serves tender steaks and prime ribs. Bar.

## PORT ANGELES

**Birney's Restaurant.** *Moderate–Expensive.* U.S. 101 E.; 457–4411. Open 24 hours a day, this popular restaurant serves breakfast, lunch, and dinner, varied menu, à la carte as well as full meals. Child's menu. Lounge.

**Haguewood's Restaurant.** *Moderate–Expensive.* 221 N. Lincoln; 457–0424. Dungeness cracked crab is a specialty at this waterfront restaurant overlooking Strait of Juan de Fuca. Wide selection of other menu items and own baked goods. Child's menu. Bar.

**Harrington's Restaurant.** *Inexpensive-Expensive.* 120 N. Laurel; 457–7363. Good food, good service, full meals or à la carte. Varied menu. Children's plates. Lounge.

## PORT LUDLOW

**The Harbormaster.** *Expensive.* Rte. 1; 437–2222. The excellent restaurant is part of the Admiralty Resort complex. A beautiful view from picture windows. Well-prepared food from a varied menu. Children's menu. Lounge and entertainment. Boat moorage. Reservations required.

## PUYALLUP

**Anton's.** *Moderate–Expensive.* Near Puyallup River bridge, on Puyallup-Sumner Hwy.; 845–7569. Varied choice of entrées, well served. Children's menu. Lounge and entertainment. Reservations advised.

## SEQUIM

**Discovery Bay Restaurant.** *Expensive.* 16 miles S. of Sequim on US 101; 385–1711. Waterfront dining. Seafood and steak, specialties are geoduck steak (sometimes called "king clam") and oysters.

**3 Crabs.** *Moderate.* 101 Three Crabs Rd.; 683–4264. Famous for its seafood dishes—crab, clams, geoduck, and oysters. This is a modest little restaurant but well worth the 7 mile drive east from center of town. It is on the water's edge with view of Dungeness Spit. A local favorite.

## TACOMA

**Cliff House.** *Expensive.* 6300 Marine View Dr. N.E.; 927–0400. Excellent spot for steak or lobster, to be enjoyed while admiring the magnificent view of Mt. Rainier and Tacoma harbor. Cocktail lounge, entertainment.

**Clinkerdagger, Bickerstaff and Pett's Public House.** *Moderate–Expensive.* 3327 Ruston Way; 752–6661. Specialty of the house here is Steak Horacio. Old English atmosphere. Waterfront view. Bar.

**Johnny's Dock.** *Moderate–Expensive.* 1900 E. D; 627–3186. One of Tacoma's fine seafood houses, located right at the waterfront. Specialties are steak, seafood, own baked goods. If you like their special seasonings they usually have a supply on hand for sale.

**Lakewood Terrace.** *Moderate–Expensive.* 6114 Motor Ave. in Lakewood Center; 588–5215. In the Lakewood Motor Inn, listed here because it is popular with the local people. Steak and seafood specialties. Children's menu. Lounge and entertainment. Reservations advised.

**Stuart Anderson's Black Angus.** *Moderate–Expensive.* Two locations: 1101 A St. in Tacoma and 9905 Bridgeport Way S.W. in Lakewood; 582–6900. Choice beef served "as you like it." Lunch and dinner. Full bar. Entertainment and dancing.

**Barbecue Pete's.** *Moderate.* 1314 E. 72nd; 535–1000. Great barbecued ribs are a specialty here. Lunch and dinner. Lounge.

**Bavarian.** *Moderate.* 204 N. K; 627–5010. German-American menu. Specialties are schnitzel and steak. Child's menu. Bar. Weekend combo.

**Raintree Pizza & Steak House.** *Inexpensive–Moderate.* 8620 S. Hosmer; 535–4044. They allow you to broil your own steaks here. That's one way to get them the way you like them. Gourmet hamburgers and pizzas are also on the menu. Salad bar. Lounge.

**Old Spaghetti Factory.** *Inexpensive.* 1735 Jefferson; 383–2214. Interesting antique décor. Large choice of spaghetti sauces. Children's menu. Lounge, cocktails, and variety of wines.

**King's Table Royal Fork.** *Inexpensive.* 9002 Pacific Ave.; 537–2933. A good place to take the family. A buffet with many choices of salads and entrées. All you can eat. One price for adults, children charged according to age.

## VANCOUVER

**Stuart Anderson's Cattle Co.** *Moderate.* 415 E. 13th; 695–1506. A member of the Black Angus chain of restaurants serving excellent steaks. Complete meals at a modest price. Lounge, entertainment and dancing.

**Holland Restaurant.** *Inexpensive–Moderate.* Main and W. McLoughlin Blvd.; 694–7842. Complete menu features children's portions; particularly fine pastries. Popular family dining spot.

**Chinese Pavilion.** *Inexpensive–Expensive.* 1401 NE 78th St.; 574–3141. Good Chinese and American food. Oriental décor. Lounge and entertainment.

**La Comida.** *Inexpensive.* 400 NE 76th St.; 695–4837. Authentic Mexican food. A la carte or complete dinners. Beer and wine. Takeout orders, too.

# BRITISH COLUMBIA

*Canada's Coastal Areas*

by
**DAVID WISHART**

*David Wishart is a freelance travel writer based in Vancouver. A former editorial writer and columnist on the morning newspaper there, he has worked as a journalist on four continents.*

British Columbia combines all the essentials for the traveler seeking a great outdoor adventure and a comfortable easygoing vacation—or both. For those interested in nature—and wishing to rough it for a while—the province encompasses 948,600 square kms. (366,255 square miles) of rugged and beautiful land. Yet coastal cities such as Vancouver and Victoria offer the tourist first-rate amenities, a rich cultural life, and the finest international cuisine.

Canada's gateway to the Pacific and the Orient, British Columbia prides itself on being the dominion's most scenic province—a land of mountain ranges and forests, rivers, streams, and lakes. Bounded by the Pacific on the west, the Rockies on the east, the United States to the south, and the Yukon and Alaska to the north, the province has developed a lifestyle quite unlike that of the rest of the nation—more tuned in to land and sea. With a mild, healthy, though often wet year-round climate, British Columbia is on the upswing economically—a land rich in minerals and wood, with waterways and coastal areas teeming with sea life. For residents and visitors alike, the province generates a great sense of vitality in the northwest stretches of the continent.

## A Bit of History

British Columbia was probably first sighted in 1579 by Sir Francis Drake, who was searching for the Northwest Passage. Instead, he saw Vancouver Island—and passed it by. It was another 200 years before anyone was interested in exploring the territory. Juan Pérez of Spain saw its shores in 1774, but it was not until 1778, when Captain James Cook sailed into what is now known as Friendly Cove, at Nootka Sound, Vancouver Island, that a white man stepped on British Columbia land. (Cook was also looking for the Northwest Passage, but settled for fur trading with the Indians instead.) By 1785, many ships were landing in the area in order to get a piece of the highly lucrative fur business.

While the Colonists were waging their War of Independence from Great Britain in the eastern United States, England and Spain were deadlocked over the rights to this vast Pacific territory. Spain assumed ownership and, in 1789, sent a ship commanded by Captain Martínez to seize all British property at Nootka Sound. The British government, by then embarrassed by its loss of the thirteen American colonies, came close to declaring war on Spain. Uneasy about forcing the issue, the Spanish declared the region open to all comers.

## England Establishes Its Claim

In 1790, the Nootka Convention between Spain and England ceded the entire northern coast up to Russian Alaska to His Majesty; two years later, the British Admiralty sent Captain George Vancouver to survey and lay claim to the territory.

At about this time, the overland route across Canada was being forged. Alexander Mackenzie reached the Pacific in 1793 in the first crossing of the country anywhere on the continent above Mexico. Mackenzie is a legend, but his journey was a search for wealth, not glory. He made the long trek as a representative of the North West Company, one of the New World trapping and trading alliances—and chief rival of the Hudson's Bay Company. Both were after the profitable fur spoils of the Northwest. Mackenzie set up a thriving fur business, and the word spread fast.

## Rivalry among Trading Companies

Unlike the eastern part of Canada and the United States, where national armies clashed, the West never saw real warfare. But there was fierce rivalry of another sort among the great trading companies that represented the competing governments of the day. The early history of British Columbia records bitter struggles on the part of these companies to establish their forts at strategic points around the area's rivers, lakes, and ocean ports.

Beginning in 1805, Simon Fraser entered the area and built several forts for his trading activities—Fort McLeod, Fort St. James, and Fort George. Other pioneers soon arrived and constructed their posts, usually at the confluence of two or more major rivers. In 1821, when the mighty North West Company sold out to the even mightier Hudson's Bay Company, the business battle was over for a time. For the next 30 years, Hudson's Bay controlled the vast territory with only nominal help from London. There were more forts, more people, more fur trapping and trading.

## The 49th Parallel

Hudson's Bay Company kept a tight rein on its land, often angering the United States government when Americans were excluded or short-changed by the company. This set the scene for a diplomatic showdown between London and Washington over the uncharted western lands. Both countries wanted title to as much land as possible. Finally in 1846, they settled on the 49th parallel, extending from the Rockies to the Pacific, as the boundary line between the United States and British holdings. Fort Victoria became the seat of government in British Columbia and, in 1849, the Hudson's Bay Company turned over all of Vancouver Island to the British.

The company installed the early governors of the territory. Richard Blanshard lasted only a year; he was succeeded by James Douglas, who ruled alone until a Legislative Assembly was formed in 1856—the first such representative body in the West. There were still less than 800 colonists in the territory at the time.

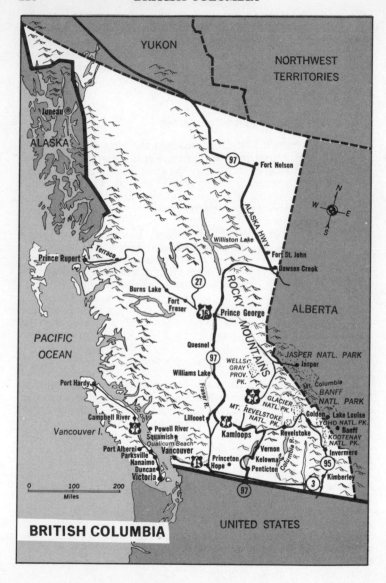

YUKON

NORTHWEST TERRITORIES

Juneau

ALASKA

97 • Fort Nelson

ALASKA HWY

Williston Lake

Fort St. John

• Prince Rupert • Terrace
Dawson Creek

Burns Lake
27
Fort
Fraser
16
Prince George

ROCKY MOUNTAINS

ALBERTA

PACIFIC OCEAN

Quesnel
97

WELLS GRAY PROV. PK.

JASPER NATL. PARK
• Jasper

Williams Lake

Mt. Columbia
BANFF NATL. PARK

Fraser R.

GLACIER NATL. PK.
MT. REVELSTOKE NATL. PK.

Golden
Lake Louise
YOHO NATL. PK.

Port Hardy

Campbell River

Powell River
Squamish
Qualicum Beach
Port Alberni
Parksville
Nanaimo
Duncan
Victoria

Lilloet

Kamloops

Revelstoke

Banff
KOOTENAY NATL. PK.

Columbia R.

Vancouver I.

Vancouver

Princeton
Hope

Vernon

Kelowna
Penticton

Invermere

95

Kimberley

3

0   100   200
Miles

97

UNITED STATES

**BRITISH COLUMBIA**

Those days were not to last long. In 1858, gold was discovered on the Fraser River, and the rush from the south was on. Within the year, close to 30,000 people invaded British Columbia, looking for instant wealth. There were many disappointments, but as one river bed dried up, another "hit" would be found elsewhere. In 1860, the Cariboo region was struck, and thousands more made the trek north. Roads were built; communities sprang up within weeks. The colony was prospering.

At the same time (1858), the colony was officially proclaimed, with Douglas serving as the first governor. In 1866, Vancouver Island and the mainland territory were officially joined; the small colony of New Westminster served as the first capital. Three years later, however, Victoria was designated the capital, which it remains today.

While British Columbia was undergoing a financial depression, the other Canadian provinces to the east were forming their Confederation. In 1867, the eastern lands joined together. Wanting to make a clean East–West sweep (and also needing British Columbia's outlet to the Pacific), they invited British Columbia to join. At issue was communications. British Columbia said it would unite with its neighbors only if a trans-Canada railroad linked them, shore to shore. The easterners agreed, and British Columbia joined the Canadian Confederation on July 20, 1871.

## Linked to the Rest of Canada

A promise to build a railroad over 8,000 kms. (5,000 miles) of difficult terrain and building it were two different things. The federal government, failing at its first attempt, had an incensed group of British Columbians on its hands, some of them shouting for secession. The second attempt, launched by a private company, was successful; by 1885, Vancouver was linked to the rest of Canada by the Canadian Pacific Railroad.

## Gold!

British Columbia's new prosperity was suddenly heightened when a large lode of gold was discovered in the Kootenay region in 1887. First came the Hall mines; the Red Mountain mines were explored three years later. Minerals were found in abundance, bringing more and more prospectors as word spread throughout the continent. The province was not yet self-sufficient, but, as its industries developed, its dependence on the federal government lessened. In the meantime, Vancouver became the primary seaport on the Pacific and, with the opening of the Panama Canal in 1915, the city shot up in size and influence, bringing prosperity to the entire province. Shipbuilding, lumbering, manufacturing, and energy all became major industries. Fishing expanded greatly. Fertile lands were farmed with excellent results. More mineral wealth was discovered. Throughout the twentieth century, British Columbia has continued to be a land of discovery, offering many challenges to man's imagination.

Today, British Columbia remains a relatively prosperous province, although her resource-based economy (logging, coal, fishing, oil, and gas) is susceptible to the ups and downs of international trade. But in good times or bad, the Canadians who live here console themselves with the thought that they are living in one of the most pleasant parts of North America—if not the world—and they are happy to share this natural beauty with visitors.

Indeed, tourism has become one of the province's biggest money-earners, a fact of life promoted by Tourism B.C., the Victoria-based provincial government agency. The rugged coast and soaring mountains of the province are advertised widely under the slogan, "Super Natural B.C." This is Canada's outdoors province, a California North if you will, where summer is for the beach, boating, and golf, and the winter for skiing—downhill and cross-country.

British Columbia's outdoor wonders may account for the fact that the pace of life in the province is slower than it is in the East, a situation that continually exasperates visiting businesspeople. But there are compensations: the people are friendly, and the various races who live in B.C. (Vancouver has the second largest Chinatown in North America after San Francisco) get along together with relatively few problems.

# EXPLORING VANCOUVER

Cosmopolitan, prosperous, multiracial, and active, Vancouver is often referred to as Canada's "Gem of the Pacific." A symbol of British Columbia, it is the largest seaport on the Pacific coast, claiming 160 kms. (100 miles) of water frontage. With mountain ranges to the east and north cutting off the cold Arctic air, and Vancouver Island, to the west, protecting it from rough Pacific winds, Vancouver has such a pleasant mild climate that on a good day in winter or spring, you can play golf in the morning, ski on Grouse Mountain twenty minutes away in the afternoon, and have a swim in the English Bay, warmed by the Japanese Current, before dinner.

But fine weather is just a start. As Canada's third largest city, with a population of 1.2 million, Vancouver offers excellent hotels and res-

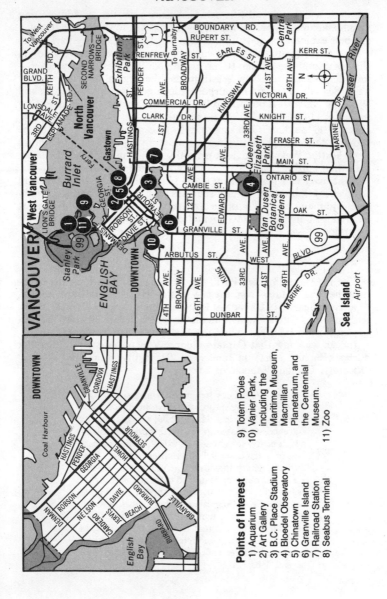

**Points of Interest**

1) Aquarium
2) Art Gallery
3) B.C. Place Stadium
4) Bloedel Observatory
5) Chinatown
6) Granville Island
7) Railroad Station
8) Seabus Terminal
9) Totem Poles
10) Vanier Park, including the Maritime Museum, Macmillan Planetarium, and the Centennial Museum.
11) Zoo

taurants, a rich cultural life, sports, leisure activities, and interesting sightseeing. Many parts of the city—such as Gastown or Chinatown—are best explored on foot; that is true for the city's many parks, too.

Vancouver is situated on a peninsula between the Burrard Inlet on the north and the Fraser River on the south. Greater Vancouver—including Vancouver, New Westminster (the original settlement), Burnaby, Sea Island (where the airport is located), North Vancouver, and West Vancouver—is connected by a series of bridges. Vancouver City measures 114 sq. kms. (44 square miles), and Metropolitan Vancouver covers 2,067 sq. kms. (798 square miles); therefore, to see many of the sights, a car or a sightseeing bus is a must. Lying 232 kms. (145 miles) from Seattle, Washington, and just 40 kms. (25 miles) from the U.S.-Canadian border, Vancouver is easily accessible by car.

Vancouver's biggest drawing card is its spectacular mountain and sea scenery. Although the city sparkles with new glass-and-steel high-rises and many grand Victorian structures, what sets Vancouver apart from almost any other North American metropolis, with the possible exception of San Francisco, is its beautiful, natural setting.

## Stanley Park

The 1,000-acre Stanley Park, the largest natural park on the continent, lies just minutes from the city center. Named after Lord Stanley, Governor General of Canada in 1889, this huge expanse of forest, trails, and man-made attractions immediately gives an idea of what Vancouver must have been like when the first white men came here.

Indeed we know that Captain George Vancouver entered the outer harbor (Burrard Inlet) on June 13, 1792. In his journal, *A Voyage of Discovery,* Captain Vancouver wrote:

> From Point Grey [where the University of B.C. now stands] we proceeded first up the eastern branch of the sound, where, about a league from its entrance, we passed to the northward of an island which nearly terminated its extent, forming a passage from ten to seven fathoms deep, not more than a cable's length in width. The island lying exactly across the channel, appeared to form a similar passage to the south of it, with a smaller island lying before it. From these islands, the channel, in width about half a mile, continued its direction about east. Here we were met by about 50 Indians, in their canoes, who conducted themselves with the greatest decorum and civility presenting us with several fish. . . .

The "island" was Stanley Park. The intrepid explorers, by the way, were showered with soft white feathers by the Indians in a welcoming gesture. Some slept on the beach that night, to be awakened by the tide lapping around their feet.

It was another 70 years, however, before white men returned to these beaches and founded the city of Vancouver. When they did, they heard the legend of "the island of the dead men," relating to a small spit of land to the east of Stanley Park (now a military reserve called Deadman's Island) where 200 men exchanged their lives for those of women and children held by an enemy tribe.

The park is 6.5 miles round, and its seawall is a favorite for walkers, runners, and cyclists. To get there, simply take a bus going west on Georgia Street and get off at the bottom of Denman Street. A taxi from the city center at Georgia and Burrard will run less than $3, but to get a taxi for the return trip you may have to walk back to Georgia and Denman and phone for one; the alternative is to call for a taxi from one of the park restaurants. A recommended plan, however, is to rent a bike (see "Participant Sports" in *Practical Information for Vancouver*); there are designated bike paths.

Going into the park from Georgia Street (there is another entrance on English Bay) the first thing you'll see is the Vancouver Rowing Club, a wooden building that sits on stilts. Although it is a private club, it is generous with its reciprocity and it's worth checking your wallet to see if your home club has an arrangement. The VRC caters to rowers, rugby, hockey, and tennis players, has numerous boating enthusiasts, and streams of runners and joggers.

Across the street is a statue of Robert Burns, the Scottish poet. First on the left is a road leading up to the zoo and aquarium, but if you keep to the seawall you'll come to the Nine O'Clock Gun, which is fired every night, and then arrive at Brockton Point Lighthouse, a good viewing point for the North Shore and Grouse Mountain.

The road continues past a group of totem poles, the cricket pitch, rugby ground, and comes to Lumberman's Arch, a tribute to the province's forestry workers, where you'll get an idea of the giants of the forest that used to stand here (most of Stanley Park's 100,000 trees, while quite impressive, are second growth). Up on the left is a children's zoo and miniature railway, as well as good picnic areas.

The seawall then winds up to Prospect Point, a superb viewpoint that also has a memorial to the S.S. *Beaver,* a British-built paddle-wheeler that was the first steamer in the Pacific Northwest. After 53 years on the coast she was wrecked below Prospect Point in 1888.

Then it's past Siwash Rock to Third Beach, then Ferguson Point (the Teahouse there is recommended for those who like a meal with a view; phone 669–3281). You'll reach Second Beach next, and across the street is a pitch-and-putt course adjacent to the fine Beach House Restaurant. Tennis courts are nearby. Lost Lagoon, with its ducks and swans, is just right for a relaxing stroll. Please note—dogs must be kept on a leash at all times.

Stanley Park is just a few minutes away from downtown, where the main hotels are located, along with the best shopping and restaurants. Major attractions here are Robson Street (often referred to as Robson-strasse), Gastown, Chinatown, and Granville Island.

## Robson Street

Buying or just window shopping is a delight in this European-style street of shops, boutiques, and restaurants. Go for a stroll between Bute and Hornby and check out the cheese shops, sausage shops, and pastry shops. You'll find fashions from around the world, and maybe your hometown newspaper at European News Import House at 1136 Robson. A good place to buy film or get any kind of photographic services is Customcolor, which has stores at 1100 Robson and another at the corner of Robson and Thurlow.

If you were to make a left off Robson at Bute and walk the two blocks to Georgia Street, you would reach the Vancouver Art Gallery. The Gallery has moved to the old Court House at 800 West Georgia after a stunning interior transformation costing $25 million. The VAG owns the largest collection of works by West Coast artist Emily Carr, but its strength lies in its programs of contemporary exhibitions.

The three city blocks running south of the 800-block of Robson Street between Hornby and Howe contain Robson Square, a complex with something for everyone: art exhibits, free lectures, concerts, and ice skating in the winter. It is a particularly pleasant place in summer, a good gathering spot or somewhere to lunch inside or out. There is often street entertainment—bands, orchestras, jugglers, and that sort of thing. The B.C. Law Courts are located here and tours are available during the summer months. And Tourism B.C. has an information office here.

## Gastown

Vancouver began in Gastown, back in the 1860s. The area later fell on hard times as Vancouver and its suburbs grew—until the 1960s, when urban renewal arrived at Gastown. Now this historic corner of town is lively and colorful. It's a good place for a stroll, to buy souvenirs or maybe antiques, and there are several restaurants and night spots. To get there head north on Granville Street—until the very end, in fact—and turn right opposite the old Canadian Pacific Railway station into West Cordova Street. (Note the beautiful First World War memorial of the soldier and the angel.) The CPR station now contains the Sea Bus terminal for the commuter ferries than run to the North Shore and back, as well as shops and offices.

Shopping in Gastown is full of surprises, particularly if you come across such fascinating little places as Uniques, 319 West Cordova, where a sign on the counter warns that "these premises patrolled by attack cockatiel." A couple of doors down is the Water Street Passage, which runs through Le Magasin into Water Street. Le Magasin is a mini-mall containing a good bistro (The Bistro at Le Magasin; phone 687–1029) and a number of boutiques, including the delightful Gallipots, which sells English toiletries and preserves.

Across the street at 345 Water is the Inuit Gallery, which sells Eskimo art and a little farther down is a steam clock, a Gastown landmark. Here are more good places to stop for a bite: the Brasserie de L'Horloge (300 Water) and Leo's, on the next corner, which does a tasty steak. Farther down Water Street is Woodward's parking lot, an inexpensive place to leave your car. The Courtyard Mall, across the street, has two interesting shops with self-explanatory names—the Doll's House and High as a Kite ("Kite" is the self-explanatory part of that name). Back across the street there is more good shopping: Railway World at 150 Water Street, for instance, and farther down, at 101, is Portobello Antiques. Have a stroll around the square where Water, Carrall, Powell, and Alexander converge. There's a statue of "Gassy Jack" Deighton, a saloonkeeper who gave his name to the area, and note the unusual wedge-shaped building—the former Europe Hotel, once the best digs in town, then a flop house, and now remodeled into condominiums. Many of the Gastown shops are open on Sunday.

## Chinatown

The second-largest Chinatown in North America is located close to Gastown on three blocks of West Pender Street between Carrall and Gore. This Oriental bazaar also takes in a couple of blocks of Main Street and one of Keefer Street, which runs south of West Pender. There's much of Chinese life here: on the corner of Carrall Street is the Chinese *Times*, two doors up at number 17 is the Hung Lin Wig Shop, followed by the Ho Tung Studio, which does portraits on plates. At number 65 there's the Yen Lock restaurant, one of many excellent Chinese restaurants in this area. If you like to cook your own, there are supermarkets, vegetable stores, and bakeries. The Yuen Fong store at 242 West Pender is a popular place, and the Kwong Hing next door does great barbecued pork. The Garden Bakery across the street has moon cakes and black-bean-paste buns. You'll also find souvenir shops and lots of import places where you can buy Chinese clothes, records, books, and newspapers. The On On Tea Garden at 214 Keefer is a popular restaurant with lots of room for family and group outings.

### Granville Island

Under the Granville Street Bridge, Granville Island is more than a brisk walk from the main Georgia Street thoroughfare, but quite accessible by bike, bus, or taxi. It is a thriving redevelopment built around a popular food market with specialty shops selling everything from pastries to nautical gear. There are several restaurants, including the chic and expensive Bridges. The Granville Island Boatel (you can dock your boat here and take a room in the hotel) is worth a visit, especially in the evening when its Pelican Bay bar, delightfully located to overlook the water, is a popular singles hangout. The place is good for strolling, watching boats and sunsets, eating ice cream, and reflecting that this is one project the federal government did well.

### Vanier Park

One of the best ways to view Vancouver's beauties is to go by car or bus from downtown, across the Burrard Street Bridge (near the Granville Street Bridge), stopping first at Vanier Park. Here you may visit the Maritime Museum, home of the ship *St. Roch,* the first vessel to sail the hazardous Northwest Passage, east and west. Close by are the Centennial Museum, containing artifacts dating from the rugged pioneer days, and the ultramodern MacMillan Planetarium, which has one of the finest planetarium shows on the continent.

### "Scenic Drive"

Continuing westward on Point Grey Road, you'll see English Bay on the north, and a stunning view of the city behind you. Called the Scenic Drive, its name lives up to its promise. You might want to make a quick stop at the Hastings Mill Store, the first store and post office built in Vancouver and now a museum. Continue on and you'll come to the 100-acre University of British Columbia. Stop by and see the beautiful Nitobe Memorial Japanese Gardens, one of the best re-creations outside the Orient. Also on the campus are the Fine Arts Gallery and the beautiful Museum of Anthropology, which features an array of shows from B.C. cultures and the totem poles of the Coast Indians.

This coastal drive lets everyone see very quickly why Vancouver is so popular—trees line the shores, and beyond is the large bay, set off against the mountains to the north. Not only is Vancouver clean and fresh and inhabited by friendly citizens, but its natural attractions are so alluring that you may want to stay for a long time.

Leaving Marine Drive and circling back eastward at 41st Avenue, continue to Oak Street and go north to the Van Dusen Botanical Gardens. Recently opened to the public, this 55-acre park is filled with native and exotic flowers and plants. Close by is one of the prettiest parks in the city: Queen Elizabeth Park, where you'll find the highest elevation in Vancouver city—and a magnificent view. There are walking paths, a rose garden, a sunken garden, an arboretum, tennis courts, and a restaurant. Aside from the view of the city and the beauty of the park, don't miss the Bloedel Conservatory, where over 400 varieties of exotic plants and flowers are nurtured.

### Artists in a Palace

From Queen Elizabeth Park you can either make the short drive downtown again or continue east to the suburb of Burnaby. There you'll find Heritage Village at Gilpin Street. The village is a fine re-creation of a typical turn-of-the century village in British Columbia. Children will be especially interested. Nearby is the Burnaby Art Gallery, featuring contemporary artists in a grand old palace of a house.

While in Burnaby, head north to the handsome Simon Fraser University campus on top of Burnaby Mountain. Here again, views of the city and the surrounding mountains are superb. The campus is well known because of its modern architectural design. Guided tours are available.

Heading west again, you'll pass Burnaby Mountain and Centennial Park, which is a good spot for a picnic. Next, in Vancouver proper along Hastings Street, you'll pass the 18-acre Pacific National Exhibition Grounds, where the Pacific National Exhibition, an agricultural show and fair, is held each August. The Grounds also include the Coliseum, home of the National Hockey League Canucks; Empire Stadium, where Roger Bannister broke the four-minute mile in 1954; and a fine racetrack, open all summer. British Columbia's Sports Hall of Fame is here, as well as the British Columbia Pavilion, housing a huge three-dimensional relief map of the province.

### North Vancouver

Leaving the Vancouver city peninsula at Exhibition Park via the Second Narrows Bridge, you'll cross the Burrard Inlet and find yourself in the suburb of North Vancouver, site of many lumberyards and shipyards. The land here is probably the most scenic in all of metropolitan Vancouver. North Vancouver is mountainous and green, with the sea at its doorstep. Just over the bridge, off Main Street and Cotton Road, is the Park and Tilford Gardens, a small but lovely series of gardens, open year round. It offers changing displays and is floodlit in summer. As with most of Vancouver's parks, admission is free.

Farther north is the 200-acre Lynn Canyon Park, a natural habitat with fine hiking trails and the Lynn Canyon Ecology Centre. The Centre displays shows, educational films, and other media presentations on the ecology of plants, animals, and man. More exciting is the Suspension Bridge, a 273-foot-high bridge that stretches across Lynn Creek. The hike across can be a bit frightening for people suffering from acrophobia, so the faint-hearted should beware. Lynn Canyon Park is one of Vancouver's treasures.

To the east is the huge Mount Seymour Provincial Park, only 16 kms. (10 miles) from downtown Vancouver, yet another world away. Skiing in winter is excellent; during the rest of the year, the natural beauties are enough to hold any visitor's attention. A convenient—and fun—way to visit North Vancouver is to take the SeaBus from the bottom of Granville Street.

### Lavish Houses, Lavish Views

But the most popular tourist spots—for Vancouverites and outlanders as well—are situated in North Vancouver but closer to West Vancouver, and are most easily reached by crossing the Lions Gate Bridge if you're coming from downtown. Sightseers interested in opulent manmade communities should head for West Vancouver's British Properties. This is the rich, secluded area featuring lavish houses with even more lavish views of the city and the terrain.

Three magnificent stops are next on your route. Going north on Capilano Road, the first is the spectacular Capilano Suspension Bridge, the world's longest, opened in 1899. You can walk across the 450-foot bridge, which spans the Capilano River and Canyon. Scenes from here are breathtaking. The bridge is safe—but, again, those with some aversion to swaying in the breeze might want to think twice before traversing it. Nearby is the Capilano Salmon Hatchery, an exciting place for anglers and those interested in fish ecology. The Hatchery offers guided tours to help the novice understand the complex world of fish life in the Northwest. Farther north, on your way to Grouse Mountain, is Cleveland Dam, a fine place to hike, rest, or picnic. The dam is known as one of the best places to see the symbol of Vancouver: two mountain peaks known as The Lions.

## Grouse Mountain Skyride

Probably the biggest tourist attraction in the city is the Grouse Mountain Skyride, north of Cleveland Dam, yet still only a short ride from town. Grouse Mountain is a favorite in winter for skiing and in summer for hiking and picnicking. The Skyride is an aerial tramway that ascends 3,700 feet above Vancouver, offering the finest view of the city, the surrounding mountains and the sea. The ride is exciting and safe; when you reach the top, there are restaurants for snacks or gourmet meals. The ride is highly recommended. In winter and spring, you can ski right there at Grouse Mountain—the skiing is quite good—and still be only fifteen minutes from downtown.

The last major site of interest in West Vancouver, and a good spot for a last look at the city, is Lighthouse Park, 8 kms. (5 miles) west of Lions Gate Bridge on Marine Drive. An idyllic park, with long walking paths and some of the area's largest trees, it yields a superb view of the skyline across English Bay.

Vancouver lives in a state of nature. While the city provides excellent entertainment, architecture, and ambiance, its parks, waterways, and mountains make the city as beautiful and refreshing as it is.

# PRACTICAL INFORMATION FOR VANCOUVER

**HOW TO GET THERE. By air:** Vancouver International Airport is a major terminal for domestic and international flights. Numerous carriers serve the city, including *Air Canada, British Airways, CP Air, Cathay Pacific, Japan Air Lines, Lufthansa, United, Western,* and *PWA.* The airport is located on Sea Island, just south of the city proper. For information on getting into town from the airport, see "How to Get Around," below.

**By train:** the *Canadian Pacific Railroad* and the *Canadian National Railroad* both service Vancouver; many of the overland trains offer glass observation cars.

**By bus:** *Greyhound* and *Trailways* both have good schedules to the city. *Pacific Coachlines* serves Vancouver Island and the Fraser Valley. (Call 683–9277 for information for PCL and Greyhound.)

**By car:** Coming from Seattle, Washington, take I–5 north to the border, where the road turns into Canada Hwy. 99. The drive from Seattle takes about 3 hours. From the east, approach Vancouver on the Trans-Canada Highway (Hwy. 1).

**By ferry:** Vancouver can be reached by ferry from Alaska, Victoria, and other points on Vancouver Island. You can get there from Seattle by changing at Victoria. (Call (604) 386–6731 for information about the Seattle–Victoria

# 240 BRITISH COLUMBIA

ferry.) British Columbia has the most extensive ferry system in the world. For more information contact *B.C. Ferries,* 818 Broughton St., Victoria, B.C., V8W 1EL; (604) 387–1401; in Vancouver: (604) 669–1211.

 **HOTELS AND MOTELS.** Most of Vancouver's hotels and motels are very comfortable. Those in the deluxe range are all excellent. Price categories (in Canadian dollars) are as follows: *Deluxe,* $105 and up for doubles; *Expensive,* $70–$95; *Moderate,* $50–$70; *Inexpensive,* under $50.

Most places accept the following major credit cards: American Express, MasterCard, and Visa; others may also be honored.

## Deluxe

**Bayshore Inn.** West Georgia and Cardero sts; (604) 682–3377. Modern 20-story tower; on harbor, near downtown; all amenities, including two swimming pools, one indoor, in new health club.

**Four Seasons Hotel.** 791 W. Georgia St.; (604) 689–9333. In shopping district; very pleasant; fine cuisine. One of the Four Seasons Group, this is one of the finest new hotels anywhere in the world; tastefully decorated, superb service.

**Georgian Court.** 773 Beatty St.; (604) 682–5555. This small, European-style hotel has an elegant clublike atmosphere. Superb William Tell restaurant. Opposite new B.C. Place Stadium.

**Hotel Vancouver.** 900 W. Georgia St.; (604) 684–3131. Beautiful older hotel in center of downtown; fine traditional décor; excellent eating.

**Hyatt Regency Vancouver.** 655 Burrard St.; (604) 687–6543. In Royal Centre, downtown; 34 stories, luxurious rooms, all amenities. Well run. Popular with upmarket meetings and conventions.

**Vancouver Mandarin.** 645 Howe St.; (604) 687–1122. New, elegant, luxurious, for the discriminating traveler. Top restaurants.

## Expensive

**Airport Inn Resort.** 10251 St. Edward's Dr.; (604) 728–9611. A few minutes from airport; spacious rooms; airport limousine. Superb health-club facilities. First-rate Japanese restaurant.

**Century Plaza TraveLodge.** 1015 Burrard St.; (604) 687–0575. 30-story, elegant; good-size rooms, nightly entertainment. Next door to St. Paul's Hospital.

**Denman Place Inn.** 1733 Comox St.; (604) 688–7711. Fine, 36-story hotel near Stanley Park; excellent rooms; splendid views. Hollywood types and showbiz people in town for extended periods like the kitchen facilities.

**Georgia Hotel.** 801 W. Georgia St.; (604) 682–5566. Newly renovated; in center of town; fine cuisine and atmosphere.

**Granville Island Hotel.** 1253 Johnston St., Granville Island; (604) 683–7373. A marine hotel on Granville Island waterfront. Limo service to airport and business district. Two restaurants; lounge; health club; docking facilities.

**Holiday Inn–Harbourside.** 1133 W. Hastings St.; (604) 689–9211. Downtown, with superb views over the harbor; revolving restaurant on 21st floor.

**International Plaza Hotel.** 1999 Marine Dr.; (604) 984–0611. Beautifully situated; a luxury resort hotel with fine views; gardens. If you have to stay on the North Shore this is the place to be.

**Miramar Hotel.** 1160 Davie St.; (604) 685–1311. Modern. 24-story. Good-size rooms; pool and restaurant.

**Palisades Hotel.** 1277 Robson St.; (604) 688–0461. Pleasant rooms, pool, convenient.

**River Inn.** 3500 Cessna Dr.; (604) 278-1411. On ten acres of parkland near river; 11 stories, very nice rooms and restaurant. Top-class airport hotel. A delightful spot for lunch.

**Sheraton-Landmark Hotel.** 1400 Robson St.; (604) 687–0511. 42 stories; revolving restaurant; near shopping; saunas, all amenities.

**Sheraton-Plaza 500.** 500 W. 12th Ave.; (604) 873–1811. Attractive, modern hotel; fine bar, restaurant.

### *Moderate*

**Park Royal Hotel.** 440 Clyde Ave.; (604) 926–5511. Ten minutes from center, located on North Shore; pleasant rooms and atmosphere. Has good neighborhood-style pub.

**Sheraton Villa Inn.** 4331 Dominion St., Burnaby; (604) 430–2828. Quiet, elegant; nice gardens, nice rooms. Restaurant.

**TraveLodge-Downtown.** 1304 Howe St.; (604) 682–2767. Good central location. Restaurant.

### *Inexpensive*

**Austin Motor Hotel.** 1221 Granville St.; (604) 685–7235. Fine, comfortable motel in downtown area. Most amenities.

**Blue Boy Motor Hotel.** 725 S.E. Marine Dr.; (604) 321–6611. Convenient location for all touring. Modern, with most amenities.

**Nelson Place Hotel.** 1006 Granville St.; (604) 681–6341. Well located for shopping. Spacious rooms.

**Sylvia Hotel.** 1154 Gifford; (604) 681–9321. Lovely old ivy-covered hotel on English Bay. Best value in town.

**HOW TO GET AROUND. From the airport:** The *Hustle Bus* runs every 20 minutes from level Two, 6:20 A.M.–12:20 A.M. Fares are $5.25 for adults and $3.75 for children 4–12. It stops at all major hotels, as well as the Bus Depot on Dunsmuir Street. Aside from catching the bus at a major hotel, travelers going to the airport can flag it down at the corners of Granville and Broadway and Granville and 41st. Call 273–0071 for more information. *Taxis* are in good supply but the run to downtown Vancouver costs almost $20. There is also a *city bus* that leaves from the airport's level 3 and costs $.75. However, you have to change at 71st and Granville (for a number 25 to downtown); this is only recommended for leisurely, impoverished travelers arriving in good weather. Call 324–3211 for information.

**By bus:** All fares are $.75, exact fare required; unlimited transfers for 1½ hours after fare is paid. For information call *Metro Transit Operating Company;* 324–3211.

**By cab:** These are plentiful but expensive if you're going any distance. They can be hailed but it's easier to go to a taxi stand or try to pick one up at a hotel.

The **SeaBus** to North Vancouver leaves from the bottom of Granville St.; call 324–3211 for information.

 **TOURIST INFORMATION.** The *Greater Vancouver Convention and Visitors Bureau* is located in Suite 1625, 1055 W. Georgia, P. O. Box 11142, Vancouver, B.C., V6E 4C8—which is above the Royal Centre Mall at the corner of Georgia and Burrard streets. It is open Monday–Saturday, 9 A.M.–5 P.M.; longer in summer; phone (604) 682–2222. *Tourism B.C.* in Robson Square (lower level) at (604) 668–2300 is mainly for out-of-town information but they do have some material on Vancouver. Open Monday–Friday, 8:30 A.M.–5 P.M.; Saturday, 10 A.M.–5 P.M.

 **SEASONAL EVENTS. January** 1 finds brave souls participating in the *Polar Bear Swim.* The *Chinese New Year* is also celebrated in January. The *Vancouver International Marathon* is in **May,** as is the three–day *Cloverdale Rodeo.* In **June,** the city celebrates *Greek Day.* **July** is the time for the *Vancouver Folk Music Festival,* the *Vancouver Sea Festival*—a beach carnival—the *World Hang-Gliding Championships* at Grouse Mountain, and *Italian Day. Loggers Sports,* showing lumberman in action, are held in **August** at Squamish, 50 miles north and well worth the trip. August also sees the *Canadian Open Sandcastle Competition* (which draws 125,000 people) in nearby Whiterock, the *Abbotsford International Air Show* (38 miles to the east), and the *Pacific National Exhibition,* an agricultural show held the second half of the month. *Octoberfest,* is held at the B.C. Place Stadium.

 **TOURS.** The *Gray Line* offers a selection of city tours, including Discover Vancouver in a British double-decker. It does the town thoroughly and offers a drop–off in Gastown. The fare is $12.95 for adults and $6.50 for children. The Discover Vancouver and the Aquarium tour costs $16.95 for adults and $8.50 for children. The North Shore tour, which takes in the Capilano Suspension Bridge, the salmon hatchery, the base of Grouse Mountain, and the opulent British Properties community, is $19.50 adults and $9.75 children. The Grand North Shore tour includes a Super Skyride to the top of Grouse Mountain (worth it for the view alone, and there's skiing in winter) and costs $25 adults and $12.50 children. The Deluxe Grand City and University goes to the University of British Columbia and the stately Shaughnessy residential area; it costs $19.50 adults and $9.75 children. The Deluxe Evening Shoreline outing, which goes to West Vancouver and Lighthouse Park, then to Horseshoe Bay and up Howe Sound to the Sunset Creek lookout, costs $14.75 adults and $7.35 children. There are also one-day and overnight trips to Victoria, costing $57.50 and $125 and up, respectively. For more information, reservations, and hotel pickup, call 872–8311.

**SPECIAL-INTEREST TOURS.** Tours of *B.C. Law Courts,* Robson Square, are available during the summer. Call 668–2830.

*Royal Hudson Steam Train,* B.C. Railway passenger depot, 1311 West First St., North Vancouver, provides a nostalgic trip in a superb old train through great scenery to the logging town of Squamish. You can combine it with a cruise up Howe Sound on M.V. *Britannia.* Fares range from $10 for the Royal Hudson trip to $34 for the combination. Bookings must be made 48 hours in advance. For more information call B.C. Railway, 987–5211; Tourism B.C., 668–2300; Harbour Ferries, 687–9558; or Vancouver Ticket Centre, 687–1818.

**PARKS AND GARDENS.** Vancouver has a wide selection of city parks and gardens, including:

*Bota Gardens,* 5 Road and Steveston, Richmond, near Vancouver Airport. Open year-round but best in spring, when 100,000 bulbs are in bloom. Admission $3; seniors, $2.50; children, $1.25. Call 271–9325.

*Botanical Garden,* University of B.C., 6501 N.W. Marine Dr. Includes an Alpine garden, a B.C. native garden, a food garden, Asian garden, and the *Nitobe Memorial Garden*—the most authentic Japanese garden in North America. Open daily Good Friday through Thanksgiving from 10 A.M. until an hour before sunset. Admission: adults $.50, children $.10. For information call 228–3928.

*Park and Tilford Gardens,* 1200 Cotten Rd., North Vancouver. Eight separate areas include a rose garden, B.C. native wood garden, and a tranquil Oriental garden. Special displays at Christmas, Mother's Day, and Easter. Open year-round 8 A.M.–11 P.M. Free. Call 987–9321.

*Queen Elizabeth Park and Bloedel Conservatory,* 33rd Avenue and Cambie Street. Superb views—the highest point in the city. There are also tennis courts, a pitch-and-putt and a restaurant. Summer hours (April 24–September 25) are 10 A.M.–9:30 P.M.; in winter 10 A.M.–5:30 P.M. Admission $2; seniors and students, $1. Call 872–5513.

*Lynn Canyon Park* in North Vancouver is a 200-acre natural area with fine hiking trails. Also here is the Lynn Canyon Ecology Centre (987–5922) with educational displays on plant, animal, and human ecology.

*Van Dusen Botanical Display Garden,* 5251 Oak St. Contains one of most comprehensive collections of ornamental plants in Canada. Open year-round from 10 A.M., closing at 4 P.M. in winter and between 6 P.M. and 9 P.M. in summer. Admission $3; seniors and children, $1.50. Call 266–7194.

*Stanley Park.* On the west end of the city. This 1,000-acre park offers space to walk, run, bicycle, swim, and play tennis, cricket, and rugby. There's a zoo and an aquarium among its many attractions. It never closes. See the section on Stanley Park in "Exploring Vancouver," above. For information call 681–1411.

**ZOOS AND AQUARIUMS.** Stanley Park has a *Children's Zoo* with domestic animals. Some petting is allowed. Open daily 10 A.M.–6 P.M.; weekends only in winter. Admission: $1.30; children, $.70.

Also in the park is the small *Stanley Park Zoo,* with bears, monkeys, and playful otters. Open daily 10 A.M.–dusk; free. For information on both zoos call 681–1141.

*Vancouver Public Aquarium,* Stanley Park. Splendid presentation of 6,000 aquatic animals; continuous displays with killer whales and dolphins, plus new Amazon gallery. Admission $4.25; seniors and children, $2. Open year-round. Open 10 A.M.–5 P.M. weekdays; until 6 P.M. weekends and holidays. July 1–September 5: daily until 9 P.M. Call 682–1118.

**PARTICIPANT SPORTS. Bicycles** can be rented year-round from *Stanley Park Rentals,* 676 Chilco St., just west of Denman; 681–5581.

**Boating.** All kinds of vessels are available, from 20-foot daysailers to the graceful 137-foot Norsal, which has seven staterooms (phone 681–8062). Try the *Bayshore Inn Marina* (689–7371), *Barbary Coast Yacht Basin* (669–0088) (both in Coal Harbor), or *Delta Charters* (273–4211). Check also *Pacific Yachting* magazine (687–1581) for charter information.

**Fishing.** By far the best is the sea-salmon fishing. The best departure point for day visitors is Horseshoe Bay, a half-hour from downtown on the North Shore. *Sewell's Landing Marina* has 15-foot boats to charter starting at $17.75 for the first hour and $9 an hour after that. Fishing licences can be bought at marinas or sports stores; they cost $5 a year for Canadian citizens, $3.50 a day or $10 for three days for foreigners. For more information, including the latest on where fish are biting, call the federal *Fisheries and Oceans Department* at 666-3169.

**Golf.** Numerous public courses include *Langara* (321–8013), *McCleery* (261-4522), *Musqueam* (266-2334), *UBC* (224-1818), and *Gleneagles* in West Vancouver (921–7353).

**Skiing.** There are three mountains on the North Shore, all within a half-hour's drive from downtown. *Grouse Mountain* has full facilities, including rentals and night skiing; write 6400 Nancy Greene Way, North Vancouver, B.C., V7R 4N4; (604) 984–0661. *Mount Seymour* also has night skiing and rentals, but has less variety; write 1600 Indian River Dr., North Vancouver, B.C., V7G 1L3; (604) 929–8172. *Cypress Bowl* does not have night skiing or rentals. Good for **cross-country.** Same address as Mount Seymour, since both are provincial parks, but phone (604) 929–8171. Bus service is available from downtown; phone for detailed information. See also "Winter Sports" in *Practical Information for Other Areas in B.C.*

There is good but cold, **swimming** at *English Bay* in West End, *Kitsilano,* and *Spanish Banks.* Just west of here is *Wreck Beach,* a mecca for nudists.

**Tennis.** There are 21 courts in Stanley Park near the Beach Avenue entrance, 20 in Queen Elizabeth Park, 10 at Kitsilano Beach Park, and pockets at smaller parks all over the city. Call *Vancouver Park Board* for information at 681–1141.

**SPECTATOR SPORTS.** Major spectator sports can be watched at the new domed *B.C. Place Stadium* in the downtown area at the north end of the Cambie Street Bridge. Here you can see the *B.C. Lions* **football** team (phone 588–5466 for game and ticket information) and the *Whitecaps* **soccer** team (291–6661). *Vancouver Canadians* **Baseball** *Club* (872–5232) plays at *Nat Bailey Stadium* on 33rd Street between Main and Ontario. *Vancouver Canucks* **hockey** team (254–5141) plays at the *Pacific National Exhibition's Coliseum.* **Thoroughbred racing** is held April to October at the Pacific National on Monday, Wednesday, Friday, and Saturday; post parade 6:15 P.M. weekdays and 1:15 P.M. Saturdays and holidays. For more information call 254–1631. There's also **harness racing** in suburban Surrey, October to April on Monday, Wednesday, Thursday, and Friday at 7:15 P.M. and Saturday at 1:15 P.M.

**FOR SPECTACULAR VIEWS.** *Capilano Suspension Bridge,* 3735 Capilano Rd., North Vancouver. This 450-foot bridge is the world's longest suspension bridge and affords a breathtaking look at the city and its surroundings. You can walk across the bridge, which spans the Capilano River and Canyon. Open September–June, 8 A.M.–5 P.M.; July and August, 8 A.M.–10:30 P.M. Admission $2.75; seniors, $2; children, $1. Call 985–7474 for information.

An aerial tram soars to 3,700-foot elevation at *Grouse Mountain,* 6400 Nancy Greene Way, North Vancouver. Price: $6; seniors and children, $3. Open summer weekdays 10 A.M.–10 P.M.; summer weekends, 9 A.M.–10 P.M.; winter weekdays, 9 A.M.–11 P.M.; winter weekends and holidays, 8 A.M.–10 P.M. Call 984–0661.

The revolving *Observation Deck* at Harbour Centre, Hastings and Seymour streets, is also a good spot from which to view the city. Call 689–0421.

**HISTORIC SITES.** *Fort Langley National Historic Park,* about 50 miles east of Vancouver on Hwys. 1 and 10. This restored Hudson's Bay Company fort shows life in pioneer days. Open June 16–Labor Day, 10 A.M.–6 P.M. daily; rest of year, Tuesday–Sunday, 10 A.M.–4:30 P.M. Admission $1; children $.50. Call 888–4424. *Heritage Village,* Century Park, Burnaby, is a turn-of-the-century village. Open Tuesday–Sunday 11 A.M.–4:30 P.M. Admission $3; seniors and children, $2. Call 294–1233. *Old Hastings Mill Store Museum,* 1575 Alma St., beside Jerico Beach. Built circa 1865, it housed the first store and post office in early Vancouver and was the only building to survive the great fire of 1886.

Open 10 A.M.–4 P.M. daily, June 1–September 15, and 1 P.M.–4 P.M., weekends only, in winter. Admission by donation. Call 228-1213.

 **MUSEUMS.** *Arts, Sciences and Technology Centre,* 600 Granville St. Three floors of exhibits where visitors can experiment with math puzzles, psycho-motor testing, illusions, and new technology, and generally absorb ideas. Good for a rainy day. Admission $2; children, $1. Open winter, Wednesday–Saturday, 10 A.M.–5 P.M., Sunday, 1 P.M.–5 P.M.; summer, Monday–Saturday until 6 P.M. Call 687-8414. *MacMillan Planetarium,* 1100 Chestnut St. Next door is *Southam Observatory.* Call 736-3656 for information on what's on. *Maritime Museum,* foot of Cypress Street near Planetarium. Houses historic vessel *St. Roch,* which has gone through Northwest Passage both ways, plus other attractions. Open winter, 10 A.M.–5 P.M. daily; summer until 6 P.M., 9 P.M. Sundays. Admission $1.50; seniors and children, $.50. Call 736-4431. *UBC Museum of Anthropology,* 6393 N.W. Marine Dr., UBC. See artistic achievements of Northwest Coast Indians. Superb totems and carvings. Admission $2, but free on Tuesdays. Closed Mondays. For more information on hours call 228-5087. *Vancouver Museum,* 1100 Chestnut St., on Kitsilano Point beside Planetarium, across Burrard Street Bridge. Displays of Vancouver's heritage. Open daily 10 A.M.–5 P.M. Admission $2, seniors and children, $.50. Call 736-4431.

 **MUSIC.** *Vancouver Opera Association* can be reached at 682-2871. Check local papers for details of performances. *Vancouver Symphony Orchestra* performs at the Orpheum, 884 Granville St., an old silent-movie house renovated with murals, chandeliers, and good acoustics. Call the VSO at 869-1411 for ticket information.

 **THEATER.** Vancouver has an active theater life. Best-known companies are the *Arts Club Theatres,* 1181 Seymour St. and Granville Island (687-5315) and the *Playhouse Company* (684-5361), which performs at the Queen Elizabeth Theatre (683-2311). *City Stage,* 751 Thurlow St. (688-7013), is a downtown group with its finger on the market, while the *Vancouver East Cultural Centre,* 1895 Venables St. (254-9578), attracts a wide range of works, including experimental. Just outside of town there is the *North Vancouver Centennial Theatre* (988-4011).

 **ART GALLERIES.** *Burnaby Art Gallery,* 6344 Gilpin St., is beautiful in itself. It houses a permanent collection of B.C. artists. Free. Call 291-9441. *Vancouver Art Gallery,* 800 West Georgia St., houses contemporary exhibitions. The renovated old Court House that it's now in is also worth a visit. Admission $2. Call 682-5621 for hours. Downtown Vancouver offers a number of good, smaller galleries. Check the *Sun* newspaper or *Vancouver Guideline* magazine to see what's on.

**SHOPPING.** *Robsonstrasse,* the *Pacific Centre Mall* (a vast mall under Georgia and Granville streets, which can be entered from Eaton's, Hudson's Bay Company, or the Four Season's Hotel), *Granville Island,* and *Gastown* are the best and most convenient places in the city for shopping. The *Royal Centre Mall* is on Georgia and can be entered from the Hyatt Regency Hotel. Vancouver is well stocked, but often expensive for all kinds of goods. The U.S. resident will find prices higher on most clothing. Some items from the Orient are less expensive, though you can do just as well in San Francisco. Vancouver does have some fine antique stores, especially good if you're hunting for British Columbia Indian goods. In Gastown, the *Inuit Gallery,* 345 Water St., sells Eskimo art; *Portobello Antiques* is at 101 Water St. If you're interested in English bone china and Irish Belleek, try the *Canyon House* at 3590 Capilano Rd. in N. Vancouver.

**DINING OUT.** Vancouver's cosmopolitan nature is reflected in its many restaurants. You'll probably be able to find just about any cuisine somewhere in the city. While beef and fish are the ready staples, you will also find excellent Chinese, Japanese, or Vietnamese food, as well as East Indian, Greek, German, Spanish, and so on. Restaurants are classified as: *Deluxe,* $20 and up; *Expensive,* $15–$20; *Moderate,* $10–$15; *Inexpensive,* below $10, for complete dinners without wine or drinks. The better hotels usually have fine cuisine. Many restaurants, with the exception of Chinese and other Asian places, close Sunday.

All of the following accept American Express, Visa, and MasterCard credit cards. However, travelers who are dependent on one card should check with the restaurant in advance.

### *Deluxe*

**The Beach House.** In Stanley Park on Beach Dr.; 681–9951. A beautiful setting and view; Continental cuisine. Quite fine in all ways.

**The Cannery Seafood Restaurant.** 2205 Commissioner St.; 254–9606. Fine seafood. Hard to do better. One of the finest restaurants in Canada. All fish is fresh daily; superb chefs, fine service.

**Chez Joel.** 217 Carrall, Gastown; 685–4910. Splendid French food.

**Harbour House.** On top of Harbour Centre at Hastings and Seymour Sts.; 669–2220. Revolving restaurant with grand view of city. Fine cuisine.

**Panorama Roof.** Top of the Hotel Vancouver; 684–3131. Nouvelle cuisine, yet traditional, with dance band. First-rate.

**Le Pavillion.** In the Four Seasons Hotel; 689–9333. Excellent French cuisine and ambiance. Expensive and worth it.

**Trader Vic's.** In the Bayshore Inn; 682–3377. One of the chain, but quite good Polynesian food and drink.

**William Tell.** 773 Beatty; 688–3504. Superb old restaurant in new hotel.

### Expensive

**Café de Paris.** 751 Denman near Stanley Park and the Bayshore Hotel; 687–1418. Superb bistro atmosphere. Best value in town.

**Château Madrid.** 1277 Howe St.; 684–8814. Fine Spanish food and surroundings.

**Guppy's Original Seafood Restaurant.** In North Vancouver at 148 East 2nd; 986–5274. Fun place to eat good seafood. Near SeaBus terminal, so sail over and have a night out.

**Maiko Garden.** 1077 Richards; 683–8812. Japanese cuisine, fine atmosphere.

**Salmon House on the Hill.** In West Vancouver, off 21st St. Exit; 926–3212. New and gracious, British Columbian Indian décor. Superb seafood menu, and salmon is king. Excellent.

**Seven Seas.** At Lonsdale in North Vancouver; 987–3344. Another fine seafood place. People come from all over for this menu. Hard to beat. Can be very expensive.

**Umberto's.** 1380 Hornby; 687–6316. Bubbly Italian restaurant, does super rack of lamb.

### Moderate

**Las Tapas.** 760 Cambie; 669–1624. Whitewashed walls, tiled floors and Latin music give good atmosphere.

**The Noodle Makers.** 122 Powell St.; 683–9196. Chinese restaurant; excellent meals.

**Orestes.** 3116 West Broadway; 732–1461. Excellent authentic Greek cuisine, good ambiance and service.

**Pepitas.** 1170 Robson St.; 669–4736. Mexican all the way. Very good.

**Puccini's.** 730 Main St.; 681–6326. Big portions and fine food. One of the most popular places in Vancouver for Italian food.

**Saigon West Vancouver.** 2508 Marine Dr., West Vancouver; 926–6001. Very good Vietnamese food.

**Schnitzel House.** 1060 Robson St.; 682–1210. German menu; quite good.

### Inexpensive

**Brodie's.** 225 Smithe St.; 685–2246. Near the stadium at B.C. Place. Superb, tasty, spicy Mediterranean food.

**Old Spaghetti Factory.** 53 Water St., Gastown; 684–1288. Serves simple dishes with family appeal.

**P.J. Burger's.** 2966 W. 4th St., Kitsilano; 734–8616. Does good hamburgers and special milkshakes.

**White Spot** restaurants, **Keg 'N Cleaver** restaurants, and **Denny's** restaurants are good chains that can be found all over town.

**NIGHTCLUBS AND BARS.** Many of the most popular nightspots are located in the better hotels in town. Other places of interest for the night crowd are: *Livingstone's,* 840 Howe St., a popular bar; *Confetti!,* 1255 West Pender; *Stage 33,* 1133 W. Hastings, a theater lounge in the Holiday Inn Harbourside Hotel; *Elephant and Castle,* Pacific Centre Mall, an English-style pub; *The Town Pump,* 66 Water St., Gastown, for rock 'n' roll; *Annabelle's,* in the Four Seasons Hotel, an elegant place to drink and dance; *English Bay Café,* 1795 Beach Ave., a fetching San Francisco–style bar with good ocean views. Also the bar at the *Sylvia Hotel,* 1154 Gifford; *Spinning Wheel Inn,* 212 Carrall St., Gastown, Irish pub-style sing-along cabaret. *Pelican Bay* at Granville Island Hotel is a delightful bar at water's edge with small dance floor.

# EXPLORING VANCOUVER ISLAND AND VICTORIA

West of the city of Vancouver, across the Strait of Georgia, are Vancouver Island and British Columbia's capital, *Victoria.* In between are the beautiful and almost empty Gulf Islands, most of which are accessible from the mainland or from Vancouver Island, by ferry.

Vancouver Island, which juts below the 49th Parallel and seems to invade the United States, is 456 kms. (285 miles) long and about 152 kms. (75 miles) across at its widest point. The east coast is built up and offers a large variety of accommodations, sightseeing, and sporting activities, but the rugged west coast has no roads and is still quite wild. Highway 4 leads from Parksville across the island to Long Beach and the haunting Pacific Rim Park that stretches for miles along the rocky coast. If you want to see the west coast, this is the place to come.

The scenery all over Vancouver Island is majestic: mountainous, forested, and filled with lakes and running streams. It's almost impossible to overemphasize the beauty of this country. The drive up or down the island's east coast, with the mountainous mainland in the distance, reminds one of Norway's fjords. You'll find very good camping sites and hiking trails here, and even the less active will enjoy the sightseeing. While the primary city of interest for many people is Victoria, the island itself yields a vast array of fascinating sights and simple entertainment.

Ferries ply the waters between Vancouver and Departure Bay, at Nanaimo, the island's second-largest town. Sidney can be reached from Anacortes in Washington State year round; Victoria is accessible from Seattle in the summer, and from Vancouver year round via the Swartz

Bay ferries (20 minutes north of Victoria). The Victoria–Vancouver ferry ride is one hour, 40 minutes; it docks at Tsawwassen, on the mainland, about 20 minutes from downtown Vancouver. Powell River, on the mainland, has a ferry service to Comox, near the *center* of the island.

If you start your journey in Nanaimo, you have your choice of going north to the resort areas and the wilderness, or south some 112 kms. (70 miles) to Victoria. We'll take the north route first.

## Petroglyphs and Pioneers

Nanaimo had its beginnings as a Hudson's Bay Company post. It has pleasant parks, the best being the Petroglyph Park, which features prehistoric rock carvings and drawings. Nanaimo has achieved real fame, however, for providing one of the most entertaining races in the world: the annual mid-July Nanaimo Bathtub Race, which runs from Nanaimo across the Strait of Georgia to Vancouver. The idea is to get across the Strait in a bathtub. They can be modified and motorized— but many don't make it all the way. It is always a festive, and usually hilarious, day.

Going north from Nanaimo on Highway 19, you'll get to Parksville, 40 kms. (25 miles) away. This popular resort town offers fine beaches and excellent trout and salmon fishing. Two provincial parks are near- by: Englishman River Falls and Little Qualicum Falls. By going west on Highway 4, you'll find Port Alberni, another resort center year- round. Fresh-water and saltwater fishing in this area is excellent. So are rafting, waterskiing, tennis, and so on. This is resort and relaxation territory, but for the sports minded, there's everything you could want. Continuing on this road will lead you to the Pacific Rim National Park—a detour that should not be missed.

Back in Parksville, again heading north, is Qualicum Beach, a resort with fine fishing opportunities. The journey through Buckley Bay and Royston brings you to Courtenay and the Comox Valley—perfect vacation land. Just to the west is the 500,000-acre Strathcona Park, the largest on the island, where you'll see Mt. Golden Hind, 7,220 feet high, and the haunting Forbidden Plateau. The scenery here is some of the finest in all of British Columbia.

About 160 kms. (100 miles) from Nanaimo is the Campbell River, famous worldwide for its fishing. Hollywood personalities have fished here for decades, and it has become a sort of mecca for serious trout and salmon fishers. This is great country for sportsmen, and people flock here for hunting and particularly for salmon fishing.

The end of the road is Port Hardy, 235 kms. (146 miles) north, and clearly in the wilds. This is where you catch the ferry to Prince Rupert (a full day-and-night journey), to the north on the mainland. From there you can connect with other ferries for Alaska. Above Port Hardy there are no public roads.

Returning to Nanaimo, head south on Highway 19 to Duncan and its interesting Forest Museum, where hundreds of tree-felling and wood-cutting implements are gathered. Before reaching Victoria, you'll ride along the Malahat Drive, which offers one of the island's most spectacular views of the city and the United States in the distance.

To the west of Victoria, on Highway 14, is Sooke, where fishing for trout and salmon is excellent, and numerous other outdoor activities are available.

## The Capital

Victoria is a city of paradoxes: it's the most westerly of Canadian cities; yet, more than any other, it will remind you of a faraway English town. The provincial capital of British Columbia, it appears more like Brighton Beach than London. Victoria is the terminus point of the 8,000-km. (5,000-mile) long Trans-Canada Highway, yet one must take a ferry boat to reach it.

With London double-decker buses (in summer) framed by mountain views, English tea at the famous Empress Hotel, and a wax museum, Victoria is a charming city that delights in putting on airs as long as tourists keep coming. Victoria is world-famous for its flowers, and hanging baskets of bright blossoms bedeck the downtown lampposts. The city has many interesting features but, on the whole, it doesn't compare with Vancouver in terms of liveliness or spirit, and sometimes appears tacky with all its tourist "shoppes" and souvenir stalls. Yet it *is* a beautiful city—clean and fresh—and a drive around the harbor area, or Beacon Hill Park, or through Oak Bay and along the Scenic Drive, will convince anyone that Victoria is a city to be looked at carefully and appreciated.

The city's main area is the Inner Harbor, where you'll see the Victorian-style British Columbia Legislative Building (1898), the Empress Hotel, the British Columbia Provincial Museum, and the curious and appealing Thunderbird Park, filled with Indian totem poles. This part of town contains the best of the past and should be seen on foot.

In a city of gardens, the most famous is the Butchart Gardens, a 35-acre area of the most beautiful flowers from all over the world. It was started over 75 years ago by a wealthy industrialist and has been well maintained and improved over the years. A must for flower lovers, this is just 19 kms. (12 miles) from town.

Other places of interest in Victoria? The Seasons of the Pacific at Oak Bay Marina where you descend beneath the sea, behind glass, to see

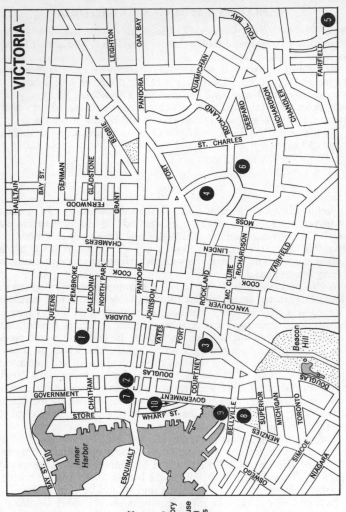

## Points of Interest

1) Arena
2) City Hall
3) Court House
4) Craigdarroch Castle
5) Gonzales Observatory
6) Government House
7) McPherson Playhouse
   (Centennial Square)
8) Parliament Buildings
9) Port Angeles Ferry
10) Baston Square

the active marine life; also see the fine Pacific Undersea Gardens; the Royal London Wax Museum, opposite the Parliament Buildings; a copy of Shakespeare's birthplace plus Anne Hathaway's cottage in Stratford-on-Avon; the museum-archive complex of Heritage Village; Craigflower Manor, an authentic 1856 home; Fable Cottage Estate, a little fantasy world of houses and animated scenes; and a Classic Car Museum.

The Bastion Square section is a favorite for most visitors. Shopping is good, restaurants plentiful, and the Olde Towne area is full of history. It was the site of the Hudson's Bay Company's building and the first courthouse—now the fine Maritime Museum. Shopping is also good on Yates Street, Government Street, and Market Square. The city features several wonderful old castles; the best are Craigdarroch Castle, built in 1888, and Helmecken House, 1853. To get away from manmade structures, head for the 140-acre Beacon Hill Park in the middle of town. Here you can stroll or picnic, and gaze at more totem poles.

To return to the mainland you have several routes: from Victoria directly, from Nanaimo, or you can ferry around, and stop off on, the Gulf Islands. These are rustic and wild, and not many people choose to live here; several have at least one good road. The best to visit are Saltspring, Galiano, Valdes, and Gabriola, the last of which figures in *October Ferry to Gabriola*, by famed British author Malcolm Lowry.

# PRACTICAL INFORMATION FOR VANCOUVER
# ISLAND AND VICTORIA

**HOW TO GET THERE. By air:** *Air Canada, CP Air,* and *Pacific Western* service Victoria. For information on getting from the airport to town, see "How to Get Around," below. **By bus:** *Pacific Coach Lines* offers bus service between Vancouver and Victoria. Fare is around $13 one-way. The bus is recommended when ferries are busy. For Vancouver information call (604) 683–9277; in Victoria, (604) 385–4411. **By ferry:** Victoria is accessible from Seattle in the summer via the *Princess Marguerite;* call (604) 386–6731. Victoria and Nanaimo are accessible from Vancouver. Contact *British Columbia Ferries,* 818 Broughton St., Victoria, B.C. V8W 1EL; in Vancouver, phone (604) 669–1211; in Victoria, (604) 386–3431. B.C. Ferries connect with Alaska Ferries in Prince Rupert. (See Alaska chapter.) Sidney can be reached from Anacortes, Washington, year-round. Contact *Washington State Ferries,* Seattle, WA 98104; (206) 464–6400. *Black Ball Ferries* run year-round from Port Angeles, WA, to Victoria; call (206) 622–2222.

**HOTELS AND MOTELS.** Elegance fades for the most part outside of Vancouver and Victoria, but all hotels and motels have basic amenities. Some of the resort complexes are close to luxurious. The price categories in this section, for double occupancy, will average: *Deluxe,* $80 and up; *Expensive,* $50–$80; *Moderate* $30–$50; *Inexpensive,* less than $30.

Most establishments accept the following major credit cards: American Express, MasterCard, and Visa; others may also be honored. Not all establishments accept credit cards, and therefore we suggest you call for information. (Accommodations on the Gulf Islands are listed in the section, *Practical Information for Other Areas in B.C.,* at the end of this chapter.)

### CAMPBELL RIVER

**April Point Lodge.** *Expensive.* Box 1, Quathiaski Cove. On Quadra Island; (604) 285–3329. Excellent salmon and trout fishing; yacht club nearby; fine amenities, dining.

**Delta's Discovery Inn.** *Expensive.* 975 Tyee Plaza; (604) 287–7155. First-class resort hotel; beside harbor; nice rooms, dining.

**The Dolphin's Resort.** *Expensive.* 4125 Discovery Dr.; (604) 287–3066. On the ocean. Resort hotel with fine fishing, spacious rooms. Open April–October.

**Painter's Lodge and Resort.** *Expensive.* Box 460; (604) 286–1102. Famous fishing resort made known to the world by Bob Hope and Bing Crosby; beautiful views; fine rooms.

**Haida Inn.** *Moderate.* 1342 Island Hwy.; (604) 287–7402. Fine inn, geared to fishing. Good cuisine, pleasant rooms.

**Vista Del Mar Motel.** *Moderate.* 920 South Island Hwy.; (604) 923–4271. Housekeeping units, next to store, boat launch.

**Rod and Reel Resort.** *Inexpensive.* R.R. 2; (604) 923–5250. Housekeeping cottages, boat and bait rentals.

### DUNCAN

**The Village Green Inn.** *Expensive.* On the Trans-Canada Hwy.; (604) 746–5126. Pleasant Spanish-styled rooms; fine *Steak House Restaurant.*

**Duncan Motel.** *Moderate.* 2552 Alexander Rd.; (604) 746–4944. Near shopping, fishing, and golf.

### NANAIMO

**Malaspina Hotel.** *Expensive.* 38 Front St.; (604) 754–3241. Overlooking harbor. Nice rooms; convenient; dining and cocktail rooms.

**Tally Ho TraveLodge.** *Expensive.* 1 Terminal Ave.; (604) 753–2241. Comfortable rooms; heated pool.

## PARKSVILLE

**Island Hall Hotel.** *Expensive.* 181 W. Island Hwy.; (604) 248–3225. Resort hotel on ten acres; good beach, tennis, fishing, dining.

**Tigh-Na-Mara.** *Expensive.* On R.R. 1.; (604) 248–3672. Log cabins with fireplaces. Lovely setting. Open all year.

**Englishman's River Motel.** *Moderate.* (604) 248–6532. Comfortable motel on river, park. Good facilities.

## PORT ALBERNI

**Hospitality Inn.** *Moderate.* 3835 Redford St.; (604) 723–8111. A fine motor hotel with all amenities.

**Timberlodge.** *Moderate.* Port Alberni Hwy.; (604) 723–9415. All amenities; close to skiing at Mt. Arrowsmith. Housekeeping units available.

**Tyee Village Motel.** *Moderate.* 4151 Redford St.; (604) 723–8133. First-class motel with cozy rooms.

## QUALICUM BEACH

**College Inn.** *Expensive.* Box 99; (604) 752–9262. Overlooking ocean with access to beach. Dining room, indoor pool. Meeting rooms.

**Sand Pebbles Inn.** *Expensive.* On the beach; rooms and dining area have fine ocean views. Sports nearby. Phone (604) 752–6974.

## VICTORIA

**Château Victoria.** *Deluxe.* 740 Burdett Ave.; (604) 382–4221. Well-located, very pleasant hotel. Good dining; all amenities.

**Empress Hotel.** *Deluxe.* 721 Government St.; (604) 384–8111. An institution in B.C. Elegant old hotel with European flavor; view of the inner harbor; excellent dining. Take tea every afternoon in the main hall. Atmosphere and service among the best in Victoria.

**Executive House Hotel.** *Deluxe.* 777 Douglas St.; (604) 388–5111. A 20-story hotel in downtown; pleasant rooms; good restaurants.

**Harbour Towers Hotel.** *Deluxe.* 345 Québec St.; (604) 385–2405. Modern, excellent hotel, also on the inner harbor; large rooms; pool; dining.

**Laurel Point Inn.** *Deluxe.* On Tuner Harbor; (604) 386–8721. Location can't be beat.

**Oak Bay Beach Hotel.** *Deluxe.* 1175 Beach Dr.; (604) 598–4556. Sea resort in garden setting for views; excellent rooms; English-style pub. Across from golf course.

**Victoria Regent.** *Deluxe.* 1234 Wharf St.; (604) 386–2211. Overlooking Inner Harbor. Big two-bath condo suites with kitchens.

**Colony Motor Inn.** *Expensive.* 2852 Douglas St.; (604) 385–2441. Tudor-style motel; pleasant rooms; pool.

**Olde England Inn.** *Expensive.* 429 Lampson St.; (604) 388–4353. Old Tudor mansion, 17th-century decor; on four acres near town; atmospheric rooms; very nice.

**Century Inn.** *Moderate.* 603 Pandora Ave., at Centennial Sq.; (604) 383–1151. Modern, pleasant rooms. *Persian Room* dining. Good location.

**Strathcona Hotel.** *Moderate.* 919 Douglas St.; (604) 383–7137. Central location. Dining and entertainment, including dancing and disco.

**Casa Linda Motel.** *Inexpensive.* 364 Coldstream Ave.; (604) 474–2141. Some units with kitchens.

**Cheltenham Court Motel.** *Moderate.* 994 Gorge Rd. W.; (604) 385–9559. Good value cottages, coffee shop.

**Ingraham Hotel.** *Moderate.* 2915 Douglas St.; (604) 385–6731. The restaurant here is inexpensive and open daily.

**CAMPING.** Camping in Canada's national and provincial parks is on a first-come, first-serve basis with nominal overnight fees. *Tourism B.C.* (117 Wharf St., Victoria, B.C. V8W 2Z2 [604] 387–1642) can provide park information (especially about provincial parks), as can *National and Provincial Parks Association of Canada,* 47 Colborne St., Suite 308, Toronto, Ont. M5E 1E3. See sections on provincial and national parks, below.

**HOW TO GET AROUND. From the airport to Victoria:** There are buses to downtown, costing about $6. Call 388–9916 for information. **By bus:** *Vancouver Island Coach Lines* and *Pacific Coach Lines* make numerous stops on the island.

**TOURIST INFORMATION.** *Tourism B.C.,* Parliament Bldgs., Victoria, B.C., V8W 2Z2. Open Monday–Friday, 8:15 A.M.–4:30 P.M. You can also write to them at 1117 Wharf St., Victoria, B.C. V8W 2Z2. Call (604) 387–1642.

**TOURS.** *Gray Line* offers tours of Victoria, starting with the Grand City Tour; $7, children $4. Butchart Gardens and the Saanich Peninsula tour is $14.50; children, $7.25. All tours depart from the Empress Hotel. For more information call 388–5248. *Pacific Coach Lines* runs a number of tours out of Vancouver and Victoria. PCL has day trips out of Victoria to Nanaimo ($7.35 one way), and on to Campbell River and Port Hardy. A two-day Island Discovery trip ($82.50) starts with the ferry from Vancouver to Port Hardy and a bus ride down the east coast of the island, back on a ferry to Vancouver. For information in Vancouver call 683–9277; in Victoria call 385–4411.

**SPECIAL INTEREST TOURS.** If you're on Vancouver Island, take a trip on the M.V. *Lady Rose,* a mail, passenger, and cargo ship that leaves at 8 A.M. from Port Alberni and sails up the beautiful West Coast. Rugged country, plus you'll see the Pacific Rim Park. The trip takes all day.

Another great West Coast cruise is on the Gold River-based M.V. *Uchuck,* which makes day trips to the logging communities of Tahsis and Zeballos and historic Nookta Island, where Captain Cook first landed in Canada. For information on the *Lady Rose* and *Uchuck* call 387–1642.

**PROVINCIAL PARKS.** There are more than 125 provincial parks in British Columbia. Camping is available at most, including *Englishman River Falls, Little Qualicum Falls,* and *Strathcona,* for a small fee in summer. No reservations. For information you can call in Victoria 387–1642; in Vancouver 668–2300. Parks are open year-round.

**NATIONAL PARKS.** *Pacific Rim National Park* on Vancouver Island's west coast is a magnificent stretch of land that offers a range of outdoor activities. The 12-mile-long Long Beach attracts swimmers, beachcombers, and even surfers. Hiking trails abound—including the famous "Lifesaving Trail": 45 miles of endurance-testing that once brought shipwreck survivors to safety. Sea lions frolic offshore. Open year-round. For more information write Box 280, Ucluelet, B.C. V0E 2S0; (604) 726–7721 or Parks Canada–Western Region, 134 11th Ave., Calgary, Alberta T2G OX5 (403) 231–4440.

**MUNICIPAL PARKS. In Victoria:** *Beacon Hill Park,* between Douglas and Cook streets. Swans and one of the world's largest totem poles are in this beautiful city park. Free. *Thunderbird Park,* at Belleville and Douglas, has open-air displays of ethnic arts and crafts, totems and carvings.

**MARINE LIFE.** *Pacific Undersea Gardens,* 490 Belleville St., opposite Parliament Bldgs.; 382–5717. World's only undersea theater features a scuba show complete with octopus. Open May 20–September 15, 9 A.M.–9 P.M. daily; winter, 10 A.M.–5 P.M. Adults $4; children $2. *Sealand,* 1327 Beach Dr., has an aquarium and whale show. For more details call 598–3373.

**GARDENS.** *Butchart Gardens* (Box 4010, Station A, Victoria) is 14 miles north of Victoria on Hwy. 17. It is considered by some to be the floral showplace of North America. Admission $6; children, $1; teens, $3.50. Call 652–2066.

**SUMMER SPORTS.** British Columbia offers every kind of sport. *Tourism B.C.* (See "Tourist Information") offers detailed information about all B.C. sports.

**Boating: Sailing** off Victoria and around the Gulf Islands is second to none. Charters are available from many companies including *Canoe Cove Charters,* P.O. Box 2099, Sidney V8L 4L4, phone 656–7131; *Sailwest Yacht Charters,* 1678 Cresswell Dr., Sidney V8L 4L4, phone 656–6348; and *Pacific Quest Charters,* Box 15, Schooner Cove Resort, Nanoose Bay V0R 2R0, phone 468-9721. **Canoes** can be rented at many resorts and at some inland hotels. Call 387–1642 for specifics.

**Fishing** licenses can be obtained from sporting goods stores and marinas. $3.50 a day or $10 for three days for non-Canadians. Fishing licenses are required in all national parks. The salmon fishing is great; there are also plentiful char, grayling, whitefish, bass, perch, trout. Port Alberni is a popular fresh- and saltwater fishing spot. Other popular fishing areas are Qualicum Beach, the Campbell River, and Sooke. Contact *Fish and Wildlife Branch,* Rm. 400, 1019 Wharf St., Victoria, B.C. V8W 2Z1; 387–6411 or *Fisheries and Oceans Dept.,* 666–3169.

**Hiking** is best in provincial and national parks where trails have been marked. The West Coast Trail in *Pacific Rim National Park* is well known as a fine, wild hiking trail—not recommended for beginners.

**Hunting** licenses cost about $25 and can also be obtained at sporting-goods stores.

Check the local telephone directories for **tennis** and **golf** facilities. You'll find over 110 golf courses in B.C. and countless tennis courts.

**Mountain climbers** will find parks the best place for climbing.

**SKIING.** It is hard to find better **skiing** elsewhere in North America. In fact, British Columbia has some of the most difficult and enjoyable runs anywhere in the world. Some areas are limited to the experts, but there are resorts that cater to every level of skier.

*Forbidden Plateau* is near Courtenay. Rentals available. Write 2050 Cliffe Ave., Courtenay, B.C. V9N 2L3; 334–4744. *Mount Washington Ski Resort* is 19 miles west of Courtenay. There's an on-mountain village. Rentals are available. Write 2040 Cliffe Ave., Courtenay, B.C. V9N 2L3; 338–1386.

**CHILDREN'S ACTIVITIES.** By and large, British Columbia is family territory; often the adults and the children end up enjoying the same things and seeing the same sights. In **Victoria,** at the Empress Hotel, is *Miniature World,* a unique and splendid show of miniature scenes. Near Victoria is *Fable Cottage Estate,* 5187 Cordova Bay Rd., 658–5741, with thatched cottages and animated characters. Open daily from last week of March–third week of October from 9:30 A.M. Admission charge. Farther north on the island is the *Forest Museum* around **Duncan;** for information call 382–2127. See also "Marine Life," above, for sea shows and aquariums, "Historic Sites and Houses," and "Museums," below.

 **HISTORIC SITES AND HOUSES.** *Anne Hathaway's Cottage and Olde Englande Inn,* the world's only replica of the birthplace of Shakespeare's wife, is at 429 Lampson St., Victoria; 388–4353. Open June 1–September 30, 9 A.M.–9 P.M.; winter 10 A.M.–4 P.M. Admission $3.75, children $2.25. The inn is a historic house converted into a 50-bedroom hotel, some rooms with canopy beds. (See "Hotels and Motels," above.) *Bastion Square,* off Government Street, between Yates and Fort Streets at the foot of View Street. Established in 1843 as the original site of Fort Victoria. Several restored buildings are open for viewing. *Craigdarroch Castle,* an 1888 castle, 1050 Joan Crescent; 592–5323. Admission by donation; open 9 A.M.–9:30 P.M.; winter 10 A.M.–5:30 P.M. *Craigflower Manor,* an authentic 1856 home, 110 Island Hwy.; 387–3067. Admission free; open May 16–September 15, 10 A.M.–5 P.M. (closed Mondays); winter 10 A.M.–4 P.M. (also closed Tuesdays). *Helmcken House,* 638 Elliot St., 387–3440. A pioneer house with early medical instruments; admission free. *Parliament Buildings* (387–3046) offer guided tours every 20 minutes, 8:30 A.M.–7:30 P.M. during summer; no charge. *Victória Heritage Village,* one block west of Parliament Bldgs.; 384–3232. Open daily 8:30 A.M.–10 P.M.; admission $5, children, $2.50. Attractions include changing of the guard, a haunted house, the "land of the little people," and Munchkin's garden café.

 **MUSEUMS. Campbell River** has an *Indian Museum.* **Courtenay** has a *historical* museum; 334–3881. **Duncan:** *The B.C. Forest Museum,* 748–9389, contains logging artifacts.

**Victoria:** *B.C. Provincial Museum,* 675 Belleville St.; 387–3701 for hours and programs. Superb heritage displays; admission free. *Classic Car Museum,* 813 Douglas St.; 382–7118. Open 9 A.M.–9 P.M.; year-round. Admission $3.50; children, $2.50. *Maritime Museum of B.C.,* 28 Bastion Sq.; 385–4222 for hours and admission charges. Outstanding exhibits, including a Captain Cook gallery. *Royal London Wax Museum,* 470 Belleville St.; 388–4461. Open mid-May–mid-September, 9 A.M.–9 P.M. daily; winter 10 A.M.–5 P.M. Admission $4; children, $2.

 **GALLERIES.** *Art Gallery of Greater Victoria,* 1040 Moss St.; 384–4101. Has European prints, English decorative art, Canadian historical and contemporary art, as well as a recognized collection of Japanese art. Admission $2; phone for other rates and hours. *Emily Carr Gallery,* 1107 Wharf St.; 387–3080. Rotating exhibits. No charge, phone for hours.

**DINING OUT.** Seafood's the thing in coastal areas, with salmon topping the list, and halibut, black cod, king crabs, oysters and shrimps crowding in for second place. Dinner in an *expensive* restaurant will run upwards of $15; in a *moderate* restaurant from $10 to $15; in an *inexpensive* one, under $10, drinks and wine excluded.

Most places accept the following major credit cards: American Express, MasterCard, and Visa; others may also be honored. Not all establishments accept credit cards, therefore we suggest you call for information.

## NANAIMO

**Harbourside Villa Restaurant.** *Moderate.* 70 Church St.; 753–1144. Downtown. Free parking. Cabaret.

## PARKSVILLE

**Island Hall Hotel Dining Room.** *Moderate.* 181 Island Hwy.; 248–3225. Outdoor garden overlooking the sea.

## VICTORIA

**Parrot House Rooftop Restaurant.** *Deluxe.* Atop Château Victoria Hotel; 382–4221. Scenic views; very good menu of mostly Continental items. Well worth it.

**Raven's.** *Deluxe.* In Harbour Towers Hotel; 385–2405. Award-winning international cuisine.

**Captain's Palace.** *Expensive.* 309 Belleville St., on the inner harbor; 388–9191. A beautiful 1897 Victorian house now reopened with a wonderful luncheon menu. House filled with antiques. Charming, and good food.

**Chauncey's.** *Expensive.* 614 Humboldt St., near inner harbor; 385–4512. Excellent seafood.

**Empress Dining Room.** *Expensive.* 721 Government St.; 384–8111. Continental cuisine, elaborate décor. Entertainment. This is *the* gem of elegant dining in the West. The room is Victorian style; the food absolutely first rate. Same for the service. *Bengal Room* does a very good curry lunch.

**Jack Lee's Chinese Village Restaurant.** *Expensive.* 755 Finlayson; 384–8151. Probably the best Chinese food on Vancouver Island.

**La Petite Colombe.** *Expensive.* 604 Broughton; 383–3234. Good French food.

**Princess Mary Restaurant.** *Moderate.* 344 Harbour Rd.; 386–3456. Extensive seafood menu. On a land-locked ship. Good for family dinners; children's portions.

**Sherwood Park Inn.** 123 Gorge Rd.; 386–1422. Robin Hood artifacts from England will please the children. Also children's portions. Entertainment, dancing.

# EXPLORING OTHER AREAS IN BRITISH COLUMBIA

If you take a look at a roadmap for British Columbia, you'll notice that the major roads are all in the south, with the exception of the Yellowhead Highway and the northerly Alaska Highway. Since most of British Columbia is mountainous, this is understandable. You'll also notice that above Powell River, some 104 kms. (65 miles) north of Vancouver, there are no roads along the rugged Pacific coast for the same reason: vast mountain ranges make highway construction prohibitively expensive.

However, you might want to take a short 72-km. (45-mile) jaunt north of Vancouver, up Highway 99, to Squamish, an old lumber town and gateway to the 480,000-acre Garibaldi Provincial Park (which connects with Golden Ears Provincial Park, to the south). Farther up Highway 99 you'll come to famous Whistler Mountain, one of the finest for winter and spring skiing in all North America. This is excellent ski territory in season and, in warm weather, good for camping and hiking. The terrain is, of course, mountainous—and glorious to see. As you drive along the coastal road, you see Vancouver Island and the beautiful Gulf Islands sparkling in the sea. On a clear sunny day, the scene of mountains and sea is magnificent. After leaving Squamish, heading south now, you can ferry from Horseshoe Bay over to Gibsons, and then proceed up Highway 101 to Powell River, a pulp-mill town offering numerous sports, primarily great fishing. If you haven't gone to Vancouver Island, you can ferry across to Comox; or you can head back to Vancouver city, and on to the east.

Although the areas discussed here are well east of the Pacific coast, visitors may want to travel in this direction to experience some of the magnificent scenery. There are three distinct touring areas in the south of British Columbia. First is the Hope—north to Cache Creek, east to Kamloops, and south to Princeton circle. Second is the summer playground in the Okanagan Valley around Penticton and Kelowna. Third is around the Alberta–British Columbia border, around Kimberley, and north to the Kootenay National Park, near Banff and Lake Louise.

## The Hope-Princeton Circle

Leaving Vancouver for Hope, you'll pass Port Moody (where Captain George Vancouver first stepped ashore in 1792) and Chilliwack, on the Fraser River. The area around Hope is built up with resorts which, again, offer very good facilities for hunting, fishing, and relaxing. Turning north on the Trans-Canada Highway (Highway 1—the longest highway in the world), you'll pass through Yale (an old trading town) and then reach the popular Hell's Gate Airtram. (Open daily 9 A.M.–6 P.M.; 681-7639.) The scenery around these parts is breathtaking, and the Airtram's descent into Fraser Canyon is one you'll never forget. The Fraser River is pounding and turbulent here, with more than 200 million gallons of water per minute beating between the shores.

At Lytton, the Fraser and Thompson rivers meet; this was busy territory a century ago when the Gold Rush was on; the original Cariboo Wagon Trail started just to the north. Today, you may search for jade in the riverbeds at Lytton.

You can veer to the west here for Lillooet, another old mining town, or continue north on Highway 1 to Cache Creek, and then east for Kamloops.

Kamloops, a thriving, modern town, is at the confluence of the North and South Thompson rivers. There are hundreds of good swimming and fishing lakes in the district, and trout is the famous specialty. This is also Cariboo Country, which means gold and fur. There's a good Gold Rush Museum in town. In July, Kamloops features an Indian Days Festival and, in April, a giant indoor rodeo. But these events pale next to the splendor of the landscape. It's difficult to imagine a place so clean and sparkling.

If you were to head north from Kamloops on Highway 5, you would reach the wild Wells Gray Provincial Park for excellent camping in the wilderness, as well as good fishing. Trail rides into Wells Gray can be arranged in Clearwater, 43 kms. (27 miles) south of the park's southern entrance.

Travel south from Kamloops on into Princeton, where the Tulameen and Similkameen rivers converge in the Cascade Mountains. This is summer rodeo territory and winter ski country.

## Okanagan Valley

Continuing southeast on Highway 3, you'll arrive in Osoyoos, on the Washington State border. Here, in Indian land, is the International Viewpoint at 4,000 feet; you can see a long distance into the United

States to the south and, to the north, far into the fertile fruit-producing Okanagan Valley.

This region is one of Canada's most popular summer resort areas. Temperatures are hot, swimming in lakes is excellent, and vineyards and fruit trees replace glaciers as the dominant part of the landscape.

Penticton is the center of the region, at the south end of the Okanagan Lake. Nicknamed "Peach City," Penticton hosts an elaborate Blossom Time Festival each May, a Peach Festival in August, and a giant Square Dance Jamboree in August. The town also offers some fine diversions aside from watersports: a huge game farm, the Pioneer Museum, and, not far from town, Copper Mountain Ghost Town.

Following Highway 97 up the west side of narrow Okanagan Lake, you'll come to Summerland, another good resort area, and Kelowna, another major center in the valley, offering a good Museum of Natural History, a zoo, and a tour of fruit-packing plants. Kelowna's big events of the summer are the International Regatta in August and the Grape Festival each September. In winter, skiing is good and trails plentiful.

Vernon, on Kalamalka Lake, is the next town north, well known for its good boating and swimming. Winter Carnival in February is the big event each year. Near Armstrong is the gracious Silver Star Provincial Park. To the north is Revelstoke, where the Monashee Mountains meet the Selkirks.

## The National Parks

Revelstoke serves as the gateway to British Columbia's inland National Parks, each of which has a particular splendor and excitement. Stop in Revelstoke before proceeding east. The town, located on the Columbia River, once served as a base town for lumberjacks, miners, and fur traders. This is superb ski country as well as a summer headquarters for hunting, fishing, and sightseeing. If you're driving through these parks in winter or spring, watch the weather closely. Roads will be closed by the Royal Canadian Mounted Police if snow conditions warrant.

## Mount Revelstoke Park

The first of the national parks to visit is Mount Revelstoke Park, just out of town. Though not very large, it has some of the most splendid scenery in all of Canada—massive peaks, running streams, glaciers, and trees. Many people contend that the Canadian Rocky Mountains are more spectacular than those farther south. It may be a debatable point, but in any case, all of these parks are glorious. By the time you reach the summit, you'll be over 8,000 feet above sea level. The views can hold a person for hours.

## Glacier National Park

Heading east on the Trans-Canada Highway, you'll come next to Glacier National Park, not to be confused with the park of the same name in the United States. Its name is apt: there are mountains in excess of 11,500 feet, glaciers, and rugged peaks. With its fine network of trails and picnic spots, you can spend an hour—or several days—in this 1,347-sq.-km. (520-square-mile) wonderland. If you travel by car (trains will take you here, too), you'll head up to Rogers Pass, perhaps the most breathtaking spectacle in all of British Columbia. This experience should not be missed. Descending the mountains, you'll come to Golden, where the Trans-Canada Highway and Highway 95 meet.

## Yoho National Park

Golden is the split-off point for the other two National Parks. To the north is the beautiful Yoho National Park. Yoho, an Indian word meaning "how beautiful," truly describes the park. There are good camping grounds and a great deal to see in its 1,295-sq.-km. (500-square-mile) territory. Drive along the Kicking Horse Trail and view the glaciers, waterfalls, Ice River Valley, and the Hoodoo Valley. Yoho Park borders on Alberta's Banff National Park, so if you're on your way east, continue through Yoho Park to Calgary.

## Kootenay National Park

Highway 1 leads south to Highway 93 and the last park, the famous Kootenay National Park, 96 kms. (60 miles) long, also on the border of Banff. The main attraction here is the fabulous Vermillion Pass, from which you'll see an assortment of canyons, lakes, and falls. The drive is a beauty. At the southern end of the park is Radium Hot Springs, where you can stop for a relaxing mineral bath, year round.

# PRACTICAL INFORMATION FOR OTHER AREAS IN BRITISH COLUMBIA

**HOW TO GET THERE AND HOW TO GET AROUND. By air:** Public and private airplanes are a way of life within British Columbia. *CP Air* has the most extensive flight pattern in the province; *Pacific Western* flies to Kamloops, Penticton, and many other towns. Also look at the schedules for *Air Canada, Air B.C., Gulf Air Aviation, Island Airlines,* and *North Coast Air Services, Ltd.* Check at any airport regarding plane rentals.

**By train:** *Via Rail* serves Kamloops; *B.C. Railway* travels between Horseshoe Bay and Prince George with many stops.

**By bus:** *Greyhound* serves B.C. *Pacific Coach Lines* serves southern B.C.

**By car:** In Canada the best highways are the *Trans-Canada* and *Yellowhead,* running an east-west route. Travel up the British Columbia coast by car is limited because of the terrain.

**HOTELS AND MOTELS.** British Columbia offers a number of resort hotels that cater to hunters and fishermen. For the traveler spending a great deal of time in British Columbia and touring some of the back roads, it would be helpful to get a copy of the booklet, *British Columbia Accommodation Guide,* which lists just about every hotel or motel in the provinces. Write Tourism B.C., 1117 Wharf St., Victoria, B.C. V8W 2Z2; (604) 387–1642.

Most establishments accept American Express, MasterCard, and Visa; other credit cards may also be honored. Not all establishments accept credit cards, so it's probably wise to check in advance.

Price categories for double rooms are: *Deluxe* $80 and up; *Expensive* $50–$80; *Moderate* $30–$50; *Inexpensive* under $30. Prices may be slightly lower in Alberta.

**ATLA LAKE-WHISTLER MOUNTAIN. Delta Mountain Inn.** *Deluxe.* 4050 Whistler Way; (604) 932–1982. Superb resort hotel near ski lifts. Pool, whirlpools. Reduced summer rates.

**Tantalus Lodge.** *Expensive.* Whistler; (604) 932–4146. Two-bedroom, two-bath units with kitchens. Pool.

**ASHCROFT. Sundance Guest Ranch.** *Deluxe.* Box 489, on Highland Valley Rd.; (604) 932–4146. Excellent dude ranch resort with fishing, riding, tennis, fine rooms, and grand scenery. Private air strip.

**CACHE CREEK. Sandman Inn.** *Moderate.* On Hwy. 1; (604) 457–6284. Nice, comfortable motel.

**CHILLIWACK. Parkwood Motor Hotel.** *Moderate.* 8600 Young St.; (604) 795–9155. Comfortable rooms, all amenities.
**Country Inns Motel.** *Moderate.* 318 Yale Rd.; (604) 792–0661. First-class; dining.

**CLINTON-70 MILE HOUSE. Flying U Guest Ranch, 70 Mile House.** *Deluxe.* Box 69; (604) 456–7717. Dude ranch open all year. Beautiful setting, horses, log cabins, winter and summer sports. Very fine experience.

**CRANBROOK. Towne & Country Inn.** *Expensive.* 600 Cranbrook St.; (604) 426–5201. First-class motel; pool; restaurant; all amenities.
**Town and Country Lodge.** *Moderate.* 1209 Cranbrook St., N. Cranbrook; (604) 489–4124. Fine motel with all amenities; licensed for liquor; dining room.
**Sandman Inn.** *Moderate.* 405 Cranbrook St.; (604) 426–4236. Central, big beds, indoor pool.
**Nomad Motel.** *Inexpensive.* 910 Cranbrook St.; (604) 426–6266. Sleeping and housekeeping units. Pool, playground.

**FAIRMONT HOT SPRINGS. Fairmont Hot Springs Resort.** *Deluxe.* Box 10, on Hwys. 93 and 95; (604) 345–6311. In Kootenay region; resort open year-round; cabins and ski lodge; 18-hole golf course, skiing, riding.

**GABRIOLA ISLAND (A GULF ISLAND). Surf Lodge.** *Expensive.* (604) 247–9231. Open year-round. On water. Dining rooms, sports, comfortable rooms.

**GALIANO ISLAND (A GULF ISLAND). Galiano Lodge.** *Moderate.* (604) 539–2233. Motel with view; on Sturdies Bay; many sports, all amenities, quiet and beautiful.

**HARRISON HOT SPRINGS. Harrison Hotel.** *Deluxe.* (604) 796–2244. Year-round resort hotel in mountains on lake; two hot-spring pools; fine cuisine, all sports.
**Harrison Lakeshore Motel.** *Moderate.* Esplande Ave.; (604) 796–2441. Large units facing lakefront, heated pool.
**Harrison Village Motel.** *Moderate.* Overlooking Harrison Lake, Box 115; (604) 796–2616. Very comfortable; sports available.
**Glencoe Motel.** *Inexpensive.* Box 181; (604) 796–2574. Sleeping and housekeeping units, opposite mineral pool.

**HOPE. Imperial Motel.** *Moderate.* On the Hope-Princeton Hwy.; (604) 869–9951. Indoor pool; all rooms with full facilities. Very comfortable.

**KAMLOOPS REGION. Coast Canadian Inn.** *Expensive.* 339 St. Paul St., in Kamloops; (604) 372–5201. Heated pool, well-done rooms. Dining rooms.

**David Thompson Motor Inn.** *Expensive.* 650 Victoria St., Kamloops; (604) 372–5282. Fine downtown motel with complete hotel facilities.

**Dome Motor Hotel.** *Expensive.* In Kamloops on Columbia St.; (604) 374–0358. First-class, pleasant rooms; dining; pool.

**Stockmen's Hotel.** *Expensive.* 540 Victoria St., Kamloops; (604) 372–2281. Centrally located in town; nice rooms; all amenities.

**Four Seasons Motel.** *Moderate.* On Hwy. 1 in East Kamloops; (604) 372–2313. Fine motel, some units with kitchens; picnic area, pool.

**Lac Le Jeune Resort.** *Moderate.* Box 3215, Kamloops; (604) 372–2722. On Lac Le Jeune; resort lodge; near Tod Mt. for skiing; other sports and dining available.

**Sandman Inn.** *Moderate.* 550 Columbia St. at 6th; (604) 374–1218. Sleeping and kitchenette units, handy to town.

**Village Hotel.** *Moderate.* 377 Tranquille Rd.; (604) 376–8811. On 3 acres between two arms of the Thompson River. Coffee shop and dining room.

**Parkside Lodge.** *Inexpensive.* 254 Lorne St.; (604) 372–7551. Older style light housekeeping rooms, shared bathrooms.

**KELOWNA. Canamara Beach Motel.** *Expensive.* On Lakeshore Rd.; (604) 763–4717. On beach; all amenities; golf, boating, etc. Pleasant.

**Capri Hotel.** *Expensive.* On Harvey Ave.; (604) 860–6060. Modern hotel; good dining; pool.

**County Inn.** *Expensive.* On Harvey Ave.; (604) 860–1212. Near golf course; tennis; private patios, heated pool.

**Eldorado Arms Resort Hotel.** *Expensive.* (604) 764–4126. Summer resort in mountains with gardens; nice rooms and cottages, all sports. May to Sept.

**Beacon Beach Resort Motel.** *Moderate-Deluxe.* 3766 Lakeshore Rd.; (604) 762–4225. A year-round resort with small or large units; private beach; boating; other sports.

**Stetson Village Motel.** *Moderate.* 1455 Harvey Ave.; (604) 860–2490. Near airport. All amenities, indoor pool. Some kitchenettes.

**Willow Inn Hotel.** *Moderate.* 235 Queensway; (604) 762–2122. Downtown, close to park and lake.

**Kelowna TraveLodge.** *Moderate.* 1780 Glenmore St.; (604) 762–3221. Opposite shopping center with restaurants and entertainment. Some kitchenettes.

**Western Budget Motel.** *Moderate.* 2679 Hwy. 97N; (604) 860–4990. Big picnic area, pets welcome.

**NELSON. Peebles Motor Inn.** *Moderate.* 153 Baker St. downtown; (604) 352–3525. Full facilities, some suites, bar and restaurant.

**"108." 108 Ranch Resort.** *Deluxe.* On Hwy. 97 and "108"; (604) 791–5211. Huge, well-planned resort hotel offering golf, tennis, water skiing, cattle drives, fishing, etc. All amenities, very nice.

**PENTICTON. Bel Air Motel.** *Expensive.* On Skaha Lake Rd.; (604) 492–6111. Sleeping and housekeeping units; heated pool. Pleasant.

**Bowmont Motel.** *Expensive.* 80 Riverside Dr.; (604) 492–0112. Rooms and suites; full amenities. Near lakes and beaches.

**Penticton Motel.** *Expensive.* On Lakeshore Dr.; (604) 492–2922. First-class motel on lake; pool, sauna.

**Penticton TraveLodge.** *Expensive.* On Westminster Ave.; (604) 492–0225. Some rooms with kitchens; full facilities; dining room and coffee shop; pools and sauna.

**Pilgrim House Motor Hotel.** *Expensive.* On Eckhardt Ave.; (604) 492–8926. Near lake and sports; fine first-class hotel.

**Log Cabin Motel.** *Moderate.* 3287 Skaha Lake Rd.; (604) 492–3155. Log-cabin housekeeping units.

**Stardust Motor Inn.** *Moderate.* 1048 Westminster Ave.; (604) 492–7015. Near lake and airport, some kitchenettes, heated pool. Restaurant.

**POWELL RIVER. Beach Gardens Resort Hotel.** *Expensive.* 7074 Westminster Ave.; (604) 485–6267. Open year-round; overlooking marina; pleasant rooms.

**PRINCETON. Evergreen Motel.** *Moderate.* Box 546. A quarter mile east of city center; (604) 295–7733. Color TV, heated pool. Sports nearby. Pretty setting.

**Sandman Inn.** *Moderate.* On Hwy. 3; (604) 295–6923. Modern, pleasant; dining.

**RADIUM HOT SPRINGS. Radium Hot Springs Lodge.** *Expensive.* Box 310, on Hwy. 95; (604) 347–9622. First-class, beautiful views; all sports, helicopter skiing available.

**Big Horn Motel.** *Expensive.* (604) 347–9522. Comfortable units, color TV, restaurant nearby. Near Bugaboo ski area.

**REVELSTOKE. Revelstoke TraveLodge.** *Expensive.* 601 1st St. W.; (604) 837–2181. Pleasant motel with full facilities and heated pool.

**Columbia Slumber Lodge.** *Moderate.* 1601 Second St. W.; (604) 837–2191. Housekeeping units, heated pool. Restaurant adjacent.

**McGregor Motor Inn.** *Moderate.* 201 2nd St. W. & Connaught Ave.; (604) 837–2121. Downtown, very comfortable.

**King Edward Motor Hotel.** *Inexpensive.* (604) 837–2104. Central location. Dining room, lounge, pub.

**Mountain View Motel.** *Inexpensive.* 1017 First St. W.; (604) 837–2057. Some waterbeds.

**ROGERS PASS. Northlander Motor Lodge.** *Expensive.* (604) 837–2126. Between Golden and Revelstoke; in park at 4,300-foot level; pool, sports, views.

**SALMON ARM. Totem Pole Resort and Marina.** *Expensive.* Located at Tappen, 17 mi. off Hwy. 1; (604) 835–4567. Chalets and nice cottages, open year-round. Fireplace, huge beach. Sports available, boat rentals. Quite nice.

**VALEMOUNT. Mount Robson Ranch.** *Expensive.* P.O. Box 301; (604) 566-4370. A true horse ranch with numerous riding plans. Cabins are rustic.

 **CAMPING.** *Tourism B.C.* (see "Tourist Information") will provide camping information. There are no reservations for camping in national and provincial parks, where in summer there are nominal overnight fees. (See the sections on these parks, below.)

 **TOURIST INFORMATION.** Write *Tourism B.C.,* 800 Robson St., Vancouver, B.C. V6Z 2C6; or 117 Wharf St., Victoria, B.C. V8W 2Z2.

 **SEASONAL EVENTS. January:** Height of ski season. **February:** *Ski competitions* on all slopes. *Winter carnival,* Vernon, B.C.

**April:** *Rodeo* at Kamloops, B.C. *Ski Competitions* on all slopes throughout the month.

**July:** July 1st is a national holiday and *Dominion Day* celebrations are held in many communities. *Indian Days Festivals* in Kamloops, B.C. and Banff.

**August:** In Penticton, B.C.: *Peach Festival* and *Square Dance Jamboree;* in Kelowna, B.C. *International Regatta.*

**September:** *Grape Festival, Kelowna, B.C.*

**December:** *Hockey* in almost every community.

 **TOURS.** Many bus tours through the Canadian west are offered by tour companies whose main booking offices are in Toronto; two such companies are: *UTL Holiday Tours,* 22 College St., (416) 967–3355, and *Horizon Holidays of Canada,* 44 Victoria St., (800) 268–7103. *De West Tours Ltd.,* 1104 510 W. Hastings St., Vancouver, (604) 684–7204, also offers Canada West packages.

In British Columbia, *Pacific Coach Lines* offers trips from Vancouver, such as a day trip up the Sunshine Coast for $33, an outing up the Fraser Valley to the delightful Harrison Hot Springs resort ($13.60), and a full day at Whistler ($16.50). There's also a Multi-Day Totem Circle ($221), which includes the famous Inside Passage waterway and return by Prince Rupert, Prince George, Jasper, Banff, Kamloops, and Vancouver. For information in Vancouver call (604) 683–9277; in Victoria, (604) 385–4411.

*Westours,* 100 W. Harrison Plaza, Seattle, WA 98119, (208) 281–3535, provides several tours of B.C. of varying length.

**SPECIAL-INTEREST TOURS.** The adventurous might want to try a *raft* trip in the white waters of the Thompson and Fraser rivers. It helps to be a swimmer, but life jackets are provided. Most tours originate in Lytton and start at $50 for a one-day outing. Contact *West-Can Treks-Adventure Travel*, 3415 West Broadway, Vancouver. Phone (604) 734–1066.

**PROVINCIAL PARKS.** There are more than provincial parks throughout Canada. Camping is available at most for a nominal fee in summer. No reservations. Popular parks in British Columbia are *Garibaldi, Manning,* and *Cathedral,* all of which are located in the southwest of the province. Open year-round. For information on the provincial parks in British Columbia's lower mainland, call (604) 929–1291.

**NATIONAL PARKS.** For complete information on facilities write to *Parks Canada*—Western Region, 134 Eleventh Ave., Calgary, Alta. T2G 0X5; (403) 231–4440. Or to *National and Provincial Parks Association of Canada,* 47 Colborne St., Suite 308, Toronto, Ont. M5E 1E3. Camping is on a first-come, first-serve basis. No pass-through charge for any motor vehicle. To spend a day or less, a 24-hour stopping pass can be purchased for $1. Most convenient is to purchase a $10 annual national parks pass, good until March 31st of the year following at any national park in Canada.

For safety reasons, visitors must register at a Parks Warden Office before embarking on or completing any climbing, extensive backpacking, hiking, or cross-country skiing expeditions. Use of open campfires is restricted to National Park Campsites specifically designed to accommodate them. Dogs and cats must be on leash. Use of firearms and bowstring equipment is forbidden; all such equipment must be sealed at park entry points. The parks are open year-round.

*Glacier National Park* (521 square miles) is in the Selkirk Mountains and contains over 100 glaciers as well as hemlock and cedar forests and excellent fishing streams. Write P.O. Box 350, Revelstoke, B. C. V0E 2S0; (604) 837–5515.

*Kootenay National Park* (543 square miles) is a narrow valley on the western slopes of the Rockies and includes colossal Sinclair Canyon and Radium Hot Springs. (P.O. Box 220, Radium Hot Springs, B. C. V0A 1M0; [604] 347–9615.)

*Mount Revelstoke National Park* (100 square miles), on the rugged western slopes of the Selkirks, is a mountaintop park with ski slopes and alpine meadows. Write P.O. Box 350, Revelstoke, B.C. V0E 2S0; (604) 837–5515.

*Yoho National Park* (507 square miles)—"How Wonderful," in the local Indian language—has spectacular Yoho Glacier, Lake O'Hara, Takkakaw Falls, and a famous pass through the Rockies following Kicking Horse River. Write P.O. Box 99, Field, B.C. V0A 1G0; (604) 343–6324.

**SUMMER SPORTS.** Contact Tourism B.C., 117 Wharf St., Victoria, B.C. V8W 2Z2; (604) 387–1642. For information on **boating** around the Gulf Islands, see "Summer Sports" in *Practical Information for Vancouver Island and Victoria.* **Canoes** can be rented at many inland resorts; call (604) 387–1642 for detailed information. For **hiking,** the wise traveler will probably stick to the provincial and national parks, where trails are marked. Register with the Parks Warden for any extended hiking or climbing.

**FISHING.** A fishing license for Canadians costs $5.00. For a nonresident or non-Canadian, it costs around $3.50 a day, $10 for 3 days. Available at sporting goods stores and marinas. A license is issued on an annual basis and is valid until the following March 31. Angling permits are required by all fishermen except children under 16 years of age. A special trophy license ($5.00) is required for some lakes which offer specimens of unusual size. A special sturgeon fishing license is required ($5.00). Spear fishermen must possess a $3.00 permit.

A fishing license is required for all national parks in Canada. It costs $4.00 and is good in every national park in Canada, again on an annual basis. Full information, sports fishing guide, and map may be obtained from Department of Energy and Natural Resources, Fish and Wildlife Branch, Rm. 400, 1019 Wharf St., Victoria, B.C. V8W 2Z1; (604) 387–6411.

**HUNTING.** The difficulty of reaching north central B.C. is rewarded by the abundance of game: mountain goat and sheep, black and grizzly bear, moose, caribou, deer, waterfowl. Hunting licenses average about $25 and are available at sporting goods stores. You can contact the B.C. Fish and Game Association, 1607 Myrtle Ave., Victoria, for more information.

**WINTER SPORTS.** The **skiing** is nothing less than splendid. Here you can even find **helicopter glacier skiing.** Heli-skiing companies in the coastal mountains include *B.C. Powder Guides,* Box 258, Whistler, B.C. V0N 1B0; 932–5331 (winter); 894–6994 (summer), *Canadian Mountain Holidays,* Box 1660, Banff, Alberta T0L OC0; (403) 762–4531, and *Coast Range Guiding,* Box 389, Squamish, B.C. V0N 3G0; 932–4477. *Big White* in the Okanagan Valley is a popular resort (Box 2039, Station R, Kelowna, B.C. V1X 4K5; 765–4411), as are *Apex Alpine* (Box 489, Penticton, B.C. V2A 6K9; 292–8221) and *Silver Star* (#1,3001 43rd Ave., Vernon, B.C. V1T 3L4; 542–0166). One of the most popular ski resorts in British Columbia is *Whistler Mountain,* two hours north of Vancouver. The village of Whistler actually has two magnificent mountains (Whistler and Blackcomb), both offering a vertical drop of more than 4,000 feet. The village has full facilities including good hotels, restaurants, bars, discos and baby-sitting. For information and reservations contact the Whistler

Resort Association, Box 1400, Whistler, B.C. V0N 1B0; 932–4222, telex 04–51208.

**Snowmobiling** is not allowed in national parks or many provincial parks although it is allowed in many of the wilderness areas. For details write Travel B.C.

 **DINING OUT.** The Okanagan Valley in British Columbia is noted for its fruit and fruit wines. Parts of British Columbia are cattle country, and the people fiercely proud of the quality of beef that the grazing lands and grain yield. With good reason, too.

Restaurants are listed by price category as follows: *Deluxe,* $28 and over; *Expensive,* $19–$28; *Moderate,* $13–$19; *Inexpensive,* under $13. Prices include hors d'oeuvres or soup, salad, main course, dessert, and coffee, but not drinks or gratuities. Entertainment (particularly good music in an appealing atmosphere) is the general rule in *Deluxe* and *Expensive* categories.

Most places accept major credit cards.

**KAMLOOPS. David Thompson Dining Room.** *Expensive.* 650 Victoria St.; 372–5282. Steak, lobster, prime ribs. Children's portions.

**China Village Restaurant.** *Moderate.* 165 Victoria St.; 372–2822. Chinese and North American food. Serves liquor.

**Oriental Gardens.** *Moderate.* 545 Victoria St.; 372–2344. Chinese and Japanese.

**Highlander Restaurant.** *Inexpensive.* 444 Victoria St.; 372–2121. Seafood, steaks, trout. Dancing. Serves liquor.

**PENTICTON. Pilgrim House Motor Hotel Restaurant.** *Moderate.* 1056 Eckhardt Ave.; 492–8926. Specializing in prime beef.

**VERNON. Vernon Lodge Hotel Restaurant.** *Moderate.* 3914 32nd St.; 545–3385. Good selection, especially seafood. Entertainment.

# SOUTHEAST ALASKA

*Few Roads Lead to the Panhandle*

by
**NORMA SPRING**

The marine and mountainscapes and multiple evergreen islands of Alaska's southeast Panhandle are the very essence of this, the largest state. Here an almost-drowned mountain range makes up the Alexander Archipelago. It parallels a strip of the United States Northwest coast, set off from Canada by mountains that are well over a mile and a half high. This narrow mainland strip, plus the mountain-top island chain, make up Alaska's five-hundred-mile-long "Panhandle." Actually it's a dipper handle which extends south and east from the main body of the peninsula state. The cup holds the other diverse areas of Alaska:

273

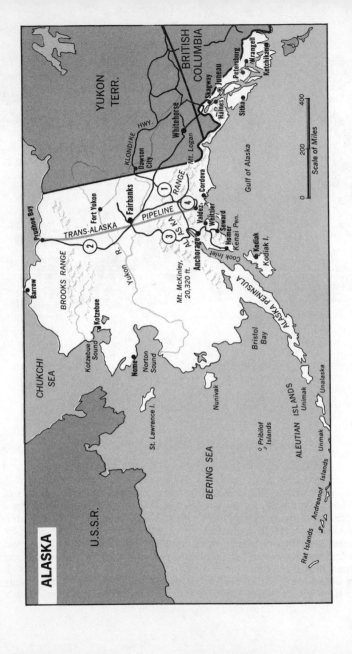

the Gulf and Interior, and the far northern and far western coastal fringes.

The scene, on a grand scale and gorgeous, continues to remain much as it was when earlier visitors admired it—canoe-paddling Indians, explorers of assorted nationalities in sailing ships, gold rushers who crowded onto almost anything that would float, and a wave of hardy tourists who came to sightsee the Great Land by steamship, before 1900.

For today's travelers, the choice is town-hopping with Alaska Airlines jets or by local air taxi services; port-calling via Alaska State Ferries or private boat; and by cruise ship. Sailing under many flags, a flotilla of cruise ships summer in southeast Alaska waters, granting shore leaves to their passengers in assorted ports.

The towns along the Inside Passage are all different, each with its distinctive flavor, from first port Ketchikan, dedicated to fish and wood chips, to Sitka, with a Russian dressing. Place names—of towns and of myriad waterways—give clues of earlier visitors, who left their mark around southeast Alaska. There's little mistaking nationalities among such labels as Baranof, Kupreanof, Prince of Wales, and Petersburg. Klawock and Ketchikan are derived from similar-sounding Indian names.

## No Roads Lead to Ketchikan

Twenty years ago, Ketchikan and other similarly isolated Panhandle towns came as close to being connected by a "road" as they are likely to, with the inauguration of the state's extensive Marine Highway System. It was an instant hit with Alaskans, who have been happily riding and singing "The Ferryboat Song" ever since.

Though there is periodic talk of a connecting combination ferry and over-island highway, it's not likely to happen very soon (if at all). The barriers are formidable for road building in the usual sense, paved or unpaved.

Ketchikan is perched on a large mountainous island underneath 3,000-foot Deer Mountain. The island's name is a jaw-breaker, Revillagigedo, named by English mariner George Vancouver who was exploring the Inside Passage in 1793. He often named things for his crew and friends, in this case the Viceroy of Mexico.

Locals say Ketchikan's name was inspired by the local Indians, who were referring to a nearby waterfall that reminded them of an eagle with its wings spread out. However, it's apt for the appearance of the town as well. Imagine that you have hiked the 5-mile trail to the top of Deer Mountain and are looking out over the town and surrounding area. Ketchikan appears squeezed onto a narrow shelf. Actually, it's

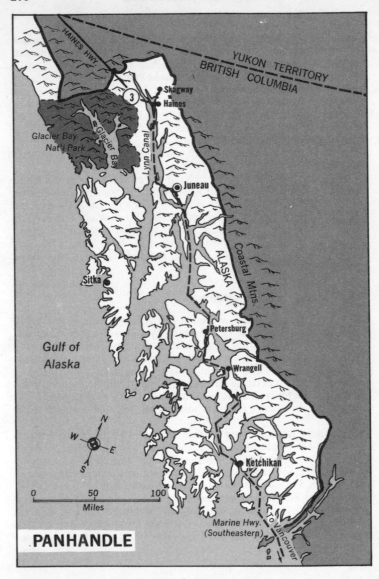

YUKON TERRITORY
BRITISH COLUMBIA

HAINES HWY.

Skagway

Haines

Glacier Bay
Nat'l Park

Glacier Bay

Lynn Canal

Juneau

ALASKA

Coastal Mtns.

Sitka

Petersburg

Gulf of
Alaska

Wrangell

N
W　E
S

Ketchikan

0　　50　　100
Miles

Marine Hwy.
(Southeastern)

TO Vancouver

**PANHANDLE**

more like an overhang, considering that much of the 3-mile-long waterfront section is built out over the water. The docks are on pilings, and with no place to grow but north and south from its center, the town has a spread-eagle shape. There is plenty of waterfront action, with ships coming and going, and small float planes and air taxis skimming off and swishing down like big insects.

It's obvious that Ketchikan's skyline hasn't been static. Some highrises mark the two up-and-coming shopping centers at both ends of town. The large pulp mill is a standout, and there are schools, including a community college, small boat harbors, parks, and many attractive homes valiantly climbing the steep backdrop.

## Ketchikan's Past

A capsulized history of Ketchikan starts with the Indian fishing camp at the mouth of Ketchikan Creek, long before white miners and fishermen came to settle in 1885. Shortly before 1900, however, the new town's future was brightened by gold discoveries and the establishment of a cannery and sawmill. Fishing industries peaked in the 1930s, but declined in the 1940s. Thick, fast-growing forests fed the growing timber industry and the mill of the Louisiana-Pacific Pulp Company. Today, along with timber, fish, and pulp, the town is banking on tourism, a molybdenum mine, and a hydroelectric project.

Ketchikan ranks fourth in Alaska city size. Population is 9,400, over 14,000 counting the surrounding communities it serves, mostly based on fishing and logging. Many of these small villages such as Klawock, Metlakatla, Hydaburg, and Craig, on neighbor islands reached by smaller ferries and smaller planes are also leaning toward tourism.

Alaska Sightseeing Company, Gray Line of Ketchikan, and Ketchikan Sightseeing Company motorcoaches offer 1- to 3-hour tours that provide a valuable orientation to the town and environs. On your own you'll find lots of atmosphere and exercise hiking the steep streets that give way to wooden staircases leading to homes and sweeping views of Tongass Narrows and islands. As they say in Ketchikan, all that's needed are "a pair of sneakers and an hour or two" to cover the high points at your own pace. Well-placed signs put up by the chamber of commerce lead you onward from the visitor center, located next to the attractive waterfront park downtown by the City Pier, where the cruise ships dock. Whether exploring by car or afoot, the Ketchikan Visitors Bureau is a good place to start.

There is interesting browsing in the Tongass Historical Society Museum in the Centennial Building, built in 1967, the 100th anniversary of the purchase of Alaska from Russia. The museum shares the building with the public library. Seasonal displays feature the arts and crafts.

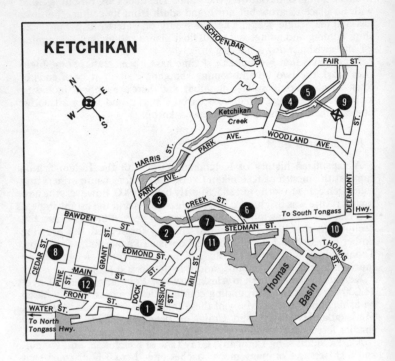

## Points of Interest

1) Visitor Center
2) Tongass Historical Society Museum
3) Fish Ladder-Salmon Carving
4) Deer Mountain Hatchery
5) World's Largest Gold Nugget
6) Dolly's House
7) Chief Johnson Totem
8) Kayan Totem
9) Totem Heritage Center
10) Ketchikan Mural painted by 21 Native artists
11) Federal Building
12) Post Office

Permanent exhibits in the museum include pioneer relics, minerals, Indian items and artifacts. Outside, Ketchikan Creek tumbles in rapids fought each season by salmon on their way upstream to spawn. Wooden Creek Street, on pilings, is across the stream from the museum. It marks what's left of a notorious part of town, including some of the infamous "houses of ill repute." Dolly's House is also a museum, but quite a contrast to its staid neighbor, the Tongass Museum. It has just recently been opened to the public. This restored house of prostitution retains the furnishings and decor picked by Dolly herself. Nearby, the Deer Mountain Hatchery in City Park offers year-round viewing of prized king and coho salmon reared for release in Ketchikan Creek.

One facet of tourism involves both trees and Indians, the art of totem carving. In Ketchikan you won't have to look far to see these "monuments in cedar." Some are downtown near the docks. Chief Johnson's totem was set in the heart of town in 1901. Chief Kyan's totem at the top of Main Street lures visitors. You'll get money within 24 hours after touching it, so they say. More are within walking distance, at the Totem Heritage Cultural Center, near the fish hatchery. This was started as a Bicentennial project for preserving the Tlingit and Haida poles from nearby Indian villages. You'll find authentic information here on the types of totems: Heraldic, depicting social standing; Memorial, usually for a dead chief; and Mortuary, with a section for ashes; devastating Ridicule, or "shame poles" for putting down an enemy; Potlatch poles for festivals; and—most common and important—House Poles, used in constructing community tribal houses.

At Totem Bight, on a point north of Ketchikan, overlooking Tongass Narrows, a stand of authentically reproduced totem poles guards a fine hand-crafted tribal house. It is a 16-minute drive and a short walk through the forest from the parking lot to the totem park.

Saxman Totem Park is about 2 miles south of Ketchikan at the Indian village of Saxman, named for a missionary who helped the Tlingit Indians who moved there before 1900. Natives can "read" the poles depicting birds, animals, and water dwellers. They (or a tour guide) can also identify the big chiefs portrayed including Abraham Lincoln, whose tall-hat makes him quite identifiable. He was honored for abolishing slavery in the U.S., which included the newly acquired Territory of Alaska. Until then, the souvenirs that warfaring tribes had been bringing home were often people, to serve as slaves. In case you wonder why the President is cut off at the knees, they say it is because the grateful Indians were working from a postcard photo, and that's where it ended. The time-rotted original of the Lincoln totem is encased in glass in the state museum at Juneau.

From town, you won't go far in either direction before running out of road. The North Tongass Highway starts at the Federal Building where area information is on display and ends about 18 miles later at Settler's Cove Campground. The South Tongass road ends at a power plant. Side roads soon terminate at campgrounds and trail beginnings, viewpoints, lakes, boat launching ramps, or private property.

If you switch to sea and air transportation, sightseeing possibilities in the Ketchikan area are expanded.

Visitors with longer time to spend can reserve one of more than 50 Forest Service cabins in the Ketchikan area. Some are accessible by hiking, or boat; most are fly-ins. There are also more luxurious accommodations.

The active Visitor Center and the Chamber of Commerce steer visitors toward what's going on. For example, visitors are welcome to fish in the April to mid-July salmon derby, where the winning fish are usually well over 50 pounds and the prizes add up to thousands of dollars. Nearby Behm Canal is one of Southeast's fishing hot spots. You can drive to Clover Pass Resort, 15 paved miles north of Ketchikan, a headquarters for the salmon derby. Hopeful fishermen strike out from here for hooking fighting king salmon. Yes Bay is 45 miles to the northwest, and besides fishing, features hiking, beachcombing, and birdwatching (see "Wilderness Lodges" in *Practical Information for Southeast Alaska*).

Bell Island, just off Behm Canal, is noted for its "fish and soak." The resort sits on hot springs appreciated by Indians and, later, commercial fishermen for their relaxing, therapeutic powers, as well as a chance for a good hot bath. Now sport fishermen go there for some of the best king salmon fishing in Alaska, from May until well into fall, plus fighting steelhead that run up a cold stream rushing past the row of guest cabins. Families of fishermen are kept happy soaking in the private tubs or swimming in the hot, spring-fed, Olympic-sized swimming pool, dropping a line off the docks, or nature watching (see "Wilderness Lodges").

## Wrangell

Next up the line is Wrangell (rang'gull), also on an island near the mouth of the Stikine (stick-een') River, but not a cliffhanger like Ketchikan. It's a waterfront town, though with a different emphasis. Here, it's the shipping point for timber processed in the town's big sawmills, a port for logging tugs, and for Japanese lumber ships.

The town might well have developed a split personality, having been exposed to motley influences over the years: soldiers, Indians, fur and gold seekers, fishermen, loggers, rivermen. With a past that goes back to the Russians, Wrangell existed under three successive flags: first Russian, then British, and finally American, accompanied by as many name changes. First it was called Redoubt Saint Dionysius. Next the British named it Fort Stikine. Then the Americans settled for the simpler name Wrangell, almost the same as the name the Russians had given to the whole island, when they named it for an early governor, Baron von Wrangel.

Don't count on much road travel while in Wrangell. Besides the two-mile loop to the airport, there is only the Zimovia Highway. It passes through town from the ferry dock and gives up at Pat's Creek campground, just over 11 miles. In between there is a short trail off the highway that goes to woodsy Rainbow Falls.

The Stikine River, however, shows possibilities of again becoming a "marine highway." In the past, the Stikine gave access to interior gold fields and was important as a mining supply route. History may be repeated, with copper the prize. Meanwhile, the Stikine has been discovered by river runners, who traverse part of its length in assorted craft. They get around its impassable Grand Canyon by making an air portage to Telegraph Creek, then running the rest of the 160 miles to Wrangell.

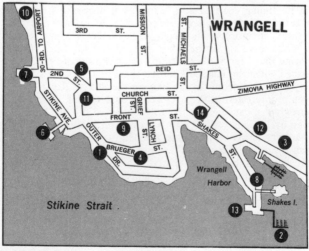

## Points of Interest

1) Visitor Information A-Frame
2) Boat Harbor
3) Chief Shakes Gravesite
4) City Hall—Totem
5) City Museum
6) Cruiseship Dock
7) State Ferry Terminal
8) Marine Bar (Fort Dionysius)
9) Petroglyph—Natl. Bank of Alaska
10) "Our Collections" Museum
11) Post Office
12) Raven Totem
13) Seaplane Float
14) Totem—Kiksadi

Tourism and services are very informal in smaller, waterfront-dominated Wrangell, still off the beaten big cruise ship path. Ferries dock just north of the pier-side Stikine Inn. Smaller cruise ships, such as the *Majestic Alaska Explorer,* tie up at the closest dock, only a short walk to the Inn and "downtown."

The town appreciates the regularly scheduled ferries, and everyone loves having the cruise ships call. In fact, they greet them with music and dance—the dancers, ranging from young tots to the young-at-heart, may turn out for a lively cancan, in costume. They may be joined by some local Stikine Indians, who dance in costume in the tribal house on special occasions.

The Wrangell Chamber of Commerce Visitor Information center is conveniently located close to the docks in a small A-frame building at Front Street and Outer Drive. It's usually open when ships are in port. On request, the center will arrange a guided tour, often led by an enthusiastic student. However, all you'll need is a free, current *Visitor Guide* put out by the *Wrangell Sentinel,* Alaska's oldest continuously published newspaper (from 1902). It tells all, with map.

The Wrangell Museum, on Second Street, north of the Visitor Information A-frame, across from the federal building, has petroglyph carvings in its Indian section, and many local historical items. Farther north, at the end of town, a private collection of artifacts and 19th- and 20th-century memorabilia is displayed in Bigelow's Museum and Gift Shop. When traveling in the other direction stop in for a refresher at the Marine Bar, near Shakes Island. It's on the site of Fort Dionysius, established when the Russians settled there in 1834, to keep the Hudson Bay Company from fur trading up the Stikine River.

If you're interested in the archaic, be sure to look along the beach for petroglyphs, carvings on the rocks believed to have been doodled long ago by Indians waiting out hunting and fishing sessions. One is near the ferry terminal; more are reached by a boardwalk trail taking off from the Airport Road.

More recent Indian art—many fine totem poles—decorate the streets, and a choice collection is on an island just offshore, reached by a foot bridge. Little mid-harbor Chief Shakes Island honors the Indian chief with a replica of his community house under the watchful eyes of superbly carved totem faces. Inside the house are more examples of Indian art, and some of their working tools.

## Petersburg

Getting to Petersburg is an experience, whether you take the "high road" or the "low road." Alaska Airlines claims the "shortest jet flight in the world" from takeoff at Wrangell to put down at Petersburg. The schedule allows 20 minutes, but it's usually more like 11. At eye level, the Marine Highway route squeaks through Wrangell Narrows, full of markers and other aids to help navigate the reefs and currents in the ticklish 23-mile stretch between Kupreanof and Mitkof Islands. It is sensationally narrow in places.

At first sight of Petersburg you might think that you are in the old country. Neat and cheery white Scandinavian-style houses and store-fronts, decked with bright-colored swirls of leaf and flower designs, and a sizeable fishing fleet adorn the waterfront.

The healthy looking people will sport fishing garb, most likely from hip boots to Norwegian knits. If you happen to land there near the 17th of May, they may be wearing old-country costumes and dancing schot-tisches on the docks. You may even hear Norwegian spoken. But don't worry about a language barrier; visitors can get by very well with "Skol!" Every year on the weekend closest to "Syttende Mai" these descendants of Norwegian fishermen, who settled Peter Buschmann's town in 1897, go all out to celebrate Norwegian Independence Day and the fame of their halibut. Though the town is devoted to fish of all kinds, scaly and shell, it's best known for having the world's largest home-based halibut fleet.

The Norwegians turn out to greet arriving visitors and summer cruise ships that are able to call now since the new, bigger dock is completed. Greeters may be a bold band of "Vikings" accompanied by a kitchen band playing a fishy tune like "I Like Hooked-nose Salmon." If your name is Norwegian, you'll have it made.

It seems that everything has a fish flavor. Eat some, for sure, in the restaurants, or if you are there during the Festival, take in a local "fish feed." And don't miss the Clausen Museum, on F Street. In front is a large bronze sculpture, called "Fisk," (fish) in honor of them all. Inside you'll see a king salmon, the record-breaker, at 126½ pounds.

Visitors can find out what they want to know about Petersburg at the museum, or at the Chamber of Commerce on Main Street, next to the Mikof Hotel. How about a hot tub, sauna, or shower? Ask Nordic Travel, also on Main Street, or phone 772-4266. Though travel, espe-cially Alaska Marine Highway and airline ticketing is their longsuit, they are also home base for Petersburg's only "spa"—a bathhouse, open evenings.

The flatter, sea level terrain in the vicinity has created some sloughs. One of them is a photographers' delight. Because of the tides, the houses bordering Hammer Slough are built on stilts. Along with ware-houses and boats reflected in the still water, they make a picture-worthy scene.

You can drive a couple of miles to Sandy Beach picnic and recreation area. Drive the 34-mile Mitkof Highway for campgrounds and a fish ladder at Falls Creek. The ladder helps migrating coho and pink salmon bypass the Falls on the way to spawning grounds; it's at Mile 10.9 of the highway and can be observed just off the roadside. Best time is late summer and early fall. Also on Mitkof Highway is the Crystal Lake Fish Hatchery. The fish hatchery is open to visitors who want to learn about this state operation which involves coho, king, and chum salmon and steelhead trout. Near the end of the highway is the Stikine River Delta; at low tide the mud flats are exposed.

Petersburg's biggest attraction, literally, is about 25 miles east of town. The LeConte Glacier is the continent's southernmost tidewater glacier. It's very active, "calving" ice chunks so big that they are far from melted down by the time they reach the main channels. The new *Explorer* ships pay weekly calls, and sightseeing charter flights and day cruises out of Petersburg are popular. Nordic Travel on Main Street will have up-to-date listings of available tours. Sightings of whales, porpoises, and seals are almost guaranteed.

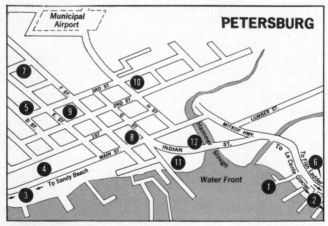

## Points of Interest

1) Alaska Island Air Charter
2) Beachcomber Inn
3) To eagle observation point
4) Buschmann Historic Marker
5) Catholic Church
6) King Salmon Hotel
7) Lutheran Church
8) C of C Info. by Mitkof Hotel
9) Museum and "Fisk"
10) Presbyterian Church
11) Visitor Parking
12) Sons of Norway Hall

### Tlingit/Russian Sitka

For centuries before the Russians came at the turn of the 18th century, Sitka had been the ancestral home of the Tlingit Indian nation. Isolated on the far west side of their large island, they cherished their affluent life, living off the land and sea. And the living was easy, with plenty of game in the forests and a wealth of seafood. It was small wonder that the Indians took a dim view of Russian intrusion.

Governor Baranof, guiding light for the settlement of Sitka, second capital of Russian America, left his name and mark. Sitka's island is named Baranof, and it is situated in the northern part of the large Alexander Archipelago. The Governor coveted the Sitka site for some of the same reasons the Tlingits did: beauty of setting, milder climate, and the forests. However, the Russians needed the wood for building craft larger than war canoes. Their ships traded far west to Hawaii and the Orient, and south along the west coast as far as Fort Ross, California. Baranof was well aware of the convenience of Sitka's location. Eventually the city grew and became so lively that it was called the "Paris of the Pacific." But not without a notable setback.

The *first* settlement site a few miles north of today's Sitka was called Fort Archangel Michael. It was established in 1799 and destroyed by the Tlingits in 1802. "I shall return," vowed Baranof, and did, in 1804, bent on building his next capital on the Tlingit's choice village property. The final "Battle for Alaska" began with the attack on their stronghold atop the hill. It ended at the Tlingit fort a few miles down the beach. Defeated, the Indians fled to the other side of the island and stayed there for the next twenty years. The battle site is now the 54-acre Sitka National Historical Park.

The Sitka Visitor Bureau headquarters is conveniently located in the beautifully designed Centennial Building on Harbor Drive. A big Tlingit Indian war canoe is displayed in front. Inside the building you'll find a museum, auditorium, art gallery, Convention and Visitor Center offices, and lots of friendly people with advice on what to see and how to do it. They'll know if the peppy New Archangel Russian Dancers are performing, if the annual Salmon Derby is in progress, and if there is a festival or contest, such as the logging championship competitions. They'll start you on your own walking tour, or direct you to a guided bus tour.

In the Centennial Building, there is also an accurate model of "New Archangel," as the Russians called the colony they built on the ruins of Indian Sitka. It shows where the Russians built boats, milled flour, cast bells for California missions, and cut ice from Swan Lake to ship to gold rush-booming San Francisco bars.

For almost ten years, Sitka's town jewel, St. Michael's Cathedral, dating from 1844, was missing. Russian-built with onion dome and carrot spire, the building burned in 1966, leaving a heart-breaking void smack in the middle of the main street. During the fire, everyone turned out. Through superhuman effort (maybe a miracle), most of the religious objects that could be carried, or that weren't fastened down, were saved.

St. Michael's Bishop Gregory was born in Kiev. He has a special affinity for the charming church. The ceremonies making him the first bishop of Sitka and Alaska to be consecrated in the Alaska diocese were celebrated in the replica of the church, even before it was completely rebuilt.

The new cathedral stands downtown in the center of Lincoln Street. The Bishop stewards the lovely old treasures with TLC. Among them are ornate gospel books, including one from Fort Ross, chalices, crucifixes, some much-used wedding crowns, and an altar cloth said to have been worked by Princess Maksoutoff herself. There are many priceless icons, religious portraits in oil with only faces and hands exposed, the rest covered with ornate silver and gold-wrought frames.

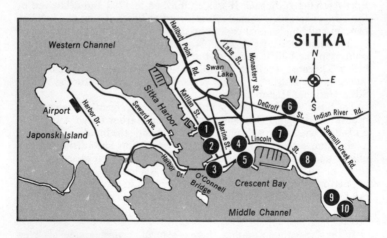

### Points of Interest

1) Russian Cemetery
2) Block House
3) Castle Hill
4) Saint Michael's Cathedral
5) Centennial Bldg., Visitor Bureau
6) Sitka National Cemetery
7) Sheldon Jackson College
8) Sheldon Jackson Museum
9) Sitka National Historical Park
10) Tlingit Fort

The Sitka Madonna icon was presented to the church by Russian American Company workers. Nearby, the Russian Mission Orphanage building dates from 1842. It is now being restored as a National Historic Landmark by the National Park Service. The staff is enthusiastic, from students to "Double O's" ("Older Ones"). Many of the latter are retired Alaskans living in the Pioneer Home, the big building dominating the downtown square and marked by a flourishing hedge of Sitka roses. On the lawn, a two-ton bronze statue of a grizzled prospector honors all "sourdoughs." Some of the Double O's are history buffs who lived through much of Alaska's lively early-20th-century history.

For photos, atmosphere, and orientation, the best spot is up some steps to the top of "Castle Hill," west of Saint Michael's. This promontory in downtown Sitka was the site of many major historical happenings. The "castle" of first Governor Alexander Baranof is long gone now, of course. What's left are some venerable cannons, a number with Russian markings. They point west to the Pacific Ocean past the lovely, island-flecked harbor and Mt. Edgecumbe, an extinct volcano that looks like a mini-Fujiyama.

Note the only other furnishing—a flagpole. Every October 18, everyone gathers around it, many wearing period costumes, the men with beards and the ladies with bonnets. Then they reenact the same ceremonies, lowering the Russian Double Eagle flag and raising the American flag that in 1867 marked the transfer of Russian America to the United States. Congress promptly renamed the new territory "Alaska." Here, too, on January 3, 1959, was raised the first 49-star American flag, signifying Alaska statehood.

From Castle Hill, the newer landmarks are obvious, such as modern hotels that contrast with the distinctive vintage buildings, and the John O'Connell Bridge. It connects Sitka's island with Japonski Island, where the Mt. Edgecumbe Alaska Native boarding high school, hospital and jet airport are located.

North of Castle Hill you can visit a crumbling old cemetery where a Russian princess is buried. She is said to have cried as she stood beside her husband, Governor Maksoutoff, during the transfer ceremonies.

Sitka's Indian side is well represented at Sitka National Historical Park, beginning with totem poles in front of the building and along a shady lane that leads to the old fort site. The Park is across town from Castle Hill and the Russian Cemetery. Inside the attractive Visitor Center, The Battle for Alaska is replayed in audio-visual, and there is a magnificent display of original totemic art. In the Indian Cultural Workshop rooms, artisans revive old crafts from wood carving to the difficult, almost lost, art of Chilkat blanket weaving.

Sitka's Russian past is reflected in the Russian Bishop's House on Lincoln Street, near Crescent Harbor. Built in 1842 for Alaska's first

Russian Orthodox Bishop, it's now part of the Historical Park. It's one of the few Russian log structures remaining in Alaska. Currently undergoing renovation, it's not open to the public.

At the nearby Sheldon Jackson College campus, the museum collection started by this early day missionary and educator also displays prized items, both Russian and Indian, including a detailed diorama of the original Indian Village. Take a walking tour of the campus and you'll see such historic buildings as Pittsburgh House, on the site of the first indoor bathtub in Sitka! The original school started in 1878 and evolved into a high school and now a college.

Before the bridge, a small ferry carried everyone back and forth for a few cents. All luggage and freight went to town aboard army "ducks," the amphibian craft developed during World War II. No one denies the convenience of the graceful-looking bridge, but visitor-wise the little ferry was a gem. Rubbing shoulders and talking with residents while crossing the harbor and admiring Sitka's marvelous setting made a captivating introduction. And it was a great unwinder after the jet speed arrival at the airport.

Over the years, Sitka's fortune has fluctuated with fishing and seafood processing plants, a Japanese-owned pulp mill, and federal government agencies. Just as the residents were adapting to sea invasion by the state ferries and a growing number of cruise ships, they were propelled into the jet set. Alaska Airlines inaugurated the Sitka air gateway to Alaska in 1967. Altogether, this has led to a fast-developing new industry, tourism, and in one way or another most of the residents are involved. There are evening cruises out of Crescent Harbor near the Centennial Building. Allen Marine Tours sail at 7 P.M. every evening in summer to touch on the scenic, the wild, the historical and even the industrial facets of Sitka as the ship sails by the pulpmill waterfront.

## Juneau, the Capital

Although the state capital is on the mainland, getting there by road is out of the question. Access is only by sea and air.

The Juneau office for Alaska Exploration Holidays and Cruises, in the Baranof Hotel, has brochures and a travel counselor with information on available optional tour packages. Gray Line, also in the Baranof, and Alaska Sight-Seeing Co., Cape Fox Sheffield House, offer local motorcoach tours daily in summer.

This northerly part of the Panhandle is set off by mountain barriers, including a formidable expanse of ice and snow, the Juneau Icefield. Lurking just beyond the mountains towering over the city, the approximately 4,000 square mile icefield is the source of all the glaciers in the

**JUNEAU**

## Points of Interest

1) Four Story Totem
2) Governor's Mansion
3) Grave of Joe Juneau and Dick Harris
4) Harris & Juneau Monument
5) House of Wickersham
6) Memorial Library and Totem
7) Native Crafts Exhibit (Federal Bldg.)
8) Old Russian Church
9) Plaque to Chief Kowee
10) State Capitol Bldg.
11) State Museum
12) State Office Bldg.
13) Log Cabin Visitor Center
14) Marine Park with Visitor Info.

area, including the Mendenhall Glacier, about 13 miles from downtown Juneau.

Besides being a main visitor attraction, the Mendenhall has been a good neighbor, obligingly retreating over some years now, making room for Juneau to expand into the suburbs. Less than 50 years ago, the glacier covered the rocks on which the Visitor Center now stands. Now the area formerly covered by the glacier is taken over by a jet airport, a modern shopping center, homes built on property with some very fine views, and camp and picnic grounds. No one seems particularly worried about the rumor that a cooler weather cycle may be due which could cause the glacier to start advancing again.

You can drive up and look the glacier in its mile-and-a-half wide, 100- to 200-foot high face. It is reflected in Mendenhall Lake, formed by melting ice, beginning about 1900. The displays in the Visitor Center tell about the plant and animal life supported in this recreational area. It's open 9 to 9 daily in summer; on weekends the rest of the year. Hiking trails take off from the center and also many other places in and around Juneau.

In 1980, the capital celebrated its centennial with special events all year. Some of the projects are now permanent attractions, such as the Visitor Center at Third and Main. This replica of an early log cabin church is a quaint contrast to the surrounding modern government buildings, the Capitol, the State Office Building, and the State Court Building, all metal and glass, and the tallest structure, the Federal Building.

Pick up a walking map (most businesses have them) and it will also lead you to some surprises, remainders from earlier days. The Governor's Mansion is colonial-style, its tall, smooth supporting pillars on the porch contrasting with nearby Indian totem poles. At Fifth and Gold streets, the tiny onion-domed St. Nicholas Russian Orthodox Church, dating from 1894, is a standout, though surrounded by other buildings now. It's not far from the landmark hotel, the Baranof. Juneau's award-winning Marine Park along the busy waterfront is a great place to meet the locals. There may be swinging entertainment, such as the "Natural Gas Jazz Band" livening up an occasion, perhaps the Fourth of July. There is also an information kiosk by the seaplane docks and Merchant's Wharf shopping mall, manned by volunteers in summer. Start from here and follow the map from the waterfront on up as high as you want to climb. Once you head away from Gastineau Channel, the route is increasingly verticle, up narrow streets and wooden stairways, past homes clinging to town-confining Mt. Juneau and Mt. Roberts.

The Alaska State Museum in the subport area houses excellent Indian displays, rocks and minerals, and mounted wildlife specimens.

Ramps instead of stairs, a boon to the handicapped, lead to upper levels. High on a slanty street overlooking Juneau is a small house-museum. James Wickersham, a judge, historian, and collector of Alaskan treasures lived here early in the century. Now, his niece, Ruth Allman, is hostess and narrator. She displays his artifacts and memorabilia, and tops the visit with her special "Flaming Sourdough Treat." Tickets and reservations are needed to put your name in her sourdough pot. (See "Museums" in *Practical Information* at the end of this section.)

A ghost of Juneau's golden past haunts the slopes of Mount Roberts. Some ruins of buildings of the Alaska-Juneau Mine that produced over $80 million in gold before it was closed in 1944 are reminders that, before government, gold was a bigger business. Rich strikes by Joe Juneau and Dick Harris were made here in 1880, before the mad rushes elsewhere. The stampede that followed their discoveries settled Juneau, the first "Alaska" town, following the Purchase. Across the Douglas Bridge and south from Sandy Beach, there are remains of the Treadwell Mine. Old pilings along the shore and rusting machinery in the woods give little hint now that here was a mine even bigger than the A–J.

By 1900, there was agitation to move the capital from Sitka to booming Juneau. The reason? Sitka was considered too isolated and far off the beaten track to be the seat of government. Legislators argued that the capital should be nearer the population center. In 1906, the deed was done.

Ironically, in 1974 the vote favored moving the capital from Juneau's 20,000 population area to a spot between the state's two largest cities. In 1976, voters approved a site near Willow, deemed within easier reach of over half of the state's residents, although it is wilderness. Since then there have been some second thoughts.

Estimates from the drawing board indicated that a lot of pipeline revenue might be consumed by rebuilding from scratch and by moving costs; the money might be used to better advantage. Then, too, many have a genuine appreciation for Juneau's capital attributes, located as it is amid Southeast Alaska's great recreational opportunities. Funding for the capital move was defeated in the 1982 election. At this writing, whether the issue is dead or dormant is anyone's guess.

## Glacier Bay

Two hundred years ago, no visitors saw Glacier Bay. It was only a dent in an icy shoreline. Captain George Vancouver sailed by an icy shoreline in 1794. Over the next hundred years, due to a warming trend and some earthquakes, the ice rivers melted and retreated with amazing speed up their fjord-like inlets, forming Glacier Bay. Nature's healing touch followed, repairing the scars of the glacier-scoured shores by covering them with lush rain forests that attracted abundant wildlife. The unusual icy wilderness also attracted naturalist John Muir, in 1879. He was fascinated by the flora, fauna and sea life. The Indians called the area "Thunder Bay," because of the sound effects caused by the calving of glaciers dropping huge ice chunks into the bay. Muir's namesake glacier has now retreated miles farther up the bay from the small cabin next to its face, where the naturalist lived while taking his notes. This glacier and others have left miles of waterways for birds, seals, whales, porpoises, and adventurous visitors.

Glacier Bay National Park, where nature has stored her great collection of tidewater glaciers, continues to attract nature lovers, wildlife watchers, and fishermen. Cruise ships bring their passengers up the Bay for closeups of glacier grandeur, the highlight of an Inside Passage voyage. Charter boats are available that explore the Bay and also other photo-worthy waters such as Tracy Arm. "On your owners" can contact the Park Headquarters for essential information on camping and recreation in the monument. Tour groups visit via Alaska Airlines scheduled flights from Juneau that take only 12 minutes to Gustavus Airport. From there it's ten miles by bus through mossy forest to overnight in Glacier Bay Lodge. Next morning, the lodge cruise boat *Thunder Bay* takes them to the glaciers.

## Gracious Living in the Ice Age

The epitome of wining and dining in unusual places is the *Glacier Bay Explorer,* forerunner of the growing fleet of Explorer Class™ ships. An evening cruise of the most active calving glaciers, Margerie and her neighbor Grand Pacific, and Lamplugh Glacier, is a highlight of the *Glacier Bay Explorer*'s day in Glacier Bay. Based in Juneau in summer, she is positioned to explore other destinations in the northern Panhandle as well. Her sister ships, the *Majestic Alaska Explorer* and the *Great Rivers Explorer,* cruise the length of the Inside Passage out of Ketchikan, and also include a memorable day in Glacier Bay.

No two cruises are exactly alike—that's part of the adventure—but glacier watching is spectacular, whether from the decks, the Vista View Lounge, or the dining room with picture windows. A tumbling icy-blue face of a glacier and the towering Fairweather Mountain Range behind is a wide-screen spectacular.

The captains are alerted for bow landing possibilities. At some glaciers they can nose the *Explorer* into shore and the crew extends a stair-stepped ramp through an opening in the bow. Then everyone can walk ashore to observe a surprising variety of small plants reinvading the recently (comparatively speaking) glacier-scoured terrain.

As the lush rain forests disappear and the vegetation dwindles, the up-Bay boat seems to be taking a trip back to the Ice Age. A Park Service naturalist is aboard to interpret the many facets of this most unusual national park, making the trip a learning experience. Everyone is encouraged to share what they see and it's relayed over the loudspeaker. Perhaps a black bear will amble over a talus slope. For sure there will be goats gamboling on 5,000-foot Mt. Wright. The *Explorer* quietly approaches nesting sites in the Marble Islands. Wherever food is plentiful—fish, plankton, shrimp stirred up in shallows by the tide—there'll be flocks of sea birds: puffins, scoters, oystercatchers, cormorants, phalaropes, kittiwakes, guillemots, murrelets, and assorted gulls. More than 200 species have been sighted, plus shorebirds, including the ptarmigan (the state bird) and the majestic bald eagle.

And you'll learn about ice, which is usually near at hand. It's scooped up, pure and crystal clear, as needed for the bar. Bartenders swear it lasts longer than the mundane ice cube. Their authority is the ranger who explains how snowflakes fall high in the mountains, granulize, and become highly compressed on their hundred-year trip to salt water; thus works nature's slow-motion, automatic ice machine.

The longer the time spent in the monument, the better. It's possible to combine tours and cruises and optional flightseeing and fishing packages available from the lodge.

Personnel of Glacier Bay Lodge and the adjacent Park Service Headquarters work together to see that monument visitors get the most out of their stay. Enlightening films and talks are scheduled in the lodge in the evening. Naturalists escort daily walks on nearby rain forest trails and along the living water line. One trek that is never the same twice is through the fleeting world of sea creatures and plants revealed for a short time at low tide before being claimed again by the sea.

### Fjord-like Lynn Canal

Captain George Vancouver, famous British explorer (and name dropper), discovered this waterway in 1794. Assuming it connected with other seas, he called it Lynn Canal, after King's Lynn, his home in England. Actually, this fjord stretches north of Juneau and after sixty scenic miles deadends at Skagway.

Almost 200 years later, a Seattle-based travel company, Westours, in a sense rediscovered Lynn Canal. They felt that this area, bordered by snowy mountains, glaciers, steep timbered slopes, and supporting a wealth of sea and bird life, should be seen in broad daylight. And so they altered their cruise pattern along the Inside Passage and added a specially built day cruiser for the best viewing of Lynn Canal's choice assets.

Their big, world-class cruise ships sail north from Vancouver, B.C., and turn around at Juneau. From there passengers switch to the *Fairweather,* which links the longer sea leg with tour destinations throughout the heart of Alaska. Though smaller, the smooth, fast *Fairweather* has maximum creature comforts. They include a narrator and four attentive hostesses, besides the captain and crew, seats that recline, and cocktails for sale. A feast for the eyes is right outside the extra-large picture windows and is augmented by complimentary beverages and a hearty snack, served up with tidbits of local lore.

Informality is the keynote during the 5½-hour cruise. You'll learn about nature and how to identify whales, porpoises, seals, and seabirds. In season fishing boats will be netting salmon, king to sockeye. And you'll have your turn to see the view from the bridge, to scan the radar, to study the charts, to peek at the log, and to pick out some landmarks.

Most Westours comprehensive Alaska itineraries include the *Fairweather,* traveling either north or south. Northbound, after overnighting in Juneau, you are taken by motorcoach to the Yankee Cove Landing. It's several pleasant miles from the city, past green islands, quiet bays, and titillating glimpses of Juneau's most famous asset, the Mendenhall Glacier. Southbound, after overnighting at Skagway, passengers step on board at the gold rush town's famous harbor.

All three Explorer ships cruise the mountain-bordered upper reaches of Lynn Canal in daylight, and also schedule a port call at hospitable Haines in time for sightseeing and an evening salmon bake. Although highway and ferry travelers have long appreciated the community's high cultural levels and superb recreational opportunities, most big cruise ships pass by what looks like an old army post. Actually, the military-style buildings from the early 1900s surround a large parade ground and house a town, Port Chilkoot, and also a national historical site, home of the Chilkat Center for the Arts. After World War II, the town's founders bought the substantial but little-used Fort William H. Seward as army surplus, and moved in. Right next door is Haines, traditional in appearance and started by Presbyterian missionaries in 1881. These adjacent towns are now incorporated.

The Dalton Trail led from this area to the Klondike gold fields before the better-known Chilkoot Trail to the north. Enterprising Jack Dalton staked it out, based on a well-used Indian route to the interior. Then he got *his* gold by charging a substantial toll to use the trail.

## Haines

A missionary, S. Hall Young, and famous naturalist John Muir picked the site for this town meant to bring Christianity and education to the native Indians. The location is a beautiful one, on a heavily wooded peninsula with magnificent views up the Inside Passage and of the Coastal Mountain Range. Its Lynn Canal neighbors are Skagway, 15 miles to the north, and Juneau, about 75 miles to the south.

From religious beginnings in 1881, Haines by 1897 was a gateway and supply route to the Klondike in the Yukon via the Jack Dalton Trail. It boomed in 1898 when gold was discovered nearby in Porcupine (now deserted). In 1903, an army post was started at Portage Cove, just south of town, and by 1905, Fort William H. Seward had a full garrison with two companies of soldiers. By 1918 there were four companies, and Alaskans were drafted from there for World War I. In 1923, they changed the name to Chilkoot Barracks, and for nearly 20 years this was the only Army post in Alaska. World War II put all of Alaska on the map, and units from Chilkoot Barracks were the nucleus for military installations in bigger cities and places such as Cold Bay and Dutch Harbor out toward the Aleutian Islands.

After the war, the deactivated Chilkoot Barracks were sold to a group of veterans "lock, stock, and barrel," you might say. They renamed their purchase Port Chilkoot and considered developing the

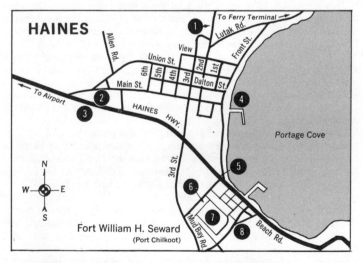

## Points of Interest

1) Mt. Ripinsky Trail
2) Visitor Information
3) Fairgrounds

4) Sheldon Museum
5) Mile 0 of the Haines Highway
6) Halsingland Hotel
7) Tribal House
8) Chilkat Center for the Arts

vast recreational possibilities of the beautiful area which so far had concentrated on such basic industries as fishing, fish processing, mining, and lumbering. The adjacent communities merged in 1970 becoming the City of Haines, combined population about 2,000.

Together, they now emphasize the hunting and fishing, and camping at Chilkoot Lake, Portage Cove, and Mosquito Lake (don't let the name deter you—it's beautiful there). They are all within easy driving distance and offer unusual bird-watching. Though eagles stay in the Chilkat Valley all year, they concentrate at about Mile 19 on the Haines Highway in the fall. Their white heads a standout against blue sky and foliage, hundreds cover the river flats and perch in the trees during November and December.

At the entrance to Haines, on Haines Highway, the Visitors Center is marked by impressive Welcome Totem Poles. They'll have maps, brochures, and suggestions for sightseeing and entertainment, camping, hiking, fishing, and other recreation. There is also an information desk at the Halsingland Hotel on the quadrangle of Port Chilkoot's Fort William Seward. They'll have information on local tours, times, and prices, and on subjects from bald eagle sightings to Indian dancing, performed frequently in summer.

"Haines Is for Hikers" is the lead for a folder describing the local trail systems. One system south of town on the Chilkat Peninsula takes in areas being developed as a large state park. Trails lead to Battery Point and Mt. Riley. The more strenuous one, the Mt. Ripinski Trail System, was named for a teacher in the Presbyterian boarding school, who settled in Haines in 1896. It's a day-long hike to the trail register on the higher northwest peak, but the view from the 3,610-foot summit is a photographer's delight on clear days: the contrasting communities; Lynn Canal bordered by its snowy mountains; waterfalls and alpine meadows.

In fact there is a great deal you can photograph in the area without such effort. You can drive toward the picturesque cannery at Letnikof Cove and take photos of the Davidson Glacier and the Rainbow, a hanging glacier that glistens in the sunshine and drops chunks of ice during rainy weather. And the walking tour of historic Fort William H. Seward is mostly a level one. A map and folder describing the buildings facing the parade ground gently guides visitors from one of the first buildings, the Cable Office, which is now an art shop, past officers' quarters, the former hospital, post exchange, barracks, and many more.

Totem Village, on the parade ground, includes a replica of a pioneer trapper's cabin and cache, a reproduction of a tribal house, an Indian drying and tanning rack for pelts, and a small collection of large totems. A totem pole 132½ feet tall, heralded as the world's largest, was carved here and dedicated to "all the Indians of southeastern Alaska." Exhibited in Japan's Expo '70 at the Alaska Pavilion, this mighty totem is now in the village of Kake, Alaska. Though not part of the original post, Totem Village belongs here as part of the heritage of the Chilkat Indians, represented in this living museum, which is still under renovation and reconstruction. You can enjoy a salmon bake here—the Port Chilkoot Potlatch. The fresh Lynn Canal salmon are baked nightly over an open fire.

There's a new museum built on the site of the surveys for the original mission, now the town of Haines. Sheldon Museum and Cultural Center is on hallowed ground donated by the United Presbyterian Church, at the end of Main Street, downtown near the waterfront. Don't miss seeing the priceless collections of community treasures, including those of the museum's founder, pioneer citizen Steve Sheldon (1885–1960).

## The Chilkat Indians

The Chilkat Indians, a branch of the Tlingits, were notoriously warlike a hundred years ago. Their strategic position helped them to guard mountain passes and waterways against most invaders who might have challenged them for the game-abundant forests and fish-filled fjords, lakes, and streams. They managed to keep most visitors at a distance, the better to enjoy their way of living, in which work alternated with periods of leisure when they had time for artistic pursuits, especially woodcarving, weaving, and dancing.

Since then, with the inevitable encroachment of people, ships, planes, and roads, much has changed—for better or worse, depending on your viewpoint.

Today some Chilkats still beat drums, flash spears, war dance, and perpetuate some of the old ways. They do it to help preserve some of the best of their culture, and for visitors. For a number of years now, friendly Chilkats in Haines have been reviving their arts and crafts under the direction of Carl Heinmiller, a white man from Ohio and an expert woodcarver. He started projects like totem pole carving, mask-and costume-making, and lively Indian dancing as antidotes for the lack of activities for young people—both Indian and white—in Port Chilkoot, then newly incorporated and isolated. An Eagle Scout himself, one of his first efforts was to organize a Boy Scout troop.

He figured Indian dancing was a logical study project for the area, as a starter. But Carl came up against a blank wall and a generation gap when he went for advice to the elders of the close-by old Indian village of Klukwan. They had to be convinced that the young people and Carl were seriously interested before they would pass on traditional dances and mask designs which had been inherited and were private clan property.

Through museum research Carl carved masks the Indians couldn't distinguish from their own, and he helped the young people study and prepare intricate dance costumes, until finally the key leaders were convinced. Once the youngsters started learning the chants and dances, there was no doubt of their enthusiasm. Girls were asked to join the activities, and the project grew into Alaska Youth, Inc., which has received some financial help from the government.

Carl was rewarded by the Indians. The Eagle (Scout) became a Raven in the clan, with a high and worthy Indian name. Since then the dancers have won honors in intertribal competitions, and have been ambassadors to cities in other parts of the world. In some places they left a souvenir at city hall—a carved totem pole.

The Chilkat Dancers are not the only result of Carl's help and concern for Native Alaskans. Alaska Youth evolved into Alaska Indian Arts, Inc. (A.I.A.), now directed by Carl's son Lee, while Carl assists and also serves as town magistrate. A.I.A., besides rekindling the natives' interest in their heritage, also provides employment for fishermen in the off-season, and for the handicapped. Handicapped himself since World War II, Carl understands the problems.

Though funding has been sporadic and the number of workers fluctuates accordingly, visitors always find the school intriguing. Inside the former fort hospital, now the Alaska Indian Arts Skill Center, people will be carving Alaska soapstone, jade, ivory, and wood, or perhaps etching silver, buffing copper, carving and painting wooden plaques, or making costumes. Outside, Tlingits may be carving a totem pole or other large item.

The fort gymnasium has been nicely remodeled as a little theater and is much used for community programs and plays. The Chilkat Dancers perform there when audiences are too big for the authentically reconstructed tribal house on the parade ground.

## The Canadian Connection via the Haines Highway

Haines is Mile 0 on the Haines Highway, a 159-mile road connecting the Marine Highway with the Alaska Highway at Haines Junction, Yukon Territory. Some people who take their cars on the ferry choose to disembark here and take this route to reach Anchorage or Fairbanks. Part of the Haines Highway follows the Dalton Trail.

The Haines Highway, skirting the eastern foothills of the St. Elias Mountains, leads over 3,493-foot Chilkat Pass, past snow-bordered lakes reflecting rugged mountains. This is the domain of snowpeaks, glaciers, glacial streams, and clear-water recreation lakes. Many travelers feel that the scenery along the Chilkat River estuary, which the highway parallels for 16 miles, is comparable to the Himalayas.

If you start early enough in the morning from either end of this highway there is time to sightsee and still reach the other end—seaward it's Haines; mountainward, the Alaska Highway—without being hampered by the lack of paving or the fact that the border closes up tight at night. If you have the time, it's well worth planning to stop over at one of the not-too-numerous resorts.

At Mile 21 a side road makes a 2-mile loop to the Chilkat village of Klukwan, one of the oldest Indian settlements of the region and for centuries before the white man a center of Tlingit culture. The American bald eagle, no stranger in southeast Alaska, arrives in the Klukwan area by the thousands in the autumn to feed on the late summer salmon run.

At Mile 27, Mosquito Lake state campground is located 2½ miles off the right side of the highway. The 33 Mile Roadhouse advertises the last gas for 92 miles; better tank up. At Mile 35, the abandoned Porcupine Mine and the ghost town of Porcupine can be seen across the Klehini River from the road. The asphalt road of Alaska gives way to the gravel of British Columbia at Mile 41. Depending on your direction of travel, you must stop at either U.S. or Canada Customs, almost next door to each other. No facilities or accommodations here, and they close up at night. Twenty-three miles onward, the road, after winding headily up a mountain, crosses 3,493-foot Chilkat Pass. At Mile 91 the road crosses into Yukon Territory. Two miles on are gas, a store, and a cafe. At Mile 97, just before the bridge, a trail leads leftward to Million Dollar Camp and waterfall, a fine picnic area. At Mile 106, a tight, twisty, rough road leads 2½ miles to the abandoned Dalton Post, established in 1892. At Mile 115, follow a sign that will send you off the road half a mile to Klukshu Indian village, a small settlement on the river of the same name. The village is on the old Dalton Trail. Good photographic possibilities in the village include: fish traps on the river banks, meat caches, log cabins, terrain of the Dalton Trail. At Mile 125, Lake Dezedeash Resort and Lodge, at the southern end of Dezedeash Lake, has rooms, horseback riding, fishing, restaurant, cocktail lounge, store, gas, garage, and complete hookups for trailers and campers open year-round, a gateway to Kluane National Park. (Write Haines Junction, Y.T., Canada YOB 1L0; [403] 634–2315.) Rooms, restaurant, cocktail lounge. At Mile 137 a side road on the left leads to Kathleen Lake Territorial Campground, with 30 campsites, kitchen, and boat launch. This lake has many grayling and rainbow trout and the rare kokanee, a landlocked salmon. Be sure to have the right license—or all three—for fishing in British Columbia, the Yukon Territory, and Alaska. Half a mile up the highway is Lake Kathleen Lodge, with rooms, restaurant, laundromat, and complete garage service (Mile 142, Haines Highway; [403] 634–2319). Haines Junction, less than 17 miles on, has tourist accommodations—rooms, store, garage. The Junction lies 98 miles west of Whitehorse on the Alaska Highway route from Dawson Creek.

## Skagway

Skagway, 17 miles north of Haines, is the last port of call on the Inside Passage. It was the end of the sea leg of a gold rusher's journey, and the jumping-off place for the arduous overland trek to reach Canada's rich Klondike gold fields. Technically, it's the same for visitors today, but they accomplish the feat in a fraction of the time, and with none of the discomforts.

Most of the cruise ships and ferries turn around here. (An exception is Westours world-class ships, which turn around at Juneau, where the *Fairweather* day boat shuttles between the capital and Skagway. Another exception is the Cunard *Princess*. She continues north to explore

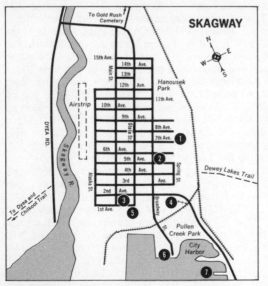

**SKAGWAY**

### Points of Interest

1) Trail of '98 Museum
2) Eagles Hall
3) Soapy's Parlor
4) RR Depot (Nat'l. Park Service Visitors Center)
5) Milepost 0 Klondike Highway 2
6) Ferry Dock
7) Cruise Ship Dock

College Fjord and Prince William Sound of the Gulf of Alaska and turns around at rail port Whittier near Anchorage.)

In Skagway, ships dock only a short walk from downtown—near the site of the famous gold rush gun duel between infamous outlaw "Soapy" Smith and good guy Frank Reid. Cruise ship passengers are primed for excursions to the summit of White Pass, or they may be on a tour continuing to the Interior and North.

By 1984, the Klondike Gold Rush National Historical Park Visitor Center is to move from the Arctic Brotherhood Hall to the refurbished vintage railroad depot. Ask them about sightseeing—even by horse-drawn buggy—about campgrounds at Prospector Park and Liarsville, and how to get to the Gold Rush Cemetery (about a mile and a half from downtown, where you can see graves of local gold rush legends), Reid Falls (a short hike from the cemetery), flower gardens, Skyline Trail to the top of AB Mountain, and to Upper and Lower Dewey Lakes for fishing. Hotels housing tour groups dispense tour and enter-tainment information and tickets at desks in their lobbies.

Skagway is an important link of the developing Klondike Gold Rush National Historical Park. It follows the historic path of the turn-of-the-century gold seekers, beginning in Seattle's Pioneer Square, the depar-ture point. In Skagway, a sizeable downtown section of business build-ings and homes—all listed in the National Register of Historic Places—is being restored. Two other segments of the Historical Park commemorate the Chilkoot Trail and the White Pass Trail. The project is international, as Canada develops portions from the summits of Chilkoot Pass and White Pass (International Boundary) all the way to Skagway's Canadian counterpart, Dawson City, of Klondike fame.

Skagway had only a single cabin, still standing, when the Yukon Gold Rush began. At first the argonauts swarmed to Dyea, nine miles west, but when it was found that a dock could be built at Skagway, this town became the great gateway to the Klondike. Skagway mush-roomed overnight into as rich and wild a mixture of people as Alaska ever knew. Three months after the first boat landed, in July 1897, Skagway numbered perhaps 20,000 persons, with well-laid-out streets, hotels, stores, saloons, gambling houses, and dance halls. By the spring of 1898, according to a Northwest Mounted Police report, "Skagway was little better than a hell on earth."

The exciting environs of Skagway, topped by 7,000-foot-high moun-tains, is matched by the flavor of the boardwalks, false-front buildings, and old stores along the dirt streets that extend from the dock. In all Alaska, there is no town to match the pioneer flavor of Skagway. "Progress," in terms of modernization, is resisted in favor of tourist appeal. However, the accommodations are not only interesting and comfortable but also most attractive, such as the lately built, modern

Westours Klondike, and Alaska's oldest, the modernized Golden North Hotel. The friendly residents will keep you busy for as long as you stay with their list of things to see and do.

In this town of about 800 people, time is kept standing still. To hear the locals talk, it was only yesterday that Soapy Smith, Alaska's most notorious outlaw, and Frank Reid, representing the forces of law and order, met in mortal confrontation.

Volumes have been written about the heyday of this lively ghost town. You'll likely see them well displayed in souvenir shops, among them Mike Miller's *Soapy,* Howard Clifford's *Skagway Story,* and Archie Satterfield's *Chilkoot Pass.*

The gist of the Smith-Reid encounter was that bad guy Smith and vigilante good guy Reid met down at the dock and shot it out on a pleasant July evening in 1898. Smith died instantly; Reid passed away 12 days later. Both men are buried in the Gold Rush Cemetery.

The town built a huge monument at Reid's grave, and with a simple inscription summed up what he meant to the honest citizens: "He gave his life for the honor of Skagway." The original gravestone of Soapy Smith was whittled away by souvenir hunters, and now only a simple plank marks his burial place.

However, his "hangout" still exists. Soapy Smith's Parlor and Museum, on First Avenue, near the site of the gun battle, is privately owned. Sometimes it's open so visitors can see inside the quaint little building. The Trail of '98 Museum, Seventh Avenue and Spring Street, is open every day in summer so that visitors have every opportunity to see a fascinating collection owned and operated by the citizens of Skagway. The museum is on the second floor of the first granite building in Alaska. It was scheduled to be a college in 1900, but became a federal courthouse instead. The city of Skagway bought it in 1956. City offices are on the first floor. Above you can browse as long as you wish over old court records preserved under glass, including Frank Reid's will and the papers disposing of Soapy's estate. Besides Native artifacts, memorabilia of pioneers, stampeders, and the Arctic Brotherhood, there are unusual miscellaneous items. How about a blanket made from the skin of duck necks and fortified by pepper bags sewn behind the skins for moth protection? The gambling paraphernalia from the old Board of Trade Saloon is on display, and on the grounds is a vintage White Pass & Yukon Route steam locomotive.

Local residents are full of enthusiasm. In summer they stage "The Soapy Smith Show" and "Skaguay in the Days of '98," with cancan girls, and preceded by play money gambling, in the Eagles Hall, 6th and Broadway.

You can drive—or take a taxi—to Dyea, where a tent city of 10,000 sprang up overnight. Here the Klondike-bound began the long, agonizing trek to a lake, where they built boats to continue onward. The fearsome Chilkoot Trail, starting from near sea level, climbed a perilous slope to 3,739-foot Chilkoot Pass. They say that if a climber had to step out of line, he could freeze to death before someone would stop long enough to let him get back in. The last half mile was so steep that some enterprising souls built a "stairway" to the top, cutting 1,500 steps—and charged those who used the stairway a heavy toll. In 1898 an avalanche at Sheep Creek swept more than 60 men to their death. Many lie in Slide Cemetery, near the Dyea townsite.

For more than 60 years the Chilkoot Trail lay silent and in time became overgrown. Then the state began to clear and restore the trail, starting from the beach at Dyea to the Canadian border. The hike today is still not an easy one, but from the heights there are impressive panoramas. Many mementos of the early Chilkoot Trail are around, so the hike is a walk through history. Each year hikers make the trip to Lake Lindeman or Lake Bennett, where they can continue to Whitehorse or return to Skagway by train, if the WP & YR is tracking again. Make arrangements for train tickets ahead, either direction. Guides are available in Skagway for those who want to follow the Chilkoot Pass Trail from Dyea to Dawson. The Klondike Gold Rush Park Visitor Center has maps and brochures. Or write to the Superintendent, Klondike Gold Rush National Historical Park, Box 517, Skagway, AK 98840.

# PRACTICAL INFORMATION FOR SOUTHEAST ALASKA

**HOW TO GET THERE. By air:** From Seattle, *Alaska Airlines* serves Southeastern points: "First City" Ketchikan, Wrangell, Petersburg, Juneau, Sitka, and Yakutat. *Western* flies to Ketchikan and Juneau via Seattle, Portland, or Salt Lake City. There are no major jet carriers that fly directly to Haines or Skagway, but *L.A.B. Flying Service* and *Air America* fly to both from Juneau. Because of deregulation, route shifting, and rumors of airline mergers, air travelers should see their travel agents or contact airlines directly for current information on schedules and fares—and Southeast gateways.

**By water.** *Ferry:* The ferries of the Southeast System of the *Alaska Marine Highway* broke the isolation of the Inside Passage towns in 1963. They connect Seattle and/or Prince Rupert with southeast Alaska ports. The main ports are Haines, Juneau, Ketchikan, Petersburg, Skagway, Sitka and Wrangell.

Largest of the ferry fleet is the *MV Columbia,* which carries 1,000 passengers, 184 vehicles, and has 96 staterooms. The *Malaspina, Matanuska,* and *Taku,* also named for big Alaskan glaciers, are not much smaller. More like liners than ferryboats, most have cocktail lounges, cafeterias, and solariums. Reserve staterooms. Otherwise it is acceptable to sleep in a reclining deck chair between ferry ports, or roll out on deck in a sleeping bag. Public washrooms with showers are available.

Whether you travel on foot, or by car or camper, motor bike or bicycle, the Inside Passage is a popular and scenic alternate route to driving the whole distance on the Alaska Highway. Passenger and vehicle fares are rated on a through basis, with no charge for stopovers. Foot passengers simply get a stopover from the purser. Vehicle space has to be reserved ahead, when you buy your ticket. Cabin fare is port-to-port for one continuous trip. Meals are not included. The fare structure is complex, depending on numerous variables including the size of the vehicle you're traveling with. The schedule is also involved, and departures sometimes depend on the right time and tide. Distances are figured in hours of running time, rather than miles. Seattle to Skagway is about a thousand miles, or about 60 hours, if all goes well. It's about 6 hours Ketchikan to Wrangell, the next port, and 3 to Petersburg, beyond. It takes only an hour from Haines to Skagway. Three smaller ferries connect with smaller ports with intriguing names: Metlakatla, Hollis, Hoonah, Angoon, and Pelican. The *LeConte, Chilkat,* and *Aurora* ferries have no staterooms, but do have cafeterias and snack and liquor bars. Write to *Alaska Marine Highway,* Division of Marine Transportation, Pouch R, Juneau, AK 99881; phone (907) 465-3941 or 465-3940. In Seattle: Pier 48, Seattle, WA 98104; (206) 623-1970. **Be sure to reserve well in advance.**

Contact the *B.C. Ferry Corp.,* 1045 Howe St., Vancouver, B.C. V6Z 2A9, Canada, about Canadian ferries operating between Vancouver Island, and Prince Rupert, B.C., Canada. These connect with the Alaska ferry system.

*Cruise ship:* The strong competition along the Alaska cruise route continues. Watch for promotional schemes, including fly-frees, or with discounts, from home to embarkation point, intended to woo cruisers. Contact your travel agent or send for information and brochures from the following companies and compare before choosing among many fine ships being dispatched to Alaska this summer.

*Canadian Cruise Lines, Ltd.* 1204 Wharf St., #401, Victoria, BC V8W 389, Canada; (604) 386-3844. 8-day, 7-night cruises on the *Prince George* from Vancouver, B.C., were priced from $695 in 1983. *Costa Cruises,* One Biscayne Tower, Miami, FL 33131; phone (800) 447-6877. 7-day round trip from Vancouver on the *Daphne* priced from $895 in 1984. *Cunard Line, Ltd.,* 555 Fifth Ave., New York, NY 10017; (800) 223-0764. 7-day cruises from Vancouver to Whittier (near Anchorage) on the *Cunard Princess,* and the reverse, from $1,090 in 1983. *Exploration Cruise Lines,* 1500 Metropolitan Park Bldg., Seattle, WA 98101; (206) 624-8551. Call collect in Washington state and (800) 426-0600 in rest of U.S. 8-day/7-night round-trip cruises from Ketchikan along the length of Alaska's Inside Passage on the *Majestic Alaska Explorer* and the *Great Rivers*

*Explorer* are priced from $1,394 in 1984. They also offer 3-night segments from $599, and 4-night segments from $789. Fares for the 1984 *Glacier Bay Explorer* Northern Panhandle (including Glacier Bay) cruises out of Juneau are from $439 for the 4-day/3-night, and from $329 for the 3-day/2-night cruises. *Holland America Cruises,* 2 Pennsylvania Plaza, New York, NY 10121; (212) 947–8959; toll-free (800) 221–3842 or 223–0550. 7-day cruises out of Vancouver on the *Nieuw Amsterdam, Noordam* and the *SS Rotterdam. Norwegian American Cruises,* 29 Broadway, New York, NY 10006; (212) 422–3900 in New York City; (800) 221–2400 rest of U.S. 14-day round trips on the *Sagafjord* out of San Francisco to the Gulf of Alaska and Columbia Glacier, from $2,890 in 1983. *Princess Cruises,* 2029 Century Park East, Los Angeles, CA 90067; (213) 553–7000. Call toll-free (800) 421–1600. 12-night round-trip cruises on the *Pacific Princess* out of San Francisco, from $2,676 in 1983. 7-night cruises out of Vancouver on the *Sun Princess* from $1,267 in 1983. 8-night cruises round trip from Vancouver on the *Island Princess,* from $1,600 in 1983. *Royal Viking Line,* One Embarcadero Center, San Francisco, CA 94111; (415) 398–8000; toll-free (800) 422–8000, 12-day round-trip cruises from San Francisco on the *Royal Viking Star,* from $2,424 in 1984. *Sitmar Cruises,* 10100 Santa Monica Blvd., Los Angeles, CA 90067; (213) 553–1666; toll-free (800) 421–0880. 14-day cruises on the *TSS Fairsea* from San Francisco, priced from $2,395 in 1984. *World Explorer Cruises,* 3 Embarcadero Center, San Francisco, CA 94111; toll-free, (800) 222–2255 in California; (800) 854–3835, rest of U.S. 14-day academic program cruises on the *SS Universe* from Vancouver, from $1,495 in 1983.

The *Cruise Lines International Association* (CLIA) keeps track of some 87 ships which practically covers the world. The rundown, including ships cruising seasonally to Alaska, is given in their *CLIA News about Cruises,* sent out from 17 Battery Pl., Suite 631, New York, NY 10004; (212) 425–7400.

**By car.** You can drive to the Southeast, but the only access highways taking off from the Alaska Highway are the 110-mile Klondike Hwy. 2 and the 159-mile Haines Hwy. leading to the two northernmost ports in the Panhandle: Skagway and Haines.

**By bus.** Bus service is available during the summer from Canada to Skagway via *Alaskan-Yukon Motorcoaches,* 327 F St., Anchorage, AK 99501; (907) 276–1305 or 555 Fourth and Battery Bldg., Seattle, WA 98121; (206) 682–4104.

 **CLIMATE AND WHAT TO WEAR.** The climate is comparable to the rest of the Pacific Northwest, but wetter. Don't complain about the rain to a native; they brag about it. It's been measured on a gauge that says at the top, "Busted in 1949—202.55 inches!" in Ketchikan. They even drink to it there in a waterfront bar, *The Rainbird.* Summer highs are in the mid-60s; winter lows, low 20s. Full raingear that is light and easy to pack is a must. Include something to keep your feet dry on city streets or while exploring and hiking farther afield. Lightweight sneakers, pants suits, and slacks are comfortable for spring and summer. In autumn, the days may still be mild, but warmer

slack outfits and perhaps a convertible-type topcoat will feel good for cooler evenings. In winter, add some wool, an overcoat or parka, heavier shoes or boots, head and hand covering, and you'll be up to anything going on out-of-doors.

Although clothing is casual aboard the cruise ships, as a rule there are also opportunities to dress up. Women may want to take an evening dress and men a jacket and tie. Just ask ahead about how formal or informal it may be aboard the particular ship you choose. Then you'll also be prepared for any special nights out in town.

**GETTING INTO TOWN. Ketchikan:** Flights land at Ketchikan International Airport on Gravina Island across Tongass Narrows from Revillagigedo Island. Ferries make the 10-minute trip every half-hour from the airport to the Airport Ferry Terminal (near the State Ferry Terminal) on Revillagigedo for $1.75. There is regular bus service to town and taxis available.

**Wrangell:** Ferries and cruise ships dock close to downtown. If you arrive at the airport, taxis are available, but may be expensive—even if shared. Inquire from your hotel about courtesy service from the airport.

**Petersburg:** The airport is a mile from town; ferries dock nearly a mile south of Petersburg. Taxis meet both planes and ferries.

**Juneau:** Docks are downtown. Air passengers can take a bus to town from the airport—about 9 miles for around $5. A Haida Cab will cost about the same per person, if you can find others to share it. Cars are for rent at the airport and in town. Reserve ahead for one if the state legislature is in town; sometimes they run into the tourist season in June and space may be tight.

**Sitka:** Ferries dock about 7 miles from town. Buses run to downtown hotels from the dock and airport. There are also taxis and cars for rent.

**Haines:** If arriving by plane, arrange for transportation in advance with your hotel. The airport is 3.5 miles from Haines. The ferry terminal, also about 3.5 miles out of town has bus service into Haines. You can also call Eagle Taxi for 24-hour service: 766–2171.

**Skagway:** There is taxi service year-round. You'll have to inquire at the *Alaska Liquor Store,* Second and Broadway, about car rentals.

**HOTELS AND MOTELS.** Lodging prices tend to be lower in the Southeast than in the big cosmopolitan areas. Mostly they fall into the *Moderate* to *Expensive* range (plus tax). *Deluxe* here will mean "Alaska Deluxe"—the best available, probably the most expensive, and considered tops by the local residents. Based on double occupancy, a *deluxe* room will probably cost over $80 per night. *Expensive* will probably be $60–80; *moderate,* $45–60; and *inexpensive,* under $45. (Be aware that the number of available rooms in hotels in small towns is not overwhelming. Reserve ahead, unless you are prepared to camp out.)

## KETCHIKAN
### (Zip Code 99901)

**Gilmore Hotel.** *Moderate.* 326 Front St.; (907) 225–2174. 42 rooms at downtown waterfront near restaurants and shopping; airporter bus service. Newly renovated with color TV; phones; cocktail lounge.

**Hilltop Motel.** *Moderate.* 3434 Tongass Ave.; (907) 225–5166. 46 units across from air and ferry terminals. Two levels, large rooms. Family-type. Restaurant and cocktail lounge.

**Ingersoll Hotel.** *Moderate.* 303 Mission St.; (907) 225–2124. Historic downtown 54-room, three-story hotel, with front rooms overlooking the waterfront. Restaurant; lounge; and deli-sandwich shop.

**Super 8 Motel.** *Moderate.* 2151 Sea Level Dr. (near Airport Ferry terminal); toll-free (800) 843–1991; (907) 225–9088 in Ketchikan. "First City" is the first Alaskan city to have a member of this chain. Newly opened with 83 rooms, among them 6 suites with view of Tongass Narrow. Many "extras" included; some rooms with water beds; some special rooms for handicapped persons; and a freezer to hold the catch of visiting fishermen.

## WRANGELL
### (Zip Code 99929)

**Roadhouse Lodge.** *Moderate.* Box 1199; (907) 874–2335. Four miles out the Zimovia Highway, but they'll send courtesy car. Lounge and restaurant; dancing. They also have bikes and cars for rent and offer hiking, charter fishing, tours, and outdoor fish bakes.

**Stikine Inn.** *Moderate.* Box 990; (907) 874–3388 or 874–3389. 16 rooms, with television; coffee shop; dining room; bar. Free phone. Liquor store. A block from ferry; overlooks city dock.

**Thunderbird Hotel.** *Moderate to Inexpensive.* 223 Front St., Box 110; (907) 874–3322. 36 rooms, all with bath, TV, phone. Free coffee in lobby; laundromat adjoining. Downtown.

## PETERSBURG
### (Zip Code 99833)

**Tides Inn.** *Expensive.* 1 mi. W. of ferry terminal, N. 1st & D Sts.; (907) 772–4288. Modest-size motel, with 23 units. Free continental breakfast. Hunting and fishing information, charters.

**Beachcomber Inn.** *Moderate.* 4 miles south of town, Box 1027; (907) 772–3215. Homey, once a cannery. Boats and float planes tie up at dock. Rooms with baths; restaurant and bar. A picturesque setting and a local favorite.

**King Salmon Motel.** *Moderate.* Box 869; (907) 772–3291. Handy to ferry dock. Restaurant and bar.

**Mitkof Hotel.** *Inexpensive.* Box 689; (907) 772–4251. Over 70 years established downtown. Color TV and phones. Has clean, comfortable rooms with and without bath.

## SITKA
### (Zip Code 99835)

**Shee Atika Lodge.** *Deluxe.* Box 78; toll-free (800) 426–0670 (inc. AK and HI); in Washington State call (800) 552–7122; (902) 747–6241. Now a Vance Corporation hotel. 97 rooms. Native Corporation-built hotel across from convention center. Features large public areas and Alaska Indian Art Shop.

**Sheffield House.** *Deluxe.* Box 318; toll-free (800) 544–0970; in Alaska call collect (907) 274–6631. On the waterfront overlooking marina. 80 rooms, banquet facilities, dining room, lounge, disco, and boat dock.

**Potlatch House.** *Moderate.* 709 Katlian St., Box 58; (907) 747–3288. Several blocks from downtown, but there is a courtesy car. Mt. Edgecumbe and harbor view.

**Sitka Hotel.** *Moderate.* 118 Lincoln St., Box 679; (907) 747–3288. Downtown hotel with elevator and 24-hour phone service. 60 rooms, some with choice harbor and island views. Easy walking to historic sites from Tlingit Indian/Russian American/Alaska Territorial past.

## JUNEAU
### (Zip Code 99801)

**Baranof Hotel.** *Deluxe.* 127 Franklin St.; toll-free (800) 544–0970; in Alaska call collect (907) 274–6631. 225 rooms, in the center of town. Telephone; TV; restaurant; bar; banquet and meeting rooms; 7-day-a-week coffee shop.

**Cape Fox Sheffield House Juneau.** *Deluxe.* 51 W. Egan Dr.; toll-free (800) 544–0970; in Alaska call collect (907) 274–6631. 104 rooms with first-run color movies. Banquet and meeting facilities. Downtown. Restaurant; lounge.

**Prospector Hotel.** *Expensive.* 375 Whittier Ave., in Sub-port area; (907) 586–3737. Modest-size hotel with full facilities. Restaurant, bar. Sightseeing tours available.

**Alaskan Hotel.** *Moderate* (for rooms with baths) to *Inexpensive* (for rooms without baths). 167 S. Franklin St.; (907) 586–1000. In downtown historic area. Rustic bar; health spa.

**Bergman Hotel.** *Moderate* (for rooms with baths) *to Inexpensive* (for rooms without baths). 434 Third St.; (907) 586–1690. A vintage hotel reflecting "old Juneau."

**Breakwater Inn.** *Moderate.* 1711 Glacier Ave.; (907) 586–6303. Three-story motel with pleasant rooms, overlooking boat basin. Dining room; bar; beauty shop. Pets OK.

**Driftwood Lodge.** *Moderate.* 435 Willoughby Ave.; (907) 586–2280. Motel with 47 units, some with kitchens. Several two-bedroom apartments. Laundromat; restaurant.

The Tides Motel. *Moderate.* Mile 4 Old Glacier Hwy.; 5000 Glacier Hwy.; (907) 586–2452. 22 rooms, 30 camper spaces; electricity; water; dump station. Kitchenettes available.

## HAINES–PORT CHILKOOT
### (Zip Code 99827)

**Captain's Choice.** *Deluxe* motel units overlooking Lynn Canal, at 2nd and Dalton. Box 392; (907) 766–2461. Captain's Suite has wet bar.

**Fort Seward Condos.** *Expensive to Moderate.* Overlooking Lynn Canal. Box 75; (907) 766–2425 or 766–2116. If you want to stay awhile, inquire about these completely furnished apartments available by week or month (3-day minimum).

**Eagle's Nest Motel.** *Moderate.* Just outside Haines. Box 267; (907) 776–2352. Open year-round; camper park full hookup May–Sept.

**Thunderbird Motel.** *Moderate.* Box 159; (907) 766–2131. Modern motel units in this small downtown facility, all with private baths. TV.

**Halsingland Hotel.** *Inexpensive.* Located in Port Chilkoot, Box 158; (907) 766–2000. Affording a view of Lynn Canal and surrounding glacial-sided mountains, this moderate-size, family-style hotel is in vintage army quarters of old Fort William Seward, facing parade ground. Cocktail lounge; family-style dining room featuring Swedish cuisine and fresh local seafood. Alaska-Yukon Motorcoach depot. Nearby wooded Port Chilkoot Camper Park with electric hookups, water, dump station, showers, laundromat.

**Town House Motel.** *Inexpensive.* At Third and Main Sts., Box 66; (907) 766–2353. Conveniently located next to post office, library, and playground in Haines, this modern motel offers free coffee in the lounge, color TV, public phone, barbershop in the premises.

## SKAGWAY
### (Zip Code 99840)

**Golden North Hotel.** *Expensive.* 3rd and Broadway, Box 431; (907) 983–2294. A gold rush remainder. All 35 rooms different; furnished with charming antique touches. You can't miss it; its golden dome is a landmark. Restaurant.

**The Klondike.** *Expensive.* Box 515; toll-free (800) 544–0970; in Alaska call collect (907) 274–6631. Next to the Historic District. 171 rooms, lounge, restaurant, banquet facilities, outdoor barbecue. Houses tour groups. Original section recreates theme of gold rush through colorful decorations.

**Skagway Inn.** *Moderate.* Box 129; (907) 983–2289. Aura of gold rush preserved in this vintage building, once a saloon, on unpaved boardwalk-lined main street. Rooms (with and without private bath) have women's names instead of numbers.

**Taiya Lodge.** *Moderate to Inexpensive.* Box 101; (907) 983–2414. 23 rooms, some with bath, next to Historic District; restaurants nearby. Off-street parking.

**Fifth Avenue Bunkhouse.** *Inexpensive.* At 5th and Broadway; Box 48. For the thrifty. Bring your own sleeping bag and they'll furnish the bunk. $10 a night; showers $1; laundromat nearby. Towels and blankets for rent if needed. No reservations.

**BED-AND-BREAKFASTS. In Ketchikan:** For information contact: *Ketchikan Bed-and-Breakfast,* Box 7814, 99901; (907) 247–8444.

**In Juneau:** Contact: *Alaska Bed-and-Breakfast Association,* 114 S. Franklin St., Suite 102, 99801; (907) 586–2959. Also: *Alaska Guest Homes,* 1941 Glacier Hwy.; (907) 586–1840.

**YOUTH HOSTELS.** No reservations at these; don't count on kitchen facilities. **In Ketchikan:** Sponsored by the First United Methodist Church, Grant and Main sts.: Box 8515, 99901; (907) 225–3331. Operates Memorial Day to Labor Day.

**In Sitka:** *Sitka Youth Hostel.* Box 1762, 99835; (907) 747–6332 or 3546 or 6839. Summer only.

**In Junea:** *Juneau Youth Hostel.* Box 1543, 99801; (907) 586–9559 or 586–6457 or 789–9229. Operates summer only.

**In Haines:** *Bear Creek Camp and Youth Hostel.* Small Tract Rd., Box 334, 99827; (907) 766–2259. Inexpensive, primitive, rustic cabins—"a step above a tent." Cook on a wood stove, haul your own water, bring own bedding. No electricity. Parking for self-contained campers; tenters welcome. Operates year-round. Stop at Rock Garden Bible Bookstore and Natural Food Store, downtown Haines, for information.

**CAMPING AND CABINS.** There are plenty of places to camp throughout the Panhandle—public and private. These charge a small fee, may limit your stay, and do not take reservations. The local visitor information center will direct you to campgrounds in the area—campgrounds within sight of mountains and glaciers, bordering saltwater beaches and freshwater lakes and streams. Or you may be invited pitch your tent or park your trailer in the yard of a new-found Alaskan friend.

The Forest Service is in charge of cabins in national parklands, including the 155 cabins in southeast Alaska's *Tongass National Forest.* More than 50 are in the Ketchikan area. Some are accessible by hiking; some by boat; most are fly-ins. The Ketchikan Area Supervisor is in the Federal Bldg., Ketchikan, AK 99901; (907) 747–6671. The Chatham Area Supervisor: Box 757, Sitka, AK 99835; (907) 747–6671. The Stikine Area Supervisor: Box 309, Petersburg, AK 99833; (907) 772–3841. Reservations are necessary for the cabins; only $10 per night per party.

See also the sections on "State Parks" and "National Forests, Parks and Preserves" later in this *Practical Information.*

**WILDERNESS LODGES. Around Ketchikan:** *Clover Pass Resort,* 15 paved miles north of the city, is headquarters for the salmon derby. Hopeful fishermen strike out from here to hook fighting king salmon. Six cabins for rent, and the RV park has complete hookups for up to 30 campers. Amenities include showers, restaurant, and laundromat, tackle and rental shop. Better check space in fishing season—especially during Derby Days. Write Box 7322A, Ketchikan, AK 99901; (907) 247-2234. Go by boat or fly to *Yes Bay Lodge,* 45 miles northwest of Ketchikan. Write The Hack Family, Yes Bay, AK 99950 for rates and reservations for packages that include all: family-style meals, room, equipment, guide, and many activities. They feature hunting, fishing, hiking, beachcombing, birdwatching and photography. From Ketchikan it's about the same distance and in the same direction to *Bell Island Resort,* noted for its "fish and soak." Just off Behm Canal, the resort sits on hot springs appreciated by Indians and later commercial fishermen for the springs' relaxing, therapeutic powers, as well as the chance they give for a good hot bath. Now sport fishermen go there for some of the best king salmon fishing in Alaska, from May until well into fall, plus a chance at fighting steelhead that run up a cold stream rushing past the row of guest cabins. Families of fishermen are kept happy soaking in the private tubs or swimming in the hot, spring-fed, Olympic-sized swimming pool, dropping a line off the docks, or nature watching. For rates, with or without fishing, write Bell Island Hot Springs Resort, 1113 5th Ave. S., #108, Edmonds, WA 98020; (206) 776-7100. Near an Indian village, Klawock, on **Prince of Wales Island** is reached by ferry, small plane, and boat. The Fabry Family Guides take over at their tenter's lodge, *Log Cabin Sports Rental,* Box 54, Klawock, AK 99925, (907) 775-2205, helping guests to learn about Tlingit Indian traditions and steering people toward wholesome outdoor pursuits in this backcountry paradise. Nearby, more elaborate accommodations—restaurants and rooms with baths—offer sport fishing and recreational packages. Contact the *Prince of Wales Lodge,* Box 72, (907) 755-2227, and the *Fireweed Lodge,* Box 116, (907) 755-2226, (both Klawock AK 99925). Besides fine fishing, this area features crabbing (cook it on the beach), and "Craiging." Craig, about 6 miles away, is where to find the stores—including three liquor stores—and the bars. *Waterfall Resort* is recycled from a historic cannery 62 miles west of Ketchikan, about 40 minutes by air. There are amenities in the restored cabins and buildings that workers of the 1910 cannery wouldn't believe. Bar, restaurant, and cabin decor are in vintage style, but with modern comforts. "Where sportfishing is for kings" is the resort motto, and they welcome visiting boats and planes. Reservations and queries go to Waterfall Resort, Box 6440, Ketchikan, AK 99901, (907) 225-9461 or (800) 544-5125. *Thayer Lake Lodge,* Box 5416, Ketchikan, AK 99901, (907) 945-3223, is on **Admiralty Island.** (From June 1–Sept. 14, contact Bob Nelson, Radio KWA 78 via Alasiom, Juneau, AK.) It's American Plan, and also has 2 cabins for up to 4 people, with cooking facilities for do-it-yourselvers.

**Around Juneau:** To the north is *Taku Glacier Lodge.* Contact Manager, 195 S. Franklin St., Juneau, AK 99801, (907) 586-1362. It is 30 air miles from

Juneau in mountain and glacier wilderness. The vintage log lodge opts mostly for day visitors, who come for the delicious salmon bake, and for the flightseeers en route over the Juneau Ice Field. Reserve ahead for overnight stays, guided trips to glaciers, and for sportfishing.

**Around Glacier Bay:** *Glacier Bay Lodge,* at Bartlett Cove, is the only overnight hotel within the National Park. For information on the abundant sightseeing, flightseeing, naturalist programs, and sportfishing from late May through late September, the year-round contact is the Reservations Manager, Glacier Bay Lodge, 1500 Metropolitan Park Bldg., Seattle, WA 98101; (206) 624–8551. Outside the park, near the jet airport serving Glacier Bay daily in summer, is small, homey *Gustavus Inn,* Box 31, Gustavus, AK 99826, (907) 697–3311, now being operated by children of the original 1928 homesteaders. *Salmon River Rentals,* Box 121, Gustavus, AK 99826, (907) 697–3291, rents economy housekeeping cabins, bicycles, and sleeping bags May through September. Grocery, showers, and washing facilities are nearby. King and silver salmon abound in the surrounding waters of Icy Strait and Glacier Bay. Cutthroat and Dolly Varden trout haunt the Salmon River. From Gustavus, bus transportation is available to Glacier Bay National Park and Preserve, 10 miles.

Lodges with some of the best all-inclusive fishing packages and live-aboard yacht charters, especially out of Ketchikan and Juneau, are rounded up in *Fish Our Alaska!* published by Alaska Exploration Holidays & Cruises. (See "Tours" section, below.) Also consult the state-compiled Travel Index of the Division of Tourism's official vacation planning guide. (Pouch E-28, Juneau 99811). Hunters should write the Executive Director, Alaska Professional Hunters Association, Box 4–1932, Anchorage, AK 99509, phone (907) 276–3236, for sporthunting and big game guide leads.

  **HOW TO GET AROUND. By air:** Check local air taxi operators for information on charter and commercial service throughout the state. The following carriers operate scheduled air service within the state. *From Ketchikan: Southeast Alaska Airlines,* 1515 Tongass Ave., Ketchikan, AK 99901—to various Southeast locations. *Tyee Airlines,* Box 8331, Ketchikan, AK 99901—to various Southeast locations. *From Juneau: Air America,* Box 2321, Juneau, AK 99803—to Haines, Hoonah, and Skagway. *Air North,* Box 60054, Fairbanks, AK 99706—to Fairbanks and Whitehorse, YT. *Alaska Airlines,* 127 Franklin, Juneau, AK 99803—to Gustavus Airport, 10 miles from Glacier Bay National Park. A bus connection can be made to the park. For many years *Channel Flying,* 2601 Channel Dr., Juneau, AK 99801, has been the charter and scheduled flying link to small Southeastern towns, always with an eye for the scenic routes that delight the passengers. Amphibious aircraft, too. *L.A.B. Flying Service,* Box 2201, Juneau, AK 99803—to Haines, Hoonah, and Skagway. *Around Glacier Bay: Glacier Bay Airways,* Box 1, Gustavus, AK 99826, has an office in the Glacier Bay Lodge lobby, as well as at Gustavus Airport, to expedite glacier flightseeing, camper drop-offs, and group transfers in the area.

**By water:** The *Alaska Marine Highway* ferries will help you travel up (or down) the Panhandle. Reservations are required for vehicles and cabins. Walk-ons may travel without reservations (except from Seattle); this means you'll be sleeping on lounge chairs or on the deck, itself. Southeast ports include Ketchikan, Wrangell, Petersburg, Sitka, Juneau, Haines, and Skagway. For reservations and information contact: Alaska Marine Highway, Division of Marine Transportation, Pouch R, Juneau, AK 99811; (907) 465–3941 or 465–3940. See also "How to Get There" earlier in *Practical Information for Southeast Alaska.*

**By car:** Only two Southeastern towns are connected to the *Alaska Highway:* Haines, via the Haines Hwy. and Skagway, via Klondike Hwy. 2.

**By rail:** The *White Pass & Yukon Route* railroad between Skagway and Whitehorse, Y.T., is not operating at press time. For the current status of the railroad contact: White Pass & Yukon Route, Box 2147, Seattle, WA 98111; (206) 623–2510. In Skagway, phone (907) 983–2214.

**TOURIST INFORMATION.** Fish and game information is freely dispensed in sporting goods and fishing gear stores, as well as at the fish and game department offices listed here. **Ketchikan:** *Visitors Bureau* office is on the downtown dock; open daily 8:00 A.M.–5:00 P.M. in summer; business hours the rest of the year. 131 Front St., Box 7055, Ketchikan, AK 99901; 225–6166. *Dept. of Fish and Game* is located at 415 Main St., room 208, Ketchikan, AK 99901; 225–2859. Open Mon.–Fri. 8:00 A.M.–4:30 P.M.

**Wrangell:** *Visitor Information Center* is in an A-frame on the corner of Brueger St. and Outer Dr., Box 49, Wrangell, AK 99929; 874–3901; open when cruise ships and ferries are in port and at other, flexible hours. *Dept. of Fish and Game,* 215 Front. St., Wrangell, AK 99929; 875–3822. Weekdays 8:00 A.M.–4:30 P.M.

**Petersburg:** *Chamber of Commerce and Information Center:* Main St., Box 649, Petersburg, AK 99833; 772–3646; open Mon.–Fri. 10:00 A.M.–4:00 P.M. *Dept. of Fish and Game:* Main St., Petersburg, AK 99833; 772–3801; open weekdays 8:00 A.M.–4:30 P.M.

**Sitka:** *Visitor Bureau,* open summer Mon.–Sat. 9:00 A.M.–9:00 P.M. Sun. noon–4:00 P.M. Weekdays 9:00 A.M.–5:00 P.M. the rest of the year. It's in the Centennial Bldg. on Harbor Dr., Box 1226, Sitka, AK 99835. *Dept. of Fish and Game:* 304 Lake St., Sitka, AK 99835; 747–5355; weekdays 8:00 A.M.–4:30 P.M.

**Juneau:** *Visitor Information Center* is in the Davis Log Cabin, 134 Third St., Juneau, AK 99802; 586–2201 or 2284. Open year-round 8:30 A.M.–5:00 P.M. Mon.–Fri.; summer 2:00–5:00 P.M. Sat., Sun., holidays. *Dept of Fish and Game,* 230 S. Franklin St., Box 3–2000, Juneau, AK 99802; 465–4270 or 4180. 8:00 A.M.–4:30 P.M.

**Haines:** *Visitor Information* on Haines Hwy. at Main St., Haines, AK 99827. Open daily Jun.–Sept. 10:00 A.M.–8:00 P.M.; 766–2202. *Dept of Fish and Game* Haines Hwy., Box 431, Haines, AK 99827, can be reached at 766–2830, 8:00 A.M.–4:30 P.M.

**Skagway:** *Convention and Visitor Bureau,* Box 415, Skagway, AK 99840; 983–2297. Hours vary. Also see *Alaska Sightseeing* at the Golden North Hotel 983–2241 or the travel desk at the *Golden North Hotel;* their desks are manned most of the time May–Sept.

**TOURS.** Names like *Misty Fiords* and *Glacier Bay* suggest a kaleidoscope of mountains, deep inlets, forests, wildlife, and glaciers—nature's spectaculars. The companies listed here have tours that visit America's newest national monument, Misty Fiords, and veteran Glacier Bay, formerly a monument, but now a national park and preserve. There are many more than these examples; the following firms can direct or take you to other worthy tour destinations also, in the Southeast–and farther north. (Note the spelling of "fiords." It was officially decided to spell it that way when the monument was established.)

*Alaska Discovery,* Box 26, Gustavus AK 99826, (907) 697–3431 majors in seven great wilderness areas including Glacier Bay. Their strong points are kayaking and backpacking adventures. For about $100 a day, or perhaps a little more than that, calculated from where the tour departs, they cover guide service, all charters involved, insurance, three meals a day, tents, cooking and camping gear, and all expedition equipment. They offer discounts if you sign up for connecting trips for their *Alaska Discovery Wilderness Series.*

*Alaska Exploration Holidays and Cruises,* 1500 Metropolitan Park Bldg., Boren and Olive Sts., Seattle, WA 98101. They also have an office in the Baranof Hotel in Juneau. Their *Majestic Alaska Explorer* and *Great Rivers Explorer* cruise from Ketchikan to Misty Fiords and penetrate deep into the heart of the monument. Dinner the first night is served among the beauty of sheer granite walls laced with waterfalls, before the ship goes north along the Inside Passage on its 8-day/7-night round-trip cruise. Besides a whole day in Glacier Bay, the ship also explores nearby *Tracy Arm,* a lovely, narrow fjord, long cherished by boaters. A smaller sister ship, the *Glacier Bay Explorer* leaves from Juneau, cruises the Lynn Canal to call at Skagway and Haines, and spends a day in Glacier Bay during her 3-day itinerary. The 2-night round-trip cruise heads directly for Glacier Bay.

*The Leisure Corporation,* 207 Main St., Ketchikan, AK 99901, handles combination cruise and air tours, a stay in Ketchikan, and a visit to Misty Fiords. They still have the limousine used by the touring Texans (mentioned in the "Touring Alaska" essay in the introductory section of this book). When not otherwise occupied, it's for hire in Ketchikan, for about $65 an hour. It can be used by a group of up to 6 people for shopping and sightseeing tours. It comes equipped with chauffeur and a cooler of mineral water, beer, and imported champagne.

*Outdoor Alaska,* Box 7814, Ketchikan AK 99901, offers assorted cruise/fly tours, some overnighting in the monument, with drop-off and pick-up service for canoers and kayakers. Dave Pihlman, a second-generation Alaskan, scheduled the first tours into solitary, little-known Misty Fiords. He also offers a

*Historical Waterfront* cruise. His narration matches Ketchikan's colorful landmarks.

*Sitka Tours* buses are waiting at the ferry to take people on a Ferry Stopover tour for $7.50 ($4 for children under 12), returning to the gangplank in time for sailing.

There has been concern that increased ship traffic in Glacier Bay may be hampering the annual whale migration. No one wants the whales to stop going there, and so the situation is being monitored. Some believe the cause may be diminishing supplies of a whale's favorite food. Meanwhile, scientists watch for signs that the whales are nervous, and the numbers and size of ships entering Glacier Bay are being regulated.

 **AIR TOURS OF NOTE IN THE SOUTHEAST.** Weather permitting, at some time during your stay try to take an air tour of the vicinity. Some are short enough to fit in between ship sailings or during ferry stopovers. You'll get an entirely different perspective of Alaska's grandeur. Small planes serve the Southeast well, and there are flying experiences awaiting you unlike any found in other places in the world.

Some favorites are flightseeing tours that include a lift off and splash down right in front of busy harbor at **Ketchikan** or **Juneau.** *Southeast Alaska Airlines,* 1515 Tongass Ave., Ketchikan, AK 99901, based on Ketchikan's waterfront, offers a 40-minute flight that covers the waterfront, during which the experienced Alaska bush pilot pinpoints totem parks, rain forests, and anything else interesting below before he heads through open spaces between the mountains for a look at the lakes behind Ketchikan. The 90-minute flight takes in the Misty Fjords National Monument and all the beautiful wilderness in between, over lakes called Mirror, Punchbowl, Goat, Swan, and Grace, and recreation area trails leading to cliffs of granite rising two thousand feet above the fjords. If you have up to 3 hours, ask about the *Bonus Bush Flight Tour* (on space-available basis only), a working trip supplying outlying communities. Fellow travelers may be loggers, Natives, and fishermen.

*Alaska Island Air* out of **Petersburg,** Box 508, Petersburg, AK 99833, operates a 9-passenger amphibious aircraft to many Southeast destinations.

In **Sitka,** *Bellair,* Box 371, Sitka, AK 99835, and *Mountain Aviation,* Box 875, Sitka, AK 99835, offer area flightseeing tours (half hour for $30 in 1983), or you can fly with *Raven Copters,* Box 2242, Sitka, AK 99835. They specialize in "personalized" photo and flightseeing by helicopter. Depending on your time and budget, you may see a bird reserve where hundreds of eagles nest, look into the once-active volcano crater of Mt. Edgecumbe, a Sitka landmark, hover around the heights where mountain goats gather—and it's likely that whales or seals will surface in the water around the many islands. The helicopter may even land for a few minutes on the top of the volcano or on an isolated scenic beach.

**Juneau** sits under the vast expanse of the Juneau Ice Field. On a clear day you can see ice almost forever on scenic charter tours of *L.A.B. Flying Service* (Box 2201, Juneau, AK 99803), sharing the cost with 3, 4, or 6 people, depending on the size of the plane. You'll want your camera as they fly over the ice fields and Glacier Bay National Monument.

You'll appreciate the planes and *Colossal Aeronautical Tours* of *Skagway Air Service,* Box 357, **Skagway,** AK 99840. They stick with the local theme in cleverly and brightly painted Cherokee Sixes, and the slogan "We Can-Can-Can!" Climbing gold rush passes and tracing the Trail of '98 by air is about a 45-minute tour, a real thriller for the money. Stop in at their office at 4th and Broadway and ask about prices of that and other air-taxi and charter flights.

 **STATE PARKS.** An ideal state park in southeast Alaska is *Chilkat State Park,* south of **Haines** on the Chilkat Peninsula. Here you can see bald eagles, fish for salmon, go beachcombing, and, of course, enjoy the breathtaking scenery. Hike and boat in the summer; cross-country ski in the winter. For further information contact Haines Chamber of Commerce, Box 262, Haines, AK 99827; (907) 766–2116. For general information about Alaska's state park system write: State of Alaska Dept. of Natural Resources, Division of Parks, 619 Warehouse Ave., Suite 210, Anchorage, AK 99501.

 **NATIONAL FORESTS, PARKS AND PRESERVES.** *Admiralty Island National Park* includes Admiralty Island, one of the largest islands in southeast Alaska. Parts of the island are less than 12 miles from Juneau, but this is still wilderness: brown bears outnumber people and there is the largest concentration of bald eagles known in North America. The principal settlement is Angoon, accessible from Juneau by scheduled flights and ferries. There are public-use cabins here (about 15). Contact the U.S. Forest Service, Admiralty National Monument, Box 2097, Juneau, AK 99803; (907) 789–3111. *Misty Fiords National Monument* displays some of Alaska's most spectacular scenery. Sheer granite cliffs rise from the ocean; crystal-clear waters and mirror lakes abound. The U.S. Forest Service maintains cabins here. Access to the monument is only by plane, boat, or occasional ferry. Information can be obtained from the Tongass Visitor Center in the Federal Building, **Ketchikan,** or from Monument Ranger, Misty Fiords National Monument, Tongass National Forest, Federal Bldg., Ketchikan, AK 99901; (907) 225–3101. For specific information on *Glacier Bay National Park and Preserve* contact the Superintendent, Box 1098, Juneau, AK 99802; (907) 586–7127. *Tongass National Forest,* America's largest, includes most of southeast Alaska and is ideal for backpackers. There are U.S. Forest Service campgrounds near **Ketchikan, Juneau, Petersburg,** and **Wrangell,** and about 150 public-use cabins in outlying areas, accessible by boat, trail, or chartered aircraft. Most of the communities in the forest are ports for the Alaska state ferry. Contact Regional Forester, U.S. Forest Service, Box 1628, Juneau, AK 99802; (907) 586–7282.

**SKIING. Juneau:** *Eaglecrest Ski Area* on Douglas Island offers 1,400-foot vertical drop, lessons, a lodge and a snack bar. Call (907) 586-3300.

**THE INDIAN HERITAGE. Ketchikan:** About 2 miles south of Ketchikan, behind Saxman Indian Village, on St. Tongass Hwy., is *Saxman Totem Park.* There are over 20 poles here, among them a reproduction of the Lincoln totem. Open year-round, no admission charge.

*Totem Bight State Historical Site,* about Mile 10 on the N. Tongass Hwy., is about 25 minutes north of Ketchikan. There are excellent reproductions of poles here and a tribal house. Open year-round, no admission charge.

*Tongass Historical Society,* 629 Dock St., exhibits Indian artifacts. Hours vary depending on whether or not cruise ships are in port. Generally open afternoons year-round. Small admission fee. 225-5600.

The *Totem Heritage Cultural Center,* 601 Deermount St., provides the background for the totemic culture, with 33 poles and fragments from old Tlingit and Haida Indian Villages. Native tour guides during summer months and a small admission fee. 8:30 A.M.–5:00 P.M. Phone 225-5900.

**Wrangell:** Cross the footbridge in the inner harbor at the bottom of Front St. to Chief Shakes Island where totems—some of the finest examples of this art—surround the restored *Bear Tribal House.* Inside, some of the chief's wealth is displayed along with other treasures. It's usually open for tour groups. Look around town for some exemplary totems tucked away in unusual places: if you aren't watching for it, you might miss the weathered mortuary pole with a kind-faced man hugging his knees; it's standing guard over by the oil docks. Nearby you'll note a house decorated with Indian carvings. Walk the beach near the ferry dock at low tide to see Indian rock carvings. Experts say these petroglyphs may have been chipped into the rocks as long as 8,000 years ago. Phone 874-3505. Free.

The *Wrangell Museum* is at the corner of Second and Bevier sts., a few blocks from the ferry terminal. Totems and local historic artifacts are inside. Open Monday–Thursday, Sat. 1:00–4:00 P.M.; Fri. 1:00–3:00, May–Sept. In winter: Wed. 1:00–4:00; also open for cruise ships and ferries and by appointment year-round. Small admission fee. 874-3770.

**Sitka:** The *Sheldon Jackson Museum* on the Sheldon Jackson College Campus houses some of the finest Indian arts and crafts, and Russian relics to be found in Alaska. Open 9:00 A.M.–5:00 P.M. daily in summer; 1:00–4:00 P.M. in winter, closed Sat. and Mon. Small admission fee. 747-5228.

At the Fort Site of *Sitka National Historical Park,* at the end of Metlakatla St., the emphasis is Tlingit Indian. Totem poles outside and inside the visitors center, excellent audio-visual programs, and people—including some natives who may be at work in the craft shops—help to interpret this side of Sitka's rich cultural heritage. The park's visitors center is open Mon.–Sat. 8:00 A.M.–5:00 P.M., mid-Sept.–mid-May; daily 8:00 A.M.–6:00 P.M., mid-May–mid-Sept. Park grounds are open daily, 7:00 A.M.–10:00 P.M., year-round. No admission fee. 747–6281.

**Juneau:** The *Alaska State Museum,* Whittier St. off Egan Dr., displays a large collection of Indian artifacts, including the Lincoln totem. Also exhibits from Alaska's gold rush period, Russian-American historical displays, natural history exhibits. Open weekdays in summer 9:00 A.M.–9:00 P.M.; weekends 1:00–9:00 P.M.; in winter, weekdays 9:00 A.M.–5:30 P.M., weekends 1:00–5:30 P.M. No admission charge. 465–2901.

If Chief Walter Williams happens to be on guide duty in town, you'll get a rundown on all he knows (considerable!) about his Indian heritage, plus his interpretation of some of his favorite dances.

**Haines-Port Chilkoot:** Indian lore, arts, crafts, and dance are perpetuated on the historic grounds of turn-of-the-century *Fort William Seward.* Artists and craftspeople work in the Alaska Indian Arts Skill Center in one of the vintage buildings; they're usually there in summer 9:00 A.M.–5:00 P.M. weekdays and when cruise ships and ferries are in town. Some may be working outside if the project is large enough—a house pole, or perhaps a dugout canoe. June through September the Chilkat Dancers perform 2 evenings a week, wearing authentic costumes crafted in the Alaska Indian Arts program. Ask at the visitor's center for a schedule for the dancers. Phone 766–2160. Small admission charge. On the post parade ground is *Totem Village,* including a replica of a tribal ceremonial house, a pioneer's cabin, pelt-drying racks, and some large totems. For information on Ft. William Seward call 766–2202, June–Sept. Free. Halsingland Hotel will also provide walking tour maps for the fort.

The *Sheldon Museum and Cultural Center,* 25 Main St., houses a collection of pioneer and Tlingit artifacts. Open 1:00 P.M.–4:00 P.M., daily in summer, by appointment the rest of the year. Small admission fee. 766–2366.

**Skagway:** Here was the namesake ancestral home of the Tlingit Indian tribe that once guarded these mountain passes. Stop in at *Native Carvings* on the main street and you may find Richard Dick, an Alaska Tlingit Indian, working in wood and stone and willing to pass on some Native lore.

Scattered around the islands, in smaller Indian villages, are many signs of Native Alaskans. *Klawock* (Kl-wahk'), an Indian community a short flight or a ferry ride from Ketchikan, has a notable collection of totems on a hill in town. Kake, Hydaburg, Angoon, and Hoonah, are also reached by air or sea. On the way, bush pilots such as Paul Breed of *SEA Airlines,* are inclined to circle and try to point out some remains of deserted village sites—perhaps a totem or part of a tribal house—if they think you are interested.

 **OTHER HISTORIC SITES. Ketchikan:** The *Creek Street Historic District,* a wooden street set on pilings along the Ketchikan Creek, was Ketchikan's "red-light district." Here, Dolly, Black Mary, and Frenchie plied their trade for over 50 years—until 1954. *Dolly's House,* 24 Creek St., is a brothel turned museum. Open during the summer for tour groups, or check at the visitors bureau (225–6166); a small admission fee. Phone 225–6329.

**Sitka:** *Castle Hill* was the site of Governor Baranof's castle. Here the first U.S. flag was raised when Alaska changed from Russian to American hands. Walkway to the site is next to the post office on Lincoln St. Open to the public free of charge, year-round.

The focal point of the town's Russian history is *Saint Michael's Cathedral,* on downtown Lincoln Street. Built in 1844–48, this building was one of the finest examples of rural Russian church architecture, until a fire in 1966 destroyed it. The rebuilt cathedral is an exact replica and contains many art treasures— including the Sitka Madonna icon—from the days of the Czarist rule. Open daily June–Sept., 11:00 A.M.–3:00 P.M., other times by appointment. Visitors are reminded that this is an active parish conducting weekly services. 747–8120.

**Haines:** *Fort William Seward* reflects the Indian heritage of this community (see "Indian Heritage" earlier in this section), as well as a military history. At the fort you can see barracks, the commanding officer's quarters, the guard-house, the mule stables, and more. Details and a map for a walking tour are available at the Halsingland Hotel, 766–2000, or call the visitor's center June–Sept. 766–2202. Free.

**Skagway:** The Skagway unit of the *Klondike Gold Rush National Historical Park* encompasses a 6-block area of the community's business district and includes many wooden buildings dating from the gold rush days. The visitor center is to move from the Arctic Brotherhood Hall to the refurbished vintage railroad depot. Open 9:00 A.M.–8:00 P.M. mid-May–mid-Sept. Phone 983–2400.

*Soapy Smith's Parlor and Museum,* on First Ave. is near the site of the duel between infamous outlaw "Soapy" Smith and Frank Reid—representing the side of law and order. The musuem is privately owned. Contact the Convention and Visitor Bureau for information, 983–2297.

*The Trail of '98 Museum,* Second and Spring sts., is on the second floor of the first granite building constructed in Alaska (1899–1900). The purpose of the museum is to preserve Alaskan historical material and to display reminders of Alaskan pioneer life. Some of Soapy Smith's personal items are here. Open daily in summer 8:00 A.M.–8:00 P.M. Oct.–May for groups by appointment only. Small admission fee. 983–2420.

 **FISH.** To learn about them visit **Ketchikan's** *Deer Mountain Hatchery* adjacent to the Totem Heritage Center. It's self-guiding, and there'll be someone on hand to interpret, too. A branch of the state Fish and Game Department looks after this city-owned birthplace and nursery for king and coho salmon. It's free, open year-round, and you can learn all you want to know about salmon, including their unusual sex life.

Besides totems, Indian community **Klawock** also majors in fish. Alaska's first salmon cannery was built in Klawock in 1878 by the Northern Pacific Trading and Packing Company. From this beginning Alaska's multi-million-dollar industry evolved.

At **Petersburg,** study the fish sculpture considered to be one of the Pacific Northwest's finest pieces of bronze art. It's outside the *Clausen Museum,* Second and F sts., and it honors all fish, including the halibut, Petersburg's mainstay. Inside the museum they boast the record-holding king salmon, 126½ pounds. The museum is open daily during the summer 1:00–4:30 P.M. 772–3598. Free.

Also in Petersburg, the *Crystal Lake Fish Hatchery* on Mitkof Hwy.—a hatchery for coho, king, and chum salmon and steelhead trout is open to visitors. No tours but personnel will explain what goes on here. Best time to visit: 8:00 A.M.–4:00 P.M., Mon.–Fri.

In **Juneau** you can watch migrating and spawning salmon, late July–Sept. Try Fish Creek, N. Douglas Hwy.; Sheep Creek, Thane Rd.; Montana Creek, Montana Creek Rd.; Steep Creek, near Mendenhall Glacier Parking Area; Peterson Creek, Glacier Hwy.

**To catch them.** All Southeast communities, regardless of their other interests, go in for sport and/or commercial fishing. And they all hold fishing derbies in the summer (usually May and June) in which visitors are invited to participate. Winning fish are usually well over 50 pounds, and the prizes add up to thousands of dollars. Local fish and game department offices, marine charters, and sporting goods stores, usually next to or on the waterfront, have current contest rules, licenses for sale, and lots of advice (free).

**To eat them.** Throughout the Southeast, visitors will meet fish on the menu, and in some places be exposed to a favorite institution, the salmon bake, a summer event, usually all you can eat for under $15. Try the *Creek St. Salmon Bake* in **Ketchikan**, overlooking the historical area. They broil fresh-caught salmon with special herbs over charcoal and alder chips. Contact Ketchikan Marketing and Management, 3420 Baranof Ave., Ketchikan, AK 99901; 225–3293 or 9505. They have a hand in many other area attractions also. **Wrangell** offers one that usually coincides with a cruise ship being in port. It's part of the sightseeing tour that ends up at the *Roadhouse Salmon Bake*, a few miles out of town.

At **Juneau**, the *Gold Creek Outdoor Salmon Bake* at Last Chance Basin, where millions in gold has been mined, has long been popular with visitors and residents. It's held rain or shine every night, 5:30–9:00 P.M. Only groups of over 20 need make reservations; 586–1424. Be at the Baranof Hotel at 6:00 P.M. for free transportation. While in Juneau it's also possible to combine flightseeing with that old Indian custom the salmon bake in a setting among glaciers and wilderness at Taku Glacier Lodge. Three-hour tours by float plane fly via the Juneau Ice Field, massive source of many mighty glaciers, including the Taku. They land at the dock of Taku Lodge, situated in a mossy rain forest. The dining room overlooks the aptly named Hole in the Wall Glacier. Coming and going, the skillful and obliging pilots identify landmarks and glaciers and watch for wildlife on the move. In the long, light summer evenings, sharp eyes may spot black bears bent on berrying, and sheep and goats on mountain ledges. Phone 586–1362 for information. The Taku Glacier Lodge office is at 195 S. Franklin St., Juneau, AK 99801.

**Sitka** is inclined to put a masterly salmon bake in the all-purpose Centennial Building, when requested by cruise ships or on other special occasions. Just ask at visitors information if one is scheduled.

Another favorite is the *Port Chilkoot Potlatch,* where fresh local salmon is prepared over an open alderwood fire, then served on the Parade Ground of Fort William Seward, adjacent to **Haines.** The potlatch is held daily 5:30–7:30 P.M. Inquire at the Halsingland Hotel nearby, facing the quadrangle; 766–2641.

 **MUSEUMS. Ketchikan:** *Dolly's House,* 24 Creek St., is a brothel turned museum. Open during the summer, small admission fee. Phone 225–6329 or the visitor bureau for information, 225–6166.

*Tongass Historical Society Museum* is in the Centennial Bldg., 629 Dock St. Collection features Indian artifacts, pioneer history, photos. Hours vary depending on whether or not a cruise ship is in port. Usually open in the afternoon throughout the year. Small admission charge. 225–5600.

**Wrangell:** The *Wrangell Museum,* Second and Bevier Sts., houses displays of local and Tlingit history, and petroglyphs. Open May–Sept., Mon.–Thurs., Sat., 1:00–4:00 P.M.; Fri. 1:00–3:00 P.M. In winter: Wed. 1:00–4:00 P.M.; also open for cruise ships and ferries and by appointment year-round. Small admission fee. 874–3770.

*Bigelow Museum,* Stikine Ave., is a private collection of artifacts and 19th- and 20th-century memorabilia. Open when ferries are in port and by appointment. Phone 874–3646 and they'll send a courtesy car.

**Petersburg:** *Clausen Museum,* Second and F sts., features the world-record king salmon caught commercially (126½ lbs.), as well as local, historical displays. Open daily in summer 1:00–4:30 P.M. 772–3598. Free.

**Sitka:** The *Sheldon Jackson Museum* was the first museum in Alaska and houses an outstanding collection of Indian and Russian art and objects. Open in summer 9:00 A.M.–5:00 P.M. daily; 1:00–4:00 P.M. in winter, closed Sat. and Mon. 747–5228.

**Juneau:** *Alaska State Museum,* on Whittier St. off Egan Dr., houses a variety of displays ranging from Indian cultural displays, exhibits on mining, wildlife, and the trans-Alaska pipeline to Russian-American exhibits and the Lincoln totem. Summer hours: 9:00 A.M.–9:00 P.M. weekdays; 1:00–9:00 P.M. weekends. Winter hours: 9:00 A.M.–5:30 P.M. weekdays, 1:00–5:30 P.M. weekends. No admission charge. 465–2901.

*House of Wickersham,* 213 Seventh Ave., houses historic collections of early 20th-century Alaska. Tours in summer by reservation only. Small admission fee. Call 586–1251.

**Haines:** *Sheldon Museum and Cultural Center,* 25 Main St., exhibits Russian and Indian items. Open 1:00–4:00 P.M., daily, in summer; by appointment the rest of year. Small admission fee. 766–2366.

**Skagway:** *Soapy Smith's Parlor and Museum,* First Ave., displays memorabilia of the outlaw. Privately owned. Contact Convention and Visitor Bureau for more information: 983–2297.

*Trail of '98 Museum,* Second and Spring sts., displays one of best collections of gold rush memorabilia in the state. You can see some of Soapy's own belongings here. Open summers 8:00 A.M.–8:00 P.M.; in winter, for groups by appointment only. Small admission charge. 983–2420.

**THEATER AND ENTERTAINMENT.** In **Ketchikan,** the farcical melodrama *Fish Pirate's Daughter* is staged June–Sept. at the Frontier Saloon, 127 Main St. Tickets available on cruise ships and from the visitors bureau, and—if available—at the door. Write Box 6653, Ketchikan, AK 99901; 225–9950.

In **Sitka,** everyone applauds the traditional Russian folk dances performed in summer by the *New Archangel Dancers* on the stage of the Centennial Bldg. Performances are timed according to cruise ship arrivals or by special arrangement. Small admission charge. Write Box 1687, Sitka, AK 99835.

In **Haines,** see *Lust for Dust,* a melodrama created by the Lynn Canal Community Players during their 3-year-long centennial celebration. Performed at the Chilkat Center for the Arts, Ft. William Seward; call 766–2160. June–Sept. the *Chilkat Dancers* also perform here about twice a week. Ask at the visitor's center for schedule information; 766–2160. Small admission charge.

In gold rush gateway **Skagway** there's no lack of 1898 atmosphere. You can count on seeing *In the Days of '98* and *Soapy Smith* shows throughout the summer. These historical comedy-dramas are performed daily mid-May–mid-Sept. Tickets sold at the door and at most hotels. Performed at Eagles Hall, 6th and Broadway, Box 1897, Skagway, AK 99840; 983–2545.

**SHOPPING.** Everywhere you sightsee and explore you'll be tempted by the myriad shops and art galleries. They'll be selling traditional and modern creations made from Alaskan materials. The source of supply may be a small "cottage industry" or a cooperative venture of several local artists and craftsmen. Some items and materials may be unique to an area.

**Ketchikan's** mix of artists and craftsmen—silversmiths, potters, sculptors, photographers, etc.—supplies the *Morning Raven,* on Mission Street. Look for paintings in art galleries such as *The Gathering* on Creek Street near Dolly's House, and *Scanlon's* near the welcome sign downtown. The *Northland Silk Screen Studio,* 309 Dock St., specializes in Indian-design prints. *Nancy's Jewelers',* 209 Main St., great variety of gold nugget jewelry includes a 14-karat-gold Rainbird charm. Look for Native crafts at the *Alaska Treasure Cache,* 224 Front St., *Trading Post,* 201 Main St., and *Authentic Alaska Craft,* 318-A Dock St. *The Foxy Lady,* 435 Dock St., not only has the latest fashions but also up-to-date information on Ketchikan's current attractions.

In **Wrangell** you can buy a garnet from a Boy Scout. An unusual garnet ledge about five miles from town near the Stikine River flats was deeded to the Boy Scouts and children of Wrangell. Garnet fanciers have to deal through them. You are bound to find an Alaskan souvenir, perhaps purchasing it from the artist who made it.

Sitka, as in its Russian past, has a reputation for having well-stocked stores. On Cathedral Circle you'll find everything from Alaska Wild Berry Products to T-shirts: *Tops & Things* has T-shirts with Alaskan motifs and phrases, created by Stella Conway, a charter member of the New Archangel Russian Dancers; The *Russian Bell* is a jewelry store also selling authentic Native handicrafts; *Old Harbor Books* has a wide selection of books, maps, and nautical charts; *Cerami- tique* makes things of native Sitka clay. *Alexanders* on Harbor Drive has Alas- kan paintings. Walk along Katlian Street behind the waterfront Sheffield House for picturesque shops in the "old town." They buy and sell old books and charts in *The Observatory* and *Books Books Books. Taranoff's Sitkakwan Shop,* also on Katlian St., like its name, reflects a Tlingit/Russian background with Alas- katique. Mrs. Taranoff designed the "Little Drook" (*friend* in Russian) button that city guests get when they sign in at the greeting desk in the Centennial Building. Wear it. Everyone is *extra* helpful when they know you are a visitor.

In **Juneau,** there are excellent modern shopping centers and fine shops dealing in original and Alaska-made products. The *Latitude 58,* on Franklin St. across from the Red Dog Saloon, displays the hand insignia, which stands for authentic native handicrafts. The *ANA (Alaska Native Arts) Cache* is on also Franklin. *Nina's Originals* on Seward Street creates distinctive fur apparel, and the *Baranof Gift Shop* off the lobby of the hotel has collector's items, including rare Russian icons, on display. The proprietress, Martha Edwards, has served as president of the Alaska Visitors Association, the first woman to be elected to that position. Her newest enterprise is the *Thane Ore House,* see "Special Interest Tours," above. If you're a bookworm, don't miss browsing in the *Baranof Book Shop* a few doors seaward. The *Merchant's Wharf,* on the water- front, of course, was recycled from the dock and an old seaplane hangar. It's now an intriguing shopping mall with restaurants and stores including the fine-quality *Ivory Cache,* with Indian arts and crafts, ivory, jade, and gold jewelry and Eskimo artwork.

As you have gathered from the exploring section, **Haines** and **Port Chilkoot** are oriented toward Indian crafts. *Helen's Shop,* on Main St., has been an outlet for fine craft work and a source of local information cheerfully dispensed for over 30 years. At Port Chilkoot, for almost as long, they have been turning out authentically designed totem poles, masks, silver etchings, soapstone carvings, and other handicrafts. What they don't use in the Chilkat Dance programs they'll sell through the *Alaska Indian Arts Skill Center.* Look for notable new- comers on the arts-and-crafts scene. They display and sell their work at the *Art Shop,* in a 1904 building, originally the telegraph office for Fort William H. Seward at Port Chilkoot. *The Sea Wolf* sculpture studio on the parade grounds has the work of Tresham Gregg, who grew up in a nearby officer's quarters made into a family residence. The *Palette and Wheel* across from Portage Cove Campground features painters and potters inspired by the magnificence of upper Lynn Canal scenery. Artists include Gil Smith, whose paintings hang in the State Museum and Governor's Mansion, the Anchorage Fine Arts Museum, and at the University of Alaska.

**Skagway** has a most interesting assortment of stores lining its boardwalk-bordered Main St. There are snack shops, restaurants and well-stocked grocery stores and bars. You can buy music, books, scrimshaw, Indian art, handicrafts, and sightseeing tours and charter flights. The *Red Onion* now sells curios, jewelry, objets d'art, and drinks, but go around back and upstairs. This 1898 building with beckoning mannikin in the window was once a bawdy house. Visitors can see and take pictures of the interior of this gold rush brothel, including the two restored "cribs." Long-established shops such as *Kirmse's Curio Store* dealt with the Yukon stampeders. *Dedman's Photo,* Broadway, has Alaska books and color slides, including a gold rush collection. And stop in at *Native Carvings,* Broadway, *Richter's Jewelry, Keller's Curios,* and the *Door Knob,* Broadway. *Artists of Skagway* is a cooperative outlet for one-of-a-kind items created by several local artists. Along with a storeful of quality merchandise, *Corrington's,* Fifth and Broadway, has an Eskimo museum and a large collection of ivory pieces for sale. In two shops on Broadway you may find "scrimshanders" at work. Both David Present and William Joseph Sidmore etch on ivory, using the same skills that were used by sailors during long periods at sea, and that are still used by Eskimos, the master ivory carvers in the Arctic. You could spend hours in Skagway browsing, buying, and talking with the friendly shopkeepers.

**PANNING FOR GOLD.** In **Juneau,** *Alaska Travel Adventures* will help arrange gold panning in gold mine tours, 2nd and N. Franklin, Juneau, AK 99811; 586–6245.

*Thane Ore House,* Juneau, combines a gold rush tour with a lunch or dinner sourdough barbeque, including beer and wine. On a working mine site overlooking Gatineau Channel, they guarantee that after lessons there will be gold in every pan. Included is a mining museum tour and transportation from hotels and cruise ships. May 15–Sept. 30. For reservations write: Thane Ore House, 200 N. Franklin St., Juneau, AK 99801; 586–6245.

 **DINING OUT.** Meals, especially if you take advantage of local specialties, are fairly reasonable in the homey restaurants of smaller southeast towns. They may run *less* in cost than this overall budget estimate: $4 to $8 for breakfast or lunch, and $8 to $30 for dinner. Major credit cards are widely accepted, but it's probably wise to call ahead to double check. The categories and ranges for a complete dinner are: *Deluxe,* $25 and up; *Expensive,* $16–24; *Moderate,* $10–15; and *Inexpensive,* under $10.

### KETCHIKAN

**Clover Pass Resort and Restaurant.** *Expensive.* Mile 15 N. Tongass Hwy.; 247–2234. Seafood specialties, probably fresh caught in their "front yard," the ocean, served with view. Salad bar and cocktail bar. Dinners only, except for Sunday brunch; open summers.

**The Helm Restaurant and Spar Tree Lounge.** *Expensive.* 2415 Hemlock (west end of Ketchikan); 225–2415. Fantastic view from top of the Marine View condominium.

**Charley's.** *Moderate.* 303 Mission St.; 255–5090. Off Ingersoll Hotel lobby; honors Charles Ingersoll, builder of this mainstay of "The Block," in the heart of historic downtown Ketchikan.

**The Fireside.** *Moderate.* 335 Main St.; 225–2006. Popular supper club located in downtown Ketchikan. Variety of dishes, with fresh seafood a specialty. Lounge, music, and dancing.

**Hilltop Restaurant.** *Moderate.* 3434 Tongass Ave.; 225–5166. Features daily specials, sandwiches, fountain. Across from ferry terminal.

**Kay's Kitchen.** *Moderate.* 2813 Tongass Ave.; 225–5860. Home cooking, especially soup and pies; crab and shrimp Louis. Lunches only. Clever decor and great location overlooking busy Bar Harbor boat traffic.

**Angela's Delicatessen.** *Inexpensive.* Mission St. Custom-made sandwiches produced cafeteria style, next to Ingersoll Hotel.

**Diaz Cafe.** *Inexpensive.* On Stedman St., across from the Salvation Army; 225–2257. Small, popular, good family food. No booze.

**The Galley.** *Inexpensive.* 2334 Tongass; 225–5400. Variety of fast food; beer and wine.

**Harbor Inn.** *Inexpensive.* Under the Welcome Arch on Mission St., 225–2850. Open 24 hours.

**Jackie's Restaurant.** *Inexpensive.* At the Midtown Mall; 225–4545. A pleasant, casual spot for tasty food.

**Stephanies.** *Inexpensive.* 1287 Tongass St.; 225–2966. Another good bet for a reasonably priced meal.

**Wheat Cellar.** *Inexpensive.* Gilmore Mall; 225–2710. Combines homey lunches and natural cosmetics.


## WRANGELL


**The Better Way.** *Moderate.* On Front St.; 874–3874. Has herb tea and vegeburgers.

**The Dockside.** *Moderate.* In the Stikine Inn; 874–3388. You can count on the fresh local seafood in season, especially the tiny shrimp, the best you'll ever eat.

**The Hungry Beaver.** *Moderate.* At Wrangell's oldest site (formerly Fort Dionysius, now the Marine Bar); 874–3005.

**The Roadhouse.** *Moderate.* Mile 4, Zimovia Hwy.; 874–2335. Lounge, evening dining. Outdoor fish bakes on request for 8 or more. Tent City Players entertain.

**Timber Room.** *Moderate.* Steak and seafood in the Totem Bar on Front St.; 874–3533.

**The Wharf.** *Moderate.* Also on Front St.; 874–3681. Come as you are. Home cooking and Alaska hospitality.

## PETERSBURG

**Viking Room.** *Expensive.* At Beachcomber Inn, Mile 4, Mitkof Hwy.; 772–3888. View of Wrangell Narrows comes with fresh local seafood and steak dinners. Shipwreck Room for cocktails. Reservations needed.

**Harvest Moon Restaurant.** *Moderate.* Indian St. Light meals.

**Irene's.** *Moderate.* Downtown, near Fisherman's Wharf, G and Main sts.; 772–3702. Seafood and salad bar.

**The Lighthouse.** *Moderate.* Indian St.; 772–3900. Deli and health foods.

## SITKA

**The Shee Atika Lodge.** *Deluxe.* Uptown, across from convention center; 747–6241. Newest, large hotel built by the Native Corporation. Fine dining and entertainment.

**Sheffield House.** *Deluxe.* Built on a former dock, overlooking the beautiful, historic waterfront and islands. 747–6616. Excellent food, entertainment, bars.

**Staton's Steak House.** *Deluxe.* Downtown overlooking Sitka Sound; 747–3396. Popular with residents. Also bar.

**Channel Club.** *Expensive.* 3½ miles out the Halibut Point Rd.; 747–9916. A local favorite for view, steaks and salad bar.

**Paul and Judy's Canoe Club.** *Expensive to Moderate.* In the Potlatch House, end of Katlian St.; 747–8606. Alaskan specialties served 7 nights a week 5–11 P.M. with piano bar and view of Mt. Edgecumbe and harbor.

**Nugget Saloon.** *Moderate.* Airport. Seafood and do-it-yourself steaks.

**Revard's.** *Moderate.* On Lincoln St. near Cathedral Circle.

**Fish Factory.** *Inexpensive.* 407 Lincoln. Menu varies with the catch.

**Marina Pizzeria.** *Inexpensive.* On Lincoln near Circle; 747–8840.

## JUNEAU

**The Diggings.** *Deluxe.* 340 Whittier Ave.; 586–3737. At the Prospector Hotel there is live entertainment nightly, dancing and cocktails.

**The Latchstring.** *Deluxe.* 2nd and Franklin; 586–2660. Alaskan paintings by Eustace Paul Ziegler and Sydney Laurence help decorate this handsome restaurant in the Baranof Hotel. Entertainment often reflects early Juneau life. Ice Worm Cocktails are the bar specialty.

**Breakwater Inn Restaurant.** *Expensive.* 1711 Glacier Ave.; 586–6306 or 6303. All remodeled, except the view of the channel. Serves seafood specialties plus regular fare.

**Ristorante Bellezza e la Festa.** *Expensive.* 171 Shattuck Way, in Alaska Steam Laundry Emporium; 586–1844. Memorable, authentic Indian.

**Woodcarver Restaurant and Lounge.** *Expensive.* 51 W. Egan Dr.; 586–6900. In the Cape Fox Sheffield House, new, elegant and excellent.

**Yancy Derringer's.** *Expensive.* At the Merchants Wharf; 586–1365. Highly recommended by the locals to those who like harbor entertainment (small boats, planes, cruiseships, sea lions) instead of the traditional. Beef and seafood specialties; try to reserve a window seat. Mon.–Fri. 4:30–6:30 P.M. is for "attitude adjustment" and the drinks are reduced.

**Beauty and the Feast.** *Moderate.* 916 Third, Douglas; 364–3307. *Billiken* bar and charbroiled burgers.

**City Café.** *Moderate.* 439 S. Franklin; 586–1363. Variety of food and quick service in this clean, convenient café across from downtown ferry terminal.

**Fiddlehead Restaurant & Bakery.** *Moderate.* 429 W. Willoughby. 586–3150. Healthful things, homemade; blueberry/buttermilk pancakes to salmon quiche; true sourdough, breads, and memorable pastries.

**Glacier Lounge and Restaurant.** *Moderate.* Located at airport. 1873 Shell Simmons Dr.; 789–9538. Usually has seafood on the menu. Overlooks Mendenhall Glacier.

**Heritage House.** *Moderate.* Above downtown in national historic site Bergmann Hotel, 434 3rd; 586–1690 or 6414.

**Mike's Place.** *Moderate.* 364–2220. A Juneau institution! Seafoods and steaks are specialties. Live music nightly for dancing. Located across the bridge in neighboring Douglas. If you don't have a ride they'll pick you up.

**Summit Café.** *Moderate.* 455 S. Franklin; 586–2050. Intimate: serves only 18 for dinner. Try the tempura prawns.

**Bullwinkle's Pizza.** *Inexpensive.* 318 Willoughby Ave.; 586–2400. When you're in the mood for pizza, this is the place to go.

**Dingly Dave's Fish House.** *Inexpensive.* 22 Egan Dr., on Merchants Wharf; 586–1322. Slogan is "More than Just for the Halibut!"

**Pattie's Etc.** *Inexpensive.* 230 Seward St.; 586–9555. A local favorite.


## HAINES-PORT CHILKOOT


**The Lighthouse.** *Expensive.* Overlooks the Haines small boat harbor and bordering snow-clad mountains; 766–2442.

**Hotel Halsingland.** *Moderate.* At Parade Ground in Port Chilkoot; 766–2641. Super Swedish and American meals. Fresh-caught salmon and other Alaskan seafood are menu favorites, along with wildberry deserts. Magnificent scenery from hotel area. Family-style meals have scheduled hours.

**The Post Exchange.** *Moderate.* On the Parage Ground; 766–2009. New restaurant in vintage Fort Seward building, once a PX and bowling alley. Varied menu offers choice international specialties.

**33-Mile Roadhouse.** *Moderate.* 766–2172. 7 A.M. to 10 P.M. daily. Also fill your gas tank; 92 miles until more.

**Annie's Sourdough Pizza.** *Moderate to Inexpensive.* Main St.; 766–2630. Tasty and fun.

**Dan and Barb's.** *Moderate to Inexpensive.* At the Main St. Y, downtown Haines; 766–2588. Good value.

**The Fog Cutter.** *Moderate to Inexpensive.* Main St.; 766–9109. A good spot for a drink, too.

The Sidewalk Sandwich. *Inexpensive.* 2nd Ave. and Main St. A fine place to stop for a bite.

## SKAGWAY

Golden North Restaurant. *Expensive.* Broadway and Third; 983–2451. Gourmet gold rush cuisine.

Irene's Inn. *Expensive.* Broadway and Sixth; 983–2520. Spacious dining room (and a few modern rooms) in once-illicit 1899 gaming parlor next door to "Days of '98" show. Family operation. Alaskan food. Good salad bar.

Chilkoot Dining Room. *Moderate.* In Klondike Hotel, 3rd and Spring; 983–2291. Bar.

Northern Lights Café. *Moderate.* Long-time Broadway favorite; 983–2225.

Salmon and Sourdough Shedde. *Moderate.* Across from the Klondike Hotel; 983–2291. Features boneless King salmon, prime steak, and sourdough rolls served from 5:30 to 9 P.M.

Sweet Tooth Saloon. *Moderate.* Broadway, between 3rd and 4th; 983–2405. Featuring home-baked goods, homemade soups, sandwiches, in attractive old-fashioned ice-cream parlor decor.

 **BARS AND NIGHT LIFE.** The favorite watering holes in towns usually are well patronized by the residents, who are quick to point them out to visitors. Some "in" places that you might want to sample include the *Fireside Supper Club,* 335 Main St., in **Ketchikan;** *Kito's Kave,* a den of many decibels, in **Petersburg;** on G St., past Main, near the new boat harbor.

In **Sitka,** the locals head for the excellent lounge and entertainment at the uptown *Shee Atika Lodge,* across from the convention center, the *Channel Club* out Halibut Point Rd., and the disco in the waterfront *Sheffield House.* In **Skagway** gold rush atmosphere can be found in *Moe's Frontier Bar,* on Broadway between 4th and 5th, and the *Red Onion Saloon,* 2nd and Broadway, with sawdust floor, antique backbar, and potbelly stove.

**Juneau's** *Red Dog Saloon,* 159 S. Franklin St., with sawdust on the floor and a bear-trap-and-snowshoe decor, may be the best known in Alaska, but don't overlook the genteel and charming atmosphere in the *Alaskan Hotel* bar at 167 S. Franklin St. It's renovated in its original Alaska-Victorian style and listed in the National Register of Historic Places. Bars at the *Prospector,* 375 Whittier Ave., and *Yancy Derringer's,* Merchants Wharf, have certain hours before dinner for "attitude adjustment" when they serve cheaper drinks. The *Marine Bar* is on the site of Ft. Dionysus; follow Front St. to Shakes St.—it's by the bridge to Shakes Island.

# INDEX

**The letter H indicates Hotels and Motels. The letter R indicates Restaurants.**

## GENERAL INFORMATION

## ALASKA PANHANDLE (Southeast Alaska)
### Practical Information

## Geographical

## BRITISH COLUMBIA
### Practical Information

## Geographical

## OREGON
### Practical Information

## Geographical

## WASHINGTON
### Practical Information

### Geographical